LONGSTREET HIGHROAD GUIDE
TO THE

COLORADO MOUNTAINS

BY HAL CLIFFORD

LONGSTREET
ATLANTA, GEORGIA

Published by
LONGSTREET PRESS, INC.
a subsidiary of Cox Newspapers,
a subsidiary of Cox Enterprises, Inc.
2140 Newmarket Parkway
Suite 122
Marietta, Georgia 30067

Great efforts have been made to make the information in this book as accurate as possible. However, over time, trails are rerouted and signs and landmarks may change. If you find a change has occurred to a trail in the book, please let us know so we can correct future editions. *A word of caution:* Outdoor recreation by its nature is potentially hazardous. All participants in such activities must assume all responsibility for their own actions and safety. The scope of this book does not cover all potential hazards and risks involved in outdoor recreation activities.

Printed by RR Donnelley & Sons, Harrisonburg, VA

1st printing 1999

Library of Congress Catalog Number 99-61764

ISBN: 1-56352-537-2

Book editing, design, and cartography
by Lenz Design & Communications, Inc., Decatur, Georgia

Cover illustration by Thomas Moran, *Picturesque America*, 1872

Cover design by Richard J. Lenz, Decatur, Georgia

Illustrations by Danny Woodard, Loganville, Georgia

Photographs: Pages 1, 117, and 161 courtesy of Grand Junction Visitor and Convention Bureau. Pages 127 and 141 (photo by Larry Pierce) and page 132 (photo by Cynthia Hunter) courtesy of Steamboat Springs Chamber Resort Association, Inc. Pages 67 and 85 by Carl Scofield. Pages 60 and 61 courtesy of Fort Collins CVB/U.S. Forest Service. Pages 27 and 50 courtesy of T.A.R.P. of Boulder County. Page 95 courtesy of the National Park Service. Page 153 by Burnie Arndt, Aspen Skiing Company. Page 177 by Tom Zuccareno, Aspen Skiing Company. Page 237 by Sven Brunso. Page 284 by Bill Bourdreax. Page 15 courtesy of Fort Collins CVB/Craig Leubben.

"We were perched on the extreme summit of the great range
of the Rocky Mountains, toward which we had been climbing, patiently climbing,
ceaselessly climbing, for days and nights together—and about us was gathered
a convention of Nature's kings that stood ten, twelve,
and even thirteen thousand feet high—grand old fellows
who would have had to stoop to see
Mountain Washington, in the twilight. We were in such an airy elevation
above the creeping populations of the earth that now and then
when the obstructing crags stood out of the way
it seemed that we could look around and abroad and contemplate
the whole great globe, with its dissolving views of mountains, seas and continents
stretching away through the mystery of the summer haze."
—From *Roughing It*, by Mark Twain

Contents

Colorado

How Your Highroad Guide is Organized

Northeast Region
Pages 27–66

East Central Region
Pages 67–94

Southeast Mountain Region
Pages 95–116

Northwest Mountain Region
Pages 117–152

West Central Region
Pages 153–236

Southwest Region and Long Trails
Pages 237–323

How to Use Your Highroad Guide

T he *Longstreet Highroad Guide to the Colorado Mountains* divides the state into six major geographic areas. The dividing lines tend to follow geographically logical paths but are somewhat arbitrary and inexact. Because this book attempts to highlight the best of Colorado, not all areas within the boundaries are discussed.

Specific boundary descriptions are included in each section. In general terms, the sections are divided up as follows:

Northeast: Rocky Mountain National Park and the northern Front Range.

East Central: Pikes Peak, Mount Evans, southern Front Range, and South Park.

Southeast: Sangre de Cristo Mountains, Wet Mountains, Spanish Peaks, and the San Luis Valley.

Northwest: Rawah Mountains, North Park, Middle Park, Park Range, northern Gore Range, Flattops, and Colorado National Monument.

West Central: Sawatch Range, southern Gore Range, Elk Mountains, West Elk Mountains, Collegiate Peaks, Grand Mesa, Black Canyon of the Gunnison National Monument, Curecanti National Monument.

Southwest: San Juan Mountains (including the San Miguel, La Garita, South San Juan, and La Plata mountains) and Mesa Verde National Park.

Within each region, sites are arranged around destination towns or cities, with the exception of national parks and monuments.

Legend

Amphitheater	Wheelchair Accessible	Special Areas	
Parking	First Aid Station	Town or City	
Telephone	Picnic Shelter	Physiographic Region/ Misc. Boundary	
Information	Horse Trail		
Picnicking	Horse Stable	Appalachian Trail	
Dumping Station	Shower	Regular Trail	
Swimming	Biking	State Boundary	
Fishing	Comfort/Rest Station	70 Interstate	
Interpretive Trail	Cross-Country Ski Trail	522 U.S. Route	
Camping	Snowmobile Trail	643 State Highway	
Bathroom	Park Boundary	SR2010 State Route	
		T470 Township Road	

Acknowledgments

No book is written in isolation; certainly, no guidebook can be created without the assistance of others. Many people have given freely of their time and expertise to help bring this project to fruition; without them, it would not have happened. While I am grateful for their contributions, I hold myself responsible for any factual errors in the text.

Maureen McDonald was kind enough to bring my previous work to the attention of Marge McDonald, project director for the Highroad Guide series at Longstreet Press. Marge set me on the path of discovery and turned me loose. Richard Lenz, John Lenz, and Pam Holliday were instrumental in converting my overwritten, badly punctuated manuscripts into the polished text contained within these covers.

On the road, on the telephone, and through e-mail I gathered facts, directions, and tips from many people, some of whom are not named here because we literally crossed paths in the woods. Public lands employees, although often overworked, remain the best, most user-friendly source of information in Colorado. I commend them to you.

Those who materially contributed to the accuracy of my text include the following:

Among the staff of the National Park Service, Libby Landreth at Great Sand Dunes National Monument, Doug Caldwell at Rocky Mountain National Park, Ron Young and Dr. Bill Hood at Colorado National Monument, Joanie Budzeleni at Curecanti National Recreation Area, Paul Zaenger at Black Canyon National Monument, Tom Ulrich at Fossil Beds National Monument, and Linda Martin at Mesa Verde National Park all were extremely helpful and gracious with their time and my errors.

Marcia Simmons of Colorado State Parks was unceasingly cheerful, helpful, and fast in providing me with information and factual corrections.

Terri Follett of the U.S. Fish and Wildlife Service returned calls promptly and caught my mistakes.

At the Colorado Division of Wildlife, Mike Jafit, Todd Malmsbury, and Russ Bromby helped me identify species and understand the wealth of the state's furred, feathered, and finned inhabitants.

Among the many employees of the U.S. Forest Service who fielded my incessant phone calls and e-mails and reviewed my texts, special thanks go to Pam Wilson, Bob Carnes, Lou French, Naomi Hifton, Bill Dunkelberger, Sandy Thomspon, Ronnie Day, Peggy Jacobson, Randy Houtz and Bill Wood.

The staffs and directors of chambers of commerce and resorts around the state were crucial to my fact-checking efforts. My thanks to Gloria Cheshier of Leadville, Judy Hassell of Buena Vista, Kristin Yantis of Vail, Joan Christensen of Winter Park, Virginia Lucarelli, Kristin Hoins, and Annie Kuhles of Telluride, Rennie Wagner of

Ouray, Dawna Moody of Crested Butte, Ed and Patti Zink of Durango, and Tracy Robertson of Silverton.

Finally, this book would never have made it into the word processor, much less out of it, without the professional support of the author Marty Carlock, my mother, who taught me to love mountains and who taught me to write. Most important of all, my wife, the writer Mary Lou Bendrick provided invaluable assistance as a researcher, editor, travel companion, muse, humorist, therapist, friend and lover. She's good at picking campsites, too.

Preface

I took on the task of writing the *Longstreet Highroad Guide to the Colorado Mountains* in the spring of 1998, captivated by the idea of traveling to remote corners of mountains I have come to love deeply. This project became an unimpeachable excuse to hike, bike, camp, listen to birds, and contemplate mountain meadows, all during working hours.

My journeys, which involved close to 10,000 miles of driving and weeks of sleeping on the ground, taught me that after living for 15 years in Colorado's high country I still had—and have—much to learn about my home. I could spend a lifetime here and not see or experience all I wish to.

I coined a private nickname for Colorado: The State That Doesn't Quit. Each day I ventured upon something that caused me to say to myself, "This is the best thing I have seen in Colorado yet." It was as sublime as the light on the Great Sand Dunes at dusk, and the dark maw of the Black Canyon of the Gunnison. It was as tiny and miraculous as a cerulean bottle gentian in a San Juan Mountain bog, and the song of a canyon wren amid the ancient rocks of the Uncompahgre Plateau. It was as simple as dawn.

This book is an attempt to capture the "best" of Colorado's mountains between bound covers, a pleasurably quixotic undertaking. It is by definition an incomplete work. Readers assuredly will find that I have overlooked a trail, a river, even half a mountain range they think worthy of inclusion here. For that omission I ask your indulgence and understanding of the limitations of any single book. In exchange, I offer amid these pages an introduction to places and experiences you may not yet have discovered and which will bring you joy.

Go into the mountains with an open heart. Be good to them, and they will nurture the willing soul.

—Hal Clifford

Colorado Mountain Ranges

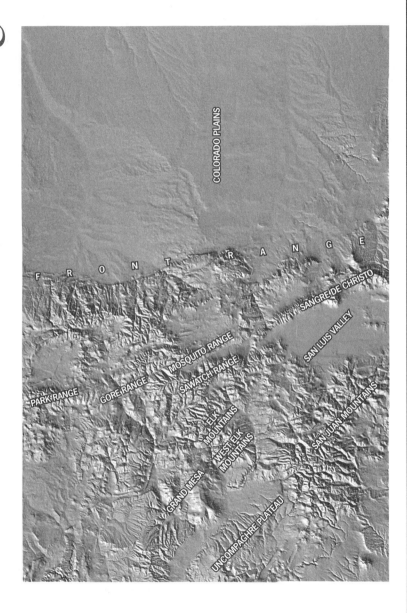

The Natural History of Colorado's Mountains

Colorado is the crown of the continent, the highest region of North America. The Centennial State's average elevation is 6,800 feet above sea level; three-fourths of the nation's terrain above 10,000 feet is contained within its borders. The result is a state that is perhaps most closely affiliated with mountains in the American mind.

The rectangular state of Colorado can be roughly divided into three sections: the High Plains, which make up the eastern third; the Rocky Mountains, comprising the central portion; and the high plateaus of the west. This book is principally concerned with Colorado's mountainous regions, which are a portion of the southern Rocky Mountains, a cordillera stretching from the Laramie and Sierra Madre mountain ranges of southern Wyoming to the southern Sangre de Cristo Mountains of northern New Mexico.

[*Above:* Colorado National Monument]

Geologic Time Scale

Era	System & Period	Series & Epoch	Some Distinctive Features	Years Before Present
CENOZOIC	Quaternary	Recent	Modern man.	11,000
		Pleistocene	Early man; northern glaciation.	1/2 to 2 million
	Tertiary	Pliocene	Large carnivores.	13 $\pm$ 1 million
		Miocene	First abundant grazing mammals.	25 $\pm$ 1 million
		Oligocene	Large running mammals.	36 $\pm$ 2 million
		Eocene	Many modern types of mammals.	58 $\pm$ 2 million
		Paleocene	First placental mammals.	63 $\pm$ 2 million
MESOZOIC	Cretaceous		First flowering plants; climax of dinosaurs and ammonites, followed by Cretaceous-Tertiary extinction.	135 $\pm$ 5 million
	Jurassic		First birds, first mammals; dinosaurs and ammonites abundant.	181 $\pm$ 5 million
	Triassic		First dinosaurs. Abundant cycads and conifers.	230 $\pm$ 10 million
PALEOZOIC	Permian		Extinction of most kinds of marine animals, including trilobites. Southern glaciation.	280 $\pm$ 10 million
	Carboniferous	Pennsylvanian	Great coal forests, conifers. First reptiles.	310 $\pm$ 10 million
		Mississippian	Sharks and amphibians abundant. Large and numerous scale trees and seed ferns.	345 $\pm$ 10 million
	Devonian		First amphibians; ammonites; Fishes abundant.	405 $\pm$ 10 million
	Silurian		First terrestrial plants and animals.	425 $\pm$ 10 million
	Ordovician		First fishes; invertebrates dominant.	500 $\pm$ 10 million
	Cambrian		First abundant record of marine life; trilobites dominant.	600 $\pm$ 50 million
	Precambrian		Fossils extremely rare, consisting of primitive aquatic plants. Evidence of glaciation. Oldest dated algae, over 2,600 million years; oldest dated meteorites 4,500 million years.	

The geography of Colorado's mountains is unique and distinctive, yet it is partly the result of events that happened thousands of miles away.

Building Mountains

The origins of Colorado's high peaks are based in Plate Tectonics, a theory which posits that the earth's crust is composed of vast, floating continental plates. These plates move imperceptibly over the eons. Along one edge, a continental plate is driven down and melted into the molten core of the earth; along the opposite edge, upwelling molten rock solidifies and builds new plate. The result is a slow-motion rolling effect, with new plate built from molten rock along one edge, and old plate melting into the earth's core at the opposite edge. It's as if each plate were a slow conveyor belt carrying its continents along.

The North American plate spans from the mid-Atlantic to the eastern Pacific, and from the Arctic Ocean to the Caribbean. The Atlantic Ocean was formed when the North American plate separated from the European plate about 200 million years ago. Since then, the North American continent has moved 1,500 miles westward as new plate formed deep in the Atlantic Ocean along the Mid-Atlantic Ridge in a process called sea-floor spreading, and existing plate was driven beneath the Pacific plate at the East Pacific Rise, west of California.

Colorado experienced two clear periods of mountain building, known as orogenies, in connection with the movement of continental plates. About 300 million years ago, when the stresses of the spreading Atlantic sea floor were greater than they had been before, the pressure on the North American plate caused it to warp and fracture in today's Colorado. The plate was weaker in Colorado than elsewhere, so this part of the crust crumpled.

Western Mountain Ash

Western mountain ash (*Sorbus scopulina*) is dramatic in the autumn, when this tree-like shrub produces fat bunches of bright orange or red berries that are visible for many yards. This ash grows up to 4 meters high and ranges from the foothills to subalpine zones. Plants grow singly through the forest.

The leaves are distinctive, each leaf a pinnately compound stem bearing 11 to 13 leaflets. The saw-edged leaflets are 1 to 3 inches in length.

The broken pieces of the plate lifted and dropped along fault lines, or cracks in the plate. This was the Colorado orogeny, which formed two ranges known together as the ancestral Rockies. The eastern mountain range, called Frontrangia, ran from near today's Rock Springs, Wyoming, southeast into New Mexico around Raton Pass. The second range, Uncompahgria, ran from eastern Utah, east of Green River, southeast across Colorado and into New Mexico around Chama.

Thimbleberry

This deciduous shrub (*Rubus parviflorus*) is sometimes confused with raspberry (*Rubus idaes*) because each produces a red, hairy, multipart berry. However, thimbleberry possesses large, broad leaves similar to those of a sugar maple, and lacks the prickling thorns of raspberries.

Look for thimbleberry along trails or other disturbed sites. The plants generally grow about 1 meter tall, often in patches. The berries may be tasteless, tart, or sweet, and are a favored food of bears and birds.

Erosion worked steadily on these mountains, which were worn down to near flatness during the next 235 million years. This erosion filled the lands around the ancestral Rockies with deep collections of sediments during the Carboniferous and Permian periods. The red rocks so common to many of Colorado's mountainous regions, for example, are the eroded remains of the ancestral Rockies, reformed under heat and pressure into sandstone and slate.

While this erosion was taking place, vast shallow seas were ebbing and flowing along eastern and western Colorado during a period from about 200 million years ago until 65 million years ago. These oceans and, in northwestern Colorado, a subsequent freshwater lake created many layers of silt and mud, sand dunes, beaches, swamps, and riverbeds. Over time, these deposits became shale, limestone, sandstone, coal, and oil shale. Colorado was probably a flat, marshy place during the most recent stages of these events, about 65 million years ago.

Then the second, more recent orogeny began. Like the Colorado orogeny, the Laramide orogeny (which started 65 million years ago) probably was related to the movement of the tectonic plates and the pressures these movements applied to the weak or faulted areas in Colorado. New mountains arose in the form of enormous, north-south blocks of Precambrian rock that split and lifted into the sky. As they rose, other blocks around them fell, forming valleys.

The Precambrian rock pushed up the overlying sedimentary rocks: Cretaceous shales, Jurassic sandstones, Permian sandstones. Erosion wore these softer rocks away, revealing the harder, uplifted cores of the new mountains.

Beginning about 28 million years ago, and continuing for 23 million years, a final spasm of the North American plate bowed the North American continent. As a result of pressure transmitted across the plate, Colorado and parts of Utah and New Mexico were heaved 1 mile into the air. The high mountains became higher, and the rivers that ran from them gained new strength and energy to carve canyons and valleys.

Two other elements added broad brush strokes to Colorado's mountains. One was volcanic activity. Volcanoes were principally responsible for the creation of the West Elk Mountains and the San Juan Mountains. The San Juan mountain range is the youngest range in the state, only about 35 million years old. It was built through multiple and complex volcanic events on the remnants of Uncompahgria and the

Precambrian rock uplifted during the Laramide orogeny. Volcanic activity also created the mineralized zones that would be seminal to Colorado's nineteenth century settlement.

The last major actor on the geological stage was ice. The Pleistocene Ice Age began about 3 million years ago. Vast ice sheets advanced southward from the polar cap, covering Canada and portions of the United States. These sheets did not flow as far south as Colorado. However, the colder climate was conducive to glacier formation within the southern Rocky Mountains.

American Kestrel

The American kestrel is often seen by roadsides, perched on telephone lines or tree limbs above open fields. *Falco sparverius* is a small falcon, no larger than a Rocky Mountain blue jay, with a rufous back and tail—all factors that make it easy to identify. Kestrels hunt mice, insects, lizards, and snakes; in flight they may hover before making a strike, beating their wings rapidly.

During an ice age, winter snow builds up year after year on the high peaks and ridges. If it does not melt (as it did not during the Pleistocene Ice Age), snow undergoes viscous deformation—that is, it flows and, under its own pressure, compacts into ice. This ice grinds slowly downhill like Silly Putty left on an angled surface.

The result is a glacier. Glaciers formed throughout Colorado's mountains during several ice ages over the last 3 million years. If glaciers did not move, they would have had little effect on the mountains. But because they follow gravity downhill they rasp enormous quantities of rock from their host peaks.

The valley left behind by a glacier is often described as U-shaped. This term refers to the cross-valley profile, which is curved and even, a distinctive shape that tells of the passage of ice. Glaciers cut rock in two ways. Near its head, glacial ice penetrates crevices with frozen fingers; as the ice moves downhill, these fingers pull and snap the rock off. Rocks embedded in the ice then become scouring tools that erode the surface over which the glacier flows. Along their sides and at their toes, glaciers push up mounds of rock and soil called moraines.

Many of Colorado's sharp peaks were formed by glaciers that carved deep bowls and long valleys, leaving behind sharp ridges and pointed summits. In most of Colorado, glaciers extended as low as an elevation of 8,000 feet before retreating. A general warming of the earth about 12,000 years ago brought an end to the most recent—but probably not the last—Ice Age.

The Major Life Zones

Imagine Colorado's life zones, or ecosystems, as bands girdling the mountains. Each band encompasses a distinct cohort of plant and animal life adapted to a particular range of temperature, precipitation, and growing season. These ranges are delimited by lower and upper elevations where different ecosystems thrive.

A note on the terminology: Different texts refer to the ecosystems with different nomenclatures. For instance, what some texts refer to as "the foothills zone" describes what others refer to as the "Lower Sonoran zone." Regardless of names, however, six widespread ecosystems are found in Colorado's mountains.

1. At the lowest elevation, the shortgrass prairie is found along the eastern fringes of the Rockies, and the Lower Sonoran ecosystem touches upon the western flatlands. Together these form the Grasslands zone.

2. Slightly higher is the Transition zone, made up of piñon-juniper forest and ponderosa pine forests.

3. At higher elevations still is the Montane zone, where aspens, Douglas fir, and lodgepole pines thrive.

4. Above this is the Subalpine zone, identified by thick forests of Engelmann spruce, subalpine fir, and blue spruce. This zone extends as high up the mountains as trees can grow.

5. Beyond this, on the summits and ridges of the high peaks, is the Alpine zone of tundra plants.

6. Through all of these ecosystems runs the Riparian zone, the wet region along watercourses that is home to a distinctive set of plant species. The Riparian zone is critical to species diversity throughout Colorado; this zone is used by 90 percent of Colorado's animal species at some point during their life cycles.

The bands that represent these ecosystems do not run in even lines of elevation, but dip lower in some areas and rise in others to accommodate local variations in precipitation, soil moisture, exposure to wind and sun, and soil type. These life zones are determined generally by elevation, then modified by the microclimates that result from the combination of elevation with these additional factors.

Among all of Colorado's life zones, the separations between them are inexact. Pockets of aspen and lodgepole pine, typical of the Montane zone, are found in the Subalpine zone, for example. These variations illustrate how local conditions— aspect, shelter from the wind, moisture, soil content—dictate which ecosystem will thrive in a particular locale. The two best indicators of ecosystem type are elevation and aspect (sun-loving species grow to higher elevations on south-facing slopes, for instance), but many factors go into the recipe that creates an ecosystem.

Because it varies so much in elevation, Colorado's mountainous terrain encompasses ecosystems that are found from Alaska to Mexico. A change in altitude of 1,000 feet brings with it a corresponding change in the ambient temperature of between 3 degrees and 6 degrees Fahrenheit. The result is that if you climb 1,000 feet up a Colorado mountain, you have entered the same climate, and therefore a similar ecosystem, as that found 600 miles north of your starting point. In terms of ecosystems, climbing to the summit of one of Colorado's 14,000-foot peaks is akin to traveling to northern Canada.

▨ GRASSLANDS

Along Colorado's Front Range, high elevation and limited precipitation create a shortgrass prairie ecosystem. This is nearly treeless terrain, home to perennial grasses, forbs, big sagebrush, and rabbitbrush. The Front Range lies in the rain shadow of the Rockies—the region in the lee of the range where relatively little precipitation falls. The scarcity of moisture limits this ecosystem's plant (and associated animal) species. Farther east in Kansas, as precipitation increases and elevation drops, medium- and tallgrass prairie displace shortgrass ecosystems. Although they once blanketed the United States from eastern Kansas to the Rockies and from Texas into Canada, most undisturbed, native prairie ecosystems have fallen to the plow or cattle grazing.

The grasslands along Colorado's Front Range, like those in most of the Great Plains region, were well adapted to the effects of vast herds of buffalo, which grazed and trampled and then moved on. Grasses grow from the base, rather than the tip, and can recover readily from short, intense periods of grazing. In addition, these plains historically were swept by fire, which may have helped keep trees from gaining a foothold in the relatively cold and arid region. Lastly, high winds, thunderstorms, lightning, and hail on the plains make them an unfriendly environment for trees.

In addition to grasses such as grama and buffalograss, common plant species in this ecosystem include cheatgrass, four-wing saltbush, rabbitbrush, prickly pear, and Russian thistle, or tumbleweed (an introduced species). Shortgrass prairie grasslands are found up to about 6,000 feet.

The vegetation found in an ecosystem helps determine the associated animal species. The black-tailed prairie dog and thirteen-lined ground squirrel thrive in traditional shortgrass ecosystems, although rampant development in Colorado's prairies is threatening the prairie dog. Raptors soar over shortgrass prairies; many species common in Colorado are found here, including red-tailed hawk, Swainson's hawk, golden eagle, and American kestrel.

On the Western Slope (that area of Colorado west of the Continental Divide), the high plateau deserts are part of the Lower Sonoran zone, an ecosystem typified by gambel oak, big sagebrush, greasewood, and rabbitbrush. In Colorado this ecosystem typifies what some might call "drive-through country"—badlands of poor, alkaline soils, little rain, and relatively barren ground. Examples are found north and south of Grand Junction, east of Delta, and in the middle parts of the San Luis Valley.

ALPINE BLUEBELL
(Mertensia alpina)
Found in the high Rockies, this tiny blue trumpet-shaped flower hangs in arched clusters from a stem.

These desert ecosystems are often founded on Mancos shale soils, which do not absorb water well and commonly are alkaline. Greasewood, four-wing saltbush, and milk vetch do well in these soils; in sandy soils, blackbrush, ricegrass, and Mormon tea may be found. Sego lilies and globe mallow are common flower species in both shortgrass prairies and the Lower Sonoran zone.

The Lower Sonoran ecosystem is rarely found above 7,000 feet. A notable exception is the arid San Luis Valley, where the Lower Sonoran species do well up to 8,000 feet. Many of the same raptor species found in the shortgrass prairie can be seen in the Lower Sonoran. Scrub jays and piñon jays are common, as are rufous-sided towhees. Around water, listen for mourning doves at morning and evening. Coyotes thrive in these ecosystems, as they do throughout Colorado and almost everywhere in the United States.

▨ TRANSITION

Along the Front Range and the southern flanks of the San Juan Mountains, the Transition zone takes the form of ponderosa pine forest. Mature, unharvested ponderosas create a cathedral feeling in the forest. The floor beneath them is dry and littered with thick carpets of long needles. Ponderosas grow from 5,500 to 9,500 feet in elevation, and may grow well up into the Montane zone. Ponderosa pine is the most widely distributed conifer in the West, and is an excellent indicator of the Transition zone—the place where arid deserts give way to moister conditions on mountain slopes. Here storm clouds begin to drop significant quantities of snow and rain; higher up the slopes, precipitation levels increase. Mountain ranges generate precipitation by forcing passing, warm, moist air to rise and cool; cool air can carry less moisture than warm air, so cooling the air causes it to release moisture as rain or snow. This ability of mountains to rake precipitation from the sky is critical to the success of Colorado's water-hungry subalpine and Montane forests, which often thrive only a few miles from much drier lowlands.

Fire and sunlight are key elements of healthy ponderosa forests, which are quite open and airy if nature has been allowed to take its course. In places where fire has been suppressed, many smaller trees may crowd together or many mature trees may shade the forest floor too heavily, preventing the growth of new trees. Like the grasslands along the eastern slopes, ponderosa pine forests evolved in the presence of frequent fire that burned litter on the relatively dry (compared to higher elevations) forest floor. Early settlers in the West reported being able to drive a wagon between ponderosas in these park-like forests.

Ponderosas don't tolerate a lot of standing snow and prefer sandy, well-drained places where precipitation amounts to about 25 inches annually. Some of Colorado's most dramatic birds—the hepatic tanager, western tanager, and western bluebird—forage in these trees. The Albert's squirrel, dependent on ponderosa seed cones for food, is unique to the ponderosa pine ecosystem. Many other species, including elk, black bear, mule deer, and chipmunks may be found here.

In some southern areas of Colorado, the Transition zone is indicated by piñon-juniper forests, an ecosystem in which the trees rarely grow taller than 30 feet. Piñon pine and juniper thrive in dry, loose soil above the Lower Sonoran zone and are sometimes described as comprising the Upper Sonoran ecosystem. Their range is from 4,500 to 8,000 feet.

Piñon pine is the ubiquitous pine of the desert Southwest, a short, round tree that is almost always found cohabitating with one or more species of juniper (Utah, Rocky Mountain, or one-seed). These species generally space themselves loosely across open, rocky slopes. gambel oak and mountain mahogany are often found with them, along with rabbitbrush, big sagebrush, and greasewood. Every three to seven years, piñon pines produce prolific crops of edible piñon nuts, an important food source for bird and other animal species. Junipers, which are evergreen and are related to pines, produce berries, another important food source for animals, every two to three years.

Sego lilies and prickly pear cactus grow on open ground amid these trees. Other common flowering species include lupines and Indian paintbrush.

Although mule deer, coyotes, and mountain lions may be found in piñon-juniper forests, the largest animal commonly seen is the jackrabbit. Bird species include piñon jay (these may travel in flocks of up to 150 birds), scrub jay, common raven, dark-eyed junco, and black-billed magpie.

MONTANE

The Montane region is the zone preferred by modern Americans who wish to live in the mountains. Cooler temperatures, greater precipitation, and heavier snow accumulations distinguish the Montane zone from the Transition zone. Soils tend to be richer in decayed vegetative matter than the rocky, sandy soil of the Transition zone, producing a denser, lusher ecosystem.

The Montane zone—the terrain between about 8,000 and 10,000 feet—is where many mountain towns and resorts are situated. Douglas fir, aspen, and lodgepole pine are the characteristic trees. In some areas, limber pine and bristlecone pine groves establish themselves at the upper edge of the Montane zone. These latter trees prefer dry, windswept ridges where other tree species cannot survive.

In many places, aspen trees are not climax species. They will be overshadowed and eventually

WESTERN GRAY SQUIRREL
(Sciurus griseus)
Active all year, this squirrel buries food and steals birdseed to eat in the winter.

killed off after a century by shade-loving conifers that grow up from beneath them. Consequently, aspen trees are the deciduous opportunists of the forest. They rely on disturbances (avalanche, fire, windthrow, logging, etc.) to create open spaces they can colonize. Aspens are unique in that many trunks (called ramets) rise from a single root system. The effect is a forest grove that appears to contain many individual trees, when in truth a single individual may send up hundreds of ramets and cover many acres.

Colorado columbine, chokecherry, and fireweed commonly grow in aspen forests. Other flowering species include cow parsnip, false hellebore, and monkshood—all species that prefer the moist, shaded forest floor found beneath an aspen grove.

Listen for the trill of a broad-tailed hummingbird in an aspen grove in midsummer. Elk winter amid aspens and scrape the bark from the trees for food with their front teeth, creating distinctive scarring 5 to 8 feet off the ground.

The coniferous version of the aspen—that is, of a tree species that depends on disturbance to gain a toehold—is the lodgepole pine. Lodgepoles grow in drier, somewhat warmer areas than aspens. Unlike aspens, which may support a lush, green ground cover, lodgepoles create dry, almost barren and inhospitable environments beneath their canopies. Little grows here; some observers describe these forests as monotonous.

Mule deer and mountain lions are commonly found in Montane regions, along with elk, red fox, black bear, and pine marten. Gray's nutcrackers, Steller's jays, white-breasted nuthatches, and pine grosbeaks are common bird species.

SUBALPINE

The dark, dense, uniform forests of the Subalpine zone are classic Colorado. These forests sweep up the flanks of dramatic mountains and line the banks of tumbling alpine streams. They are composed principally of Engelmann spruce and subalpine fir, along with scattered blue spruce, which grow in damp areas. The forests are dim and moist, and may surround wet meadows and fields of wildflowers. The Subalpine zone extends to the limit of tree line, about 11,500 feet in Colorado.

Here the average annual temperature is 35 degrees Fahrenheit. Snow and frost occur in every month of the year. Precipitation may amount to 40 inches annually. The forest floor in the Subalpine zone is dark and wet and often covered by a thick layer of dead limbs and downed trees. Many fungus species thrive in this environment. So does grouse whortleberry, a low groundcover species that does well in the acidic soil created by decomposing needles.

The gray jay, or camp robber, is a common denizen of this forest, and one of the few birds likely to come toward humans in search of a handout, rather than flee. Other common birds include the ruby-crowned kinglet, hairy woodpecker, pine grosbeak, and blue grouse. Broad-tailed hummingbirds inhabit summer mountain meadows.

Kinglets and mountain chickadees overwinter in these forests. These small birds are able to survive in part because they are extremely adept at finding insects such as spiders even when the prey does not move—a significant advantage over other foraging birds, which rely on movement to reveal prey.

Near tree line Engelmann spruce trees are beaten and twisted by harsh weather into short, stunted, bush-like forms known as krummholz. Fir trees, unable to adapt to the harsh weather, do not grow at tree line. Tree line is higher than timberline, which is the elevation above which commercially valuable timber cannot grow.

The Subalpine is terrain where snowshoe hares and pine squirrels thrive. Elk and deer shelter in the deep timber in summer. Porcupines are common.

ALPINE

From 11,500 feet to the summits of Colorado's 14,000-foot peaks lies Alpine tundra. Tundra plants are both tough and fragile. They survive extreme conditions and must reproduce in a region where growing seasons are only a few weeks long and every night the temperature drops below freezing. Yet wet Alpine meadows, if they are sheltered from the wind, can support astonishing arrays of wildflowers, including bluebell, columbine, Indian paintbrush, and larkspur.

In the highest regions, moss campion, alpine forget-me-not, cinquefoil, and hundreds of other species eke out an existence in the wind shadows of boulders and along the edges of melting snowfields.

The key to understanding a tundra ecosystem is understanding how many discrete ecosystems are contained within the larger environment above timberline. One plant community grows at the edge of a snowbank, another in the lee of a boulder, another where meltwater accumulates in a low spot.

Lichens on dry rock begin the process of turning rock into soil. Mosses colonize the first, granular bits of rock and add a little decaying vegetative matter. In fellfields (stony, rocky ground), cushion plants such as moss campion dig in. At its lower edges and in sheltered pockets, tundra can include sedges, grasses, and larger flowering plants.

The adaptations of tundra plants are plain to the careful observer. Lichens on bare rock can go months without liquid water. Cushion plants hold warmth and moisture in the tight weave of their vegetation. Nothing sticks up into the air any farther than it has to—usually a few inches at most—to minimize exposure to the constant, dessicating wind whipping across Colorado's highest places.

Tundra's fragility is a result of its

MARTEN
(Martes americana)

environment. Tundra plants, although well adapted to a life in hard, cold places, live close to the edge of existence. They possess little reserve energy and have short growing seasons to recover from damage caused by trampling, mountain bikes, motorized vehicles, or other abuse. Damaged tundra can take decades to regrow.

Tundra is home to the pika, marmot, bighorn sheep, and mountain goat. In summer, elk forage on tundra above dark forest groves that provide cover. Ptarmigan raise their young on tundra, protected only by superior camouflage.

RIPARIAN

Colorado's riparian regions are typified by the cottonwood, a broad-leaved, thick-barked, twisting, deciduous tree. In the eastern portions of the state, plains cottonwood dominates. In the west, Fremont cottonwood grows up to about 7,000 feet, and narrowleaf cottonwood grows above that, up into the Montane zone. Other plant denizens of this ecosystem include the willow, alder, Russian olive, chokecherry, and box elder. Aspens and blue spruce, both of which do well in wet soils, are commonly found along streambanks.

Riparian zones are home to many distinctive wildflower species, including Parry's primrose, cow parsnip, marsh marigold, yellow monkeyflower, bluebells, and gentian.

Almost all animal species use the Riparian zone at some point in their life cycle, and Riparian zones can form critical seasonal migration corridors. Those species that spend a great deal of time in the Riparian zone include beavers, moose, raccoons, flycatchers, great blue herons, and belted kingfishers. The most common bird seen in Riparian zones, especially within the Montane zone, is the American dipper, which nests and feeds within the splash of waterfalls. Many varieties of waterfowl can be found here at lower elevations. Flycatchers and swifts often hunt insects near the water, and American goldfinches will nest in streamside willows.

Riparian areas are home to the carnivorous tiger salamander, which grows to 13 inches and is the largest salamander found on land.

People In Colorado

Precisely when man first came to Colorado is a matter for conjecture. In 1932, evidence of man in the form of bones and projectile points was found near Clovis, New Mexico. Archeologists determined the remains were about 12,000 years old. Distinctive in their manufacture, Clovis projectile points eventually were found in all 48 of the lower United States, and Mexico.

Similar evidence at Folsom, New Mexico, from an excavation begun in 1926, revealed a different and more recent habitation, from perhaps 9,000 to 11,000 years ago. Folsom points were found near Fort Collins, Colorado and in other locations in Colorado and New Mexico. Thus it seems certain that man hunted in Colorado

12,000 years ago. Some scientists believe that man was present in the region much earlier.

Folsom peoples appear to have been principally hunters and gatherers who preyed on the extinct big-horned bison (an animal significantly larger than today's bison) and other animals.

The most prevalent and significant archeological evidence of prehistoric habitation is found in the cliffs and mesas of southwestern Colorado in and around Mesa Verde National Park. The earliest evidence of habitation by what has come to be known as the Anasazi culture dates from around 500 B.C. The Anasazi lived and thrived in southwestern Colorado and the rest of the Four Corners Region until the end of the thirteenth century, when the region was depopulated suddenly for reasons that are unclear today.

RED FOX
(Vulpes vulpes)
Notorious for preying on chickens, the red fox feeds mainly on small mammals and birds.

When Spanish explorers first ventured into Colorado's mountains during the 1760s and 1770s they encountered the Ute tribe. Ute Indians (pronounced "yoot") lived in 11 identified bands occupying the mountains of northern New Mexico, eastern Utah, southern Wyoming, and Colorado. They migrated into the high country during the warm months, hunted buffalo on the plains and skirmished with the Indians of New Mexico's pueblos and those of the grasslands east of the Rockies.

By the beginning of the nineteenth century explorers and trappers, later known as mountain men, were taking the measure of Colorado's mountains both on behalf of the Spanish to the south (who controlled Mexico until the revolution of 1821) and the land-hungry United States to the east. The first village settlement in Colorado was established by Mexican authorities in 1851, at San Luis. The Ute Indians, however, were relatively unaffected by immigration from afar until 1859, when gold was discovered at the site of Central City.

Then the boom was on, and it came fast. For almost two decades the Utes were continually pushed by settlers, miners and government officials to cede more and more of their traditional land. Following the Meeker massacre of 1878 near the headwaters of the White River, Utes were forced by federal troops onto reservations in southern Colorado and eastern Utah. These reservations remain today.

Gold & Silver

The heady boom days from 1859 to 1893 brought Colorado into the fold of the United States and the industrial world. Lured by the prospect of riches, would-be miners poured into the Colorado Territory and began a mad scramble across the peaks and valleys in the quest for precious metals. All the enterprises attendant upon mining, from railroads to ranches to whorehouses, followed hard on the miners' heels.

It was one of the great mining and industrial booms in American history. Colorado joined the Union during the middle of the mineral boom in 1876 (earning the sobriquet Centennial State), after having fought on the Union side in the Civil War. Colorado troops had stopped a Confederate advance on Denver at Glorieta Pass in northern New Mexico.

The boom years lasted until the federal government withdrew its guaranteed purchase price for silver in 1893. That action caused the silver market to collapse and took the wind out of Colorado's sails. Many mining towns folded and died. A few did well by mining gold or other metals. Others struggled on as dim silhouettes of their former selves.

Through the first half of the twentieth century, Colorado was—like much of middle America—a backwater. It was hard to get to, distant from the cultural mainstream on the coasts, a place of small cities and smaller towns. The state's economy was based largely on the exploitation of natural resources. Miners pursued lead, gold, uranium, coal, and tungsten. Oil men drilled for oil and gas. Cattle and sheep ranching and logging were the industries of the mountains.

Recreation

The end of World War II saw the beginning of a profound shift in Colorado's economy. Although tourism had come to Colorado in the late nineteenth century with excursion trains and dude ranches, it did not develop as a major industry until after the second world war.

Recreational skiing had come to the state in a small way in the 1930s with a lift here, a ski club there. Skiing wasn't fancy, just an inexpensive sport designed to take advantage of the long winter months. In some cases skiers were reviving a sport miners had partaken of in the 1870s and 1880s. A few ski areas, such as Winter Park, opened before the war.

After the war ended, however, the idea of a ski industry was born, incubated, and brought to maturity in Colorado's mountains. Many veterans of the U.S. Army's 10th Mountain Division who had trained near Leadville and relaxed in Aspen, returned to their stomping grounds to pick up the thread of their lives. Development of Aspen as a ski area got underway—a chancy thing when few people skied. But the sport caught on, and entrepreneurs began to build ski resorts.

By the 1960s the ski industry was growing fast. Colorado's mountain towns were becoming a place for young Americans to go to drop out of the mainstream culture and find an alternative, back-to-the-land life. Ski areas continued to grow and

Boating, fishing, hiking, biking, and rock climbing are some of the activities to enjoy in the mountains of Colorado.

expand until the early 1980s. By then, the state had been discovered by the rich and famous who followed in the wake of hippies, artists, and writers who had created a new life in the mountains, then told the world about it.

Many mountain towns found themselves in the middle of a recreational and resort development boom in the flush years of the 1980s. Mountain biking had been invented in the 1970s simultaneously in northern California and in Crested Butte; soon Crested Butte was a Mecca for devotees to the new sport. Durango became home to professional mountain bikers and bicycle manufacturers.

Rock climbing took off as a popular form of recreation with the development of better, more reliable equipment, and Boulder became a climbing center. Fly-fishing was discovered by Americans trying to get back in touch with nature, spawning a fly-fishing industry. Thousands, then tens of thousands, of hikers were drawn annually to the challenge of Colorado's 14,000-foot peaks.

By the end of the 1980s, Colorado had become a place with a full-fledged recreational industry. People today can and do pay for the opportunity to partake of almost every possible outdoor activity: hang-gliding, hunting, ice-climbing, cattle driving, powder skiing, horse-packing, four-wheeling, mushroom hunting, nature photography, cross-country skiing, bicycle racing, and on and on.

Extractive industries such as logging and grazing continue in Colorado's mountains, although many pundits expect these traditional uses of public and private land will fade away in the face of regulation, development pressures, and dubious profitability. Such a loss would leave Colorado a poorer place, for any region with an economic monoculture—even a monoculture based on recreation—is both less interesting and less economically secure.

At the end of the 1990s, Colorado is a state with 3.8 million residents, many of whom have come in search of what is commonly called "quality of life." That quality is inextricably tied to Colorado's natural beauty and recreational opportunities. As is true with all beautiful places in the modern world, Colorado is valued by many people; consequently, it is a place where many people argue passionately about its future.

Such debate bodes well, for it implies that Colorado's millions of residents and visitors understand the uniqueness and value of the state's natural wonders.

Public Lands

America is clearly divided between states that are principally composed of private land, and states with a large proportion of public land. That dividing line runs north to south, slightly east of the Rocky Mountains.

East of the Rockies, no state contains more than 13 percent public land, and most contain only 2 or 3 percent. West of this line, and including the Rocky Mountain states, no state contains less than 28 percent public land. Nevada, the most public of states, is 83 percent federally owned.

This ownership pattern, more than any other factor, gives the states of the West their character. The America found here is still a land of open spaces. Public land brings with it public acrimony, for different interest groups have different designs on public property—logging, grazing, mining, ski area development, wilderness establishment, off-road-vehicle riding.

Many Americans conceive of public land in the West exclusively as national parks, yet parks make up only a small percentage of the region's public lands. Nationwide, the Bureau of Land Management (BLM) is responsible for 264 million acres, the U.S. Forest Service for 191 million acres, the U.S. Fish and Wildlife Service for 91 million acres, and the National Park Service for 81 million acres.

Colorado is the eighth largest state in the nation, covering more than 67 million acres. Thirty-six percent of this land is publicly held by federal agencies, principally in the mountains and deserts of the central and western portions of the state. In Colorado, the BLM manages 8 million acres; the U.S. Forest Service, 14.5 million acres (of which 600,000 are National Grasslands in eastern Colorado); the Fish and Wildlife Service, 57,000 acres; and the National Park Service, 657,000 acres. The balance of the state's public land is managed by state and local governments.

The BLM and the Forest Service are the progeny of the General Land Office, which picked up the unclaimed pieces of the public domain after homesteading ended in the 1890s. In general the Forest Service was given domain over the timbered, higher-elevation country, while the BLM got the lowlands and deserts. The Forest Service is a part of the U.S. Department of Agriculture; the BLM, Park Service, and U.S. Fish and Wildlife Service are elements of the U.S. Department of Interior.

Traditionally, the Forest Service managed its lands primarily for grazing and timber production, while BLM properties were given over to mining and grazing. U.S. Fish and Wildlife refuges were managed to provide food and cover for game species, and the Park Service lands were managed as showcases of America's natural splendor.

Those management patterns have changed radically in the last two decades. Recreation is becoming one of the most, if not the most, significant uses of many public lands. Managers of federal lands struggle to catch up with recreational demands. In some instances, such as in national parks and popular wilderness areas, too much recreation threatens to damage or destroy natural and archeological resources.

Not surprisingly, many Colorado visitors are confused by the public land ownership patterns and use designations of the state's public lands, but the differences are significant. For instance, very little of Colorado is protected by the National Park Service. Most of the state's mountainous country falls under the purview of the U.S. Forest Service. Here, development of ski areas, hunting, off-road vehicle riding, logging, and mining are permitted—uses that are not allowed in national parks.

NATIONAL PARK SERVICE

Colorado includes national parks, national monuments, and national recreation areas, all of which are managed by the National Park Service, part of the Department of the Interior. These include Rocky Mountain National Park, Florissant National Monument, Colorado National Monument, Black Canyon National Monument, Curecanti National Recreation Area, and Mesa Verde National Park.

The Park Service's management theory is dictated by the Organic Act of 1916, which prescribes "such means and measures as conform to the fundamental purpose of said parks, monuments, and reservations, which purpose is to conserve the scenery and the natural and historic objects and the wild life therein and to provide for the enjoyment of the same in such manner and by such means as will leave them unimpaired for the enjoyment of future generations."

Park managers thus try to balance the need to preserve natural resources with the imperative of making them available to the public, a constant juggling act.

Colorado's National Park Service holdings include the following:

National parks, defined by the Park Service as "generally large natural places having a wide variety of attributes, at times including significant historic assets. Hunting, mining, and consumptive activities are not authorized."

National monuments, defined as "landmarks, structures, and other objects of historic or scientific interest situated on lands owned or controlled by the government to be national monuments."

National Recreation Areas (NRAs). According to the National Park Service, 12 NRAs in the system are centered on large reservoirs and emphasize water-based recreation. Five other NRAs are located near major population centers. Such urban parks combine scarce open spaces with the preservation of significant historic resources and important natural areas in locations that can provide outdoor recreation opportunities to large numbers of people.

UNITED STATES FISH AND WILDLIFE SERVICE

The U.S. Fish and Wildlife Service manages more than 500 wildlife refuges nationwide, including four in Colorado. Wildlife refuges were established for many purposes, although many focus on preserving wetlands for migratory birds, particularly ducks, geese, and other game birds, as well as songbirds. Some refuges are managed to provide habitat for endangered species.

Wildlife refuges are often aggressively managed to provide food, water, and nesting sites to resident or transitory species. This management can include creating impoundments, pumping water into the refuge, farming, grazing, and hunting.

UNITED STATES FOREST SERVICE

The U.S. Forest Service, a division of the U.S. Department of Agriculture, manages Colorado's national forests. The forest service is the principal landowner within Colorado's mountain regions. National forests in Colorado are Arapaho, Grand Mesa, Gunnison, Manti-La Sal (most of which is in Utah), Pike, Rio Grande, Roosevelt, Routt, San Isabel, San Juan, White River, and Uncompahgre.

National Forests are managed under the Multiple Use-Sustained Yield Act of 1960, legislation which yielded the slogan "Land of Many Uses" evident on some forest signs. The multiple-use concept is to manage forests for wood products, livestock grazing, water supplies, fish and wildlife habitat, recreation, and wilderness.

As more people take to the high country for recreation, frictions develop among those holding conflicting visions of how public lands should be managed. Forest managers sometimes try to address various demands on the public lands by segregating uses.

UNITED STATES BUREAU OF LAND MANAGEMENT

The Bureau of Land Management, a division of the Department of the Interior, is landlord to much of the lower-elevation terrain in western Colorado. The BLM became the catch-all agency in the early twentieth century, gaining control over public land not designated to the Forest Service or other agencies. Although the BLM does manage a few high country parcels, most BLM land is in river valleys and the western plains and mesas of the state. Like the Forest Service, the BLM manages for multiple uses, including grazing, mining, wilderness recreation, water management, off-road vehicle riding, and so on.

The stated mission of the BLM is "to sustain the health, diversity, and productivity of the public lands for the use and enjoyment of present and future generations."

WILDERNESS

The National Park Service, Forest Service, and BLM all manage a portion of their Colorado holdings as designated wilderness or Wilderness Study Areas (WSAs). WSAs lack formal designation but are managed as if they were protected by wilderness legislation. While the concept of wilderness can vary greatly among individuals, the government definition is spelled out in the 1964 Wilderness Act, which created the nation's first formal wilderness areas.

The legislation is surprisingly lyrical for a legal document. Congress defined wilderness in the law this way: "[I]n contrast with those areas where man and his own works dominate the landscape, [wilderness] is hereby recognized as an area where the earth and its community of life are untrammeled by man, where man himself is a visitor who does not remain."

This definition was designed to protect certain public lands in their preindustrial state. In practice, it means that access to wilderness lands is limited to foot and horseback. Motorized vehicles are prohibited, as are mountain bikes, which are considered mechanized transport.

One way to understand the management and significance of wilderness is to imagine concentric circles. In the center is wilderness, where you can cover ground only as fast as you can walk. Thus, a destination 5 or 10 miles distant is a day's travel away. Consequently, a wilderness area like the Weminuche, covering 790 square miles of southwestern Colorado, seems quite large to the person walking through it.

The next ring is nonwilderness public land open to mountain biking or jeeping. Here you might be able to cover 20 or 30 miles in a day's travel, an act that can shrink the landscape. The third ring encompasses public lands that are traversed by forest roads, where you might cover 100 miles in a day in a jeep or truck.

Beyond this is the rest of the modern world, where we can drive 500 miles in a day or fly to Europe overnight. An airliner passes over the Weminuche wilderness in a few minutes. The effect of wilderness, then, is to slow us down and bring us closer to the land. While it is true that a hiker or backpacker can partake of his or her sport in nonwilderness areas, if the journey is interrupted by mountain bikes or motorized vehicles, it is degraded and less enjoyable.

All of this is a way of encouraging you to respect wilderness and other designations on public land. You will enjoy the beauty and gifts of these places best by seeing them on their own terms.

COLORADO STATE PARKS

This book also describes lands managed by another public land agency, Colorado State Parks, a division of the Colorado Department of Natural Resources. The first state parks were created in 1957. Thirty-two of the 40 state park holdings were built around man-made reservoirs, adding a recreational element to water storage facilities. Today Colorado State Parks manages approximately 160,000 acres of land and 46,000 surface acres of water.

Safe Mountain Travel & Equipment

Safe travel in Colorado's mountain regions requires the traveler to recognize that he or she is entering an environment in which nature can and will have something to say about the itinerary. Thunderstorms, blizzards, and avalanches are part of the natural environment here. Rapid changes in the weather are the norm, not the exception. Even for drivers, the weather can be a significant factor in your trip, not simply a minor inconvenience.

Recognition of this reality can help place a visitor in the frame of mind to enjoy the challenges of mountain travel, rather than be frustrated or endangered by them.

Road Safety

Mountain roads, even interstate highways, can be treacherous in Colorado. Don't attempt mountain passes without proper equipment. This equipment may include snow tires or chains in the winter—often required by the Colorado State Patrol on Colorado's high passes during bad weather.

Don't travel without warm clothing, food, and water. A minor inconvenience such as getting stuck in a ditch on a back road can turn into an ordeal for the unprepared. A cellular phone can be handy, but cell phones often do not work in Colorado's mountains, due to poor reception. This is true even on many roads.

Do not be deluded into thinking that a four-wheel-drive vehicle makes you a better driver or enhances your safety on the road. Statistically, sport utility vehicles (SUVs) have a higher accident rate in Colorado than passenger cars. Although SUVs may provide better traction for accelerating in slippery conditions, four-wheel-drive gives no advantage when braking or turning. SUVs tend to be heavier and more prone to rollover accidents than many passenger cars.

Be aware of wildlife, livestock, rockfall, black ice, cyclists, pedestrians, and agricultural equipment on mountain roads.

Weather

Changing weather is the nature of Colorado's mountains. Snowfall is the rule, not the exception, every month of the year at elevations above 10,000 feet. Afternoon thunderstorms should be expected throughout the summer months. Autumn often brings a brief, clear window of Indian summer, but this can be eclipsed quickly by the first major storm of winter, which can strike in the mountains any time from September on.

A simple rain shower can lower ambient air temperatures 30 degrees Fahrenheit on a summer day. For the unprepared, this can turn a day hike into a miserable, even dangerous outing. Consequently, visitors to Colorado's high country must be prepared for changing weather conditions. Even day hikers should expect bad weather. Carry warm clothing. Avoid cotton, which does not insulate when it is wet and can quickly chill the person wearing it. Carry water, food and a waterproof shell layer to ward off wind and precipitation.

Water

Although the water coursing in brooks and streams through Colorado's high country appears pure, prudent travelers treat all raw water throughout the western United States as potentially contaminated with *Giardia lamblia,* which causes acute and prolonged intestinal sickness. Giardiasis is caused by *giardia lamblia* cysts transmitted by fecal matter in water sources.

Treat all drinking water. The most effective treatments are filtration through a hand-held water purification system or iodine pills. Both are available at outdoor equipment stores.

Hypothermia

Hypothermia is the lowering of an individual's core body temperature. It is potentially fatal and is often referred to in the press as "exposure." Hypothermia can occur at almost any temperature below 90 degrees Fahrenheit; it commonly strikes travelers who are wet and tired. Hypothermia is a significant risk for hikers and others who are exposed to summer wind and rain in the high country.

Hypothermia victims rarely recognize what is happening to them. Lack of coordination, stumbling, inability to make decisions, lethargy, and shivering are some of the early symptoms of hypothermia. Action must be taken to reverse the condition's course. Hypothermia victims may be physically unable to warm themselves and will continue to lose body heat without help. Warming may be as simple as getting into a warm, dry environment, changing the victim out of damp clothing into dry gear, and administering warm fluids and food. In more acute situations in the field, victims may need to be physically warmed by another person in the same sleeping bag.

Prevent hypothermia in the first place by staying warm, dry, and hydrated (dehydration limits metabolism). Change out of wet clothes quickly. Smaller people, especially small women and children, are more prone to hypothermia because of their higher ratio of skin surface to body mass. Watch your partners for hypothermia and take quick action to head it off.

Wild Animals

Colorado's animals should be enjoyed from a distance. In some areas, such as Rocky Mountain National Park, animals are habituated to human presence, but they are not tame. Approaching a wild animal of any size is often illegal and always unwise, for animals can and will hurt people if they feel cornered or threatened. Approaching an animal will raise its stress level. Most of Colorado's wildlife is busy through the warm months preparing for winter. Disturbance by humans of feeding patterns and other natural cycles may force the animals to flee, and flight burns calories animals need to store as fat for winter. Human disturbance costs the animal a second time because it loses feeding opportunities, takes in fewer calories, and puts on less fat. Simply put, disturbing wildlife in the summer can keep animals from preparing adequately for winter, a potentially fatal situation for the animals involved.

Do not feed wild animals, even those that frequent campsites such as chipmunks and gray jays. Feeding animals can cause them to develop a fatal dependence on humans, cause them to be aggressive, and disrupt the natural relationship between the animal and its environment. In addition, many animals cannot easily digest human food.

Take precautions when camping, even in drive-in campgrounds, not to leave out food, trash, garbage, barbecue grills, coolers, or other temptations which might attract animals. Lock these securely in your vehicle at night or when you are not present. In the backcountry, hang your food and trash at least 200 feet from your campsite. The best way to hang items is to suspend them at least 10 feet off the ground and 4 feet away from anything that can be climbed. String a rope between two trees, throw another rope across the middle of it, and raise your food out of reach.

Never keep any food, even gum or candy bars, in your tent. Raccoons, bears, mice, and many other denizens of the forest have excellent senses of smell and will seek food out wherever it is.

Altitude Sickness

Because air pressure diminishes as elevation increases, Colorado's air is thinner than what many visitors are accustomed to. Diminished air pressure lowers the amount of oxygen available to your lungs. As a general rule of thumb, each 1,000 feet of elevation reduces available oxygen by approximately 3 percent.

Consequently, the air in Denver (5,280 feet high) provides about 85 percent of the oxygen found in San Francisco or New York. On the slopes of Breckenridge, around 10,000 feet, there's 70 percent as much oxygen. Atop Colorado's 14,000-foot peaks, there's around 58 percent as much.

The human body can adjust to Colorado's thin air, although full acclimation takes months. If possible, travel to Colorado's high country in stages. Spend a night or two in Denver, for example, before heading up to the ski areas or Rocky Mountain National Park.

Altitude sickness, also called acute mountain sickness, can be fatal, although it rarely is at Colorado's elevations. As many as 30 percent of Colorado visitors experience mild altitude sickness. Symptoms include restless sleep, headaches, and nausea. Remedies include avoiding alcohol, drinking lots of water, sleeping at a lower elevation than where you spend your day, and avoiding strong physical exertion for several days. If altitude sickness symptoms persist or worsen, the only solution is to travel to a lower elevation.

If severe symptoms occur, such as staggering or persistent coughing, seek medical attention without delay.

Suggested Hiking Equipment

What you take into the woods is, of course, a personal decision. However, some basics can make your trip more enjoyable. These basics include the following:

Warm clothing. Even in summer, travel with warm gloves, a warm hat, and an insulating layer such as a pile pullover. Avoid cotton, which wicks body heat away when it is wet. Use polyester pile or wool.

A shell layer. A windproof, water-resistant layer will keep you warm and dry during the inevitable afternoon rainstorm or on a windy pass.

Sturdy boots. Light hiking boots are fine for day hikes. Waterproof leather boots provide ankle support for backpackers.

Sun block and sunglasses. Ultraviolet radiation at altitude is significantly stronger than at sea level. If there is snow on the ground, this radiation is reflected. Use at least SPF-15 in Colorado.

Water. Carry at least one quart, more if you plan to be traveling for more than an hour or two. Dry mountain air will dehydrate you quickly. If necessary, carry water treatment equipment (*see* page 22).

Food. An energy bar or a handful of peanuts and raisins is sufficient for a short hike.

Maps. Know where you are, where you're going, and how to read the map in hand.

Hiking poles. Several manufacturers making hiking poles similar to ski poles. These poles provide stability and traction and let you transfer some of the work of hiking to your upper body.

Rescue

Search and rescue operations in Colorado's backcountry are the responsibility of each county's sheriff. In the event of a backcountry emergency, dial 911 or the local sheriff's office.

Cellular telephones rarely work in Colorado's mountains beyond the confines of mountain towns; ridges block the signals. Consequently, a cell phone in your backpack is unlikely to be useful in summoning help. The most important thing to take into the woods is self-reliance. Even when help is on the way, mountain rescue response times in Colorado are measured in hours, not minutes. Be prepared for a long wait which may well entail spending a night out.

Before you head into the woods, tell someone you trust where you're going, when you'll be back, and what to do if you don't show up. This information can be invaluable to searchers if you become lost or hurt.

Search and rescue typically is provided free of charge in Colorado, although in certain cases—such as when skiers or snowboarders ignore closure signs at ski area boundaries—victims may be assessed for the cost of rescue efforts. If a victim is a holder of a current Colorado fishing license, hunting license, boat registration, snowmobile registration, off-road-vehicle registration, or Colorado Hiking Certificate, a state fund will reimburse county sheriffs for rescue costs.

Leave No Trace

As the wild lands of Colorado—indeed, of the world—become increasingly popular among visitors, the need grows to tread lightly upon the land. If wild land visitors follow the ethic of "Leave No Trace," those who follow should not know that anyone has passed this way before them.

When hiking, stay on designated trails. Although you may be tempted to circle around muddy and snowy parts of a trail, don't. Doing so only creates a wide area of braided trails and damaged vegetation.

Don't cut switchbacks; this can cause significant erosion. If you are hiking cross-country in the absence of a trail, don't walk single-file. Instead, spread out to minimize the impact of your travel on any one area. Try to walk on durable surfaces, such as rock, rather than easily damaged ones, such as wet meadows.

Be courteous to other forest users. Mountain bikers should yield the trail to hikers and equestrians; hikers should yield to equestrians. When encountering a horse party, make your presence known at a distance, then step aside, stand quietly, and let horses pass. Cyclists should dismount. Don't ride off a trail to pass a group.

When choosing a campsite, two schools of thought exist. Vegetation in the high country and the deserts of Colorado recovers from trampling very slowly; how you camp determines how well the land accommodates your visit.

In some locales such as national parks, land managers encourage or require campers to use existing campsites again and again, in order to concentrate impact in one small area. In other areas, particularly in designated wilderness, campers should avoid using the same site repeatedly. Instead, camp lightly in a new place and avoid creating a visible site that will attract others and damage the area's vegetation. Spreading light usage over a wide area keeps a place wild.

Wherever you camp, be sure that you are at least 200 feet from the nearest open water.

Never cut or scar live vegetation, never ditch the ground around a tent, and never build a new fire ring. All these actions damage a special place for decades to come. In general, backcountry campers should carry a camp stove and cook on that. Dead and dry wood for fuel is scarce at high elevations. Collecting it disturbs the ecosystem, and the scar left on rocks and soil by even a small campfire sterilizes the area. Backcountry campfires are antithetical to the Leave No Trace ethic; they should be enjoyed only in fire rings in designated campgrounds.

Pack out everything you pack in, even toilet paper (use doubled Zip-Loc or other sealable plastic bags). Human waste should be disposed of in a cat hole, dug approximately 6 inches deep and filled in after use.

If you choose to travel in the woods with a dog, keep your pet leashed. Dogs are predators, and are viewed by prey animals with the same alarm as coyotes, wolves, and foxes. The presence of dogs adds significant stress to animals for hundreds of yards around you, including ground-nesting birds, rabbits, squirrels, marmots, and pika, as well as coyotes, foxes, deer, elk, bears, and so on. In many places on Colorado's public lands your dog is in danger of being shot—legally—if a citizen or wildlife officer witnesses it chasing deer, elk, or other game. In other places, land managers issue citations for dogs running off leash on public lands. Do yourself and your dog a favor by keeping him leashed in the backcountry.

Horse packers and other livestock users should check with local land managers about party size limitations, camping restrictions, and other regulations. Tether stock at hitching posts, if provided, or on a highline between trees, rather than against a tree or other natural element. Minimize damage to riparian areas by tethering livestock well away from wetlands.

Northeast Mountain Region

FIGURE NUMBERS

5 Rocky Mountain National Park

6 Arapaho National Recreation Area

7 Winter Park Region

8 Nederland Region

9 Cache la Poudre Wilderness

Northeast Mountain Region

T he drama of the Rocky Mountains is underlined by the view from the High Plains and Denver Piedmont, a broad, almost imperceptible valley stretching north from Denver along the foothills. Approaching from the east, visitors today see what explorers saw 150 years ago: A wavering line of blue mountains rising from the flat landscape in a broad, apparently unbroken front. This is Colorado's Front Range. It was a major impediment in the nineteenth century to travelers headed west, since mountain passes through it rise to 9,000 feet and higher. From the State Capitol steps in Denver, which rest at 5,280 feet, the land climbs 8,000 feet or more only 30 miles to the west. But the Front Range also was—and is—a region that hides vast wealth and marvelous beauty in its folds and upon its peaks.

The northern Front Range described in this section is bounded by Interstate 70 from Denver west to the Eisenhower Tunnel, then north along an imaginary line west

[*Above:* Snow-capped peaks are the backdrop for the 67-mile Peak-to-Peak Scenic Byway]

of Byers Peak to the intersection of US 40 and CO 25 west of Granby, then north again along CO 25, across Willow Creek Pass to the southern tip of North Park. From here our imaginary line runs northeast across Cameron Pass, then turns north up the east side of the Rawah (also called Medicine Bow) Mountains to the Wyoming border.

The gold and subsequent silver booms of the nineteenth century brought Americans to every nook and peak of Colorado's mountains and drove the indigenous Ute Indians out of their traditional lands. But the mineral booms began here, in this corner of Colorado's mountains. Like the scenery, the history of the state is due to geology, for it was geology that created the vast, 50-mile-wide "mineral belt" that stretches from the Central City-Blackhawk area to the southwest corner of Colorado.

The core of the Front Range is a great block of Precambrian rock that was lifted during the Laramide Orogeny, which began about 65 million years ago. Evidence of that uplift is strikingly clear along the Front Range, particular in the Flatiron Mountains immediately west of Boulder. These red sandstone slabs, perhaps 300 million years old, rest directly against Precambrian granite a billion years old or older, the rock that forms the core of the mountains. The slabs' steep angle was created as the Precambrian mountains were lifted up from the plains, so that the sandstone lies like shards of ice along the hull of a submarine that has surfaced through a frozen sea.

As the Laramide uplift continued, the resulting mountains continued to erode until about 28 million years ago. This process filled the basins on the eastern and western sides of the Front Range with great deposits of eroded material. Today, when you drive along the eastern edge of the Front Range in the flatlands around Denver and Boulder, you are driving atop the Denver Basin, which is layered with the remnants of rocks which once overlaid today's mountains. At its deepest point, the Denver Basin's bottom lies 13,000 feet below the land's surface. By contrast, Longs Peak, in the southern part of Rocky Mountain National Park, rises more than 8,000 feet from the High Plains. Yet at one time, the top of Longs Peak and the bottom of the Denver Basin, lay on the same level. The total vertical displacement, which took place over a time period from 65 million to about 5 million years ago, amounts to roughly 4 miles.

The erosion that occurred during this period removed the Paleozoic rocks which overlaid the oldest rocks of all, the Precambrian rocks, leaving this ancient rock exposed. Thus, Longs Peak, although it reaches toward the heavens, is made of rocks from the earth's basement—rocks a billion or more years old. Much of the erosion took place from 65 million to 28 million years ago, wearing the mountains back down. But then the mountains, and the entire region, lifted again, during an event called the Miocene-Pliocene uplift. Geologists aren't sure why this happened, but apparently the great pressures of continental plates grinding on one another caused the southwestern United States to bow and lift about 5,000 feet. This lifting flexed and cracked the old mountains, opening weaknesses in the crust that led to an era of volcanic activity. The volcanic action created the mineral belt. Gold, silver, lead, zinc, and other mineral ores were transported into cracks and crevices in the rocks by hot, volcanic solutions during eruptions or when molten magma approached, but did not break through the land's surface. Where these minerals crystallized around veins of quartz—as was the case around Central City, site of the first major gold strike in the state—or in other formations, they concentrated in quantities sufficient to attract miners and lead to the Anglo-American settlement of the state. The mineral belt begins south of Rocky Mountain National Park; even though the fracturing typical of the mineral belt occurred within park boundaries, it was not followed by volcanic intrusions into those fractures. Had miners found wealth in the cracks and crevices of that region, it's quite likely the land would have been settled and despoiled before it could have been protected.

During the last ice age, 12,000 to 18,000 years ago, glaciers put the finishing touches on the Front Range, carving deep valleys, scooping cirques from the peaks, sharpening some summits into pointed glacial horns, filling valleys with moraines.

The Rush For Wealth

Colorado's Front Range was first sighted by an American in 1806, when the explorer Zebulon Pike saw the peak that was to bear his name, Pikes Peak, on the far western horizon. Pike, reconnoitering the South Platte and Arkansas rivers, attempted to climb but never summited the mountain that rises above today's Colorado Springs and bears his name. Mountain men and trappers came in following decades to prowl the high, wild country, but few settled there. It was miners, lit with gold fever, who led the United States west into the mountains a half century later.

Only a year after the California gold rush, in 1850, Colorado's first gold strike was made at the confluence of Ralston and Clear creeks—what is now the intersection of Sheridan Avenue and US 76 in downtown Arvada. But the discoverer of that gold, Lewis Ralston, only lent his name to the creek that flowed out of the mountains. He moved on to California, convinced the placer gold he had found in the sands at the foot of the Rocky Mountains was a fluke.

Not until 1858 did the true Colorado gold rush begin, resulting in the creation of Denver City, a canvas tent boom town, in the area where Cherry Creek and the South Platte River converge (what is now lower downtown Denver, or LoDo). Rival Auraria was settled nearby, but the two towns soon consolidated. This strike, too, seemed to amount to more sound and fury than gold, and many miners moved on. But in the spring and summer of 1859, solid gold strikes were made in Front Range gulches that would become the towns of Idaho Springs and Central City, and then the rush was on for good; by early 1861 Colorado had become a United States Territory and contained 25,242 Anglo-Americans—97 percent of them men.

These strikes were made in gold veins, the so-called mother lodes that had released the eroded gold particles found downstream in sand bars and creek bottoms. They promised—and delivered—vast riches. If you drive up Clear Creek Canyon, between Golden and Idaho Springs, you will still see the old piles of rock and gravel shifted by miners methodically working the placers (pronounced "plah-surs"), or sand bars, of the creek. Placer mining involved running gravel and water through sluice boxes; heavier gold flakes would settle to the corrugated box bottom and be caught there. Most of the region's mining, however, was hard-rock mining, which meant blasting and tunneling into the mountains in pursuit of the ore-bearing veins of rock. More than 500 mineral veins were mined in the Central City-Idaho Springs area surrounding the headwaters of Clear Creek. In the decades that followed the first strike, these veins produced almost $200 million worth of gold, silver, lead, zinc, and copper.

Montane Forests

The steep terrain between the High Plains and alpine tundra of the high Front Range peaks encompasses most of Colorado's major life zones, rising rapidly from grasslands through foothills shrublands, to montane forest, subalpine forest, and tundra.

Starting at Denver, the land climbs through shrublands into a broad band of montane forest, an ecosystem that characterizes the foothills of the Front Range. This is ponderosa pine and lodgepole pine country—an excellent mountain lion habitat.

These montane forests, which characterize much of the country up to and inside the borders of Rocky Mountain National Park, may be found as high as 9,000 feet, depending upon the exposure. A warmer forest type, such as a montane shrubland (characterized by gambel oak [*Quercus gambelii*]) may dominate the south-facing side of a valley, while an aspen (*Populus tremuloides*) forest grows on the cooler, wetter, north-facing slope of the same valley.

Inside the park, and in the Indian Peaks area (the large chain of mountains

MOUNTAIN LION
(Felix concolor)
This solitary and nocturnal animal stalks its prey from trees or high rocks before pouncing; it is one of the few cat species without spots or stripes.

extending south from the park between Nederland and Fraser), lodgepole pine forests—characterized by small, tightly-packed trees and very little underbrush—give way to subalpine forests, limber-bristlecone, and finally tundra. Tundra is one of the dominant features of Rocky Mountain National Park and most of Colorado's high mountains. Yet today, it is only a remnant of what it was following the last Ice Age, about 12,000 years ago. Then, tundra extended as low as 9,500 feet. Today it has retreated to mountaintop islands, usually appearing at around 11,500 feet.

Mountain Lions

Although they prefer wild country, mountain lions (*Felis concolor*) have made a significant comeback in Colorado since bounty hunting ended in 1965, and seem to be willing to adapt themselves to human populations, at least to a degree. Colorado Division of Wildlife officials estimate between 1,500 and 3,000 of the big, elusive cats now reside in the state, many in the Front Range, where the cliffs and ledges of the hills offer preferred hunting perches. While mountain lion encounters remain few and far between, they are becoming more frequent. Between 1991 and 1997, five people were killed by mountain lions in the western United States, including two in Colorado. If you do spot a lion, you're lucky, for they are very secretive. Lions hunt by leaping on prey (usually deer) from above, which is why they prefer broken country containing cliffs and ledges, or by stalking unsuspecting animals from behind. If you encounter a lion, don't run, since this is prey behavior and may prompt the animal to attack. Instead, if it approaches, make yourself appear larger by raising your arms and shout or wave to scare it off.

Lodgepole pine (*Pinus contorta*) is quite prevalent throughout Colorado and is the dominant tree in the Fraser Experimental Forest west of Fraser, a state forest managed for timber and water yields. In the Experimental Forest the trees are thinned and grow quite large, but in much of the state—for instance, below Bierstadt Lake in Rocky Mountain National Park—the lodgepole grows in spindly thickets referred to as "dog hair."

Lodgepole pines, like many species in the west, evolved in the presence of fire, which played a major role in shaping the region's ecosystems. Prior to the twentieth century, relatively cool fires burned through lodgepole ecosystems every 10 to 25 years, clearing out brush, downed trees and smaller trees. Lodgepole cones exhibit a quality called serotiny; they generally remain closed until they are subjected to heat. Temperatures between 113 and 122 degrees Fahrenheit cause the cones to pop open and fling their seeds outward. During a fire, vast quantities of seeds are released, setting the stage to produce dense stands of similar-age trees (lodgepole can grow at densities of up to 100,000 trees per hectare). Susceptible to fire, these trees will burn in the future, and the cycle is renewed.

Mountain Meadows

Another common ecosystem type in the area is mountain meadows, often called parks. Estes Park, the eastern entrance to Rocky Mountain National Park, is just such a place. Visitors often wonder why natural meadows occur in the middle of forests in the Colorado Rockies. The answer depends on the type of meadow.

Natural dry meadows occur on very deep, very well-drained soils, and may include pockets of ponderosa pines (*Pinus ponderosa*), which have found a toehold in rockier areas of the meadow. Typically, ponderosa grow in mountain meadows on south-facing slopes, ridgetops, or the upper levels of floodplains. Natural wet meadows contain water-saturated soils, at least for part of the year. They may be found where glacial debris has blocked a valley—Moraine Park in Rocky Mountain National Park, for example. In both wet and dry meadows, trees cannot sustain themselves except in occasional open, scattered formations. The reasons for this are several. In wet meadows, the water table may be too high for trees to tolerate. In dry meadows, successful competition from grasses and herbs can prevent tree seedlings from gaining a toehold. Dry meadows also may have so little water available that they experience occasional microclimate drought and dry out sufficiently to kill seedlings.

Successional meadows, however, are temporary, the result of a disturbance (fire, beaver pond, grazing or logging). In time they will be replaced by climax forests. A third kind of meadow, mountain grasslands, characterizes certain broad mountain valleys (examples include North Park, Middle Park, Wet Mountain Valley, South Park and the San Luis Valley). These are generally too dry and windswept to sustain extensive tree stands.

Look for mountain bluebirds (*Sialia curricoides*) around meadows, particularly in spring, when the flash of blue in tree branches is most visible. Bluebirds nest in cavities in forest trees but, like many of Colorado's song birds, feed in meadows. Many landowners, and some public land agencies, place small bird houses on fenceposts to entice bluebirds to nest, not only in Colorado but across the country. These houses are a common roadside sight, and are often found in groups, since bluebirds can be pushed out by other species and therefore need several nesting opportunities. More than 85 other North American bird species, including aggressive introduced species like the English sparrow (*Passer domesticus*) and European starling (*Sturnus vulgaris*), compete for nesting cavities.

Another common bird in meadow environments is the American kestrel (*Falco sparverius*), a tiny, compact raptor generally seen perched on telephone wires along roadsides. It is most easily identified by its perch, its flights (short and relatively close to the ground), and its small size.

Perhaps the most significant animal of mountain meadows is not the majestic elk or furtive mule deer that occasionally browse in them, but the northern pocket gopher (*Thomomys talpoides*). Evidence of the gophers' work is apparent to anyone

Fires and Forests

Like storm, flood, and avalanche, fire is a natural and cyclical phenomenon in western American forests. Fires create opportunities for certain plant and animal species to thrive, and allow the strongest trees to survive by removing competition from smaller and weaker trees. Beginning in the first quarter of the twentieth century, forest managers—failing to understand the role of fire in forest health—aggressively attacked fires as a threat to forests. Many eventually adopted the "10 a.m." policy, which stipulated that all fires, whether man-made or caused by lightning, should be extinguished by 10 a.m. the day after they were discovered.

The result was a short-circuiting of natural cycles and a dangerous buildup of forest fuels. The cataclysmic 1988 fires in Yellowstone National Park were in part the result of this policy, and almost exclusively burned lodgepole pine, a species that depends on regular fire. Park managers found themselves in a no-win situation. In keeping with the tenets of wilderness area management, they wanted to allow the fires to burn naturally. But man had unnaturally suppressed fire at Yellowstone for a century. Consequently, the Yellowstone fires appeared to the public to be destroying the park, and many critics demanded that they be extinguished. Firefighters worked through much of the summer to limit fire damage near popular tourist attractions; winter snows eventually extinguished the blazes.

Public land managers are coming around to the idea that fire is a natural and necessary part of good stewardship, but it is often difficult to implement. Few people favor actively burning national parks and forests, and in many cases—including along the foothills of Colorado's Front Range—residential development in forest lands over the last 50 years precludes any such action. Even where burning is possible, local political opposition is often vocal and effective, and the potential for forest fires to degrade air quality in nearby urban areas can hamstring fire managers.

The opportunities for controlled burning are thus limited, and the potential for catastrophic fires—such as the 1994 Storm King blaze near Glenwood Springs, Colorado, which killed 13 Forest Service firefighters—continues to grow. The question is not if the forests will burn, only when.

who walks through a meadow, for the gophers leave large, mysterious dirt piles in their wake. Their continual churning of the soil creates opportunities for new plant species to gain a foothold, aerates the soil, and increases a meadow's ability to retain water. Their elaborate tunnel systems occasionally wash out, creating gullies across meadows.

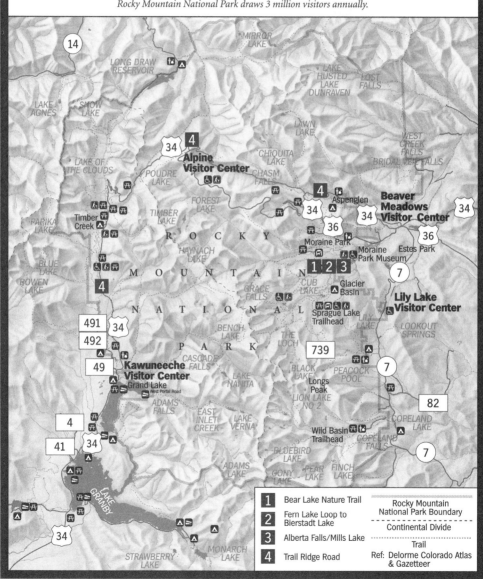

Rocky Mountain National Park

Rocky Mountain National Park draws 3 million visitors annually.

Legend:

1. Bear Lake Nature Trail
2. Fern Lake Loop to Bierstadt Lake
3. Alberta Falls/Mills Lake
4. Trail Ridge Road

Rocky Mountain National Park Boundary
Continental Divide
Trail
Ref: Delorme Colorado Atlas & Gazetteer

Rocky Mountain National Park & Arapaho National Recreation Area

[Fig. 5] Rocky Mountain National Park is often called one of the crown jewels of the National Park System, placed in the same category as Yellowstone, Yosemite, Mount Rainier, and Denali. Its extraordinary beauty and proximity to the major population centers along Colorado's Front Range draw 3 million visitors annually, mostly in the summer months. At peak times the park can be crowded, particularly at the eastern entrance in Estes Park, around Bear Lake, on Longs Peak and along Trail Ridge Road. Nevertheless, the park offers extraordinary scenery and opportunities to see Colorado's mountains. It is rewarding to all visitors, from those who drive through in a half-day to those who backpack deep into its wilds, seeking solitude and self-reliance.

The park was created by Congress on January 26, 1915, thanks largely to the efforts of Enos Mills, a man described as "the John Muir of Colorado." Mills had met Muir on a California beach and been deeply affected by Muir, who spearheaded the fight to protect the Yosemite valley. Through a six-year campaign, Mills (an erstwhile miner-cum-conservationist who would climb 14,255-foot Longs Peak 297 times in his role as a mountain guide), fought off miners, loggers, ranchers, and even the U.S. Forest Service to prevail in his goal of protecting the northern Front Range mountains for future generations. Such protection was a countercultural idea. National parks were an American invention, and a young one at that. Nevertheless, in 1915 Congress protected 350 square miles, making Rocky Mountain the 10th national park. Subsequent expansions brought the park to its current size of 415 square miles—265,727 acres.

Today the park maintains 355 miles of hiking trails, 260 miles of which are open to horseback and other stock users. Trail Ridge Road, which climbs to 12,183 feet, is a 48-mile scenic drive across the top of the park, one of the major attractions for visitors. The park contains 113 named mountains and 147 lakes and is home to 260 bird species, along with numerous mammalian species including bighorn sheep, elk, mule deer, black bear, moose, and coyote.

The park is an extraordinary example of the effects of glaciation on mountain environments. Fed by high mountain snows, glaciers flowed down from these peaks several times during the last 100,000 years, most recently about 18,000 years ago (they retreated 12,000 years ago). The largest glacier in the park was on the west side at the headwaters of the Colorado River, which rises in the Never Summer Range. Ice ran 20 miles down today's Kawuneeche Valley and approached depths of 1,500 feet at the glacier heads.

In the wake of the Laramide Orogeny, the last great mountain building period in Colorado, glaciers gave the park its finishing touches. Indeed, the Colorado Rockies

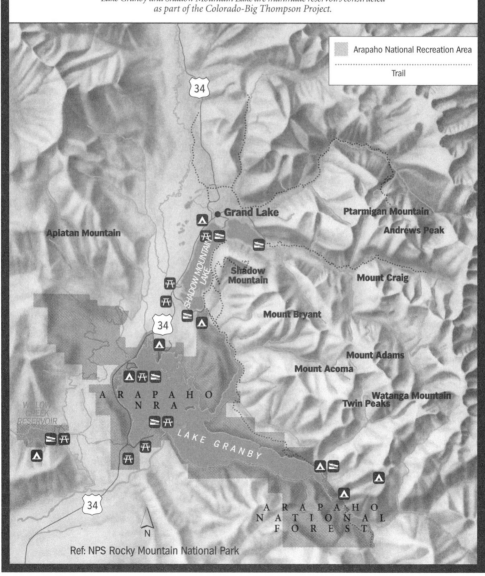

Arapaho National Recreation Area

Lake Granby and Shadow Mountain Lake are manmade reservoirs constructed as part of the Colorado-Big Thompson Project.

Arapaho National Recreation Area

Trail

Grand Lake

Ptarmigan Mountain

Apiatan Mountain

Andrews Peak

SHADOW MOUNTAIN LAKE

Shadow Mountain

Mount Craig

Mount Bryant

Mount Adams

Mount Acoma

A R A P A H O N R A

Watanga Mountain

Twin Peaks

WILLOW CREEK RESERVOIR

LAKE GRANBY

A R A P A H O NATIONAL FOREST

N

Ref: NPS Rocky Mountain National Park

owe their sharp, distinctive shape to ice. Without it, they would be broad, rounded peaks. The deep, circular bowls at the heads of mountain valleys are cirques, carved out of the Precambrian granite by the ice, which bit into the rock and then broke it off as the glaciers flowed slowly downhill like taffy. In places—most spectacularly The Diamond, a 945-foot-high sheer cliff on the east face of Longs Peak—glaciers cut vertical faces out of the rock, probing their icy fingers deep into cracks and then snapping the rock off as they moved downhill. Where glaciers carved away more than one side of a peak they created a horn or an intervening knife-like ridge known as an arête.

Most of the park's lakes are glacial in origin. Some lakes are situated in kettle holes—depressions created as ice melted at the end of glacial periods. Bear Lake, Bierstadt Lake, Sheep Lake, Dream Lake and Copeland Lake are examples. These lakes rest upon moraines.

Tarns, formed at the bottom of cirques where ice ground out a deep hole, include Blue Lake, Black Lake, Chasm Lake, Shelf Lake and Tourmaline Lake.

The third type of lake visible in the park is "paternoster lakes," so named because they run through the valley in a chain that resembles the beads on a rosary (paternoster is Latin for "our father"). They are formed when a glacier excavates a valley unevenly, digging more deeply into weaker rock. Paternoster lakes are connected by a single stream. Examples include Cub Lake, Inlet Lake, Loch Vale, and Ouzel Creek Lake.

On the western side of the park, the Kawuneeche Valley runs straight, thanks to the straightening effect of the glaciers that once inhabited it (glaciers don't like to go around corners, and so they set about breaking off rock that lies in their way). The western entrance to the park is marked by Grand Lake, which was formed when the terminal moraines of two glaciers—one descending the Kawuneeche Valley, the other descending Paradise Creek—dammed their waterways. The other two lakes in the area, Lake Granby and Shadow Mountain Lake, both part of Arapaho National Recreation Area [Fig. 6], are manmade reservoirs constructed as part of the Colorado-Big Thompson Project.

Authorized in 1937, this massive water project stores and diverts water from the Colorado River through a 13-mile tunnel beneath Rocky Mountain National Park to the Big Thompson River on the eastern side of the Continental Divide. Colorado-Big Thompson is one among several massive water projects to shift water from Colorado's Western Slope to the population centers of the Front Range—a political point of contention in a state where water means wealth. Observing the American West, Mark Twain noted, "Whisky is for drinking, and water is for fighting."

Down in the valleys of the park, the remnants of glaciation can be seen in lateral moraines, most notably in the long, timbered ridges that enclose Moraine Park, near Estes Park. These piles of rock and gravel mark the side boundaries of ancient glaciers and were pushed up and out of the way by tongues of ice. The terminal moraines, which mark the ice floes' toes, are often harder to pick out, since they may have been washed out by wandering streams meandering over the valley floors.

Because it encompasses so much high-elevation country, one-third of Rocky Mountain National Park is tundra, the ecosystem above treeline. As you drive or climb up through treeline, you'll notice trees getting shorter and more stunted, their limbs and trunks twisted and gnarled by the wind. Above 11,500 feet (a number that varies with aspect, latitude and the nuances of local geography), trees cannot grow. Long, brutal winter weather and scouring winds prevent seedlings from taking hold in the thin or almost non-existent soil here. Growing seasons sometimes last only a few weeks, and even then, temperatures drop below freezing almost every night.

Although it may seem barren or lifeless, tundra is simultaneously fragile, tough, and complex. Park tundra supports 200 species of flowering plants, many blooming only centimeters from the ground's surface. Some types of tundra contain as much lushness, in their own way, as rich prairie lands. To appreciate tundra, shift your sense of scale; rather than scanning the horizon for vast and sweeping illustrations of majesty, get down on your hands and knees and marvel at the community of life that exists above where the last tree grows.

Hikers may see small birds foraging on summer snowfields. These are brown-capped rosy finches (*Leucosticte arctoa*), which pick up insects that have been blown in from surrounding areas and then been immobilized by the snow's chill. The American pipit (*Anthus spragueii*) nests in tundra, and can sometimes be identified by its flapping song flight. The white-tailed ptarmigan (*Lagopus leucurus*) lives year round on tundra, molting to pure white in winter and mottled brown in summer. This latter camouflage is so good that hikers may walk within a few feet of ptarmigan, which rarely flush, without seeing them on the open tundra.

Two small mammals are common in tundra, the yellow-bellied marmot (*Marmota flaviventris*) and the pika (*Ochotona princeps*). The marmot, a woodchuck-like rodent, is often seen sunning on large rocks in boulder fields near or above timberline, or lumbering across the rocks for cover. Pikas look like fat, light-colored mice but are in fact a member of the rabbit family. Both animals will whistle at the approach of an intruder, but the pika's whistle is more of a "cheep."

Directions: From Estes Park, drive west 2 miles on US 36 to the Beaver Meadows entrance station and park headquarters, or west 4 miles on US 34 to the Fall River entrance station. From Grand Lake, travel east on US 34, 1 mile to Kawuneeche Visitor Center and Grand Lake entrance station.

Activities: Hiking, camping, fishing, photography, climbing, mountaineering, horseback riding, picnicking, bicycling. Interpretive programs are offered by park staff and volunteers days and evenings at a variety of locations during the summer. These include walks and talks about cultural history, wildlife, geology, and other aspects of the park for adults and children, both at park visitor centers and on park trails.

Facilities: The park headquarters and Beaver Meadows Visitor Center are near Estes Park, as is Moraine Park Museum. The Alpine Visitor Center is on Trail Ridge

Road, just west of the summit. On the west side of the park, Kawuneeche Visitor Center is located near Grand Lake.

Five campgrounds, including 1 group site, with 592 sites for car camping. Longs Peak, Moraine Park, and Timber Creek campgrounds are open all year. Moraine Park, Glacier Basin, and Timber Creek have dumping stations. None of the campgrounds provide showers or hookups. All provide firewood and water; public phones are available at all except Longs Peak. Additionally, there are 267 backcountry sites, available only on a permit basis and managed by the Backcountry Office. Some backcountry sites have pit toilets; some do not. Specifics on each site are available from the park, and are provided with permits.

Dates: Year round.

Fees: There is a fee to enter the park, plus an additional fee to camp, both in the campgrounds or backcountry. A backcountry permit must be obtained prior to camping by writing the Backcountry Office at the park, calling (970) 586-1242, or stopping in at the Backcountry Office (next to park headquarters) or the Kaweneeche Visitor Center.

Closest town: Estes Park on the east side, Grand Lake on the west.

For more information: General information phone: (970) 586-1206. For summer camping reservations in Moraine Park and Glacier Basin, call Biospherics Inc. Phone (800) 365-2267. Web site: www.nps.gov. Aspenglenn, Longs Peak, and Timber Creek do not take reservations, and offer sites first-come, first-served.

DAY HIKING IN ROCKY MOUNTAIN NATIONAL PARK
BEAR LAKE NATURE TRAIL

[Fig. 5(1)] This is a handicapped-accessible nature trail that is extremely popular and can become quite crowded. Nevertheless, it's a good introduction to some of the park's drama and beauty. The lake, a small jewel set amid spruce and fir, is surrounded by steep, glaciated peaks. Waterfalls careen down adjacent slopes; afternoon thunderstorms boil up over the high ridges. Everywhere one senses the great forces of nature at work.

Directions: Immediately after the Beaver Meadows Entrance Station (past park headquarters), turn left onto Bear Lake Road. Because Bear Lake parking lot is usually full, rangers encourage use of the free shuttle bus, which runs daily from June through August. Park in the lot opposite Glacier Basin Campground; the bus stops in the middle of the lot by the information kiosk. The bus also stops at Bierstadt Lake trailhead and Glacier Gorge Junction. For Bear Lake, stay on until the end of the road. The Bear Lake Nature Trail begins at the top of the parking lot.

Trail: 0.6 miles. Elevation change is 20 feet.

Degree of difficulty: Easy.

Surface: Smooth, packed dirt.

ALBERTA FALLS / MILLS LAKE

[Fig. 5(3)] Alberta Falls is a short hike, good for families with small children. Mills Lake is significantly farther up the valley. From the Glacier Gorge trailhead, proceed directly up the valley to Alberta Falls, 0.6 mile up. If you elect to continue to Mills Lake, climb until you meet the North Longs Peak Trail. Bear right here for 0.4 miles to a fork; bear left toward Mills Lake, crossing Glacier Creek on the way. Follow rock cairns to the lake itself, and notice the "glacial pebbles"—big, stranded boulders sitting on open rock—left when the last glacier melted.

Directions: Follow the directions for the Bear Lake Nature Trail (*see* page 39) but debark at Glacier Gorge.

Trail: Alberta Falls: 0.6 mile. Mills Lake: 2.5 miles.

Elevation: Alberta Falls: Change of 160 feet. Mills Lake: Change of 700 feet.

Degree of difficulty: Alberta Falls: Easy. Mills Lake: Moderate.

Surface: Rough dirt and rock.

OVERNIGHT CAMPING IN ROCKY MOUNTAIN NATIONAL PARK

There are five improved campgrounds in the park for vehicle camping. Reservations are accepted three months in advance at two of the campgrounds (*see* page 39 for details). Backcountry camping is allowed in two types of areas: In improved and marked sites, which are reserved on a permit basis, and in remote areas of the park designated "cross country areas," which are open to no-impact camping with a maximum one-night stay at any locale. Permits are required for all camping and are available at the Backcountry Office at park headquarters, or at the Kawuneeche Visitor Center.

OVERNIGHT BACKPACKING TRIP, EASTERN SIDE: FERN LAKE LOOP TO BIERSTADT LAKE

[Fig. 5(2)] This trail begins at the Bear Lake trailhead and includes a number of possible variations. The trail climbs 1,215 feet to an extraordinarily sublime view into the headwaters of Fern Creek, overarched by snowfields, waterfalls, and Little Matterhorn Peak. Glaciated cirques rise up all around the lake and nearby Spruce and Odessa lakes. From here hikers can look down at Odessa Lake and Fern Lake in the subalpine forest below. The trail descends 800 feet to Fern Lake, where a ranger cabin stands and is occasionally occupied by backcountry rangers working in the area. Fern Lake was the site of a lodge used by outing club members from Denver, who would ski up to the valley during the winter to play and party. The lodge has been removed and the site is being revegetated.

Several backcountry campgrounds are situated on this loop. Those closest to the midway point are at Odessa Lake, Fern Lake and Spruce Lake. Camping at any of the sites requires a permit from the Backcountry Office (*see* page 39).

Look for rare greenback cutthroat trout (*Salmo clarki stomias*), which may be spotted spawning during the summer in the outlet stream of Fern Lake. The outlet is quite shallow; watch for the telltale flash of a female turning on her side to beat out her redd, or nest, with her tail in the gravel. Dawn and dusk are good times to see wildlife, including elk and snowshoe hares, around the lake and in the woods.

From Fern Lake, the trail descends past Margeurite Falls and Fern Falls into Spruce Canyon. Here, hikers catch glimpses of Moraine Park to the east. Notice the high, rounded slabs of stone on the far side of the canyon. This is glacially polished rock, rounded back a bit by a process known as spalling, in which the freezing action of water breaks off surface rock.

It is possible to follow the Fern Lake Trail down Spruce Canyon to the Fern Lake trailhead. To reach Bierstadt Lake, turn right at the next trail intersection and climb toward Cub Lake, then right again after 1 mile toward Bierstadt Lake (the trails are clearly signed). The trail progresses up through Engelmann spruce and subalpine fir forest, over the crest of the low ridge dividing Spruce Creek from Bear Creek, and into lodgepole pine forest, which surrounds Bierstadt Lake.

This small, round jewel of a lake seems perched in the sky. It was a favorite spot for the nineteenth century landscape painter Alfred Bierstadt, who painted dramatic, sometimes overwrought scenes of the American West, including the mountains visible from this location. His work added to the romance, mystery, and sublimity of the West, particularly as it was perceived by easterners and Europeans.

Bierstadt Lake is quite popular, since it's only a short hike from the bus stop and trailhead. Hikers can follow the Bierstadt Trail, which breaks off the southern side of the loop around the small lake to that trailhead, or go east downhill for 1 mile to the shuttle bus parking lot.

Directions: Begin at the Bear Lake trailhead (*see* page 39).

Trail: 12.7-mile loop

Facilities: Phone, rest rooms at Bear Creek trailhead.

Elevation: Fern Lake to shuttle bus changes 2,515 feet in two climbs from Bear Creek drainage over to Spruce Canyon, and then back again.

Degree of difficulty: Moderate.

Surface: Rough dirt and rocks.

OVERNIGHT BACKPACKING TRIP, WESTERN SIDE: EAST INLET CREEK

[Fig. 5] The western side of the park is less developed, and less crowded, than the eastern side. The mountains rise up more gently, their drama less apparent from roadways in and around the park.

East Inlet Creek dives deeply into the southwestern corner of the park. The trail is wide, flat, and very popular for the first 0.3 mile to Adams Falls. After this, crowds thin significantly. The trail winds along wide, wet riparian meadows, giving views up the valley to 12,007-foot Mount Craig.

Several campsites exist in the valley. The trail climbs past a series of lakes through lodgepole pine to Engelmann spruce-subalpine fir forest. Along the way, notice the beautiful, swirling mica schist and gneiss in the ancient rock along the trail. Both schist, which is easily identified by the shiny flakes of mica, and gneiss, a banded or streaky rock, are metamorphic rocks. They started out as some other kind of rock but through heat and pressure have been turned into what they are today. Sometimes it's hard to tell what a metamorphic rock was originally. Gneiss generally was sandstone or granite in its earlier incarnation.

In the first 2.3 miles to Lower East Inlet Campsite, the trail rises only 300 feet. Then the trail climbs steadily, opening up to views back toward Grand Lake and up to the high ridges that define the East Inlet Creek drainage. Keep an eye peeled for Rocky Mountain columbine (*Aquilegia saximontana*), which favors rockfields around the several lakes in the valley, and Parry's primrose (*Primula parryi*), which can be spotted in wet spots along the very edges of mountain streams.

It is possible, if you wish to undertake a multiday backpacking trip, to continue up out of the valley and onto the great, broad spine of the Front Range, connecting to trails that lead in all directions, or to strike out cross-country. Such an expedition, however, should not be undertaken by those unfamiliar with high altitude mountain travel, safety, and orienteering.

Directions: At the intersection of US 34 and West Portal Road, bear east on West Portal Road, toward Grand Lake. Almost immediately you face a fork; avoid the right-hand fork, which leads into Grand Lake. Stay left on West Portal Road to the end of the road, about 1 mile. The trail begins beside the outhouses on the east side of the parking lot.

Facilities: Restrooms and boat-launching ramp for Grand Lake at trailhead.

Trail: Adams Falls: 0.3 mile. Lone Pine Lake: 5.5 miles. Lake Verna: 6.9 miles. Spirit Lake: 7.8 miles. Six permit campsites are located in the valley between East Meadow (1 mile from the trailhead) and Lake Verna.

Elevation: Adams Falls: Change of 59 feet. Lone Pine Lake: Change of 1,494 feet. Lake Verna: Change of 1,809 feet. Spirit Lake: Change of 1,899 feet.

Degree of difficulty: Easy to Adams Falls, moderate beyond that.

Surface: Rough dirt and rock.

BICYCLING IN ROCKY MOUNTAIN NATIONAL PARK

Bicycling is allowed only on paved or graded roads in the park. No mountain biking is allowed on trails or cross-country.

The park includes 60 miles of hard-surface roads and grades of 5 to 7 percent. Because Trail Ridge Road climb as high as 12,183 feet, cyclists need to be prepared for bad weather, which is a daily and potentially dangerous occurrence. In addition to the obvious risks from lightning, thunderstorms chill the air and can soak unprepared riders. Hypothermia can set in quickly, even on summer days.

Cyclists are urged to ride early in the day to avoid both bad weather and heavy vehicular traffic. Trail Ridge Road attracts many large recreational vehicles and has little shoulder space, making for harrowing bicycling.

There is a fee to enter the park on a bicycle.

▦ FISHING IN ROCKY MOUNTAIN NATIONAL PARK

Four trout species are found in the park: German brown, rainbow, brook, and cutthroat. Only cutthroat (in two subspecies, greenback and Colorado River [*Salmo clarki pleuriticus*]) is a native, and it has been extirpated from large portions of Colorado by more aggressive, introduced salmonid species such as rainbow trout (*Oncorhynchus mykiss*), brown trout (*Salmo trutta*), and brook trout (*Salvelinus fontinalis*, which aren't trout at all, but are a kind of char). The park has been working with the Colorado Division of Wildlife since 1980 on reviving greenback cutthroat populations, and it now has the largest population in the state. Greenback cutthroats have been reintroduced into the Fall River, Big Thompson and Saint Vrain Creek drainages.

No bait fishing is allowed in the park; only flies and lures are permitted. Some park waters are closed to fishing to protect the greenback cutthroat trout. Other park waters are catch-and-release areas. No greenback cutthroat trout may be kept; daily bag limits are a total of two rainbow, brown, or Colorado River cutthroat trout (minimum length 10 inches), plus six brook trout of any size (eight if no other species are possessed), and 10 additional brook trout under 8 inches in length. Check with a ranger for current regulations.

All anglers must possess a valid Colorado fishing license, which can be bought at most sporting goods stores.

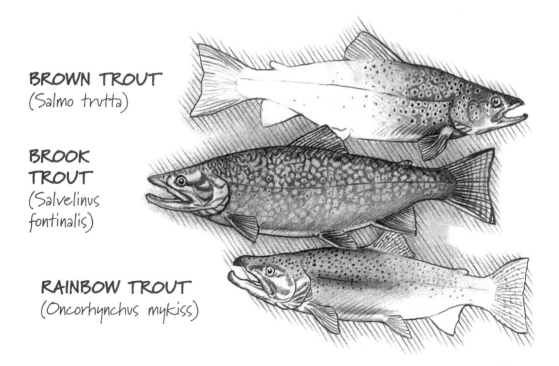

BROWN TROUT
(Salmo trutta)

BROOK TROUT
(Salvelinus fontinalis)

RAINBOW TROUT
(Oncorhynchus mykiss)

Tundra

Tundra starts above treeline at altitudes of 11,000-12,000 feet, and rises to the peaks of Colorado's mountains. Tundra represents an extreme environment, and plant adaptations here are similar to those found in arid desert environments. The harsh characteristics of tundra sites include a very short six-week growing season, 40 to 60 inches of annual precipitation (mostly snow, and much of it either blown away or packed to great depths over the plants, creating micro-environments to which individual species have adapted), wind speeds in excess of 100 miles per hour, and an average annual temperature below freezing.

Leaves, stems, and other parts of tundra plants are tiny, often protected by a waxy substance to prevent moisture loss—yet flowers can be quite showy. Alpine sunflower (*Tetraneuris grandiflora*, also called *Rydbergia grandiflora*) is a good example, producing a sulfur-yellow bloom several inches across that nods just above the ground's surface in alpine breezes. Some plants live with 90 percent of their mass underground; others can function in temperatures below freezing, or before snow around them is fully melted. Tundra plants flower and set fruit in only a few weeks, and some, such as alpine bistort (*Polygonum bistortoides*), can reproduce asexually. In bistort's case, some flower buds turn into "bulblets," which sprout leaves, fall from the plant and immediately take root as new plants.

Much of the variety of tundra plant species is a result of variations in site characteristics. One side of a rock may be dry and exposed to the wind; the other side may collect snow and water. Each will host a different plant community. Dry areas may be colonized by a cushion plant like moss campion (*Silene acaulis*), while depressions that hold snow and water may be sprinkled with snow buttercup (*Ranunculus adoneus*).

HORSEBACK RIDING IN ROCKY MOUNTAIN NATIONAL PARK

Horses are allowed on 260 miles of trails in the park during the summer season. Livestock must stay on trails; no horse or stock travel is permitted cross-country. Many trails are closed to stock; if you have your own animals, contact the park for specific rules and regulations.

Stock and riders are welcomed in many areas of the park, including Big Meadows, East Inlet Creek, Lawn Lake, Lost Lake Trail, and Finch Lake (in Wild Basin).

More than a dozen concessionaires offer guided horse packing trips in the park. A complete list is available from the park. Two concessionaires' livery stables are located within the park.

For more information: Moraine Park Stables, Rocky Mountain National Park, Estes Park, CO 80517. Phone (970) 586-2327. Glacier Creek Stables, Rocky Mountain National Park, Estes Park, CO 80517. Phone (970) 586-3244.

CLIMBING IN ROCKY MOUNTAIN NATIONAL PARK

Home to 71 peaks over 12,000 feet high, Rocky Mountain National Park is a magnet for alpinists and technical rock climbers. The park's climbing season runs from June through September, with periods of good weather in May and October. Rain and thunderstorms are a daily occurrence; to avoid lightning, try to be off your route by noon. Summer snow on the high peaks is not unusual. Anyone attempting the high peaks here or anywhere in Colorado's mountains should be fully prepared (*see* Safe Mountain Travel and Equipment, page 20).

No climbing permit is necessary for day climbs. Climber bivouacs for technical climbers are allowed near climbing routes that are more than four pitches long and are situated at least 3.5 miles from a trailhead. Bivouac permits are required and are available at no charge to climbers from the Longs Peak Ranger Station or the Backcountry Office at Park Headquarters. Permits are issued to climbers from June 1 through September 30.

For more information: The park licenses a climbing guide service, Rocky Mountain Climbing School, as a concessionaire. Phone (970) 586-5758.

LONGS PEAK

[Fig. 5] Longs Peak, at 14,255 feet, is the highest point in the park, and draws the most attention from mountaineers. The first recorded climb to Longs' summit was in 1868, led by the one-armed Civil War veteran John Wesley Powell, who would go on to command the first expedition through the Grand Canyon. The National Park Service considered the 945-foot east-facing wall known as The Diamond to be an impossible climbing route until 1960 and banned anyone from trying it. That year it relaxed its regulations and the first party, two Californians, conquered it in three days. Since then, The Diamond has been climbed as many as three times in a single day by the same climber (Derek Hersey).

Most people, of course, prefer to walk up. Longs is the second most popular 14,000-foot-plus peak in the nation after Mount Whitney in California, receiving as many as 10,000 summit visitors annually. Such peaks are commonly called Fourteeners; of the 68 Fourteeners in the Lower 48 United States, 54 are found in Colorado. The standard route up Longs Peak is strenuous, climbing 4,800 feet in 8 miles (beginning at the Longs Peak Ranger Station), and requires a 3 a.m. start in order to make the summit and get off the approach ridge before afternoon thunderstorms. It also includes exposure to dangerous vertical drops.

WINTER ACTIVITIES IN ROCKY MOUNTAIN NATIONAL PARK

On weekends from January through March, rangers lead free, two- to four-hour snowshoeing tours on the east side of the park. Rangers on the west side lead weekend cross-country skiing trips of the same duration. The tours are geared toward beginners and designed to introduce people to the equipment, to safe winter travel, and to animal tracks and track identification. For information and reservations, contact the park's

Elk Rebound

In 1910 Colorado contained an estimated 500 to 1,000 elk (*Cervus elaphus*). The animals, which had once ranged over much of North America, had been pushed out of traditional range by settlement, and hunted to the point where only about 40,000 remained, all in the West. A program of protection and reintroduction has given Colorado the largest elk herd in North America, estimated at 200,000 animals.

This has been the result of aggressive wildlife management and the elimination of key predators, wolves and grizzly bears, which have been extirpated from most of their range by hunting and loss of habitat. Grizzlies, for example, were principally predators of the Great Plains prior to settlement of the West. The last verified grizzly in Colorado was killed in the South San Juan Mountains in the late 1970s.

Only in recent decades have large predators been intrinsically valued by Americans. Bears, wolves and mountain lions traditionally were viewed as a danger to humans and their livestock, and were regularly shot on sight. As recently as 1965 Colorado offered a bounty on mountain lions. The U.S. Department of Agriculture continues to run an agency, Animal Damage Control, that kills predators on public and private lands in the belief that this action aids farmers and ranchers.

Mature bull elk stand five feet at the shoulder, grow to 1,000 pounds and carry a rack of antlers (grown and shed each year) that may weight 30 pounds. Bull elk "bugle" in the autumn, challenging other bulls at dawn and dusk with a high-pitched, squealing call that is hauntingly evocative of wilderness.

Little information exists on how many elk may have lived in Colorado prior to 1900. Today, elk are so numerous that in many parts of the state they are outstripping the carrying capacity of their range. Unlike deer, however, elk do not easily adapt to humans presence and generally only venture into developed areas when pressed by extreme hunger to graze in their former wintering grounds.

information office at (970) 586-1206. Snowshoeing and cross-country skiing equipment may be rented at several stores in Grand Lake and Estes Park.

The park is open year-round, providing opportunities for winter mountaineering and wilderness cross-country skiing. Longs Peak, Timber Creek and Moraine Park campgrounds remain open, but Timber Creek is not plowed. Backcountry camping permits are required year-round. Winter camping is not for the unprepared; blizzards, avalanches, and hypothermia are all real dangers in the park during the cold months.

Several concessionaires offer guided winter snowshoeing and cross-country skiing trips in the park. Contact the park for an updated list.

TRAIL RIDGE ROAD

[Fig. 4] Opened in 1932, Trail Ridge Road remains one of the most scenic drives in the United States. The 48-mile road from Estes Park to Grand Lake climbs 4,000 feet to a maximum elevation of 12,183 feet. Eleven miles of the route are above treeline, and numerous pull-outs offer extraordinary views, from Wyoming to Denver to the Never Summer Range. Allow approximately half a day to complete the trip; driving speeds tend to be relatively slow, and most visitors take time to stop and gaze at the views.

More than 200 plant species survive in the tundra environment, which is more like the environment of northern Alaska than the High Plains around Denver. The Tundra World Nature Trail is a self-guided, half-hour walk that begins at the parking area by Rock Cut, east of the Alpine Visitor Center. Tundra is the summer home to many of the park's larger species; drivers may spot mule deer (*Odocoileus hemionus*), elk (*Cervus elaphus*), or bighorn sheep (*Ovis canadensis*) grazing on the open slopes around the road. Do not attempt to approach any wildlife you see. Doing so is both potentially dangerous to you and stressful to animals.

Trail Ridge Road is open only in summer, usually by Memorial Day, depending on snowfall. It generally closes in mid-October. Expect air temperatures between 20 to 30 degrees Fahrenheit cooler than in Grand Lake or Estes Park and, as is true every-where in the park, be prepared for afternoon thunderstorms.

Directions: Trail Ridge Road is a section of US 34, but travelers on it must pass through a park entrance station. From Estes Park, go west 2 miles on US 36 to the Beaver Meadows entrance station and park headquarters, or west 4 miles on US 34 to the Fall River entrance station and then directly onto Trail Ridge Road. From Grand Lake, drive east on US 34, 1 mile to Kawuneeche Visitors Center and Grand Lake entrance station.

ELK
(Cervus elaphus)
Also called "wapiti" — an Indian word for "white" — referring to the light color of the animal's rump, elk herds are distributed through mountain forests and valleys in the West.

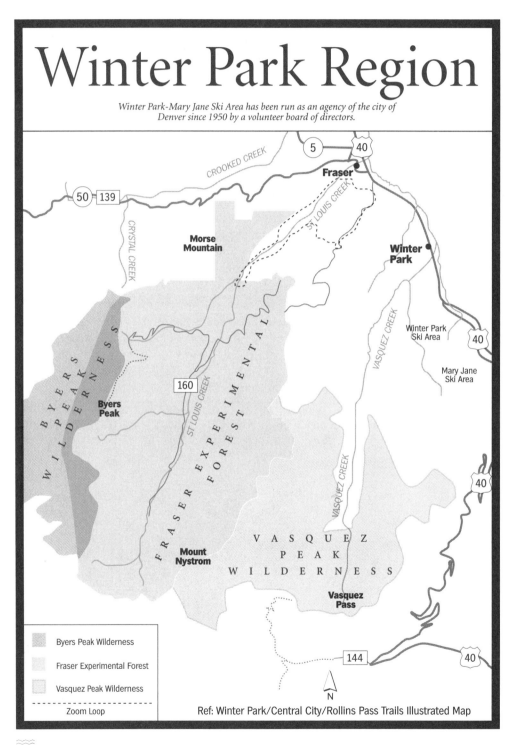

Winter Park Region

Winter Park-Mary Jane Ski Area has been run as an agency of the city of Denver since 1950 by a volunteer board of directors.

CROOKED CREEK

5 · 40

Fraser

50 · 139

ST LOUIS CREEK

CRYSTAL CREEK

Morse
Mountain

Winter
Park

Winter Park
Ski Area

40

VASQUEZ CREEK

Mary Jane
Ski Area

B Y E R S
W I L D E R N E S S

Byers
Peak

160

ST LOUIS CREEK

F R A S E R   E X P E R I M E N T A L   F O R E S T

40

VASQUEZ CREEK

40

Mount
Nystrom

V A S Q U E Z
P E A K
W I L D E R N E S S

Vasquez
Pass

144

40

Legend:
- Byers Peak Wilderness
- Fraser Experimental Forest
- Vasquez Peak Wilderness
- - - - - Zoom Loop

N

Ref: Winter Park/Central City/Rollins Pass Trails Illustrated Map

Winter Park Region

[Fig. 7] The mountain-ringed Fraser Valley was once covered by glaciers, a fact evident in the composition of the valley floor itself, which is glacial moraine—the gravel and rock accumulated and then left behind by glaciers that ground slowly down from the mountains that ring the north-facing valley. Fraser, a small town at 8,574 feet in the flat, high Fraser Valley regularly debates International Falls, Minnesota as to which is the coldest community in the Lower 48 (Fraser's average January low is -11 degrees Fahrenheit).

The Fraser Valley is a bit of a geological jumble. Berthoud Pass, at the southern end of the valley, is a natural low point in the ridge at the head of the valley. A fault runs through the Front Range mountains here, creating a weak area that has eroded over the ages. The shattered rock revealed in road cuts near the top of the pass is evidence of the fault's movement. US 40 careens down from the pass through Precambrian rock, the stuff that is the core of the Front Range and makes up the Indian Peaks, which run along the eastern side of the valley, and the Vasquez Mountains, curling up to the west. At the northern base of the Berthoud Pass you come to Winter Park-Mary Jane ski area and the western entrance to the Moffat Tunnel.

North of the town of Winter Park, about 3 miles farther on, the valley floor is comprised of Tertiary Era sediments and volcanic ash, although much of this is covered with glacial outwash—rocks and gravel carried from glaciers by streams.

Much of the forest cover on the surrounding peaks is lodgepole pine. This is a common forest type in northern and central Colorado, but less so in the south. If you walk through a lodgepole forest you are likely to notice charred stumps, evidence of logging, or other hints that some other forest existed before the present one. This was probably the case, since lodgepole is generally not a climax forest type, but a successional one that gives way to Douglas fir (*Pseudotsuga menziesii*) in montane environments, or Engelmann spruce (*Picea engelmannii*) and subalpine fir (*Abies bifolia*) at higher elevations.

However, lodgepole does very well in disturbed environments. Fire and logging both create opportunities for lodgepole, which may hold old cones on its branches for up to 40 years, waiting

LODGEPOLE PINE

(Pinus contorta)
Growing up to 80 feet tall, this pine has needles growing in twisted pairs and cones that are closed and prickly pointing away from the branch.

Nordic skiing and downhill skiing are both popular activities, especially near the Peak-to-Peak Scenic Byway.

for the heat of a blaze to loosen the sticky sap holding the cone closed and protecting the seeds. If a region is regularly logged or burned, lodgepole is likely to result.

Lodgepole grows densely, killing off many smaller trees and providing little opportunity for understory plants. One of the few that does survive in lodgepole groves, and is quite common, is heartleaved arnica (*Arnica cordifolia*), easily identified in this environment by its bright yellow blooms.

Relatively few animals thrive in lodgepole. The most common—or at least the most apparent—is the pine squirrel, or chickaree (*Tamiasciurus hudsonicus*), which will chatter furiously if it detects and intruder. The squirrels' tendency to cache large quantities of cones benefits another common, but less visible denizen, the red-backed vole (*Clethrionomys gapperi*), a rodent that looks like a mouse and lives off the squirrels' stores of cones. Other rodents, including deer mice (*Cricetidae*) and Uinta chipmunks (*Eutanias*) make their homes here, attracting the pine marten (*Martes americana*), a small, shy predator.

Directions: From I-70, take Exit 233 to US 40, which leads over Berthoud Pass to Winter Park and the Fraser Valley.

For more information: Fraser Visitors Center, 120 Zerex Ave, Fraser, CO 80442. Phone (970) 726-8312. Grand County Tourism Board Phone (800) 247-2636.

WINTER PARK

[Fig. 7] Winter Park is just that, a "winter park" owned and operated by the City of Denver. Following the 1940 opening of the Winter Park-Mary Jane ski area, a small town (Winter Park) coalesced near the base. One of the state's oldest ski areas, Winter Park-Mary Jane has been run as an agency of the city since 1950 by a volunteer board of directors. The resort now tallies more than a million skier days each winter. In terms of skiable terrain it is the third largest ski area in the state, with 2,886 acres. The rail line through the Moffat Tunnel to Front Range cities has carried skiers to the slopes since 1940. The Ski Train runs between Union Station in Denver and the base of Winter Park on Saturdays and Sundays from mid-December to mid-April, and on Fridays as well in February and March. The ride takes about two hours. Amtrak also provides daily service between Denver and Fraser, four miles north of the slopes.

Winter Park Resort (which runs the ski area) and the Fraser Valley promote themselves as Mountain Bike Capital, USA. The town and resort of Winter Park and nearby Fraser have aggressively developed mountain biking trails in recent years, and the valley's businesses generally seem to appreciate mountain bikers; many businesses adopt individual trails and make sure they are kept in good shape. More than 600 miles of bike trails exist in the valley, including many at Winter Park Resort, in the Fraser Experimental Forest, Silver Creek Resort, and Snow Mountain Ranch. From paved valley paths to demanding single track trails, the Fraser Valley is committed to providing bicycling opportunities for everyone.

Summer chairlift operations at Winter Park Resort enable bicyclists to take the easy way up, then ride a maze of trails down to the ski area base. A chairlift carries bike and rider from the base area to the Winter Park summit, Sunspot, at 10,700 feet. From here, a network of marked and accurately rated trails, patrolled by the bicycle equivalent of ski patrollers, extends to the summit of adjacent Mary Jane (11,200 feet) and Vasquez Ridge (10,700 feet).

Directions: From Denver, take I-70 west to Exit 233, then US 40 over Berthoud Pass to Winter Park. The resort is 67 miles from Denver.

Winter Activities: Skiing, snowboarding, snowshoe tours, snowcat tours, snowmobile tours. Cross country skiing on groomed trails is available for a fee at two areas in the Fraser Valley: Devil's Thumb Ranch (970-726-5632) and Snow Mountain Ranch (970-887-2152)

Summer Activities: Mountain bike tours, mountain bike clinics, mountain bike rentals, guided hiking tours, guided mountain adventures for kids ages 5-16.

Facilities: Information kiosk staffed daily, telephones, restrooms, summit and base restaurants. 2,886 acres of terrain, including 134 ski trails. Winter Park is home to the National Sports Center for the Disabled and hosts many disabled athletes.

Dates: Winter activities are generally available from early or mid-November to mid-April, depending on snow. Mary Jane remains open on weekends into May, conditions permitting. Summer activities are available from June through October.

Fees: There is a fee for skiing, mountain biking and chairlift rides.

Closest town: Winter Park, about 3 miles north on US 40.

For more information: Winter Park Resort, PO Box 36, Winter Park, CO 80482. Phone (970) 726-5514. For train information and reservations phone (800) 729-5813. Chamber of Commerce Web site: www.winterpark-info.com

MOUNTAIN BIKE RIDE: UPPER ROOF OF THE ROCKIES TO FANTASY MEADOW TO MOUNTAIN GOAT TO LITTLE VASQUEZ TO LOWER ARAPAHOE

The chairlift ride to Sunspot provides excellent views of Rollins Pass and James and Parry Peaks, at the south end of the Indian Peaks Wilderness. Riders should be in good shape to attempt single-track routes, not only because of their difficulty but because of their high elevation between 8,600 and 12,000 feet. Easier alternatives tend to stick to the ski area's service roads, but still involve occasional uphill sections. As with most mountain activities, an early start is a good idea, since afternoon often brings thunderstorms.

This is a moderate and strenuous ride, with the strenuous segment being Mountain Goat Trail. However, riders can easily avoid this black diamond-rated route (the ratings system is the same for a ski area going from green [easiest] to black diamond [expert only]) by taking alternate trails. Trail ratings are very accurate, and signage is excellent. This route takes about two hours to ride. It is a mix of uphill switchbacks through subalpine forest and meadows, steep descents along a tumbling mountain brook, dirt roads across the ski area, and swooping descents through lodgepole forest to the base of the ski area.

Trail: This particular trail combination amounts to about 10 miles, but many combinations are possible at the ski area.

Elevation: About 180 feet of climbing, followed by 1,740 feet of descent.

Degree of difficulty: Moderate and strenuous.

Surface: Dirt and rock, with some dirt roads. Signage at intersections.

MOUNTAIN BIKE RIDE: ZOOM LOOP, FRASER EXPERIMENTAL FOREST

[Fig. 7] Fraser Experimental Forest is managed by the U.S. Forest Service, which tests different logging methods to compare how logging affects water runoff in alpine and subalpine ecosystems. Established in 1937, the Experimental Forest has been selectively logged in small plots since 1955. Although the name may suggest a mishmash of logging roads and clear-cuts, the Fraser Experimental Forest presents a generally uniform facade from a distance. Only by traveling through it does the visitor see how and where it has been logged in small patches over the years.

Despite its emphasis on logging, the forest is a great place to mountain bike, and a number of trails have been cooperatively developed there, along with a campground inside the forest.

This trail winds from the tiny railroad community of Fraser, past wet meadows into the lodgepole pine of the Fraser Experimental Forest, along the verdant bank of Saint Louis Creek, and back past meadows to town. Along the way it gives nice views of the valley and the summit of Byers Peak to the west, a mountain that lies at the heart of a 100,000-acre roadless area.

Directions: Park in Fraser. Head west on County Road 73 / Saint Louis Creek Road. Ride 2.5 miles to Saint Louis Creek Campground, on the left. Turn onto the campground road, then turn right after a few hundred yards onto a single track trail just before the campground entrance (Creekside Trail). Follow this about 2 miles up to County Road 159. Turn left and head up the hill, then turn right on King Creek Road to reconnect with County Road 159. Stay straight for 0.5 mile, then turn left onto Zoom Trail. Descend 1.5 miles to a T intersection; bear left here onto Chainsaw

Trail to Elk Creek Road. Turn left and follow this road back to Fraser.

Fees: None to ride in the Fraser Experimental Forest, but there is a fee to camp at Saint Louis Creek Campground.

Closest town: Fraser, 2.5 miles east of Saint Louis Creek Campground.

Trail: 12 miles.

Elevation: Change of 1,000 feet.

Degree of difficulty: Moderate.

Surface: Dirt trails and gravel roads. Signage at intersections.

For more information: Fraser Visitors Center, 120 Zerex Ave, Fraser, CO 80442. Phone (970) 726-8312. Grand County Tourism Board Phone (800) 247-2636. A number of shops and facilities, including some campground hosts, provide free biking trails maps, which are indispensable.

VASQUEZ PEAK & BYERS PEAK WILDERNESSES

[Fig. 7] Vasquez Peak Wilderness (12,300 acres), and Byers Peak Wilderness (8,095 acres) make up two ends of the small Vasquez Mountains. The middle comprises the headwaters of St. Louis Creek in the Fraser Experimental Forest, an area that has not been logged. Both Vasquez Peak and Byers Peak were added to Colorado's wilderness inventory by Congress in 1993. Although small, these wilderness areas lie at the center of a 100,000-acre roadless area that includes the upper elevations of the Fraser Experimental Forest, the Williams Fork headwaters and the Ptarmigan Peak Wilderness Area (both lie to the south of the Vasquez Mountains). The Byers Peak and Vasquez Peak wilderness areas offer stunning ridge walks, mile after mile of open ridgeline; Vasquez Peak Wilderness includes seven miles of the Continental Divide Trail, all above timberline.

The idea of a "small" mountain range is a somewhat humorous one, particularly since Byers Peak rises to 12,804 feet. But given that Colorado has about 50 mountain ranges (a precise number depends on how you count), these mountains—which would form the heart of a national park in many other states—lie relatively unnoticed between the dramatic cordilleras of the Indian Peaks and Rocky Mountain National Park to the east, and the Gore Range to the west.

Directions: From Fraser, reach the Byers Peak Wilderness by taking Saint Louis Creek Road west to Forest Road 111 (West Saint Louis Creek), then following this to the end of the road, where you pick up the Byers Peak trailhead, which leads to the 12,804-foot summit of Byers Peak. Vasquez Peak Wilderness can be reached from Berthoud Pass. On the west side of the pass, hike up an old road marked by a Continental Divide Trail sign (CDT). At the top of the road, the trail picks up, climbing to a high point of 12,280 feet after 1.5 miles, which is the wilderness area boundary.

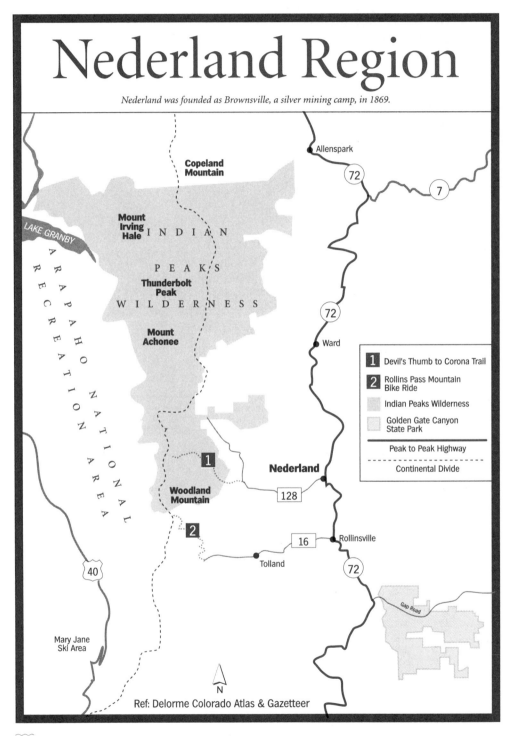

Nederland Region

Nederland was founded as Brownsville, a silver mining camp, in 1869.

Allenspark

72

7

Copeland Mountain

Mount Irving Hale

LAKE GRANBY

I N D I A N

P E A K S

Thunderbolt Peak

W I L D E R N E S S

72

Mount Achonee

Ward

A R A P A H O   N A T I O N A L   R E C R E A T I O N   A R E A

1

Woodland Mountain

Nederland

128

2

16

Rollinsville

40

Tolland

72

Mary Jane Ski Area

Gap Road

N

Ref: Delorme Colorado Atlas & Gazetteer

1 Devil's Thumb to Corona Trail

2 Rollins Pass Mountain Bike Ride

Indian Peaks Wilderness

Golden Gate Canyon State Park

Peak to Peak Highway

Continental Divide

Nederland Region

[Fig. 8] Located 16 miles west of Boulder on CO 19, Nederland was founded as Brownsville, a silver mining camp, in 1869. As was the case with many mining camps, the name kept changing. By 1871 it was known as Middle Boulder. In 1875 the town was given its present name because the principal mine and mill in the area had been purchased by a Dutch company, which operated as Mining Company Nederland. Much of Colorado's mineral exploitation depended on investors from the East Coast and overseas; to honor their Dutch employers, citizens changed the town's name to Nederland, which stuck.

Nederland's biggest boom came not from the usual gold or silver strikes, but from tungsten, a mineral used to strengthen steel. Ironically, tungsten had little value for the miners who were looking for silver and gold in the nineteenth century. But tungsten laced the hills around Nederland, and with the rise of steelmaking and the onset of war in the twentieth century, its value rose tenfold. Between 1900 and 1915, three-fifths of the tungsten produced in the United States came from Nederland. Then the tungsten market crashed, and with it the town. Today Nederland is a tourist and bedroom town, the eastern gateway to the Indian Peaks Wilderness and home to Eldora Ski Area.

Directions: From I-70, take Exit 244, US 6. After about 4 miles take CO 119 toward Black Hawk; stay on this route through Black Hawk to Nederland. From Boulder, take Canyon Boulevard west through town; this is the eastern end of CO 119; stay on it to Nederland.

INDIAN PEAKS WILDERNESS

[Fig. 8] This midsize (73,391-acre) wilderness area, easily visible from Denver, includes a jumble of sharp and dramatic peaks that rise south of the distinctive, flat-topped form of Longs Peak, which dominates the southeastern corner of Rocky Mountain National Park. Because it is so easily reached from the population centers of Denver and Boulder, the Indian Peaks Wilderness—particularly on its eastern side—is very heavily used. Forest Service regulations to manage this use require backpackers to obtain permits if they intend to camp inside the Indian Peaks Wilderness Area. This is the only wilderness area outside the national parks in Colorado with such a regulation. Permits are available from local Forest Service offices.

The Indian Peaks Wilderness contains several small glaciers, remnants of the last ice age. The city of Boulder's main water supply is Arapaho Glacier, just outside the eastern boundary of the wilderness. To protect the watershed, this area is closed to hikers and patrolled by rangers. The glaciers are replenished annually by winter snows. As the southernmost glacial remnants in the U.S., these ice fields may serve as the alpine equivalent of canaries in coal mines in that they are indicators of global warming. A rise of only a degree or two in annual average temperature could throw the balance toward melting and cause the glaciers to shrink or disappear.

Other reminders of the last Ice Age include the many glacial lakes and tarns that dot the landscape, and the north-facing cirques and steep slopes carved from the Precambrian rock by the ancient ice.

Directions: Several roads out of Nederland lead to eastern trailheads. Take County Road 130 west to County Road 111, then follow this to the trailhead for Arapaho Pass. For the Brainard Lake trailhead, take County Road 102 (Brainard Lake Drive) west out of Ward. For access on the west side, take US 34 north from Granby to Arapaho Bay Road, a right along the south short of Lake Granby. Follow this to the end of the road and the trailhead for Cascade Creek and Buchanan Pass.

Closest town: Nederland on the eastern side, Fraser on the western side.

For more information: Boulder Ranger District, Arapaho and Roosevelt National Forest, 2995 Baseline Road, Room 110, Boulder, CO 80303. Phone (303) 444-6600. Sulphur Ranger District, Arapaho and Roosevelt National Forest, 62429 Highway 40, PO Box 10, Granby, CO 80446. Phone (970) 887-4100.

DEVIL'S THUMB TRAIL TO CORONA TRAIL

[Fig. 8(1)] Devils's Thumb Trail (Forest Service Trail #902) begins at 9,100 feet. The trail crosses Middle Boulder Creek to a junction with King Trail; stay right on the old road. After 2.5 miles, another fork leads to Woodland Lake; stay right again. At the next intersection, Diamond Lake Cutoff, stay left. The trail crosses the outlet from Jasper Lake and passes along the south side of Devil's Lake, then climbs steeply to Devil's Thumb Pass at 12,100 feet.

Directions: From Nederland, go four miles west on CO 130 to the Hessie Trailhead, turn left and park at the trailhead.

Trail: 6 miles.

Elevation: Change of 3,000 feet.

Degree of difficulty: Moderate to Devil's Thumb Lake, strenuous to Devil's Thumb Pass.

Surface: Dirt and rock.

ROLLINS PASS MOUNTAIN BIKE RIDE

[Fig. 8(2)] This ride reaches the Continental Divide, yet it is moderate because it lies upon an old railway roadbed that was abandoned when the Moffat Tunnel was opened beneath Rollins Pass in 1927. From the top you can look west at Winter Park-Mary Jane ski area, down into the Fraser Valley, and on to the Vasquez and Byers Peak wilderness areas, as well as north into the Indian Peaks Wilderness. Because the last several miles of this route are above timberline, get an early start and keep a close eye on the weather.

Directions: From Nederland, follow CO 119 south about 4 miles to Rollinsville. Go west on Forest Road 149 (CO 16) for 9 miles. At the T-intersection (you can see the entrance to Moffat Tunnel to your left), park and begin riding up the old railroad bed to your right.

Moffat Tunnel

The opening of the 6.2-mile Moffat under the Continental Divide in 1927 greatly improved access into the Fraser Valley. Previously, trains traveled over the Indians Peaks to the east via Rollins Pass, a route first used by Ute Indians.

The trains started running over Rollins Pass in 1909, after Denver railroad investor David H. Moffat built a route for his Denver and Salt Lake Railroad over the pass, laying track over a toll road that John Quincy Adams Rollins had opened in 1873. At 11,680 feet, the pass was the highest railway route in the nation. The railroad bed and the remains of trestles and ruins of a boarding house at the pass are about all that's left of the great effort to get over Rollins Pass, for Moffat quickly learned that snow on the pass was a constant problem; clearing it consumed up to 40 percent of the railroad's budget. He convinced the federal government to build a tunnel under the Continental Divide instead, a project that cost $3 million a mile and was finished 16 years after Moffat's death.

The town of Arrow was built in 1902 at 9,580 feet on the western approach to Rollins Pass as a railroad camp during the construction of the railway route. It subsequently became a depot and mining supply town and was the first incorporated town in Grand County. But it lasted all of two years and has now vanished.

Closest town: Nederland, 13 miles east.

Trail: 15 miles.

Elevation: This trail rises 2,490 feet from the T-intersection, starting at 9,190 feet and ending at 11,680 feet.

Degree of difficulty: Easy to moderate, since the entire trail is on an old railway bed.

Surface: Graded roadbed, with some washouts and fallen rock.

🏞 GOLDEN GATE CANYON STATE PARK

[Fig. 8] Golden Gate Canyon State Park offers 14,000 acres of public lands and 35 miles of hiking trails in the foothills between Boulder and Golden. The park is relatively young; the first land purchase of 198 acres was made in the early 1960s.

The canyon took its name soon after the discovery of gold in Central City and Black Hawk in 1859. The region apparently was named by Joel Estes, a Kentuckian who later settled the area that would become Estes Park. Around 1859, Estes and his family established a settlement several miles north of Golden and named it Golden Gate, evidently in tribute to his successes in California during the gold rush of 1849. Estes stayed only a few months, then moved on. Shortly after the discovery of gold around Central City, the Golden Gate Canyon Toll Road was built and opened to accommodate miners seeking their riches.

Since no gold was found in the lands now enclosed by the park, the region became

Cache La Poudre Wilderness

The Cache la Poudre is Colorado's only federally protected Wild and Scenic River. This designation prohibits construction of dams or other man-made interference with the natural character of the river.

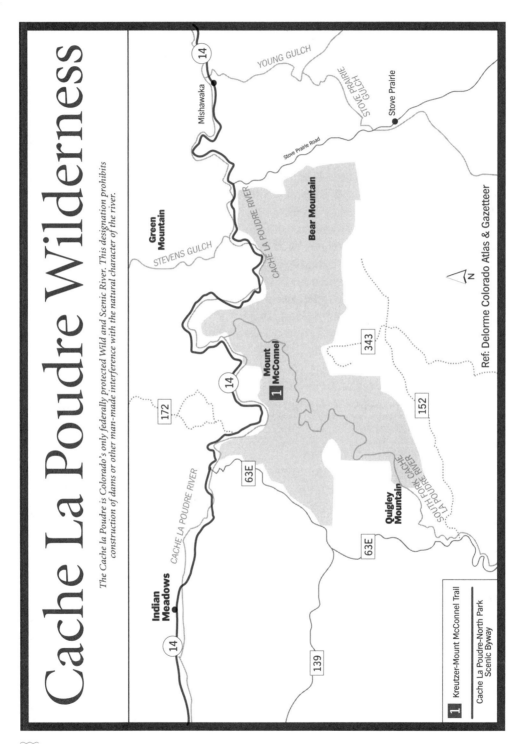

Ref: Delorme Colorado Atlas & Gazetteer

Mishawaka

YOUNG GULCH

STOVE PRAIRIE GULCH

Stove Prairie Road

Stove Prairie

Green Mountain

STEVENS GULCH

CACHE LA POUDRE RIVER

Bear Mountain

Mount McConnel

Quigley Mountain

SOUTH FORK CACHE LA POUDRE RIVER

CACHE LA POUDRE RIVER

Indian Meadows

14

172

63E

63E

139

343

152

1 Kreutzer-Mount McConnel Trail

Cache La Poudre-North Park Scenic Byway

home to farmers, ranchers, and loggers. During Prohibition, moonshiners found the rugged country good terrain for making and storing illegal liquor, for it was a good place to hide yet close to markets in Denver.

The park ranges in elevation from 7,400 feet to 10,388 feet. Panorama Point, on the northwestern edge of the park, offers dramatic views of the Indian Peaks and Continental Divide to the west—a view that usually includes snowy mountains until midsummer.

Directions: South entrance: Take I-70 west from Denver to Highway 58; follow this 5 miles west to CO 93; take this road two miles north to the sign for Golden Gate Canyon Road. Turn left, proceed 13 miles to the park entrance. West entrance: Follow CO 119 south from Nederland for 10 miles; turn east onto CO 46, proceed 5 miles to the visitor center.

Activities: Hiking, biking, horseback riding, interpretive programs, camping, picnicking, cross-country skiing.

Facilities: 168 campsites, including a group site; 288 picnic sites; dump station, showers, and laundry.

Dates: Open year-round.

Fees: There is a fee to enter the park, and a fee to camp.

Closest town: Nederland, 15 miles west; Golden, 15 miles east.

For more information: Golden Gate Canyon State Park, 3873 Highway 46, Golden, CO 80403. Phone (303) 582-3707.

Cache La Poudre Region

[Fig. 9] The Cache La Poudre River gained its name quite early in Colorado history, in 1836. Trappers affiliated with the Hudson Bay Company became bogged down while trying to bring wagons up the river. They stored barrels of gunpowder near the banks of the river until the next year, and named the place "store the powder" river. (It's pronounced "cash-la-pooh-druh.")

The river canyon, stretching from Fort Collins up into the northern reaches of Rocky Mountain National Park, was first formed by glaciers. Great tongues of ice extended down from the mountains in the Never Summer Range in the northern part of the park, turned east and carved the typically U-shaped valley formed by ice. Then the river took over as the glaciers receded, cutting a V-shaped gorge through the bottom of the older, glaciated canyon.

The Cache La Poudre is Colorado's only federally protected Wild and Scenic River. This designation, which covers the Little South Fork of the river and the entire main stem above Poudre Park, was granted in 1986. It prohibits construction of dams or other man-made interference with the natural character of the river. In addition, the Cache La Poudre Wilderness, Colorado's smallest (9,238 acres), protects the Little

The Cache La Poudre River is Colorado's only federally protected Wild and Scenic River.

South Fork and land along the south side of the main river. This wilderness area is almost completely undeveloped, largely because of the ruggedness of the land, but it does include one trail, the Kreutzer-Mount McConnel Trail (*see* page 61).

The vegetation in the Cache La Poudre canyon varies sharply depending on the exposure. For instance, near the mouth of the canyon, north-facing slopes host ponderosa pine and Douglas fir (*Psuedotsuga menziesii*), while hotter, south-facing slopes are populated by mountain mahogany (*Cercocarpus montanus*) and rabbitbrush (*Chrysothamus*).

Fire suppression and overgrazing of ponderosa parklands have exposed ponderosa pines to natural hazards, in particular the mountain pine beetle. Without fire, ponderosa may grow in dense, weak stands. Pine beetles, which are always present in low levels, take advantage of weakened trees, which cannot effectively defend themselves against the beetles. (Defense consists of trying to push boring beetles out by extruding pitch.) The beetles lay eggs between the bark and wood of the tree. During the winter, the eggs hatch and larvae eat the wood. A fungus carried by the beetles then kills the trees when it plugs up the cells that transport nutrients.

Ponderosas and other conifers are also vulnerable to dwarf mistletoe (*Arceuthobium americanum*), a parasitic plant that weakens and kills trees. When it is present in the branches of trees, dwarf mistletoe leads to the development of "witch's broom," a dense, twisted growth of twigs.

Look for evidence of porcupines (*Erethizon dorsatum*) in ponderosa forests. These slow-moving animals are found throughout Colorado but are particularly abundant in ponderosas. They do not hibernate, but eat forbs during the summer, then climb ponderosas and other conifers to eat the nutritious inner bark of the trees in winter. Large, uneven patches of missing bark on a green tree indicate that a porcupine has been dining there.

The Albert's squirrel (*Sciurus alberti*) depends almost entirely on ponderosa pines for food and nesting. Easily identified by its tasseled ears, the Albert's squirrel does not cache food for the winter. Instead, it eats the seeds of ponderosa pine cones during the summer and the inner bark from twigs during the winter. The Albert's squirrel will often select particular trees as food trees, a choice scientists discovered is based on the taste of the tree. They prefer trees with few aromatic chemicals in the sap.

During the spring and well into the summer, the Cache La Poudre River swells with snowmelt, making it ideal for whitewater rafters and kayakers.

Directions: From I-25, take Exit 269 to CO 14 and turn west toward the mountains. Follow this through Fort Collins to US 287; take this north. After about 10 miles, turn left onto CO 14 (west again); this road follows the Cache La Poudre River up to North Park.

KREUTZER-MOUNT MCCONNEL TRAIL

[Fig. 9(1)] This is the only official trail in the Cache La Poudre Wilderness. It switchbacks up out of the Cache La Poudre canyon to provide good views of the Mummy Range, Comanche Peak, and the Poudre Canyon, as well as a view into the rugged Little South Fork of the Cache La Poudre River.

Directions: From US 287 and CO 14, drive approximately 26 miles west on CO 14 to Mountain Park Campground. Turn south into the campground on the paved road. Southeast of the road is the Kreutzer Trail, Forest Service Trail #936. At the top of this trail—7,520 feet—the Mount McConnel trail begins.

Dates: This trail can be hiked all year, but may be partially covered by snow or ice during the winter.

Closest town: Fort Collins, 35 miles east.

For more information: Estes-Poudre Ranger District, 1311 South College, 2nd Floor, Fort Collins, CO 80526. Phone (970) 498-1375.

Trail: 4 miles round-trip.

Elevation: Change of 1,280 feet.

Degree of difficulty: Moderate.

Surface: Rough dirt and rock.

Scenic Drives

▨ THE PEAK-TO-PEAK SCENIC BYWAY

This route stretches 67 miles from Estes Park to Clear Creek, running almost directly north-south along the Front Range and passing through some of Colorado's richest mining country.

Estes Park was founded in 1860 by Joel Estes, who decided the meadows at the headwaters of the Big Thompson River created an ideal location for ranching. Today the town is the major entryway to Rocky Mountain National Park; on peak weekend days as many as 50,000 visitors can pass through Estes Park—an excellent reason to visit at other times. The great white hotel on the hill north of downtown is the Stanley Hotel, built by the F.O. Stanley who created the Stanley Steamer motorcar. The hotel served as the film location for the movie *The Shining*.

Heading south from Estes Park, the byway slowly descends. Much of its route,

Ponderosa Pine

Pinus ponderosa is perhaps the most distinctive forest type of the Front Range foothills and can be found the length of the state on the eastern side of the mountains. Ponderosa pines are easy to identify at close range, for they have much longer needles than any other Colorado conifer: 4 to 7 inches, growing in bunches of two or three needles. The bark of mature ponderosas smells faintly of vanilla or butterscotch if you put your face against it. Middle-aged trees have great, round crowns; old trees, which can grow to 150 feet, have flattened tops.

Ponderosas dominate the second warmest conifer forest sites in the state; only piñon-juniper forests prefer warmer sites. Typically, precipitation in areas ponderosas prefer is less than 25 inches annually, and snow rarely accumulates to a depth of greater than 1 foot. This preference for relatively dry terrain, and for elevations from 5,600 feet to 9,000 feet, explains why ponderosas thrive on the Front Range foothills. Although vast quantities of precipitation fall from winter storms in the mountains, relatively little falls immediately east of Colorado's peaks. This area is known as a "rain shadow" (*see* page 64).

Ponderosa pines often grow in distinctive parklike settings, creating a savannah-type environment that includes rich blankets of forbs and grasses beneath the large, widely scattered trees. Like other western pine species, ponderosas evolved to take advantage of fire. A thick, corky bark protects mature trees from smaller fires that clear out underbrush and younger trees. Ponderosas thrive in drier soils but also compete for moisture, sending out lateral roots as far as 100 feet, and tap roots as deep as 40 feet.

however, runs through the montane ecosystem of ponderosa pine, Douglas fir, blue spruce, aspen, and lodgepole.

Many visitors come to the area, and to nearby Rocky Mountain National Park, to observe elk. The big ungulates are commonly seen during winter months, when they are forced toward towns and residential developments that have been built in areas such as valley floors where they traditionally foraged. Look for them at dawn and dusk, especially in winter.

At Mile 29.5 the byway passes the turnoff to Ward, once a rich mining town and the upper end of the vanished Colorado and Northwestern Railway, which traveled so tortuously up Left Hand Canyon from Boulder that locals dubbed it "the Whiplash Route." Gold was first found here in 1860 by Calvin M. Ward. The next year the Columbia vein was located; it would eventually produce $5 million worth of ore.

PONDEROSA PINE
(Pinus ponderosa)
Also called the western yellow pine, this tree grows to 180 feet tall with needles up to 7 inches long.

Ward didn't incorporate until 1898, when it had about 1,000 residents. But a 1900 fire that burnt down all but one of 53 buildings in the business district doomed the town, which was only partially rebuilt.

Fire was a common scourge in mining towns, which were thrown up in a matter of days with little consideration for safety. Almost inevitably, a mining town had to burn to the ground at least once before the locals decided to build in brick and stone. This approach may seem foolhardy, but it did have a certain crazy logic. Many mining camps were just that—camps. They were built in a few weeks and sometimes amounted to only a few tents. If the strike turned out to be a bust, miners moved on. There was no point in building a real town until you knew whether you had real wealth to build it with.

One town that did was Central City, just up Gregory Gulch from Black Hawk. This was the site of the gold strike that started Colorado's half-century mineral boom on May 6, 1859. John Gregory hit the ore vein that had been leaching gold into Clear Creek. Within weeks, thousands of men were working the steep hills around what would become Central City. New York newspaper editor Horace Greeley came to see all the commotion and soon publicized the news of the discovery to the world—apparently unaware that the placer he examined had been salted with gold dust in advance. When Greeley panned for gold—surprise!—he found some. Greeley, Colorado, is named for the man who is famously (but wrongly) believed to have said "Go west, young man."

What Greeley really said was, "If you have no family of friends to aid you, and no prospect opened to you there, turn your face to the great West, and there build up a

Rain Shadows

The jet stream generally carries storms from west to east across Colorado's mountains. When warm, moist air from the Pacific Ocean encounters mountain ranges it rises and cools (generally at a rate of 3 to 5 degrees Fahrenheit for each 1,000 feet). Cooler air cannot hold as much moisture as warmer air, so water vapor condenses into visible clouds and precipitation, which falls on the cordillera. Mountains literally make their own weather by this process; visitors unfamiliar with mountain weather may, when they are in the mountains, expect storms to come from somewhere else when in fact the day's thunderstorms are forming all around them.

This cooling process squeezes much of the moisture from the Pacific air flow. As the air continues west over the Front Range foothills and out onto Colorado's plains, significantly less moisture is available in the sky to fall as rain or snow. Sometimes, however, the weather pattern is reversed. Warm winds occasionally bring moisture from the Gulf of Mexico into Colorado from the southeast (a process called an "upslope"). Such winds can produce fierce blizzards along the eastern side of Colorado's Front Range as moist air crashes into the eastern side of the mountains.

home and fortune." John Soule wrote "Go west, young man," in an 1851 Indiana newspaper article.

Central City burnt down in 1874, but by then it was well established as a mining center, and it was immediately rebuilt in brick and stone. Gilpin County, which includes Central City, has produced $500,000,000 dollars in mineral wealth since that first strike, much of it in the early, frantic years. Central City was home to Clara Brown, a black woman who bought her own freedom from slavery for $100 and moved to Colorado. As the operator of a laundry, and an occasional grubstaker of miners, she earned enough money to buy the freedom of 29 other slaves. Today her image graces a stained glass window in the State Capitol.

Central City and nearby Black Hawk, along with Cripple Creek, are the only towns in Colorado to allow gambling. Limited stakes gambling was approved by voters and began on October 1, 1991. Since then, all three towns have been largely reconstructed as theme-park versions of their former selves, catering to vast numbers of tourists but now bereft of their authenticity.

Length: 67 miles

Dates: Open year-round.

For more information: Central City Chamber of Commerce, 281 Church Street, Central City, CO 80427. Phone (303) 582-5077.

▩ CACHE LA POUDRE-NORTH PARK SCENIC BYWAY

This scenic byway runs 103.5 miles from Fort Collins to Walden. This section describes the first 72.5 miles, from Fort Collins to Cameron Pass. The balance of the route is included in the Northwest Mountains Region section of this book (*see* page 117).

The route up the Cache La Poudre Valley from the High Plains is one of the few natural breaks in the Front Range, and it has been used by travelers for millennia. Evidence of the Folsom people, early hunter-gatherers who are believed to have roamed the area 10,000 years ago, was first found in 1924 in the foothills above Fort Collins. In more recent centuries, the region was a contact point between Ute Indians, who resided principally in the interior mountains, and the Arapaho, Cheyenne, and Sioux of the Plains. The explorer John C. Frémont traveled the area twice during the mid-1840s, although trappers and mountain men had worked the region previously.

Because this area is north of Colorado's mineral belt, there is almost no mining history or activity in the region at all, although there is some quarrying of limestone.

From the junction of US 287 and CO 14, the route climbs west on CO 14 along the river. At Mile 11.5 you can see a hogback to the northwest. The term "hogback" describes the uneven ridgetop and refers to a particular type of ridge that is formed when sedimentary layers of rock are lifted up on edge and erode unevenly. This particular hogback is Dakota Sandstone, formed about 135 million years ago. It is harder than the Lower Cretaceous shale and Jurassic shale which lie on either side of it (once above and below, now east and west respectively), and so has withstood erosion more fully during the eons since these rocks were first lifted and displaced by the great Precambrian block that formed the Front Range. The Dakota Hogback is visible along much of the Front Range where the plains and mountains meet.

At Mile 51 there is a pulloff for the Home Moraine Geologic Site. This is the terminal moraine of the glacier that carved much of the Cache La Poudre canyon. Generally, glaciers along the Front Range did not descend below 8,500 feet. More glacial evidence can be found around Mile 63 where glacial till—a mix of many sizes of rock—was left by retreating glaciers along the west side of the valley.

At Cameron Pass, Mile 72.5, you have reached the Continental Divide at 10,276 feet. Just to the south are the 12,485-foot Nokhu Crags, the dramatic exclamation point at the northern end of the Never Summer Range, which comprises the northwestern corner of Rocky Mountain National Park. The Crags are actually within the Colorado State Forest, which encompasses both sides of the road and the forested western slopes of the Medicine Bow Mountains, which are run north from the pass toward Wyoming (*see* the Northwestern Mountain Region section, page 117).

Length: 72.5 miles.

Dates: Year-round.

For more information: Fort Collins Chamber of Commerce, 225 South Meldrum Street, Fort Collins, CO Phone (970) 482-3746.

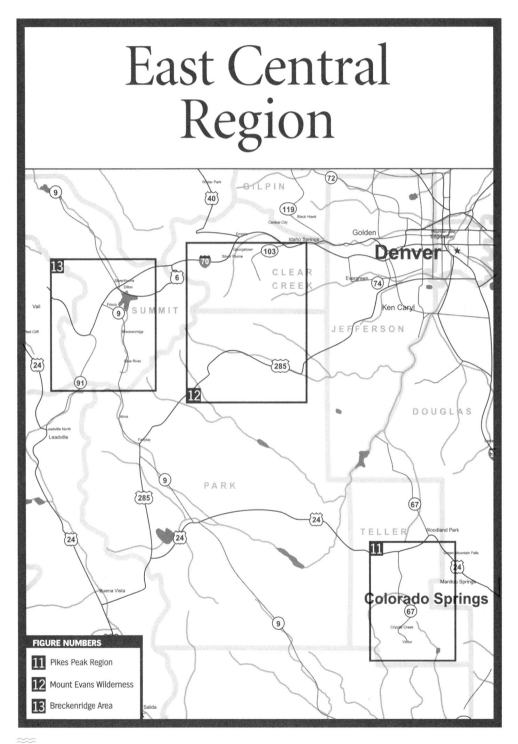

East Central Region

FIGURE NUMBERS

11 Pikes Peak Region

12 Mount Evans Wilderness

13 Breckenridge Area

East Central Region

The southern half of Colorado's Front Range is punctuated by the broad, distinctive frame of Pike's Peak, a mountain that intrigued early explorers and is still easily picked out by visitors driving or flying into Denver. Like the northern Front Range, Pikes Peak and much of the southern Front Range, as well as the mountains lying immediately west, contain enormous mineral wealth—an enticement that drew midnineteenth century miners and settlers to what had been, until then, the province of Indians, beaver trappers, and explorers.

The East Central Region lies southeast of Denver. It is defined along its northern edge by Interstate 70 from Denver to Vail Pass. The border turns south here along an imaginary line to Fremont Pass, then—tracing the summit ridge of the Tenmile and Mosquito ranges—follows the western boundaries of Park and Fremont counties to the hamlet of Cleona, on the Arkansas River. The southern boundary turns east here,

[*Above:* A view of snow-covered mountains from Breckenridge]

following and encompassing the Arkansas River out to the plains.

This area includes South Park, one of four intermontane parks in the state. It is a region with a colorful mining history and a booming ski industry—both the result of geology.

As is true throughout the state, history is a function of geology and geography. The entire Front Range is what geologists call a "faulted anticline." An anticline is an upward fold in the earth's crust (the opposite, a syncline, is a downward fold); this one is "faulted" because of the way its Precambrian granite core is broken by fault lines.

The basis for today's mountains was laid 300 million years ago, during the Colorado orogeny in the Pennsylvanian Epoch. The ancestral Rockies formed then were comprised of two enormous ranges: Uncompahgria, covering much of the southwestern quadrant of Colorado; and Frontrangia, extending from south-central Wyoming southeast across Colorado into New Mexico. Erosion of these mountains produced sedimentary rocks known as the Fountain Formation (seen at Garden of the Gods, *see* page 72), the Maroon Formation (shown most dramatically in the Maroon Bells near Aspen, *see* page 178), and the Sangre de Cristo Formation, now situated high in that uplifted eponymous mountain range (*see* page 76).

After the ancestral Rockies had been worn by erosion to mere nubs of their former grandeur, the Laramide orogeny began about 65 million years ago, lasting about 20 million years. Great spines of Precambrian rock were forced upward. This was followed, in the period from 45 million to 28 million years ago, by volcanic incursions and eruptions. Masses of hot lava and superheated fluids pushed up into the cracked overlying rocks, both the Precambrian rock and the younger sedimentary rocks. In many places it did not erupt through the surface, but slowly cooled in place, only to be revealed by millions of years of erosion as softer, overlying rock was stripped off. This is how Pikes Peak was formed. Other volcanic intrusions weren't revealed until miners discovered and chased them, following the "veins" of white quartz and other minerals that often contained gold or silver.

But that's getting ahead of ourselves. Beginning 28 million years ago, the Miocene-Pliocene uplift raised the entire state of Colorado, and surrounding regions, about 5,000 feet. This uplift gave new energy to streams running off the mountains, allowing them to cut deep gorges in the rock. Royal Gorge was formed by the Arkansas River cutting through the rock as it was slowly raised. So was the Black Canyon of the Gunnison River (*see* page 218).

Pleistocene-age glaciers put the finishing touches on the peaks, carving deep cirques and broad valleys during three distinct glaciation periods called the Wisconsin glaciation.

The southwestern flanks of Pikes Peak were, in 1890, the site of the largest and most profitable gold strike in the state—a discovery that came 31 years after the first Colorado gold rush. To the north, Idaho Springs, Georgetown, Silver Plume, Breck-

Zebulon Pike

United States Army Lieutenant Zebulon Montgomery Pike departed in the spring of 1806 from Fort Belle Fontaine, near Saint Louis, with 22 men to survey the southwestern portions of the new Louisiana Purchase. Lewis and Clark had not yet returned from their expedition to the northwest and the Pacific Ocean when Pike began his trip across the Great Plains in search of the headwaters of both the Arkansas and Red rivers.

The Spanish governor in Santa Fe, who had heard about Pike's expedition and worried about American incursions into Spanish territory, sent an armed force of 600 men to intercept him, but they failed to find the small American group. By November 1806, Pike had established a small log stockade near the site of present-day Pueblo, and set out to climb the mountain to the northwest he described as "a small blue cloud." Two-and-a-half days of labor left Pike in waist-deep snow and seemingly no closer to the peak, so he retreated. He was the first known American to attempt the summit.

His expedition covered an extraordinary amount of territory in the following months, especially given that the men were traveling in winter. They found the mouth of Royal Gorge, then traveled north away from the Arkansas River, up through South Park, and over the Mosquito Range to the upper reaches of the Arkansas. Thinking they were now on the Red River, they descended down through the Royal Gorge, thus making a loop, before realizing their mistake.

Still seeking the Red River, and plagued by hunger and frozen feet, Pike's expedition traveled in January over the Sangre de Cristo Mountains to the San Luis Valley, then to the Conejos River, a tributary of the Rio Grande, which they again mistook for the Red River. Well inside Spanish territory, Pike's group was discovered by Spanish scouts and "invited" to the territorial capital of Santa Fe. Considering discretion the better part of valor, they went. From there the Spanish governor sent them south to Chihuahua, Mexico for interrogation. After confiscating Pike's papers, Spanish officials marched the expedition to the Texas-Louisiana border and released Pike and his men in July 1807.

enridge and Fairplay were part of the early mining booms that began with John Gregory's gold strike in nearby Central City. Today they are tourist attractions and resort towns that continue to find their appeal in the mountains around them.

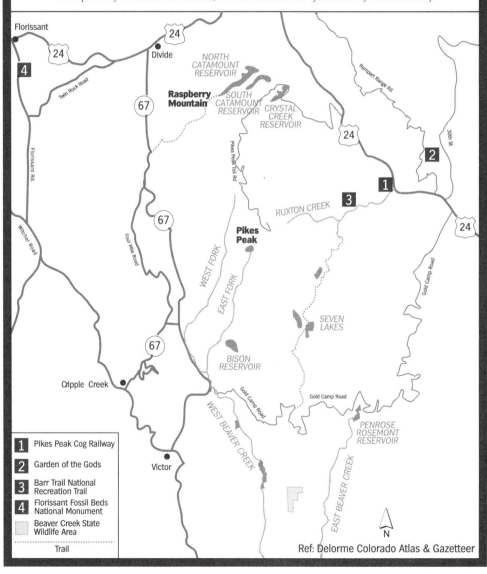

Pikes Peak Region

The inspiration for America the Beautiful, *Pikes Peak attracts tens of thousands of visitors annually.*

Florissant

24

Divide

NORTH
CATAMOUNT
RESERVOIR

Rampart Range Rd

24

4

Twin Rock Road

67

**Raspberry
Mountain**

SOUTH
CATAMOUNT
RESERVOIR

CRYSTAL
CREEK
RESERVOIR

24

30th St.

Florissant Rd.

Pikes Peak Toll Rd

2

1

3

RUXTON CREEK

67

Witcher Road

Four Mile Road

WEST FORK

EAST FORK

**Pikes
Peak**

24

Gold Camp Road

SEVEN
LAKES

67

BISON
RESERVOIR

Cripple Creek

Gold Camp Road

Gold Camp Road

WEST BEAVER CREEK

PENROSE
ROSEMONT
RESERVOIR

Victor

EAST BEAVER CREEK

1 Pikes Peak Cog Railway

2 Garden of the Gods

3 Barr Trail National
Recreation Trail

4 Florissant Fossil Beds
National Monument

Beaver Creek State
Wildlife Area

Trail

N

Ref: Delorme Colorado Atlas & Gazetteer

Pikes Peak

[Fig. 11] Said to be the inspiration for Katherine Lee Bates' 1893 song "America The Beautiful," conjuring the lines "purple mountain majesties / above the fruited plain," Pikes Peak is a very popular destination. Tens of thousands of people travel annually by car, foot, and cog railway to the 14,109-foot summit.

A landmark for settlers coming across the Great Plains, Pikes Peak was first described by Zebulon Pike in 1806. Its summit was not climbed by an American until July 1820, when Edwin James, a scientist accompanying Major Stephen H. Long on a military survey of the region, ventured to the top. The naming of mountains got a little confusing then, in part because maps and navigation tended to be rough. Long, for whom Longs Peak in Rocky Mountain National Park is named, didn't know James had climbed the mountain already called Pikes Peak, so he named the mountain James Peak in honor of his comrade's success. Long thought he already had passed by Pikes Peak as he traveled south along the foot of the Front Range; in fact, the mountain he thought was Pikes Peak would later be named after Long himself. What he had seen was not Pikes Peak, but what we know today as Longs Peak, in Rocky Mountain National Park (*see* page 35).

Needless to say, "James Peak" didn't stick, and Pikes Peak retained its original appellation.

BARR TRAIL NATIONAL RECREATION TRAIL

[Fig. 11(3)] Built between 1914 and 1921 by Fred Barr, this trail is the traditional, and most popular hiking route up the northeastern side of Pikes Peak. Many trailheads leading to the summits of Colorado's Fourteeners start at 10,000 feet or higher; the Barr Trail begins at 6,720 feet. Because of its length (13 miles one-way) and very low starting elevation, the trail is usually attempted as a two-day hike to the summit.

Directions: Pick up the trailhead above the Pikes Peak Cog Railroad Depot, off Ruxton Avenue in Manitou Springs.

Facilities: Barr Camp, a lodge and camping site at 10,840 feet. There is a fee for overnight use, and reservations are required.

Trail: 13 miles one-way.

Elevation: Gain of 7,390 feet.

Degree of difficulty: Strenuous.

Surface and Blaze: Dirt and rock.

For more information: Pikes Peak Ranger District, 601 South Weber Street, Manitou Springs, CO 80903. Phone (719) 636-1602.

PIKES PEAK COG RAILWAY

[Fig. 11(1)] This cog railway has operated for more than a century and currently uses modern, Swiss-made vehicles. Rides to the top and back, including about 30 minutes on the summit, take slightly more than three hours.

Directions: From I-25, take Exit 141 to US 24 west to Manitou Springs, about 8 miles, then left on Ruxton Avenue. The depot is at 515 Ruxton Avenue.

Dates: Open late Apr. to late Oct., weather permitting.

Fees: There is a fee to ride the train.

For more information: Pikes Peak Cog Railway, PO Box 351, Manitou Springs, CO 80829. Phone (719) 685-9033. Reservations recommended.

PIKES PEAK TOLL ROAD

[Fig. 11] This is a 19-mile drive, beginning at 7,400 feet. Allow at least two hours to reach the summit. The road is paved on the lower sections, gravel above. Six miles up is the Crystal Visitors Center, which provides interpretive information on the mountain and the various life zones, from the high plains to alpine tundra, that the road traverses. At the 13-mile mark the Glen Cove Inn offers refreshments. From the summit, views on clear days stretch to New Mexico to the south, Kansas to the east, west toward the Collegiate and Sangre de Cristo Mountains, and north along the length of the Front Range.

Directions: From I-25, take Exit 141 to US 24 West. Follow this 14 miles to Cascade, then turn left on Pikes Peak Road.

Facilities: Visitors center, restaurant en route.

Dates: Year-round, weather permitting.

Fees: There is a fee to drive the road.

Closest town: Manitou Springs, six miles east of Pikes Peak Road.

For more information: Pikes Peak-America's Mountain, PO Box 1575, Mail Code 060, Colorado Springs, CO 80901-1575. Phone (719) 684-9383.

Garden of the Gods

[Fig. 11(2)] This spectacular city park is popular with walkers, bikers, picnickers, climbers and drivers because of its geology and its location. Situated along a fault line where the Plains crash into the mountains, the garden is a fantastic collection of geology, a place that seems like a collision of titanic forces, frozen in time—which it is. Beautiful spires of peach-colored rock rear into the sky here, framing dramatic views of Pikes Peak, which shoulders its way 7,000 feet into the sky almost directly above Colorado Springs.

Garden of the Gods was created by Frontrangia, the easternmost of the two ancestral Rockies ranges. The rocks which today comprise the striking vertical walls and fins in the eastern shadow of Pikes Peak were laid down as eroded Fountain Formation sediments by streams and rivers that cut the ancestral Rockies down to nubs. This occurred from Pennsylvanian time, about 300-plus million years ago, down into the Permian Period, which ended 240 million years ago. That's what scientists think, anyway; a lack of embedded fossils has made dating these rocks problematic.

The monoliths of the park were tilted into their vertical position by the uplift of the Precambrian core of the Front Range. These salmon-colored rocks are more erosion-resistant than others because they were hardened by groundwater that carried silica and hematite into the sandstone, cementing the individual grains together and giving the rock its distinctive color.

The visitor center on the eastern edge of the park provides dramatic views through the Garden of the Gods formations up toward Pikes Peak. Southeast of the main peak, Cheyenne Mountain is an example of a thrust fault. Relieved of the enormous pressure of overlying rock by erosion, the internal grains of the hard, cold rock actually expanded like a chewing gum bubble, pushing horizontally out over younger, sedimentary layers as far as 1 mile. This faulting layered older rock on top of younger rock, which is uncommon in geology.

Directions: From I-25, take Exit 146 and drive west on Garden of The Gods Road 2.3 miles to 30th Street. Turn left, south, and go 1.5 miles to the visitor center, on the left.

Activities: Walking, bicycling, rock climbing, picnicking, horseback riding. Check at the visitor center for regulations regarding climbing, bicycling, and horseback riding.

Facilities: Visitors center, bookstore, restaurant, phone, restrooms. More than 4 miles of trails, many handicapped accessible.

Dates: Open year-round.

Fees: None.

For more information: Colorado Springs Parks and Recreation Department, 1401 Recreation Way, Colorado Springs, CO 80905. Phone (719) 578-6640.

ENGELMANN SPRUCE
(Picea engelmannii)
This spruce grows up to 120 feet tall and is identified by four-sided blue-green needles and cones with wavy edges on the scales.

Cripple Creek and Victor

[Fig. 11] These two towns formed around the fifth richest goldfield in the world, producing more than $500 million of the mineral. Although Pikes Peak is not a volcano, the area between Victor and Cripple Creek is an ancient volcanic caldera, or crater. The core rock is known as breccia, a rock that has been broken and consolidated repeatedly, the result of the caldera forming and collapsing several times during eons of volcanic activity.

The ore-bearing veins in the region were formed by mineral-rich fluids that seeped into the cracked rock, veining the old volcano with gold, silver, and other minerals. Erosion eventually stripped off 1,500 feet of overlying rock, preparing the way for cowboy Bob Womack, who discovered gold in a pasture in 1890.

Cripple Creek quickly became one of Colorado's greatest mining towns. Three railroads served the region. Two devastating business district fires hardly slowed the work, and enormous fortunes were made. By 1900 an estimated 30,000 people lived in the region.

Today, Victor retains a few hundred residents and a dilapidated feel. Cripple Creek, by contrast, has been radically altered by the introduction of limited stakes gambling, which has taken over and sharply altered what was once a fading mountain belle.

Directions: From I-25, take Exit 141 and turn west on US 24, which offers two choices. You may take Gold Camp Road (left after about 3 miles) to Victor, a winding route along an old railroad bed. Or, follow US 24 through Woodland Park to Florissant, then take Cripple Creek Road (County Road 1) south to Cripple Creek.

For more information: Cripple Creek Chamber of Commerce, 337 Bennett Drive, Cripple Creek, CO 80813. Phone (719) 689-2169.

Florissant Fossil Beds National Monument

[Fig. 11(4)] Unprepossessing from a distance, this small national monument is a window into an ancient world, the site of a prehistoric lake, and home to some of the earth's most extraordinary fossils.

The 6,000-acre monument was created in 1969 after scientists threatened to lie down in front of bulldozers that were about to gouge out a subdivision on the site of an ancient lake bed. This lake, about 12 miles long and 2 miles wide, existed during the Oligocene epoch, 34 or 35 million years ago. Although the site probably lay near today's elevation of 8,000 feet, the climate—according to the fossil record—was more like that of today's San Francisco, warmer and wetter than it is now.

The lake bed turned out to be a paleontologist's dream. Since it was discovered in 1874, fossilized leaves, fruit, flowers, pollen, and even tree stumps of 150 ancient plant species have been discovered, plus 1,200 insect species, along with fossilized fish, mammals, birds, snails, and clams.

The most striking natural phenomena at the monument are the enormous, fossilized stumps of ancient redwood trees, several of which have been excavated but remain in place where the trees once grew. The largest stump is of an ancient, extinct giant redwood, *Sequoia affinis*. This fossil stump is 13 feet in diameter and 42 feet in circumference.

At one time these trees grew on the shore of the ancient lake. A volcano located near the site of Pikes Peak, 15 miles to the southeast, erupted, sending a wall of mud flooding down to the lake and its surroundings. This mud entombed the trees 15 feet up their trunks. Eventually the mud hardened into volcanic tuff. Ground water soaking through the tuff dissolved silica; as the water penetrated the wood, the silica hardened, petrifying the tree stumps.

Many of the insect, leaf, and flower fossils are extraordinarily preserved, so that even the veins in insect wings may be discerned. Mud, silt and volcanic ash preserved these fossils in shales. Taken all together, they paint a picture of a very different time, when plants and insects that now live in much more temperate climates, such as Mexico and coastal regions of the United States, thrived in Colorado.

Directions: From US 24 in Florissant, take County Road 1 south 2 miles to the signed monument entrance.

Activities: Interpretive trails, including a 0.5-mile and 1-mile loop that are handicapped accessible. Another 10 miles of trails are open to hiking, horseback riding, and cross-country skiing in winter. No fossil collecting is permitted.

Facilities: Visitor center with museum, restrooms, phone, 2 picnic areas.

Dates: Open daily except for Thanksgiving, Christmas, and New Year's Day.

Fees: There is a fee between Apr. and Nov.

Closest town: Florissant, 2 miles north.

For more information: Florissant Fossil Beds National Monument, PO Box 185, Florissant, CO 80816. Phone (719) 748-3253.

Mount Evans Area

Mount Evans is the Fourteener that dominates Denver's skyline, clearly visible immediately to the west. Mount Evans and Pikes Peak are the only Fourteeners with roads to their summits. Their geology, too, is similar; both are batholiths. About 1.7 billion years ago, molten granite welled up into the overlying rock but did not break through in an eruption. The intrusion cooled slowly, a fact evidenced by the large grains of quartz, feldspar, and mica in Mount Evans's rock. Such old rock as this has

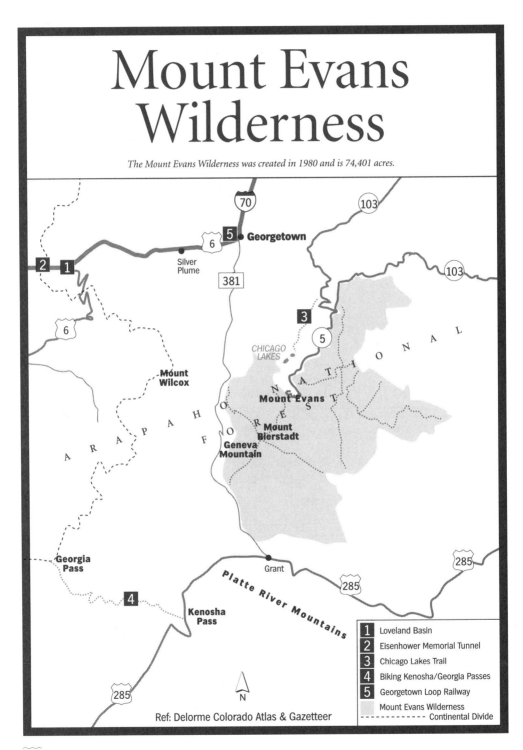

Mount Evans Wilderness

The Mount Evans Wilderness was created in 1980 and is 74,401 acres.

Georgetown

Silver Plume

381

CHICAGO LAKES

Mount Wilcox

Mount Evans

Mount Bierstadt

Geneva Mountain

Georgia Pass

Grant

Kenosha Pass

Platte River Mountains

1	Loveland Basin
2	Eisenhower Memorial Tunnel
3	Chicago Lakes Trail
4	Biking Kenosha/Georgia Passes
5	Georgetown Loop Railway
	Mount Evans Wilderness
	- - - - Continental Divide

Ref: Delorme Colorado Atlas & Gazetteer

N

been through a lot; it experienced both the creation of the ancestral Rockies and the Laramide orogeny.

All that lifting, twisting and shaking fractured the batholith, creating opportunities for mineral-carrying volcanic solutions to impregnate the mountain with veins of quartz, and sometimes gold and silver. Mount Evans is part of the mineral belt, a broad swath stretching from the northern Front Range southwest into the San Juan Mountains created in this manner. The Miocene-Pliocene uplift eventually raised the batholith and set the stage for erosion to remove overlying layers of softer stone.

Along the base of surface rocks you will find a coarse, granitic sand, the first step in soil building. These grains are broken off because the mica, or biotite, included within the rock decomposes into clay when exposed to water. This clay expands, breaking grains off of the granite surface. On both Mount Evans and Pikes Peak, this weathering of ancient granite tends to round the rock and separate boulders along exposed cracks.

The montane environment extends up to 7,000 feet on Mount Evans, and is characterized by ponderosa pine and Douglas fir. Above this point you'll encounter the aspens and lodgepole pines, which give way to subalpine fir, Engelmann spruce, and bristlecone pines (*Pinus aristata*). Timberline and alpine tundra begin at about 12,000 feet.

The summit drive takes you past Echo Lake at 10,600 feet, Lincoln Lake at 11,700 feet, and Summit Lake at 12,830 feet. If you're not accustomed to altitude, take it easy when walking down to these lakes or from the parking lot to the summit, where your body is able to obtain only about 60 percent of the oxygen you would at sea level.

Directions: From I-70 take Exit 240 to CO 103. At the intersection with CO 5, turn right, south, toward the summit, which is 28 miles away from I-70.

Facilities: Seasonal road to summit. Day hiking at several trailheads, including Mount Goliath Natural Area and Summit Lake. Picnicking and fishing at Echo Lake Park.

Dates: Year-round, although summit road is closed in winter.

Fees: There is no fee.

Closest town: Idaho Springs, 13 miles north.

For more information: Idaho Springs Chamber of Commerce, 2200 Miner Street, Idaho Springs, CO Phone (303) 567-4382.

MOUNT EVANS WILDERNESS

[Fig. 12] Created in 1980, this 74,401-acre wilderness area excludes the road to the summit but encompasses both Mount Evans (14,264 feet), and nearby Mount Bierstadt (14,060 feet). Mount Evans is home to some of the best examples of bristlecone pines in the area, along with bighorn sheep (*Ovis canadensis*) and mountain goats (*Oreamnos americanus*), animals that are often furtive and rarely seen in other parts of the state, but seem to be more accustomed to human presence here.

Directions: The wilderness can be reached from several points, including the summit road (*see* page 77), the Guanella Pass (*see* page 91), and the Chicago Lake Trail (*see* page 78).

Closest town: Idaho Springs, 13 miles south.

For more information: Clear Creek Ranger District, Arapaho-Roosevelt National Forest, 101 Chicago Creek, PO Box 3307, Idaho Springs, CO 80452. Phone (303) 567-2901.

CHICAGO LAKES TRAIL

[Fig. 12(3)] This trail drops down through bristlecone pines and past a small reservoir before crossing a zone where the subalpine forest is slowly recuperating from a forest fire. The trail follows the glacially carved Chicago Creek valley. Great, sloping domes of ancient granite line the walls, shaped by spalling, when freezing water flakes off chunks of rock. Near the head of the valley, which pushes up underneath the summit of Mount Evans, hikers encounter several paternoster lakes, created when the glacier carved divots out of the valley floor.

The open upper valley is often lush with alpine flowers, including scarlet paintbrush (*Castilleja miniata*), common toadflax (*Linaria vulgaris*) (also called butter-and-eggs because of the orange and yellow coloring of its blossoms), and Rydberg's arnica (*Arnica rydbergii*), distinguished from other arnica by the spray of basal leaves.

Directions: Take CO 103 south from Idaho Springs (Exit 240 off of I-70) 13 miles

GLACIER LILY
(*Erythronium grandiflorum*)
Found in mountain meadows, streambanks and woods near melting snow, this lily's yellow, upswept tepals arise from a leafless stalk.

to Echo Lake State Park, on your right. Turn into the park along a gravel road, follow this around to the left for 300 yards. Park at the end of the road, walk up the bank to Echo Lake, turn right (south) along the shore, and look for the trailhead sign in the trees on the south shore, about 200 yards from the parking lot.

Trail: 4 miles one-way.

Elevation: Change of 1,200 feet.

Degree of difficulty: Moderate.

Surface: Dirt, dirt road, and rock.

Glacier Lilies

Also called snow lily, *Erythronium grandiflorum* is easily identified by its six, lancelike yellow petals, which curve back and around behind the downward-facing flower, like someone holding his hands behind his back. The corms, or root tubers, are an important food source for black bears and rodents, while the seed pods are grazed by elk, deer, and bighorn sheep. They were an important food for humans, too; at one time the dried bulbs were traded by native Indians. Harvesting, however, kills the plant, and overharvesting has sharply reduced plant populations in some areas. Glacier lilies can be found singly or in great profusion in moist, rich sites from montane to alpine regions.

GEORGETOWN LOOP RAILWAY

[Fig. 12(5)] Georgetown was a jumping off point for the silver boom town of Leadville in 1879. But the route from Georgetown to Leadville was long and difficult, 60 miles by horse or wagon over bad roads. New York robber baron Jay Gould, who had gained control of the Colorado Central and Pacific Railroad, decided to extend the line—which had reached Georgetown in 1877—west in a bid to be the first railway into Leadville.

The result was the Georgetown Loop, an extraordinary feat of engineering that lifted the railway 638 vertical feet to the town of Silver Plume, 1.5 miles west, by folding 4.5 miles of track into a twisted loop. The tight valley above Georgetown obliged engineers to curl the train tracks back over themselves along a 90-foot-high viaduct know as the Devil's Gate.

The engineering was extraordinary, but the construction wasn't; the Devil's Gate trestle had to be dismantled and rebuilt due to shoddy work. Consequently, the job wasn't finished until 1894, and that only got the train as far as Silver Plume. By then the Denver, South Park and Rio Grande Railway had laid track up the Arkansas River valley to Leadville, beating Gould to the punch. Gould's railway only went a short distance past Silver Plume, where construction stopped.

In 1939 the Georgetown Loop was dismantled, but it has been rebuilt as a summer tourist attraction, offering spectacular narrow-gauge railway rides since 1984.

Directions: From Denver, take I-70 west to Georgetown, Exit 228. Go left on 15th

Street across Clear Creek to Rose Street, then right to the Old Georgetown Station, on your left. Boarding is at the Devil's Gate boarding area, on the western end of town, but tickets must be bought at the Old Georgetown Station. Alternatively, get off I-70 at Exit 226 and turn south to the Silver Plume Boarding Area, where tickets are sold.

Facilities: Cafe, restrooms, ticket sales.

Dates: Open from May to early Oct.

Fees: There is a fee to ride the train.

Closest town: Georgetown is at the eastern end of the railroad, Silver Plume at the western end.

For more information: Georgetown Loop Railroad, 1106 Rose Street, Georgetown, CO 80444. Phone (970) 569-2403 or (800) 691-4386.

BIKING KENOSHA-GEORGIA PASSES ON THE COLORADO TRAIL

[Fig. 12(4)] Where US 285 drops into the northeastern corner of South Park, bikers and hikers can intercept the Colorado Trail, which runs from Durango to Denver. The trail to the east runs toward Lost Creek Wilderness (no bikes allowed inside the wilderness area). To the west is a long, beautiful, and moderate ride to the Continental Divide at Georgia Pass.

The ride is not overly steep anywhere, but the steady ups and downs, the occasional roots and rocks, and the bumpy tundra, all combined with the steady grade, altitude, and long distance, can make this a tiring undertaking. Riders who don't want to do the full 24-mile ride may cut the distance in half by beginning at Lodgepole Campground and riding only the western half to the divide.

The trail begins at Kenosha Pass in lodgepole pine, then quickly breaks out to an extraordinary view of South Park. Aspen trees make this a very scenic ride during the autumn. The trail drops and climbs over two gulches before crossing Forest Road 401 near Lodgepole Campground, at the 6-mile mark. From here, the trail climbs steadily through lodgepole pine up to tundra, angling toward the massive, rusty red bulk of 13,370-foot Mount Guyot, named for Princeton geography professor Arnold Guyot. In the tundra, follow the cairns to the jeep track, then bear left to the shallow saddle.

The views to the north reveal Breckenridge and the Tenmile Range, and farther north the Gore Range. Georgia Pass is actually below this saddle, on a small jeep road visible down to the left.

The last 1.5 miles of this route are in open terrain, so be aware of weather changes and head down if thunderstorms threaten.

Directions: Take US 285 to Kenosha Pass, 40 miles west of Fairplay. Park on the west side of the pass, then cross the highway into the Kenosha Pass Campground. The trailhead is straight ahead. Pick up the trail and head right, west. To begin at the Lodgepole Campground, take US 285 south over Kenosha Pass to the hamlet of Jefferson, then turn north on 35 Road (Forest Road 400) for 3 miles to FR 401, a right. Take this past Lodgepole and Aspen campgrounds, about 3 miles. Look for the trailhead registers on both sides of the road. Park and take the trail heading west (left) toward Georgia Pass.

Closest town: Fairplay, 40 miles west of Kenosha Pass on US 285.

Trail: 12 miles one-way from Kenosha Pass, 6 miles one-way from FR 401.

Elevation: Net gain of about 1,600 feet, with several hundred additional feet of up and down.

Degree of difficulty: Moderate.

Surface: Single-track dirt.

SKIING LOVELAND BASIN

[Fig. 12(1)] One of Colorado's oldest ski areas (opened in 1934), Loveland is located around and above the eastern slopes of Eisenhower Tunnel on Interstate 70. It is Colorado's second highest ski area, with a summit elevation of 13,010 feet, and a base elevation (10,600 feet) that is higher than the summit of Steamboat Ski Area. Loveland encompasses 1,365 acres with a vertical drop of 2,410 feet. Snowfall averages 400 inches annually.

Lacking any base village or associated real estate development, Loveland is one of Colorado's vanishing old-style ski areas, where ski runs were built because people wanted to ski, rather than as an adjunct to real estate development. (Other remaining examples include Arapaho Basin, on the far side of Loveland Pass, and Ski Cooper near Leadville.)

Loveland's high altitude gave it an advantage in the early days of skiing, before snow-making allowed ski areas in Colorado to open in early November, as several now do. In 1961, taking advantage only of natural snow, Loveland opened on September 30—two months before ski areas typically opened at the time.

Directions: From Denver, drive west on I-70 to Exit 216, just east of the Eisenhower Tunnel. From the west, east on I-70 through the Eisenhower Tunnel to Exit 216. The ski area is located at the exit.

Activities: Skiing, snowboarding, lessons.

Facilities: 3 on-mountain picnic cabins, 9 ski lifts.

Dates: Open approximately mid-Oct. to mid-May, depending on snow conditions.

Fees: There is a charge to ski.

Closest town: Silver Plume, 12 miles east.

For more information: Loveland Ski Area, PO Box 899, Georgetown, CO 80444. Phone: (970) 569-3203 or (800) 736-3SKI.

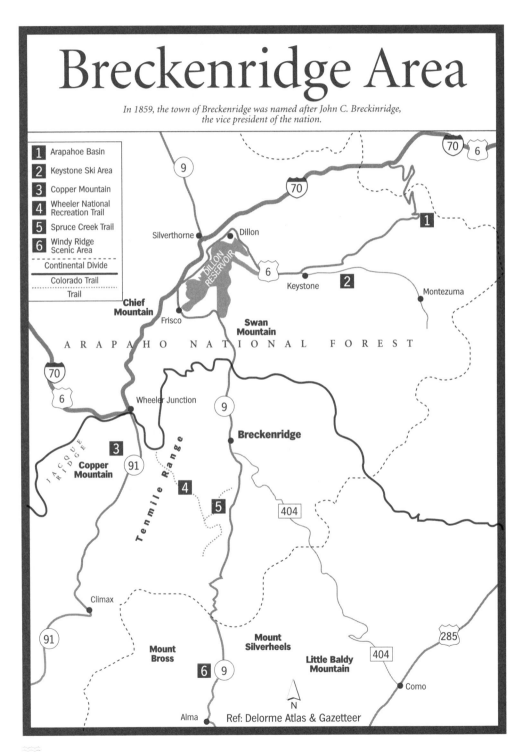

Breckenridge Area

In 1859, the town of Breckenridge was named after John C. Breckinridge, the vice president of the nation.

1 Arapahoe Basin
2 Keystone Ski Area
3 Copper Mountain
4 Wheeler National Recreation Trail
5 Spruce Creek Trail
6 Windy Ridge Scenic Area
--- Continental Divide
--- Colorado Trail
······ Trail

Silverthorne
Dillon
DILLON RESERVOIR
Chief Mountain
Frisco
Swan Mountain
Keystone
Montezuma

ARAPAHO NATIONAL FOREST

Wheeler Junction

JACQUE RIDGE
Copper Mountain
Tenmile Range
Breckenridge

Climax

Mount Bross
Mount Silverheels
Little Baldy Mountain
Como

Alma
Ref: Delorme Atlas & Gazetteer

N

Breckenridge Area

[Fig. 13] Breckenridge and the Blue River Valley have become a locus of what writer Edward Abbey called "industrial tourism." Extensive ski area development at Keystone and Breckenridge, and associated residential and commercial development around Lake Dillon, Silverthorne and down the Blue River valley, have altered much of this region. Nevertheless, many recreational opportunities remain.

Attentive drivers descending west from the Eisenhower Tunnel may see rock formations familiar from the eastern side of the Front Range: Pierre Shale and Dakota Sandstone, now evident on the western border of the Precambrian core of the Front Range. In many places these rocks are occluded by the Precambrian granite, which expanded west in a thrust fault over the younger rock, just as Pikes Peak expanded east. Farther west, just past Copper Mountain Ski Resort, I-70 passes through red sandstones identical to those found along the Front Range foothills and particularly noticeable at Garden of the Gods near Colorado Springs (*see* page 72). This is the Pennsylvanian-Permian rock which once eroded from the summits of the ancestral Rockies.

Like so much of Colorado, the upper Blue River valley was the site of feverish mining activity from the 1860s through the 1890s. At one time, as many as 18 distinct mining communities were scattered through the hills and valleys from Grays Peak to the Tenmile Range, which lies west of Breckenridge and connects the Gore Range, north of Interstate 70, to the Mosquito Range, south of Hoosier Pass (the Mosquito Range defines the western limit of South Park).

Breckenridge, settled in 1859 by prospectors from the southern United States, was named after John C. Breckinridge, then vice president of the nation. But as the Civil War approached, and Breckinridge seemed to sympathize with the Confederate cause, easterners sympathetic to the Union cause, who had moved into the mining camp, insisted the spelling of the town's name be modified by replacing the first "i" with an "e."

Directions: From I-70, take Exit 203 and drive south on CO 9 approximately 10 miles to the town of Breckenridge.

For more information: Breckenridge Chamber of Commerce, 137 South Main Street, Breckenridge, CO 80424. Phone (970) 453-5579.

▓ SPRUCE CREEK TRAIL-WHEELER NATIONAL RECREATION TRAIL TO MOHAWK FALLS

[Fig. 13(5)] This is an easy hike through dark, Engelmann spruce forest to views up the Mohawk Lakes drainage on the northeast side of Quandary Peak, to a dramatic, cascading waterfall. After 1.8 miles on the Spruce Creek Trail, turn right (north) on the Wheeler National Recreation Trail. After a half-mile, at the intersection with a dirt road, turn left on the road, which turns into the Mohawk Lakes Trail; follow this to Mohawk Falls.

The Other Sam Adams

Sam Adams is known to school children as a Revolutionary War patriot. But a second Sam Adams, a century later, was a scoundrel. In 1869, one Captain Samuel Adams departed in six boats down the Blue River, determined to follow the tributary to the Colorado and then the Colorado down through the unexplored Grand Canyon. Adams had tried to join John Wesley Powell's crew, which would depart from Green River, Utah a few months later and successfully navigate the unknown canyon, but had been rebuffed. He launched his own expedition instead, getting only as far as Glenwood Canyon (west of Eagle, Colorado). His trip a failure, he hiked back to Breckenridge but managed to convince promoters in the East for many years that he had, in fact, been successful in exploring the Grand Canyon.

Ironically, Adams's wholly mythical vision about the ease of exploiting and settling the arid lands of the desert southwest were gratefully received by East Coast boosters trying to encourage settlers to move to the region. Powell argued for decades after his trip through the Grand Canyon that settlement in the West would be greatly circumscribed by the limited availability of water—a message the region's promoters didn't want to hear.

Directions: From Breckenridge, south on CO 9 to "Blue Lake" town limits sign. Continue 0.1 miles, take the next right, Crown Road. Follow this to an intersection with Spruce Creek Road, about 0.25 mile, then to a parking lot at the trailhead, 2 miles farther up.

Closest town: Breckenridge, 5 miles north.

Trail: 1.8 miles to intersection with Wheeler National Recreation Trail; 3 miles to Mohawk Falls.

Elevation: Change of 700 feet to trail intersection and 1,500 feet to falls.

Degree of difficulty: Easy.

Surface: Packed dirt.

For more information: Dillon Ranger District, White River National Forest, 135 Highway 9, Blue River Center, PO Box 620, Silverthorne, CO 80498. Phone (970) 468-5400.

WHEELER NATIONAL RECREATION TRAIL

[Fig. 13(4)] This trail ranges across the top of the peaks above the Breckenridge Ski Area, crossing the Tenmile Mountains from southeast to northwest and terminating near Copper Mountain Ski Area. From its high points hikers can see the Gore Range to the north, Sawatch Range to the southwest, and Flat Tops Mountains to the northwest.

Directions: Follow the directions to the Spruce Creek trailhead, (*see* page 83), and hike the Spruce Creek trail to the T-junction with the Wheeler National Recreation Trail. Follow the trail right, north, across Spruce Creek Road and along an aqueduct for 200 yards, then pick up the trail where it turns left into the woods.

Trail: About 6 miles from the Spruce Creek junction to Copper Mountain.

Elevation change: Gain of 1,500 feet.

Degree of difficulty: Strenuous.

Surface: Dirt, rock, and tundra.

For more information: Dillon Ranger District, White River National Forest, 135 Highway 9, Blue River Center, PO Box 620, Silverthorne, CO 80498. Phone (970) 468-5400.

Extensive ski area development surrounds downtown Breckenridge.

WINDY RIDGE SCENIC AREA

[Fig. 13(6)] A gravel road and short hike lead to this grove of ancient bristlecone pines overlooking Mount Silverheels, Fairplay, and South Park.

Directions: Take CO 9 north from Fairplay or south from Breckenridge to Alma. Turn west on Forest Road 416 opposite the Alma Grocery and Liquor Store. Follow signs for Windy Ridge. After 2.5 miles turn right on FR 415. If you are driving a two-wheel-drive vehicle, you may park at the Mineral Park Mine ruins at timberline and walk the road for another 0.25 mile to the signed parking area. From the parking area head northeast across the tundra about 200 yards to the trees.

Activities: Scenic walk.

Facilities: None.

Dates: Open summer and fall, when the gravel road is passable.

Fees: None.

Closest town: Alma, 5 miles southeast.

For more information: South Park Ranger District, Pike National Forest, PO Box 219, Fairplay, CO 80440. Phone (719) 836-2031.

MOUNT SILVERHEELS

[Fig. 13] At 13,822 feet, Mount Silverheels is a broad, open, near-Fourteener at the top of South Park. Its summit provides views up into the Blue River valley and Gore Range to the north, down into South Park, west to the Mosquito and Tenmile ranges, and east along the Continental Divide.

Directions: From Como, take Forest Road 404 north. Do not take the turnoff to Boreas Pass after about 3 miles, but stay left; after another 0.5 mile, stay left at a second fork. Approximately 0.5 mile farther on, park near the cabin on the left bearing the number 1187. Follow the dirt road next to the cabin west toward Tarryall Creek (don't park here, since this is a private road). Cross on the footbridge. You're now on a jeep road which crosses Silverheels Creek, passes through a small meadow, and drops down to cross Silverheels Creek a second time. The trail climbs from this point, reaching a saddle between Little Baldy and Silverheels that is the halfway point to the summit, which is an open climb for about 2,000 feet along the ridge.

Closest town: Fairplay, 14 miles southwest.

For more information: South Park Ranger District, Pike National Forest, PO Box 219, Fairplay, CO 80440. Phone (719) 836-2031.

Trail: 5 miles one-way.

Elevation: Change of 3,600 feet.

Degree of difficulty: Moderate.

Surface: Packed dirt, rock, and tundra.

SKIING IN SUMMIT COUNTY

Summit County lies at the heart of Colorado ski country, with four major ski areas, plus Loveland to the immediate east and Vail and Beaver Creek to the west. Here is basic information on each of the Summit County ski areas:

BRECKENRIDGE

[Fig. 13] Laid across the Tenmile Range, Breckenridge has 2,043 acres of skiing and a 3,398-foot vertical drop. Adjacent to the oldest inhabited mining town on Colorado's Western Slope, the ski area is the second-most popular in the United States, after Vail. The resort is particularly popular with British visitors, perhaps because a large portion of its terrain—approximately 800 acres—is above timberline and provides European-style, wide-open skiing and snowboarding. There are 139 trails and 23 ski lifts. Average snowfall is 300 inches; base elevation is 9,600 feet.

Directions: From I-70, take Exit 203 to CO 9 south. Breckenridge is about 14 miles down CO 9.

For more information: Phone (970) 453-5000. E-mail: breckenridge@vailresorts.com

KEYSTONE SKI AREA

[Fig. 13(2)] Keystone sprawls over several ridges southeast of Lake Dillon. Unlike Breckenridge, it did not have an old mining town at its base, but an alpine resort village is being built there now. Its modern claim to fame is that it is usually one of the first resorts to open in Colorado, generally in late October. The ski area's high elevation and extensive snowmaking capacity combine to give it a jump start on other resorts. Two attributes help Keystone stand out among skiers and snowboarders: The Outback, a large gladed bowl offering extensive tree skiing; and night skiing. Keystone keeps the lights on along 17 trails and a 20-acre snowboarding terrain park until 9 p.m. for those who just can't get enough time on the snow during daylight hours.

Keystone has 1,861 acres of terrain encompassing 116 rails and 20 lifts. Average annual snowfall is 230 inches; base elevation is 9,300 feet.

Directions: From I-70, take Exit 205 to CO 9 South, then bear right on US 6 east. Keystone Ski Area is about 10 miles up the road.

For more information: Phone (970) 496-2316. E-mail: keystone@vailresorts.com

ARAPAHOE BASIN

[Fig. 13(1)] Set on CO 6 on the west side of Loveland Pass, Arapahoe Basin just tops nearby Loveland with the claim for the highest lift-served terrain, reaching 13,050 feet. A-Basin, as it is known, prides itself in being rough around the edges and lacking in frills. It's a ski area that caters to a retro crowd, to skiers and boarders who think that skiing doesn't need

RED-TAILED HAWK
(Buteo jamaicensis)

fancy lifts and restaurants. Each spring, the A-Basin parking lot, known as "the beach," hosts serious tailgate parties. Revelers have been known to truck portable hot tubs and even sailboats to the parking lot at 10,780 feet in order to convey the right beach ambience. Skiing is usually available until early July.

Arapahoe Basin has 61 trails on 490 acres and relies entirely on natural snowfall (an average 367 inches annually). Five lifts service the ski area.

Directions: From I-70, take Exit 216 to US 6 West over Loveland Pass to the ski area, about 6 miles. Do not, however, attempt this during bad weather, as the road can be especially dangerous. Alternatively, take Exit 205 to CO 9 South, then bear right on US 6 East past Keystone to Arapahoe Basin, about 20 miles.

For more information: Arapahoe Basin Ski Area, Box 8787, Arapahoe Basin, CO 80435. Phone (970) 468-0718.

COPPER MOUNTAIN

[Fig. 13(3)] At the Intersection of I-70 and US 24, Copper Mountain is sometimes overshadowed by surrounding ski areas. But its three high peaks—Copper Peak, Union Peak and Tucker Mountain—provide extensive, open, expert terrain with multiple slopes and aspects, so good snow is almost certain to be found somewhere, particularly by skiers willing to hike the ridges for the right line.

Copper Mountain's base village is currently undergoing a massive redevelopment. The ski area has 2,433 acres, with a base elevation of 9,712 feet, a summit of 12,313 feet, and a vertical drop of 2,601 feet. It offers skiing on 118 trails, serviced by 20 lifts, and is open from mid-Nov. until May. Cross-country skiing is offered on 25 kilometers of machine-set tracks and skating lanes.

Directions: From I-70, take Exit 195 to CO 91 South for 0.25 mile to the Copper Mountain Road, a right.

For more information: Phone (970) 968-2882.

Big Horn Sheep Canyon

The Arkansas River runs 1,400 miles to the Mississippi River, but in the first 125 miles, as it pours out of the Colorado Rockies, it drops 5,000 feet. This descent has given the Arkansas a reputation as one of the best whitewater rivers in the state.

Rafting and fishing are popular throughout the portion of the river that cuts between the Mosquito Range, Sangre de Cristo Mountains, and Wet Mountains, a section known as Big Horn Sheep Canyon. This 40-mile canyon of old granite, ponderosa pine, and cane cholla cactus (*Opuntia spinosior*) is traced by US 50 and includes seven boat-launching ramps for rafters and kayakers. The river contains rapids rated from Class II (moderate) to Class VI (generally unrunnable). Detailed maps and information about river conditions, as well as information on commercial rafting operators, may be obtained from the Arkansas Headwaters Recreation Area office in Salida.

Directions: From I-25, take Exit 101 to US 50 West, which follows the river to Salida.

Activities: Rafting, kayaking, fishing.

Facilities: There are 2 public campgrounds and 7 boat ramps in Big Horn Sheep Canyon, along with numerous public fishing easements.

Fees: There are fees for use of some of the public facilities.

Dates: Open year-round.

Closest town: Salida at the western end of the canyon, Parkdale at the eastern end.

For more information: Arkansas Headwaters Recreation Area, PO Box 126, Salida, CO 81201. Phone (719) 539-7289.

Scenic Drives

GOLD BELT TOUR

The Gold Belt Tour runs through the complex geology south and west of Pikes Peak, site of an 1891 gold strike that, in following decades, produced 17 million ounces of gold, which would be worth more than $4 billion at today's prices. Cripple Creek's gold fields were so prolific that they had the effect of flooding the world's gold markets and depressing prices. The trip section described here is from Cripple Creek to Florence, 40 miles of the 132-mile double-loop.

In Cripple Creek, take CO 67 south toward Victor. In 1991, Cripple Creek was one of three Colorado towns to begin allowing limited stakes gambling (the other two are Black Hawk and Central City). The corporate development accompanying gambling has turned all three towns into commercial visions of their former selves.

During the 1890s, Cripple Creek was where the majority of the miners lived, but most of the mines were in Victor, 6 miles away. A pair of electric trolley lines was run as commuter lines for miners and was considered the best trolley system at the time in the world.

At Mile 4, modern mining shows itself. The Cripple Creek and Victor Gold Mining Company here moves vast quantities of earth containing tiny amounts of gold. The earth is piled up and sprinkled with a dilute cyanide solution, which dissolves the gold as it drains through the soil. The gold is then chemically retrieved from the solution. This is how most gold is now mined in the world. It is a process far removed from the romantic notion of the pick-and-shovel prospector, and one that can be vastly more destructive to the environment. Cyanide spills such as occurred in Summitville, Colorado in the early 1990s poison miles of river. Modern miners still operate under the same rules as miners did when the federal Mining Act

Bighorn Sheep

Bighorn rams can grow to 350 pounds, and an old ram's skull and horns (which are never shed, but grow until death) can weigh 50 pounds. Competing males will charge each other, ramming their horns together at speeds up to 54 miles per hour, creating an ear-splitting crack and often settling the matter in one blow as to who will mate with the ewe in question. Colorado's bighorn population now numbers around 6,000 animals, thanks to efforts to revive a waning population. But the animals' tendency to favor old habitat over new terrain, and the loss of winter range to ski areas and valley development, limit population recovery efforts.

was passed in 1872, and pay no royalties to the government on the minerals they extract from public lands.

Mile 5 brings you into Victor, where most of the Pikes Peaks mines were located. At Mile 7, take Phantom Canyon Road, featuring 30 miles of extraordinary twisting canyon, once the route of the first of three trains to service Cripple Creek, the Florence and Cripple Creek narrow gauge railway. The route runs through Precambrian granite before exiting into the Arkansas River valley and the town of Florence.

Dates: Not recommended during winter weather, since much of the road is dirt.

Fees: There is no fee to drive the road.

Closest town: Cripple Creek on the northern end, Florence on the southern end.

For more information: Cripple Creek Chamber of Commerce, 337 Bennett Drive, Cripple Creek, CO 80813. Phone (719) 689-2169.

MOUNT EVANS SCENIC BYWAY

The 49-mile Mount Evans Scenic Byway runs east from Bergen Park up to the flank of the peak, then branches south to the summit (generally open Memorial Day to Labor Day) before retracing back to the fork and then turning north to Idaho Springs.

Highly popular, Mount Evans draws 120,000 visitors annually to the summit, so avoid peak times if possible. Begin the route at Exit 252 (westbound) on I-70. Take CO 74 west toward Bergen Park. After two miles, bear right onto CO 103 (Squaw Pass Road). The route passes through mature ponderosa pine, then "dog hair" stands of closely-packed lodgepole pine. After Mile 15 you have climbed sufficiently to be in Engelmann spruce-subalpine fir forest. At Mile 18 you have a good view out the windshield to Gray's Peak (14,270 feet) and Torrey's Peak (14,267 feet), located west of Mount Evans and named for the geographers John Torrey and Asa Gray.

At Mile 21, turn left (south) on CO 5. Keep an eye peeled for both bighorn sheep, which are native to the area, and mountain goats, which are not.

Native to the Northwest, mountain goats (actually related to African antelope and

European chamois) were introduced to the state between 1948 and 1971. Weighing up to 300 pounds (males) and half that size for females, mountain goats will clamber up near-vertical cliffs with impunity. Baby goats (kids) can climb within a few hours of birth.

Unlike bighorn sheep, goats stay in the high country all winter, seeking out windblown areas to graze and waiting out weather that drives all other mammals under the snow or down to lower elevations.

The Mount Goliath Natural Area parking area is at Mile 24. The nature trail accessed here provides a walk through one of the state's largest stands of bristlecone pine. These trees range to about 1,700 years old here, but some stands in California are three times as venerable.

The summit gate is located at Mile 30; the summit itself is at Mile 36, providing views up to 100 miles in all directions on a clear day.

The route retraces back to the intersection with CO 103, then descends 13 miles to Idaho Springs and Interstate 70.

Dates: Open year-round, although the spur to the summit is closed in winter.

Fees: There is no fee to drive the byway.

Closest town: Bergen Park on the eastern end, Idaho Springs on the western end.

For more information: Idaho Springs Chamber of Commerce, 2200 Miner Street, Idaho Springs, CO Phone (303) 567-4382.

BIGHORN SHEEP
(Ovis canadensis)
Called the Bighorn because its horns measure up to 4 feet, this mountain sheep have hooves that separate, allowing it to climb and jump along uneven terrain.

Beavers

The most evident animal in alpine riparian systems is the beaver (*Castor canadensis*). Visitors rarely see him, because he is generally nocturnal, but often see his work. Beavers drew some of Colorado's earliest Anglo-American explorers. Mountain men tramped the region in the first half of the nineteenth century, seeking pelts so valued in Europe they sold for $6 to $8 on the East Coast during the 1820s. Regulation of trapping has allowed beavers to recolonize many mountain waterways where they had been trapped out 150 years ago.

Beavers dam flowing water so that they can build a lodge in the resulting pond. Beaver families may grow to a dozen individuals, but the animals eventually eat most of the nearby aspen and willows they prefer, leading to the abandonment of the pond. Over time, beaver ponds drain as unmaintained dams are breached by floods, and as stream-borne silt fills in the pond. Colonization of the beaver-made wet meadow begins by a variety of plant species, eventually reaching the climax aspen and willow, which may draw beavers back in a few decades. Evidence of old beaver dams and ponds is quite common in many mountain valleys.

GUANELLA PASS

This scenic byway is short, 24.3 miles, and relatively close to Denver. It is particularly popular during late September and early October (too popular on weekends), when city denizens come up for a half-day drive to see the fall colors in the many aspen groves and alpine bogs characteristic of the route.

The byway starts in Georgetown at 8,519 feet and climbs up the South Clear Creek Valley. Georgetown was named George's Town when four rude cabins were built here in 1860 in honor of Kentuckian George Griffith, who had found a small gold vein the year before, and convinced several relatives to join him in working it. They followed their vein, digging through apparently worthless rock but not coming out much richer for it. What they failed to realize was that the rock they were discarding was high-grade silver ore. In 1864 more astute prospectors recognized the rock for what it was, and the boom was on. Georgetown became the state's first great "silver queen," joined later by the likes of Leadville and Aspen.

To begin the scenic byway, take Exit 228 off of I-70. Drive south along Second Street to the south side of town. Pick up Guanella Pass Road where it starts to climb steeply up the hillside. The road, completed in 1952, is gravel for its length but passable in summer and fall by two-wheel-drive vehicles.

After Mile 1, notice the long fingers of aspen trees growing up the slopes of the mountains on either side of the road. Because they grow faster than conifers, aspen often colonize avalanche zones where full-bore, climax avalanches only run every 25 years or so (open slopes are swept more frequently). The trees can survive smaller slides but are often bent over by the force and weight of the snow. Look for groves of smaller trees and willows that have been bent downhill, and for the debris of broken trees, both on the hillsides and in the valleys, that shows where avalanches have cleared out sections of forest.

At Mile 6 you will pass an electric generating facility. The Cabin Creek Hydroelectric Generation Station is what is known as a pumped storage facility; its operation actually results in a net loss of electricity. Water flows from Upper Cabin Creek Reservoir (uphill to the west) through turbines here, at Lower Cabin Creek Reservoir, when demand for electricity is highest (mornings and evenings). During slower demand periods, such as late at night, excess electrical generating capacity is available at coal-fired generating plants around the region; this electricity is used to pump water back uphill to the Upper Cabin Creek Reservoir, refilling it like a battery so the peak demand may be satisfied again.

Around Mile 7, alpine bogs become quite evident in the valley. These are profuse on this byway and comprise one of the richest mountain ecosystems. At the higher altitudes found on Guanella Pass, these riparian areas are characterized by alder (*Alnus incana*), river birch (*Betula fontinalis*), and low willows (*Salix*). The wet thickets, sometimes no more than waist high, are called "carrs," and can be almost impossible to walk through, as any fisherman who has tried knows.

Common flowers in these bogs are cow parsnip (*Heracleum sphondylium*), with its great dishlike galaxies of tiny white flowers, and chiming bells (*Mertensia ciliata*), pendulous and blue and favoring the sides of tumbling creeks.

Mile 11 brings you to Guanella Pass at 11,669 feet. Immediately east is 14,060-foot Mount Bierstadt, named after the landscape painter Alfred Bierstadt, who chronicled the sublime beauty of the nineteenth-century American West. Continuing to the south you descend through subalpine and then lodgepole forests. At Mile 19 is Falls Hill, site of a waterfall, but once the toe of the glacier that flowed down this valley from the pass. The waterfall cascades down the terminal moraine. After 24 miles the byway ends at US 285.

Facilities: There are no commercial services except at the ends of by the byway.

Dates: Open year-round, but may be closed in winter due to avalanche hazard.

Fees: There is no fee to drive the byway.

Closest town: Georgetown, at the northern end of the byway.

For more information: Georgetown Chamber of Commerce, 613 Sixth Street, Georgetown, CO 80444. Phone (303) 569-2888.

BEAVER
(*Castor canadensis*)

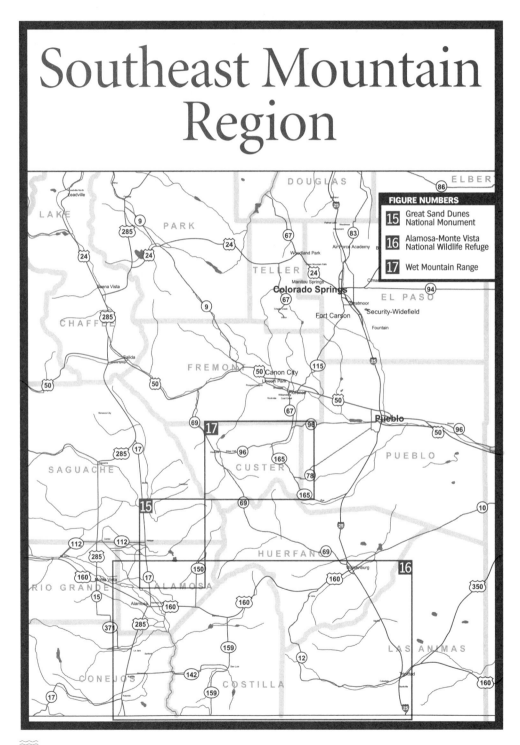

Southeast Mountain Region

FIGURE NUMBERS

15 Great Sand Dunes National Monument

16 Alamosa-Monte Vista National Wildlife Refuge

17 Wet Mountain Range

Southeast Mountain Region

The Southeastern Mountain Region encompasses an area of profound cultural history in Colorado, the state's only true mountain desert and a variety of arid, semiarid and alpine landscapes. This is mythical country, at times hotly contested by its residents. It is a land where prehistoric peoples hunted huge, now vanished buffalo, and where they mined turquoise. Much of this country was claimed by Mexico in the nineteenth century, then lost to the United States in the Mexican-American War. Yet, Hispanic culture is still alive and vibrant here, so that a visitor might feel he or she were in New Mexico rather than Colorado. It is a region of striking geography and geology, where vast lakes underlie arid lands and a rift valley separates two of the state's most dramatic mountain ranges.

The Southeastern Mountains are defined in this book by a line running west from Pueblo along US 50, paralleling the Arkansas River up to Salida but excluding it (the

[*Above:* The Great Sand Dunes National Monument in the San Luis Valley contains 39 square miles of dunes]

river is discussed in the East Central Region chapter), then turning south along US 285 over Poncha Pass. From here, our imaginary boundary traces the western edge of the San Luis Valley south to the New Mexico border.

This delineation of the region encompasses the San Luis Valley, Wet Mountain Valley, and three mountain ranges: the Sangre de Cristo Mountains, Wet Mountains, and Spanish Peaks. The region's geology is both volcanic and the result of faulting in the earth's crust.

Some of the most striking volcanic effects can be seen in the southeasternmost mountains in the region, the Spanish Peaks. This dramatic pair of summits rises 7,000 feet from the surrounding plains. The mountains are relatively young, the result of an igneous intrusion up through the Pierre Formation shale and Upper Cretaceous sandstone of the High Plains, an event that occurred after the Rockies had been formed. These mountains were formed from "stocks," volcanic intrusions that pushed up into, but not through, the overlying sedimentary layers during the Tertiary Period, which began 65 million years ago. Since then, the softer rock around the Spanish Peaks has eroded, exposing not only the peaks themselves but numerous surrounding dikes, which radiate from the peaks like nature's version of the Great Wall of China.

To the north of the Spanish Peaks lie the Wet Mountains, a relatively low and undramatic range south of Pikes Peak. Like the Front Range, this range is a "faulted anticline," an upward fold in the ancient, Precambrian rock that forms the core of so many of Colorado's mountains, which then faulted, or broke.

West of the Spanish Peaks is the great, ranging cordillera of the Sangre de Cristo Mountains, the heart of this region. One of the longest and narrowest ranges in the world, the Sangre de Cristos stretch 100 miles from Poncha Pass to Santa Fe, New

BALD EAGLE
(Haliaeetus leucocephalus)
It is believed that bald eagles mate for life. The 40-inch-long bird, which can have a 7½-foot wingspan, builds a large nest in trees, cliffs, or on the ground that can weigh up to 1,000 pounds. Eagles eat carrion, fish, and waterfowl.

Mexico, but the range is no wider than 10 miles.

Between the Wet Mountains and the Sangre de Cristos lies the Wet Mountain Valley, and then between the Sangre de Cristos and the eastern edge of the San Juan Mountains is the San Luis Valley. Both are grabens, while the Wet Mountains and Sangre de Cristo Mountains are horsts. Grabens are places where the earth sank, and horsts, places where it rose. Imagine the landscape as a sort of checkerboard; some squares sank, other squares rose and, in the case of the Sangre de Cristos, tilted down to the east. Thus the eastern side of the Sangre de Cristos is relatively gently sloped, while the western face is steep, almost vertical in places.

The reason the grabens formed isn't clear to geologists. One theory is that as the earth's crust pulled apart during the Miocene-Pliocene Era uplift that raised the Rockies to their present elevation (a process that lifted the region 5,000 feet), the crust expanded, causing the grabens to drop as the horsts separated. The resulting San Luis Valley, part of the headwaters of the Rio Grande River, is a true rift valley.

Eagles

The eagle most commonly seen in Colorado is the golden eagle, *Aquila chrysaetos*, an almost wholly brown bird that subsists on rabbits and rodents. Bald eagles (*Haliaeetus leucocephalus*) are more common in coastal environments, since they prefer dead and dying fish. In Colorado, look for them in or near river valleys, where they may nest and feed. Both species, however, soar great distances. Eagles are easily identified overhead by their great, straight wingspans—7 feet for a golden eagle, up to 8 feet for a bald eagle. Balds can also be picked out by their white heads and tails. Eagles are sometimes confused at a distance with turkey vultures (*Cathartes aura*); they can be distinguished by the way eagles soar with flat wings, versus a shallow V dihedral for turkey vultures.

A Frontier Between Mexico and The United States

The San Luis Valley, although altered by modern man, was once a vast grassland visited by indigenous peoples throughout the region. Here, the Folsom people roamed 11,000 years ago, hunting an extinct species of bison about one-third larger than those that exist today. The Tewa Indians of northern New Mexico speak in their myths of a "sandy place lake far to the north," an apparent reference to the San Luis Lakes near Great Sand Dunes National Monument. Pueblo Indians came north to the King turquoise mine, located near Manassa, in search of this gemstone formed by hydrothermal alteration of copper. Navajo myth describes 14,338-foot Blanca Peak,

PIÑON PINE
(Pinus edulis)
This pine grows to 40 feet tall, has needles in twos and egg-shaped cones.

which towers over the rest of the Sangre de Cristo range, as one of that tribe's four sacred mountains.

The first town anywhere in what would become the state of Colorado, San Luis, was founded on the Culebra River, in the southeastern corner of the San Luis Valley, in 1851. (Colorado was declared a United States Territory in 1861 and gained statehood in 1876.) San Luis was built on the Sangre de Cristo Land Grant, one of several enormous gifts of land in what would become southern Colorado and northern New Mexico, gifts made by the Mexican government in 1840 to Mexican landowners. At the time, the entire region was claimed by Mexico; the government in Mexico City hoped to solidify those claims with settlements. But the Mexican-American War of 1846 put an end to Mexico's dreams of northward expansion. All of Colorado—indeed, all of what is today's southwestern United States—was ceded to the United States with the 1848 Treaty of Guadalupe Hidalgo.

San Luis's settlers built in the traditional Hispanic adobe style and farmed in a manner that included treating the high country of the Culebra Mountains to the east (a subrange of the Sangre de Cristos) as common land. This was in keeping with the Spanish and Mexican traditions of the land grant, but those traditions conflicted with the United States' legal concepts of property. Even today, court battles are being waged in San Luis over whether the lands granted as common property 160 years earlier are, indeed, still common property for the community.

The United States explorers John Frémont and John Gunnison traversed the region several times, beginning in 1848, in search of a viable cross-country railroad route (*see page 309*). He thought there might be a route over 9,413-foot La Veta Pass, the saddle that demarcates the Culebra subrange, a flank of the Sangre de Cristo Mountains that runs south from the pass to the New Mexico border. The pass provided an easy and popular trail into the Rio Grande drainage from the east. The U.S. Army opened Fort Massachusetts in 1852 at the western entrance to the pass. In 1858, the fort was moved to its current location a few miles closer to San Luis and renamed Fort Garland.

Significant Anglo-American immigration didn't begin in the region until relatively late. Silvercliffe got its start in the Wet Mountain Valley in 1877 with the discovery of low-grade silver ore, 18 years after the first major gold strike in the state. A major silver strike was made there the following year, and Silvercliffe boomed. Gold was discovered at the western edges of the Sangre de Cristo mountains in 1879, leading to the founding of Crestone. Crestone became a significant gold mining town, but mining activity was sharply curtailed after an 1898 U.S. Supreme Court ruling that the owners of the Luis Maria Baca Grant—another of the old Mexican land grants—had the right to control the mines there.

At almost the same time gold was being discovered in the nearby mountains, the San Luis Valley was being settled by Mormons. Mormon leader John Morgan and a band of disciples built the town of Manassa on the banks of the Conejos River in 1878. (Its latter-day claim to fame has been as the home of boxing champion Jack Dempsey.)

At the higher elevations, visitors find Douglas fir, lodgepole pine, subalpine forests, and bristlecone-limber pine communities, as they will in other Colorado mountains. But along the skirts of the peaks are plant communities not found in the northern part of the state, most notably desert shrublands and large expanses of piñon-juniper forest.

Arid Country, Desert Plants

Piñon pine (*Pinus edulis*) is broadly spread over southern Colorado and New Mexico and is associated with one-seed juniper (*Juniperus monosperma*). Piñon is easily identified both by its location—warm, dry, desert-like sites from 4,000 to 9,000 feet—and its size. Rarely does the shrubby tree grow over 30 feet tall. Piñon is an important food source for birds, animals, and man. Piñon nuts, found in the sticky pine cones, were a significant food source for Native Americans in the region. They are avidly collected today and form an important part of a traditional Indian and Hispanic diet in the region. Individual trees set fruit only every three to seven years.

Piñon jays (*Gymnorhinus cyanocephalus*) and scrub jays (*Aphelocoma ceoerulescens*) are easily spotted in piñon forests—and because the raucous, blue-grey birds look similar, they are easily confused. Look for the white throat and buff shoulders to identify the scrub jay.

Desert shrublands characterize much of the valley terrain in the Southeastern Mountain Region. Good examples of big sagebrush (*Artemisia tridentata*) can be found along Poncha Pass and the northern end of the San Luis Valley. Farther south in the valley, and north of the Spanish Peaks between La Veta and Walsenburg, are extensive stands of greasewood. Often confused with sagebrush, greasewood (*Sarcobatus vermiculatus*), four-wing saltbush (*Atriplex canescens*), and shadscale (*Atriplex confertifolia*) form large stands in the flat, hot alkaline soils of the southern valleys. One of the most beautiful of the shrubland species is rabbitbrush (*Chrysothamnus*), also called chamisa. A late bloomer, its several species flower in vast sulphur billows in early autumn, drawing birds, butterflies, and other insects.

Great Sand Dunes National Monument

*At least 5 billion square yards of sand lies in the Great Sand Dunes;
no one knows how deep these deposits actually go.*

● **Moffat**

T Road

● **Crestone**

T Road

WILLOW CREEK LAKES

1 Medano Creek

2 Mosca Pass Trail

3 San Luis State Park

Great Sand Dunes National Monument

Great Sand Dunes Wilderness

.... Trail

17

SAND CREEK

Sangre De Cristo Mountains

NATIONAL FOREST

S A N
L U I S
V A L L E Y

1

112 ● **Hooper**

12NLN

HEAD LAKE

3

● **Mosca**

10NLN

SAN LUIS LAKE

6MLM

2

150

RIO GRANDE NATIONAL FOREST

17

Blanca Peak **Mount Lindsey**

Hamilton Peak

↑
N

Ref: DeLorme Colorado
State Atlas & Gazetteer

Great Sand Dunes National Monument

[Fig. 15] Although Colorado is a land of extremes and of superlatives, the Great Sand Dunes undoubtedly make the Top 10 (even Top Five) list of extraordinary natural phenomena in the state. Dunes are popularly associated with Africa's Sahara desert, but a corner of the San Luis Valley contains 39 square miles of dunes, including the highest dunes in North America: Piles of sand rise 750 feet from the valley's floor. The dunes exist here thanks to a combination of factors: Sand, of course, but also aridity; wind; terrain; and (surprisingly) water.

The San Luis Valley is a true desert, receiving less than 8 inches of precipitation annually. At one time, however, the upper valley was the waterway for the Arkansas River, which flowed into the valley from the north at a place west of Poncha Pass. Regional uplift about 12 million years ago blocked that channel off, and now the Arkansas turns southeast at Salida and carves its way north of the Sangre de Cristo and Wet mountains. But during its time in the San Luis Valley, the Arkansas and other streams carried eroded material into the graben, or depression, between the Sangre de Cristos and San Juans. Alluvial fans of eroded material are quite evident in the gentle slopes that rise all along the eastern edge of the valley toward the mountains. In fact, the rivers carried an enormous amount of material. The bedrock floor of the valley lies 10,000 to 13,000 feet below the current surface. The intervening space is a layer cake of sand, gravel, water, volcanic ash, lava, and clay.

The sand in the Great Sand Dunes is mostly clear or light-colored grains of quartz and other volcanic rocks eroded from the San Juans. At least 5 billion cubic yards of sand lies in the dunes; no one knows how deep the sand deposits go. Test drillings to 135 feet have found pure windblown sand all the way down, drawing into question the common belief that the sand dunes have existed only for about 12,000 years, or since the last Ice Age. Perhaps, say geologists, they are much deeper—and much older.

Prevailing winds in the valley blow from the southwest. The Sangre de Cristo range runs generally northwest to southeast, perpendicular to the wind. But south of Crestone the range doglegs a little more to the east, then back to the southwest, creating a pocket in the side of the valley. In addition, three low passes—Mosca, Medano, and Music—are situated in this dogleg. These terrain features funnel the wind into and over the mountains here.

As the wind rises up over the ridge toward the passes, it slows, dropping the heavier sand grains it has blown across the Connecticut-size San Luis Valley. The ability to fetch sand from such a large area, and concentrate it in such a small one as the wind rises over the passes, appears to have been critical to the creation of the Great Sand Dunes.

Once deposited, the sand is held in place by water. Two waterways, Sand Creek on the northwest and Medano Creek on east, line the northern and southern flanks of the dunes. As the dunes advance to the east they collapse into the creeks, which carry sand back out to the west before disappearing into the porous soil of the San Luis Valley. There the wind picks the sand up again. This recycling of sand seems to account for much of the dunes' stability.

Additionally, a good deal of water flows directly beneath the dunes. Although the dunes' surface is dry and easily blown about, their interior appears to be wet and much less mobile. The sand has a moisture content of about 7 percent, which adds to the dunes' stability.

The 60-square-mile Great Sand Dunes National Monument, established in 1932, is a study in both continuity and change. Visitors are encouraged to climb on the dunes at random (although shoes are suggested, since the surface temperature can rise to 140 degrees Fahrenheit); their footprints will vanish in a day. Climbing in sand is, of course, tiring; reaching the tops of the highest dunes can take an hour or more and is best attempted during the cool hours of the day.

Footprints are, in fact, one of the most rewarding aspects of a visit to the dunes. Both the dunes and the wide, sandy creeks alongside them tells stories of the creatures that have passed here. In addition to the fresh prints of various visiting *homo sapiens*, keep an eye peeled for the tracks of kangaroo rats, mule deer, bobcats, coyotes, ravens, and magpies.

Narrowleaf cottonwood trees (*Populus angustifolia*) line the creek banks at the dunes' base, creating a broad, dark band of vegetation that turns brilliant yellow in autumn. The trees are a good indicator of water in desert environments throughout the Southwest, and grow lushly along waterways in the Southeastern Mountain Region. Typically, narrowleaf cottonwood grows to a height of 50 feet and a diameter of 18 inches. Other cottonwoods may grow larger.

In places along the dunes, cottonwoods and other trees have been killed by the shifting sand. Across the creek in the foothills look for ponderosa pines, which create open, airy groves where they grow together. (*See* the Northeastern Mountains Region, page 62, for a discussion of ponderosa pine ecosystems). The dunes themselves, possessing little organic material and forever on the move, are essentially bare of plant life.

The San Luis Valley contains a wealth of bird species. Several frequently encountered in the National Monument are the northern flicker (*Colaptes auratus*), a resident woodpecker that nests in the adjacent forests and is easily identified in flight by its rusty wings and white rump; the western tanager (*Piranga ludoviciana*), perhaps the most brilliant bird in the state, unmistakable with its black wings, white wing bars, yellow body and red head; and the green-tailed towhee (*Pipilo chlorurus*), a bush nester that scurries along the ground in the scrub, searching for insects. Water in the nearby streams and on the flats of the San Luis Valley provides a wealth of insect life for many bird species (*see* Alamosa-Monte Vista National Wildlife Refuge, page 105).

Directions: From Alamosa, go north on Colorado Highway 17 for 14 miles to Six Mile Lane, then east 14 miles CO 150. Turn left for 2 miles to the monument entrance.

Activities: Hiking, birding, tracking, dune climbing, camping.

Facilities: Campground and visitor center. Interpretive exhibits, phone, restrooms at visitor center. Restrooms are also at the campground and at dunes parking.

Dates: Open year-round. Visitor center is open daily except for federal holidays in winter.

Fees: There is a fee to enter the monument and another fee for camping.

Closest town: Alamosa, 38 miles southeast.

For more information: Great Sand Dunes National Monument, 11999 Highway 150, Mosca, CO 81146. Phone (719) 378-2312.

WESTERN TANAGER
(Piranga ludoviciana)
The male tanager is bright yellow with a red head and black upper back, wings and tail; the female is greenish above and yellowish below.

🦶 MEDANO CREEK

[Fig. 15(1)] Although monument staff encourages people to walk on the dunes, you can walk in the water, too. This trail really isn't a trail at all; one simply follows the creek, looking for tracks in the water and the sand and marveling at the vast, shifting piles of sand and their ever-changing patterns. Particularly in evening, when the western light cuts sharply across the San Luis Valley, the dunes are a study in light and shadow, shape and form.

Directions: Past the visitor center, park at Amphitheater Parking. Follow Medano Pass Road 200 yards east to a utility building, then turn left (north) toward the dunes, following the path through rabbitbrush for 0.25 mile to the creek. Bear right up the creek for as far as you would like to go. To return a different way, climb out of the creek to your right (south) and intercept the Medano Pass Road, then turn right again (west) back toward the parking area. Medano Pass Road is a four-wheel-drive road; driving in its soft sand often necessitates low tire pressure.

Trail: Up to 5 miles one way.

Elevation: Changes up to 600 feet to Little Medano Creek overlook.

Degree of difficulty: Easy.

Surface: Sand and water.

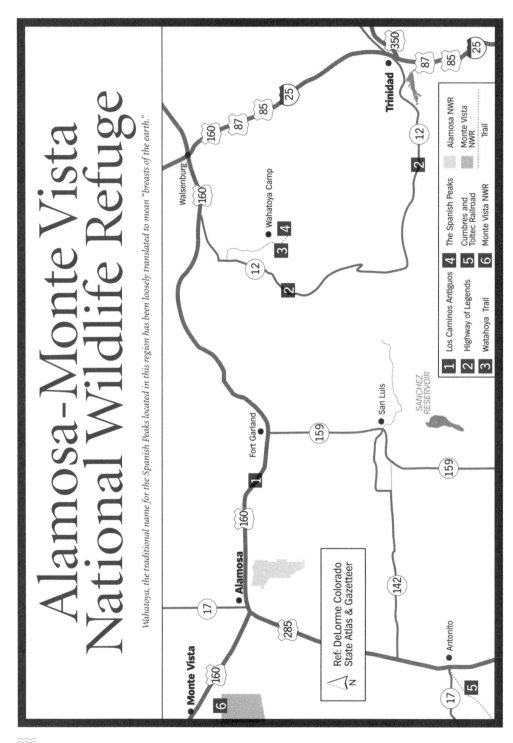

Alamosa–Monte Vista National Wildlife Refuge

Wahatoya, the traditional name for the Spanish Peaks located in this region has been loosely translated to mean "breasts of the earth."

Ref: DeLorme Colorado
State Atlas & Gazetteer

N

1 Los Caminos Antiguos **4** The Spanish Peaks
2 Highway of Legends **5** Cumbres and Toltec Railroad
3 Watahoya Trail **6** Monte Vista NWR

Alamosa NWR
Monte Vista NWR
Trail

Alamosa-Monte Vista National Wildlife Refuge

[Fig. 16] Monte Vista National Wildlife Refuge, encompassing 14,189 acres, was created in 1953 to provide nesting and feeding grounds for migratory birds. In 1953 the nearby Alamosa Wildlife Refuge (11,169 acres) was created in the Rio Grande floodplain. The two were combined for administrative purposes in 1979.

The most dramatic event at the refuges is in spring and fall, when thousands of sandhill cranes (*Grus canadensis*) stop at refuges. Several very rare whooping cranes (*Grus americana*) also migrate with the sandhills from Bosque del Apache National Wildlife Refuge in central New Mexico to their summer feeding grounds at Grays Lake National Wildlife Refuge in southeastern Idaho. In 1997, only 335 whooping cranes existed in the world; wildlife officials are trying to bring the species back through intensive breeding efforts. In 1997, the whoopers that stopped here had been taught to migrate by biologists flying tiny, ultralight aircraft along the migratory route. The birds, believing the aircraft to be their parents, followed along.

The two wildlife refuges offer extraordinary opportunities to see many bird species, including waterfowl such as cinnamon teal (*Anas cyanoptera*), American coot (*Fulica americana*), ruddy duck (*Oxyura jamaicensis*), American avocet (*Recurvirostra americana*), and Wilson's phalarope (*Phalaropus tricolor*). Northern harrier hawks (*Circus cyaneus*) are common throughout the valley, and yellow-headed blackbirds (*Xanthocephalus xanthocephalus*) can be seen in the rushes along the many waterways that line the refuges.

Both refuge units are actively managed to provide food, cover and nesting sites for migratory birds. Water is key to this effort; much of the water in Monte Vista National Wildlife Refuge is pumped in to replace natural flows used by valley farmers. Farming, grazing, and hunting are allowed on the refuges, with an eye toward managing for the migratory birds.

Directions: For Monte Vista National Wildlife Refuge, drive south from the town of Monte Vista on County Road 15 approximately 6 miles to the beginning of the auto tour route, on left (east). For Alamosa National Wildlife Refuge, travel 4 miles east of Alamosa on US 160 to El Rancho Lane, then 2 miles south to refuge headquarters.

Activities: Bird-watching, photography, hiking, hunting under special regulations.

Facilities: At Monte Vista, self-guided auto tour only (visitors are not allowed to leave cars, but birds are not spooked by cars, either) through the western corner of the refuge. This refuge unit is occasionally staffed by volunteers. Alamosa offers a visitor center, interpretive exhibits, hiking trail, and auto route to a bluff overlook.

Dates: Open year-round.

Fees: None.

Closest town: Monte Vista, 6 miles north from Monte Vista National Wildlife Refuge; Alamosa, 6 miles north from Alamosa National Wildlife Refuge.

For more information: Refuge Manager, Alamosa-Monte Vista National Wildlife Refuge, 9388 El Rancho Lane, Alamosa, CO 81101. Phone (719) 589-4021.

San Luis Lakes State Park

[Fig. 15(3)] This 2,054-acre park includes more than 800 acres of open water, surrounded by low dunes of four-wing saltbush, rabbitbrush and greasewood, desert species growing incongruously on the verge of a lake. Although the valley appears to be dry from a distance or from CO 17, which bisects it, in fact there are billions of gallons of water here, the vast majority of it beneath the surface. San Luis Lakes represent the surface of that water table. The lakes are a natural collection area, or sump. Groundwater flowing south down the valley beneath the land's surface rises here and forms the lakes because of a subterranean rock barrier that prevents the water from continuing its southerly movement.

Ditches and wet meadows are common in this part of the valley during the summer, and the presence of red-winged blackbirds (*Agelaius phoeniceus*) and yellow-headed blackbirds on roadside fences is a good indicator of nearby water.

The northern half of the valley is a "closed basin"—it has no outlet to the sea. An almost imperceptible rise in the valley floor north of Alamosa prevents surface water from running south to the Rio Grande River. Billions of gallons of water are stored as groundwater in aquifers that stretch down two miles below the land's surface. Prior to Anglo-American and Hispanic settlement in the region, the San Luis Valley was a rich grassland. Despite the water, and in part because of its mismanagement, over-grazing and other agricultural activities destroyed much of the grasslands. In many places, grasses have been killed by saline deposits left in the soil from poor irrigation practices. Unable to recover, the historic grasslands have mostly been replaced by desert scrub vegetation.

Directions: From Alamosa, north on CO 17 for 14 miles to Six Mile Lane, then east 6 miles to park entrance. From Great Sand Dunes National Monument, go south on CO 150 for 2 miles from the monument entrance to Six Mile Lane, then west 8 miles to the park entrance.

Activities: Camping, fishing, interpretive programs, boating (sailing and power boating), sailboarding, hiking, wildlife watching. The northern portion of San Luis Lake is closed to boating to protect waterfowl nesting areas.

Facilities: 51 campsites, 27 picnic sites, boat ramp, dump station, laundry, showers.

Dates: Open year-round.

Fees: There is a fee for entry and camping.

Closest town: Alamosa, 17 miles south.

For more information: San Luis Lakes State Park, PO Box 175, Mosca, CO 81146. Phone (719) 378-2020. Reservations phone (800) 678-2267.

Crestone/Sangre de Cristo Mountains

[Fig. 15] The village of Crestone, an oasis of cottonwood trees tucked against the base of some of the Sangre de Cristos' most dramatic peaks, is quiet and tiny. It's also an access point into a group of four Fourteeners: Kit Carson Peak (14,165 feet), Crestone Peak (14,294 feet), Crestone Needle (14,197 feet), and Humboldt Peak (14,064 feet). Most alpinists, however, choose to attempt the summits of the latter three peaks from South Colony Lakes, reached from the eastern side of the range.

Because the western side of the Sangre de Cristos is the side of the great fault block that rose while the eastern side sank, hikes in this area tend to be steep and strenuous.

Directions: From CO 160, take CO 17 approximately 37 miles north to Moffat, then east on T Road 18 miles to Crestone.

WILLOW CREEK LAKES

[Fig. 15] This spectacular hike provides extraordinary views out over the San Luis Valley as it climbs an improbable route into a hanging valley at the base of Kit Carson Peak. (A hanging valley leads out to a cliff or steep incline, and then drops off.) Once they reach the valley, hikers will be rewarded by Lower Willow Lake's waterfalls: A 20-footer at the outlet, and a fall of approximately 120 feet that plunges cleanly and directly into the water at the lake's head. Some of the upper switchbacks, just below the lip of the hanging valley, can feel exposed and may be covered with avalanche debris or old snow in early summer. Prevailing southwest winds can really howl through the venturi that forms at the lip of the hanging valley, so hang onto your hat.

Directions: Follow Crestone's Main Street north to the only stop sign. Turn right, east, on Galena Avenue. After 1 mile the road becomes Forest Road 49. After an additional 1.2 miles, park at the South Crestone trailhead. Go right at the trailhead sign for Willow Lake, cross a small creek, and bear left into the meadow to the trail register.

Trail: 5 miles of well-made trail.

Elevation: Change of 2,900 feet.

Degree of difficulty: Strenuous.

Surface: Dirt and rocks.

The Spanish Peaks

[Fig. 16(4)] The dominant geographical element of the La Veta region is the great, twin Spanish Peaks. Rising up from the verdant Trinchera and Huatajolla valleys, the peaks bear a striking resemblance to Mount Sopris, near Carbondale.

Mythology surrounding the peaks is evident in regional names. Huatajolla (also spelled Watahoya or Guatajolla, and pronouned wah-TOY-yuh), the traditional name for the peaks, has been loosely translated to mean "breasts of the earth." The twin peaks can present that visual impression, but the name also implies the mountains' nurturing effects. Because they create localized rain (all mountain highlands generate their own weather in the sense that they force passing air to rise, thus cooling it and causing the moisture carried by the air to fall as precipitation), the Spanish Peaks breed the streams that irrigate the surrounding valleys, thus literally feeding the residents.

The obverse of the "mother" image associated with the peaks is darker deities. Names such as the Devil's Staircase are applied to the various volcanic dikes radiating out from the peaks like long walls or isolated plugs. These igneous formations are unique in Colorado; the region was designated a National Natural Landmark in 1977. The distinctive dikes and plugs were formed when hot magma pushed up against the

BLUE COLUMBINE
(*Aquilegia caerulea*)
Colorado's state flower,
the blue columbine has five
spurs stretching from the
petals to give it a birdlike
form and inspiring its name
— "columbine" means dove.

overlying sedimentary Cretaceous rock. The pressure cracked the sedimentary layers, and those cracks were filled with magma which, like the mountains, cooled in place beneath the Cretaceous surface of the earth. Over time, erosion removed the softer sedimentary layers to reveal both the Spanish Peaks and the distinctive dikes and plugs. The longest dike runs for 14 miles.

Directions: From I-25, take Exit 50 at Walsenburg to US 160 west. Travel west 12 miles to CO 12, take a left-hand fork, then travel 5 miles to La Veta. Follow Watahoya Trail directions (*see* page 109) from here if you wish to continue up into the mountains, or pick up the Highway of Legends scenic byway (*see* page 114).

WATAHOYA TRAIL

[Fig. 16(3)] The Spanish peaks are not a wilderness area, so you may encounter jeeps, mountain bikers or others on this trail. Although this route does not lead to either of the summits, it does climb up into a northeast-facing bowl on West Spanish Peak (13,626 feet), granting views north along the Great Plains toward Pikes Peak, the Wet Mountains, and the Blanca Peak massif north of La Veta Pass.

Directions: From La Veta, take CO 12 south to the edge of town. Turn left on Cuchara Street. Go 0.2 mile to a T intersection; follow the main road around to the right. Go 1 mile, then left (follow signs for Huatajolla Valley). Go 0.5 miles, turn right at another Huatajolla Valley sign, then go 3.5 miles to the small sign on the right for Forest Service Trail 1304. Park on the left. After about 3 miles the hiking trail forks; climb left here to get into the West Spanish Peak bowl.

Trail: 4 miles one-way.

Elevation: Change of 3,000 feet.

Degree of difficulty: Moderate.

Surface: Dirt and rocks.

Blue Columbine

The state flower, *Aquilegia coerulea* was so popular with urban residents during the late nineteenth and early twentieth centuries that excursion trains departed for day trips to Colorado's mountains so that people could pick great heaps of the flowers. Now protected by a law that prohibits picking wild blooms, columbines have been bred into an array of domesticated blossoms of many colors. The original flower, with its blue and white leaves, evolved in conjunction with the hummingbird. The flower's deep, distinctive spikes contain nectar which draws hummingbirds, helping to pollinate the flowers. Columbines thrive in rocky scree slopes as well as in groves of aspen trees.

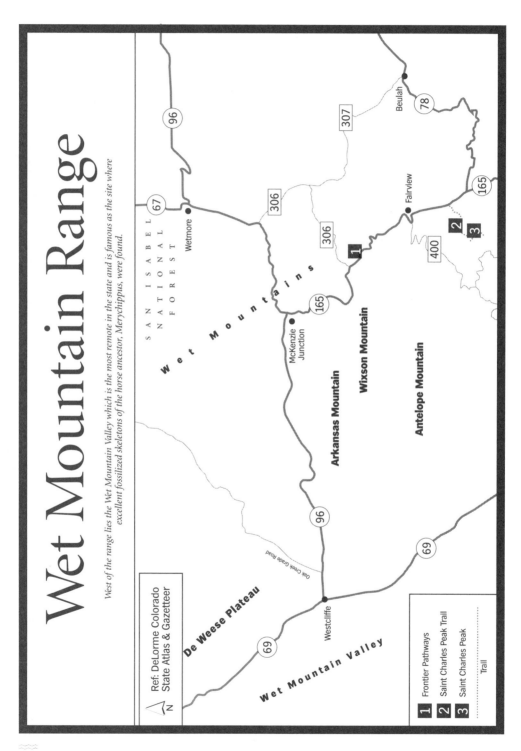

Wet Mountain Range

West of the range lies the Wet Mountain Valley which is the most remote in the state and is famous as the site where excellent fossilized skeletons of the horse ancestor, Merychippus, were found.

Ref: DeLorme Colorado State Atlas & Gazetteer

N

SAN ISABEL NATIONAL FOREST

Wet Mountains

Wetmore

McKenzie Junction

Arkansas Mountain

Wixson Mountain

Antelope Mountain

Fairview

Beulah

De Weese Plateau

Oak Creek Grade Road

Westcliffe

Wet Mountain Valley

96

67

306

306

165

1

400

2

3

165

307

78

96

69

69

1 Frontier Pathways
2 Saint Charles Peak Trail
3 Saint Charles Peak

Trail

Wet Mountain Range

[Fig. 17] The Wet Mountains were created as part of the Laramide orogeny, the great uplift that formed the core of the Colorado Rockies. As a mountain range they stand, relative to so many of Colorado's dramatic and spectacular peaks, as a sort of ragged afterthought, unimpressive in the shadows of Pikes Peak and the Sangre de Cristos.

The Wet Mountains are mostly timbered and lack both Fourteeners (the highest peak, Greenhorn Mountain, is 12,349 feet) and lakes—both attractions that draw visitors. However, the Wet Mountains have their charms, not the least being the solitude visitors are likely to find here. In 1993, 22,040 acres in the southern portion of the range were designated the Greenhorn Mountain Wilderness, in part because the region contains such a broad mix of ecosystems. The Wets rise directly from the High Plains, so that a traveler can begin hiking in gambel oak at 7,200 feet near the town of Rye and climb a vertical mile to Greenhorn Mountain's summit, passing through aspen, white fir, Engelmann spruce, subalpine fir, limber pine, and ultimately tundra ecosystems.

Greenhorn Mountain was named for *Cuerno Verde*, or "Green Horn," a chief of the Comanche Indians. He was killed near the base of the peak in 1779 by a Spanish expedition sent out from Santa Fe to crush the tribe. The Spanish victory led to a treaty and, in 1787, an attempt to convert the nomadic Comanches to a sedentary life in a Spanish-funded village called San Carlos, situated near the present site of Pueblo. However, the Comanches abandoned the village in less than a year, and no permanent settlement was created in the state until San Luis was built in 1851 on the western side of the Sangre de Cristo Mountains.

The valley west of the range, the Wet Mountain Valley, is one of the most remote in the state. It is famous among paleontologists as the site where excellent fossilized skeletons of an ancestor of the horse, *Merychippus*, were found in Tertiary Period sediments. (The horse was introduced to the Americas by Spanish conquistadors, but its progenitors evidently evolved on the North American continent, migrated to Eurasia over the Bering Strait land bridge, and then died out here.) Like the San Luis Valley, the Wet Mountain Valley lies in a rain shadow, drawing little direct rain but thriving as an agricultural area on the streams that flow down from the surrounding peaks.

Directions: From I-25, take Exit 52 and pick up CO 69 West into the Wet Mountain Valley; Exit 74 to CO 165 West; or Exit 97, at Pueblo, to CO 78 West. Both of these last two roads lead into and through the Wet Mountains.

🦫 SAINT CHARLES PEAK

[Fig. 17(3)] At 11,784 feet, Saint Charles is the second highest peak in the Wet Mountains. Its summit is a rounded meadow of tundra, ringed by limber pine and subalpine fir. Limber pine (*Pinus flexilis*) is sometimes called Rocky Mountain

Broad-Tailed Hummingbird

Perhaps the most common hummingbird in Colorado, *Selasphorus platycercus* is relatively large, up to 4.5 inches long. Like many hummingbirds, the males are iridescent green, with buff underbellies and a glittering red throat. Females are slightly smaller and lack the red patch. These hummers are usually the first to arrive in the mountains each spring, migrating from Central America. They particularly prefer red flowers such as scarlet gilia (*Ipomopsis agregata*) and can often be heard or seen flying in mountain meadows. Watch for the males' territorial flight. The bird climbs higher and higher, the pitch of its wings rising until it stops and dives with a screaming buzz in a great, U-shaped arc, pulling up from the ground at the last moment and towering up 100 feet or more for another dive.

white pine and easily confused with bristlecone pine (*Pinus aristata*). Both species grow to 1,000 years old or more, and both become twisted and gnarled and generally grow near treeline. Limber pines, however, have longer needles (4 to 7 centimeters, versus about 4 centimeters for bristlecone) and do not have prickles on their cones. Limber pines appear to depend to a large degree on Clark's nutcrackers (*Nucifraga columbiana*) for seed dispersal. The big birds cache seeds and then forget them. Biologists think the location of limber pines may have as much to do with where the birds put the seeds as with the site preferences of the limber pines themselves.

Directions: Drive north on CO 165 to CO 178 (the turn to Beulah). From this point, continue north on CO 165 for 0.8 mile. Pass South Creek Trail on the right; park at the next right-hand pullout. The trailhead is across the road on the west side.

Trail: 5 miles one-way.

Elevation: Change of 2,700 feet.

Degree of difficulty: Moderate.

Surface: Dirt, rocks, and tundra.

Scenic Drives

LOS CAMINOS ANTIGUOS

[Fig. 16(1)] This byway runs 136.7 miles from Mosca to the New Mexico state line in the South San Juan Mountains. The discussion here covers the first 97 miles of the route.

The byway begins at Mosca near the heart of the San Luis Valley, and runs due east from CO 17 along Six Mile Lane. Low, vegetated dunes along the route, around Mile 7, are a continuing source of sand for the Great Sand Dunes, visible to the northeast. Blanca Peak is the large summit visible to the southeast. At Mile 16 turn right (south) onto CO 150 (left leads to the Great Sand Dunes). The route parallels the flanks of the Blanca Peak massif until it meets US 160 at Mile 28. On the right, as you pass Blanca Peak, is the Baca Grant, an old Spanish land grant now home to cattle and domesticated bison.

Turn left on US 160 at Mile 28 and travel to the town of Fort Garland, at Mile 40. This is the site of the renamed and relocated Army Fort Massachusetts, built here in 1858. Turn south (right) on CO 159. At Mile 54 there's a good view of Culebra Peak, the only privately owned Fourteener in Colorado (14,069 feet). It is part of the Taylor Ranch, a now-private ranch comprised of lands that were held in common by citizens of San Luis until the early 1960s. A legal battle is continuing over whether the ranch should be reopened to locals for hunting, grazing, and firewood collection. Meanwhile, much of the timber on the ranch is being logged, a practice that worries locals who depend on runoff from the ranch's mountains to irrigate their fields. Too much logging will diminish the land's capacity to retain snowmelt and rainwater and release it slowly over time. Instead, heavily logged lands tend to drain quickly, sometimes catastrophically. This possibility threatens the traditional irrigation methods of the San Luis community, which depends not on reservoirs but on an acequia (pronounced ah-SAY-kee-ah), or common ditch, to carry water diverted all summer long from creeks to farmers' long, narrow fields.

These fields can be seen around San Luis, at Mile 55. Turn right (west) here onto CO 42. Cross the Rio Grande at Mile 75. Throughout its length, much of the water in this river, which flows from the San Juan Mountains to Brownsville, Texas, is appropriated for agricultural and urban uses, which means the river isn't as grand as it once was. Pass the King turquoise mine at Mile 76, a site where this gemstone has been sought for centuries. At Mile 89 turn left, south, on US 285 to Antonito, a small farming community. South of Antonito is the rounded hump of San Antonio Peak, marking the New Mexico border. This and several other low peaks and flat mesas to the east are the remnants of small volcanoes and lava flows which keep groundwater dammed up in the San Luis Valley.

BROAD-TAILED HUMMINGBIRD
(Selasphorus platycercus)
These tiny birds (4.5 inches long) can fly backward or straight up and down, as well as hover and drink nectar without actually landing on a flower.

CUMBRES AND TOLTEC RAILWAY

[Fig. 16(5)] Antonito is the eastern terminus of the Cumbres and Toltec Scenic Railroad, a narrow-gauge steam train operated between here and Chama, New Mexico. Until World War II, the railroad continued south to Santa Fe, New Mexico, and was known colloquially as the Chile Line.

Directions: From Alamosa, take US 285 approximately 50 miles south to Antonito. Drive through town and follow US 285 around to the west; the train station is on the left (south) approximately 0.25 mile from town.

Dates: Mid-May to mid-Oct.

Fees: There is a fee to ride the train.

For more information: Cumbres and Toltec Scenic Railroad, Box 789, Chama, NM 87520. Phone (505) 756-2151.

HIGHWAY OF LEGENDS

[Fig. 16(2)] This 82.3-mile scenic byway stays on the eastern side of the Sangre de Cristo Mountains, carving an east-facing arc from Walsenburg to Trinidad, cities set out in the Plains. The central portion passes between the Spanish Peaks and the Culebra sub-range.

From Walsenburg, drive west on US 160 to CO 12 at Mile 11. Turn left here to La Veta, and follow the highway through town. This approach shows a number of the volcanic plugs and dikes unique to the region; at Mile 22 you can see the Devil's Staircase, a long dike rising toward West Spanish Peak.

The Dakota Sandstone that forms a hogback all along the mountain ranges edging the High Plains appears here on the right at Mile 24. It looks like a volcanic dike but is sedimentary in nature. From the top of Cuchara Pass (9,941 feet), at Mile 33, you can look south to New Mexico. From the aspen ecosystem present on the pass you

COYOTE
(Canis latrans)
Easily adapting to the presence of man, the coyote often preys on rodents, small animals, and livestock. It is a member of the dog family and has been known to mate with domestic dogs.

drive down through gambel oak and mountain mahogany, then follow the Purgatoire River through Stonewall. The Dakota Sandstone rears up again here. As you follow the river, coal-bearing sedimentary rocks are visible along the sides of the road. This was and remains coal country.

BLACK RACER
(*Coluber constrictor*)

The route ends at Trinidad. Between Trinidad and Walsenburg is the town of Ludlow, site of a bitter coal strike in 1914 that ended when local militia slaughtered striking men, women and children here in an attack that shocked the nation and stands as one of the battle cries of the American labor movement.

FRONTIER PATHWAYS

[Fig. 17(1)] This scenic byway has an extra leg, so that it looks like a T. The right-hand leg of the T is not covered here, since it runs out toward the Plains.

This route tracks up through the heart of the Wet Mountains, in the San Isabel National Forest. Pick up CO 165 in Colorado City, and follow it west toward Rye. Around Mile 8, Greenhorn Mountain, the highest peak in the Wet Mountains at 12,349 feet, is clearly visible to the south (left). Continue on CO 165 around the hamlet of Rye and up into the mountains. Around Mile 13 you climb out of the sedimentary rock and into the Precambrian core of the Wet Mountain Range.

Much of this range is timbered, some quite lushly, thanks in part to the precipitation that gave these peaks their name. Notice the heavy timber around Mile 21. At Mile 24 you'll pass Bishop's Castle, a medieval architectural oddity being built by Jim Bishop, who welcomes visitors.

Pass over Bigelow Divide at Mile 29 (9,400 feet), then Wixson Divide at Mile 33. At Mile 37 you reach MacKenzie Junction, a T intersection with CO 96. Turn left (west) here. In a couple of miles the Sangre de Cristo Mountains present themselves over the horizon. Around Mile 46, volcanic activity is evident to the south. The town of Silver Cliff, at Mile 52, got its name—and its wealth—from mineralization brought to the surface by volcanic intrusion. The namesake ore was discovered in 1877; by 1880 the town had 5,000 residents. But when the Denver and Rio Grande Western ran its line up the Wet Mountain Valley through Westcliffe in 1881, the community faded in favor of the railway town. Westcliffe, it seems, was built on land owned by a friend of the president of the railroad.

Westcliffe, with its views up into the glacial North Colony Valley in the Sangre de Cristo Mountains—surrounded by Humboldt Peak, Crestone Peak and Crestone Needle—is the end of the byway.

Northwest Mountain Region

FIGURE NUMBERS

19 Arapaho National Wildlife Refuge
20 Steamboat Springs Area (North)
21 Steamboat Springs Area (South)
22 Hot Sulphur Springs
23 Flattops Wilderness
24 Colorado National Monument

Northwest Mountain Region

C olorado takes a little bit from each surrounding state and sweeps it within its own borders: from the east, the grasslands of Kansas and Nebraska; from the south, the high desert and mysterious light of New Mexico; from the west, the red and yellow sandstones of Utah's canyon country; and from the north, the high, windswept grasslands of Wyoming. In the Northwest Region of Colorado's mountains lie the transitional lands that lead from the dramatic cordillera of central Colorado toward the mesa, canyon, and rangeland country of Utah and Wyoming.

Here, on the Pacific side of the Continental Divide, the land opens itself to the sky. Long vistas draw the traveler westward, as if toward the edges of the earth. A visitor to the northwest edge of the state's mountains may feel as if he or she can almost see Wyoming just over the horizon, or feel the canyon zephyrs of Utah, for the land here changes perceptibly from the sharp relief of the Front Range.

[*Above:* Multicolored sedimentary rocks characterize the Colorado National Monument]

Pronghorn Antelope

The pronghorn is extraordinary for several reasons: A denizen of the high plains, it can see a human 4 miles away, run at speeds of up to 84 miles an hour, and is related to no other mammal. *Antilocapra americana* is the fastest animal on the continent, and one of its truest natives. It is the only modern hooved animal to have evolved on the North American continent, and has been around since the late Cenozoic Era, approximately 10 million years ago. Once as many as 20 million pronghorn ranged across the American steppes. After dwindling to a total population of only 13,000 in 1920, the animal has made a comeback. About 60,000 now live in Colorado. Most reside on the eastern plains, but they are also found in North Park, South Park, Middle Park, and the San Luis Valley.

There are mountains here, to be sure, dramatic ranges and alpine plateaus—although no 14,000-foot peaks. The land relaxes slightly. It has a different feel, a different rhythm on the western side of the divide, where it's all downhill to the Pacific Ocean.

The Northwest Mountain Region is defined by an eastern boundary that begins at the Continental Divide at Eisenhower Tunnel on I-70 and runs generally north, passing west of Byers Peak to the intersection of US 40 and CO 25 west of Granby. From here, it follows CO 25 north across Willow Creek Pass to the southern tip of North Park, then northeast to Cameron Pass. At this point, the border turns north up the east side of the Rawah (also called Medicine Bow) Mountains to the Wyoming border.

The southern border of this section follows I-70 west from Eisenhower Tunnel to Silverthorne, then jogs north up CO 9 along the east side of the Gore Range, curls west through the Gores where they are split by the Colorado River, and runs southwest to Wolcott. Then the border resumes its course along I-70, following this main artery west to Grand Junction, where this region encompasses the Colorado National Monument.

The geography of the Northwest Region is profoundly different from the bold, big-shouldered mountains of the Front Range and the jumbled, volcanic mountains of the Southwest Region. There are classically glaciated cordilleras here, yes: the Park Range and the Rahwahs. But this is more generally a land of high, flat volcanic plateaus, broad, sere parklands and hot, sedimentary mesas.

This section does contain a portion of the state lying on the eastern side of the Continental Divide: North Park and the Rahwah Mountains, as well as the eastern flank of the Park Mountains, which carry the divide on their spine up into Wyoming. Edging up to the northern border of the state, running almost due north-south, the Park and Rahwah ranges flank North Park, a high, naturally dry valley made rich in agriculture and wildlife by the waters running off the surrounding mountains.

Moving south and west, travelers encounter a different geography of vast, table-like mesas (the word actually means "table" in Spanish). The Flattop Mountains and nearby Grand Mesa (*see* the West Central Mountain Region—page 153) are two of a kind. These mountains exist because the world around them eroded away. They did not erode significantly themselves because each was capped by volcanic rock— basalt—during the Tertiary Period, which began 65 million years ago. The volcanoes that produced this rock did not erupt in the traditional sense. Instead, the lava oozed out of the ground and spread over the land, flattening like a pancake. The basalt, as much as 600 feet thick, is harder than the underlying sedimentary rock, and serves as a caprock that protected the softer stone from erosion that wore away the surrounding lands.

Colorado National Monument, the westernmost portion of this region, was formed in a very different manner, although it, too, appears as a long, low, flat-topped mountain. It is in truth the northwest corner of the Uncompahgre Plateau, which runs from Ridgway, at the northern edge of the San Juan Mountains, almost to Cisco, Utah.

The Uncompahgre Plateau is the easternmost extension of the red rock canyon country associated with southeastern Utah. This plateau was uplifted—probably as a result of the pressures created by the grinding together of the earth's continental plates—in the Pennsylvanian Period, about 300 million years ago. This uplift formed Uncompahgria, one of the two main ranges of the ancestral Rocky Mountains.

The erosion of that set of ancient mountain ranges down to plains deposited the multicolored sedimentary rocks that characterize Colorado National Monument and the surrounding desert lands. The monument itself is an excellent example of a monocline; the sedimentary layers fold down from west to east over a core block of Precambrian rock underlying the monument, dropping across a fault that demarcates the western side of Grand Valley and the eastern side of the monument.

PRONGHORN
(Antilocapra americana)
Sometimes called an antelope, the pronghorn is North America's swiftest mammal, with speeds of 84 miles per hour and 20-foot leaps.

Moose

The largest ungulate in North America, *Alces alces shirasi* can be one of the most dangerous animals found on land. Cow moose, which can weigh up to 700 pounds, become aggressive in defense of their young, charging any perceived threat—including humans—with sharp teeth and sharp hooves. Bulls, perhaps less dangerous, are more impressive to watch: Adult males stand 6 feet at the shoulder and weigh 1,100 pounds. Moose love water and are usually found in or near it, although occasionally they travel to high altitudes to avoid summer insects. Unlike deer and elk, they do not migrate to lower elevations in winter but will tolerate snow depths of up to 5 feet, continuing to browse on willows and other riparian vegetation.

Throughout northwestern Colorado the eroded detritus of the ancestral Rockies forms the basis for the region's geography. This geography is quite different from the uplifts that distinguish the state's more mountainous regions. Western Colorado simply was not disturbed as much as other parts of the state during the mountain-building periods. Thus, sedimentary layers remained relatively (although not completely) horizontal and undisturbed.

One of the most widespread rocks here is Mancos Shale that, like the Pierre Shale on the eastern flanks of the Continental Divide, was deposited by a sea that once covered the region. As much as 5,000 feet of Mancos lies above Dakota Sandstone and below the Mesaverde Group. Mesaverde sandstones and shales often weather into distinct honeycomb pockets (examples can be seen along I-70 in Debeque Canyon). These sandstones and shales contain frequent coal deposits (they were once the littoral of a shallow sea, a coastline created as the Cretaceous sea that created Mancos Shale slowly withdrew from the region), and are prominent east of Rifle, at the Grand Hogback, and above Palisade, where they cap the Book Cliffs.

West of Rifle, the Roan Cliffs are largely comprised of Green River Shale, which contains keragen, the substance that is the "oil" in oil shale. Theoretically, one of the earth's great oil fields lies in northwestern Colorado in the form of oil shale. But getting oil from the rock requires enormous quantities of water—quite sparse in the region—and development of this resource, despite a frantic boom in the early 1980s, does not appear likely in the foreseeable future.

Green River Shale was not formed as a deposit at the bottom of a sea, but rather as the mud at the bottom of an enormous freshwater lake, Lake Uinta,

MOOSE
(*Alces alces shirasi*)

which covered northwest Colorado, southwest Wyoming, and northeast Utah during the Tertiary Period (after the Cretaceous sea had vanished).

Last Stronghold of The Utes

The northwestern mountains were generally passed by during the hectic settlement years of the latter half of the nineteenth century, when so much of Colorado was being turned inside out in search of mineral wealth. Because it was not as radically disturbed during the orogenies that created many of Colorado's other mountains, the land here was not veined with gold and silver. The Anglo-American history of the area is principally one of agriculture, although not entirely. Significant coal, oil, gas, and oil shale deposits are found here, particularly in the mesa country northwest of the major mountain ranges. Exploitation of these resources, however, came relatively recently in the state's history.

The eastern portion of the Northwest Mountain Region is Colorado's moose country; 24 moose (*Alces alces shirasi*) were transplanted from Utah and Wyoming to the North Park area in 1978 and 1979. Today, the herd numbers 600, and animals have ranged as far south as Tennessee Pass, near Leadville. In addition, the region is home to the largest elk herd in the state; Colorado, possessing 200,000 resident elk, has the largest elk herd of any state or province in North America.

Two particularly significant events in the region's recent human history occurred shortly after the end of the Civil War. John Wesley Powell, a one-armed veteran of the war and a major in the Union Army, spent the winter of 1868—1869 with his Rocky Mountain Scientific Exploring Expedition along the banks of the White River west of Meeker. The following summer, he began a journey that led him down to Green River, Utah, and then into *terra incognita*.

Powell and his party became the first Anglo-Americans to traverse the length of the Grand Canyon, the mysterious heart of a portion of U.S. territory that, even at that late date, had not been seriously explored. Powell lost two men when they abandoned the expedition and climbed out to the Grand Canyon's rim, where they were killed by Indians. The entire expedition had been given up for dead when Powell and his remaining party appeared at the mouth of the canyon in Arizona. Powell went on to found what became the United States Geological Survey, and became a cogent, although widely ignored, voice in Washington on the limitations of human settlement and development in the arid regions of the West.

A decade later, in September 1879, the Meeker Massacre drew the curtain on the Ute Indians' historic occupation of most of Colorado. The Utes had been steadily pushed west out of the mountains as Anglo-Americans agitated for more access to and control of the Indians' traditional lands. But, as was true in so much of western history, no concession seemed sufficient for the settlers. Boostering newspapers championed the cause of "intelligent and industrious citizens" who should be given traditional lands, and a campaign on the slogan "Ute Must Go" gained political strength.

The situation was primed to come to a head, and it did in the White River valley. Here Nathan Meeker, an Indian agent, was attempting to "civilize" nomadic Utes by forcing them into an agrarian lifestyle. The Utes perceived Meeker to be an oppressor; as tensions at the agency escalated, Army troops were sent to round up Indians who had fled and to protect the agency from possible attack. Instead, an Indian ambush left 14 soldiers dead, as well as Meeker and 11 men at the White River Agency. Five women were taken hostage by the Utes but were eventually released.

This incident produced an outcry in Denver and other Colorado towns, where settlers demanded the ouster of Ute Indians. The result, in 1881, was the exile of the Utes to the Uintah Reservation in eastern Utah and to lands around Sleeping Ute Mountain along the southwestern Colorado border. Today, the Utes reside principally on the Ute Mountain and Southern Ute reservations, which lie in Colorado and New Mexico.

North Park Area

North Park can be one of the most beautiful, and one of the loneliest places in Colorado's mountains. Encircled by three mountain ranges—the Park Range to the west, Rahwahs to the east, and Rabbit Ears Range to the south—North Park is a high, fertile valley of hayfields, braided streams, and gentle hills, running 45 miles north to south and 35 miles wide at its broadest point. Jackson County, with a population of one person per square mile, is among Colorado's least populous counties. The region has almost no commercial development, and is anchored at its center by Walden, a tiny agricultural service town that describes itself as The Moose Viewing Capital of Colorado.

Yet North Park has a great deal to recommend it. At dawn and dusk, alpenglow lights up the surrounding mountains. Summer thunderstorms sweep across the sky and pile against the peaks, throwing a brilliant, elemental chiaroscuro of light and shadow, rain and sun across the valley and the surrounding mountains. The Arapaho National Wildlife Refuge dominates the center of the valley, while the Colorado State Forest, crown jewel of the state park system, rolls across the western flank of the Rawahs.

Like Colorado's three other structural basins—Middle Park, South Park, and San Luis Valley—North Park is a valley rimmed by geologic faults that allowed the valley to drop as the mountains around it rose over the eons. All of these valleys then filled with eroded sediments from the surrounding higher ground. During the Miocene-Pliocene uplift, some of those sediments were scrubbed out of the valley floor as

North Park's streams were reinvigorated by steepened terrain. Today, the streams move rather sedately. The Michigan, Canadian, Grizzly, and North Platte all wind in dense, complex braidings across the valley floor, creating a profusion of willows and other riparian habitat—excellent country for moose, which have flourished here. North of Walden these rivers combine into the North Platte, which flows into Wyoming.

North Park was not easily settled, largely due to the harsh winters found at the valley's altitude of about 8,300 feet. The first year-round residents, the Fordyce family, settled in 1878, 58 years after the first trapper had traversed the region. North Park was described by the explorer John C. Frémont in 1844. His words are accurate even today:

"A beautiful circular valley of 30 miles in diameter, walled in all around with snowy mountains, rich with water and grass, fringed with pine on the mountain sides below the snow, and a paradise to all grazing animals."

COLORADO STATE FOREST

[Fig. 19] This is a prime holding of the Colorado state park system, a 71,000-acre park that runs 28 miles along the western flank of the Rawah Mountains and is up to 8 miles wide. It is an anomaly in the system in that it is managed, in part, for timber harvest, but it is nevertheless considered a park by the Colorado State Parks, the administrative agency in charge of it.

The state forest encompasses the state's largest moose herd, numerous lakes and streams, the dramatic Nokhu Crags at the northern tip of the Never Summer Mountains, and 400 acres of sand dunes—a smaller incarnation of the Great Sand Dunes National Monument in the San Luis Valley (*see* page 100).

The state forest is actively managed for multiple use. Power boating is allowed on Michigan Reservoir, although at wakeless speeds, and in the northern reaches of the park, one of the two sand dune complexes is open to off-road vehicles (North Sand Hill Recreation Area). Six backcountry yurts—round, Mongolian, tentlike structures that sleep up to nine people and include wood stoves—are open on a reservation basis for winter and summer use, and primitive cabins may be rented from the park along the shores of Michigan Reservoir. Most noticeably, the forest is logged. Approximately 280 acres, on average, are cut each year. Most of the timber is lodgepole pine. Higher elevations (the park climbs to 12,400 feet) encompass subalpine forests and alpine environments. Several jeep roads are open in the park, and the area is popular with hunters in the fall.

The state forest is contiguous with the western edge of the Rawah Wilderness Area, which covers a portion of the eastern side of the Rawah Mountains.

Directions: From Walden, drive south on CO 14 approximately 30 miles to the park entrance station, located 2 miles north of the hamlet of Gould. The visitor center is located 7 miles west of Cameron Pass on CO 14.

Arapaho National Wildlife Refuge

Created in 1967, this 18,000-acre refuge is home to 198 species of birds, 33 mammals, and 15 other vertebrates.

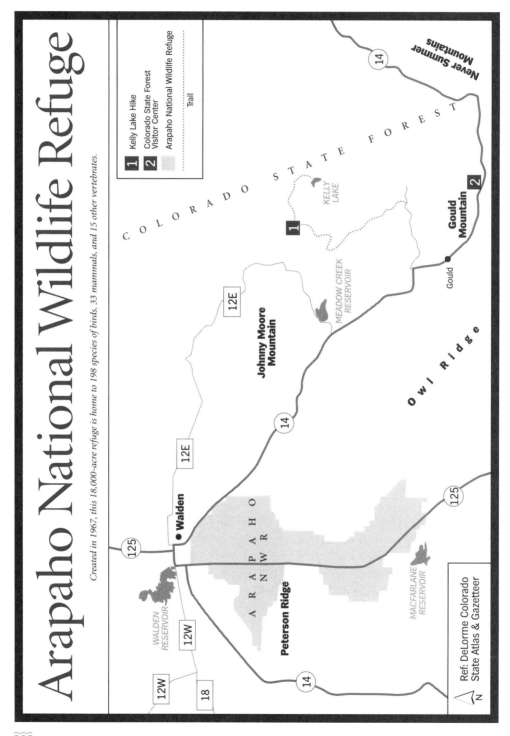

1 Kelly Lake Hike
2 Colorado State Forest Visitor Center
   Arapaho National Wildlife Refuge
   .... Trail

Never Summer Mountains

COLORADO STATE FOREST

KELLY LAKE

1

Gould Mountain

2

Gould

MEADOW CREEK RESERVOIR

12E

Johnny Moore Mountain

Owl Ridge

14

12E

Walden

125

A R A P A H O N W R

Peterson Ridge

125

MACFARLANE RESERVOIR

WALDEN RESERVOIR

12W

12W

18

14

14

Ref: DeLorme Colorado State Atlas & Gazetteer

N

Activities: Hiking, camping, picnicking, boating, biking, horseback riding, backpacking, weekend interpretive programs, cross-country skiing, cabin and yurt rentals.

Facilities: 104 campsites, 16 picnic sites, 2 boat ramps, rental cabins, yurts.

Dates: Open year-round.

Fees: There is a fee to use the park.

Closest town: Walden, 30 miles northwest.

For more information: Colorado State Forest, Star Route Box 91, Walden, CO 80480. Phone (970) 723-8366. For information and reservations on cabin rentals, contact the park; for information on the yurt system, contact Never Summer Nordic, PO Box 1983, Fort Collins, CO 80522.

KELLY LAKE HIKE

[Fig. 19(1)] This hike winds through sage meadows, aspen, lodgepole, and subalpine forest to a jewel of a lake tucked beneath the craggy ridge of the Rawah Mountains.

Directions: From the entrance station, drive east toward North Michigan Reservoir, bear left toward Bockman Campground, pass along the north shore of the reservoir, then turn left at the T-intersection toward the Kelly Lake trailhead. Park here and begin hiking on the road past the locked gate; follow the signs for Kelly Lake. The distance to the trailhead is about 10 miles.

Trail: 4 miles one-way.

Elevation: Change of 1,200 feet.

Degree of difficulty: Moderate.

Surface and Blaze: Dirt road and natural rock and dirt footpath.

ARAPAHO NATIONAL WILDLIFE REFUGE

[Fig. 19] Created in 1967, this 18,000-acre refuge is home to vast flocks of migrating waterfowl, wintering deer and elk, moose, pronghorn antelope (*Antilocapaa americana*), trout, and the dramatic sage grouse (*Centrocercus urophasianus*). This bird—as large as a small turkey—is noted for courtship displays in which the male inflates his white chest, which exposes two yellow sacks amid the feathers, and simultaneously lifts and fans the spiky feathers of his tail.

A total of 198 species of birds, 33 mammals, and 15 other vertebrates have been sighted on the refuge, which is principally managed for waterfowl nesting and production. As many as 5,000 ducks are present on the refuge during spring migrations (peaking in numbers in May); in September and October as many as 8,000 birds gather. Commonly sighted species include mallard (*Anas platyrhynochos*), northern pintail (*Anas acuta*), gadwall (*Anas strepera*), American widgeon (*Anas americana*), lesser scaup (*Aythya affinis*), and redhead (*Aythya americana*). Each year approximately 7,000-8,000 ducklings and several hundred Canada goslings are raised by their parents on the refuge.

Fig. 20: Steamboat Springs Area (North)

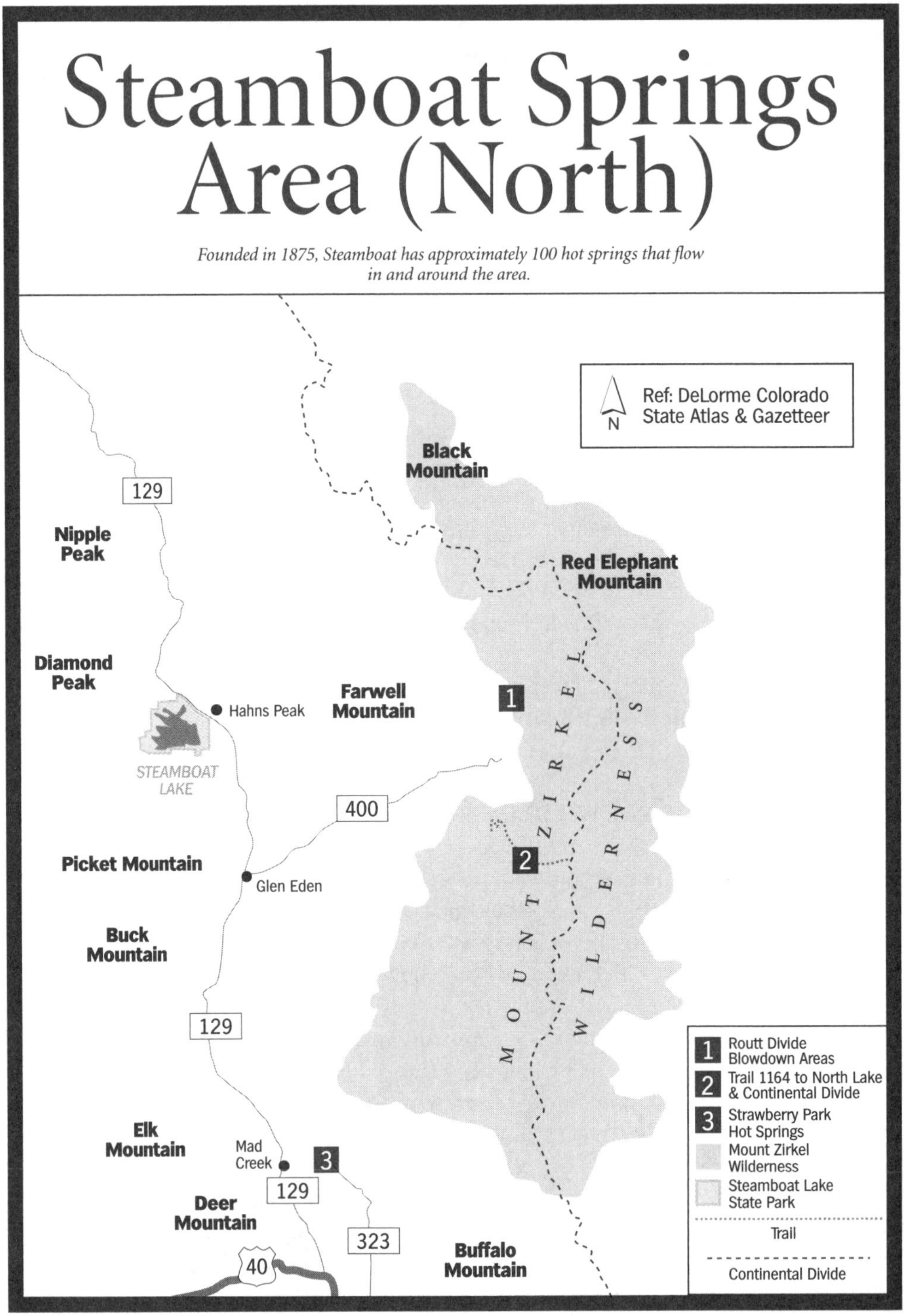

Steamboat Springs Area (North)
Founded in 1875, Steamboat has approximately 100 hot springs that flow in and around the area.
Ref: DeLorme Colorado State Atlas & Gazetteer
N
Black Mountain
Red Elephant Mountain
129
Nipple Peak
Diamond Peak
Hahns Peak
Farwell Mountain
1
STEAMBOAT LAKE
400
MOUNT ZIRKEL WILDERNESS
2
Picket Mountain
Glen Eden
Buck Mountain
129
Elk Mountain
Mad Creek
3
129
Deer Mountain
323
40
Buffalo Mountain
1 Routt Divide Blowdown Areas
2 Trail 1164 to North Lake & Continental Divide
3 Strawberry Park Hot Springs
Mount Zirkel Wilderness
Steamboat Lake State Park
Trail
Continental Divide

In addition to ducks, birders may see (depending on the season) birds as varied as Virginia rails (*Rallus limicola*), eared grebes (*Podiceps nigricollis*), mourning doves (*Zenaida macroura*), Swainson's hawks (*Buteo swainsoni*), and killdeers (*Charadrius vociferus*). Black-crowned night herons (*Nycticorax nycticorax*) have established a rookery in the bulrush and cattail on one of the refuge ponds.

Directions: From Walden, drive south on CO 125 approximately 3 miles to a right (west) turn onto the 6-mile, self-guided automobile tour. The refuge headquarters, open during regular business hours, is 5 miles farther south on CO 125, on the left (east) side of the road.

Activities: Bird-watching, self-guided auto tour, hunting and fishing (in season and subject to refuge restrictions), hiking (the entire refuge is open for walking unless posted otherwise).

Facilities: Refuge headquarters, auto-tour route, handicapped-accessible nature trail.

Dates: Open year-round during daylight hours. However, winter weather closes most roads and trails, including the auto-tour road, from Oct. until Apr. or May. Headquarters open during office hours Monday through Friday.

Fees: None.

Closest town: Walden, 7 miles north of refuge headquarters.

For more information: Arapaho National Wildlife Refuge, Box 457, Walden, CO 80480. Phone (970) 723-8202.

Steamboat Springs Area

[Fig. 20] This euphoniously named town was christened in 1875 by its first settler, James H. Crawford, who built a cabin near the banks of a river, beside a chugging natural hot spring that mimicked the sound of a paddlewheel steamboat. The springs were silenced in 1908 when the Denver and Rio Grande Railroad arrived in town and graded over them while laying track.

Approximately 100 hot springs continue to flow in and around the area today, including one at the public pool on the eastern end of Lincoln Avenue, Steamboat's main street. Steamboat (as it is commonly known) has been rediscovered in the last decade, as evidenced by sprawling residential development along US 40 and ongoing expansion of the Steamboat ski area. But the town retains much of its mining and ranching roots.

Steamboat Lake State Park offers fishing, boating, water skiing, swimming, camping, and picnicking in view of historic Hahns Peak.

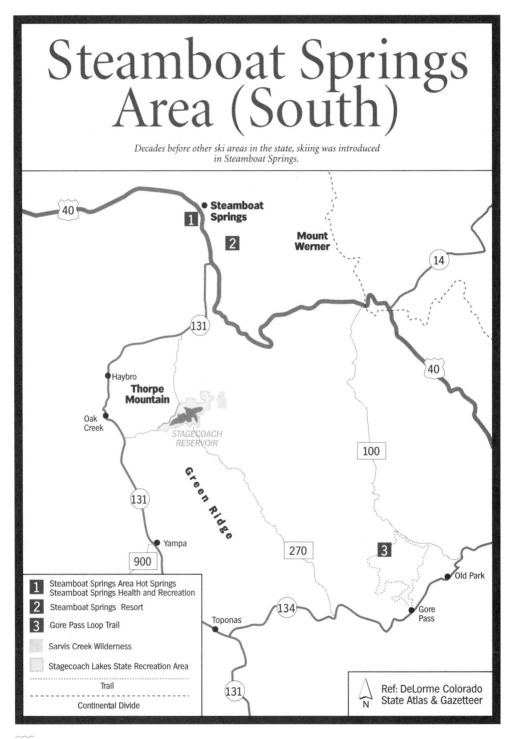

Steamboat Springs Area (South)

Decades before other ski areas in the state, skiing was introduced in Steamboat Springs.

Legend:

1. Steamboat Springs Area Hot Springs
   Steamboat Springs Health and Recreation
2. Steamboat Springs Resort
3. Gore Pass Loop Trail

Sarvis Creek Wilderness

Stagecoach Lakes State Recreation Area

····· Trail

- - - Continental Divide

N — Ref: DeLorme Colorado State Atlas & Gazetteer

These activities remain viable, even vibrant, in surrounding Routt County.

Steamboat is also the catalyst for an innovative approach to open space conservation. Like many mountain valleys, the lands around Steamboat Springs are rapidly being developed. Colorado, in fact, is one of the fastest growing states in the nation. Between 1990 and 1995, the population grew 13.7 percent. Much of this growth appears in the cities of the Front Range, but much also comes in mountain valleys, precisely because they are nice places to live. On average, 90,000 acres of Colorado's open space disappeared under development each year during the 1990s. The state's population is projected to rise from 3.5 million in 1990 to 5 million by 2010.

This growth is problematic for areas like Routt County, where valley lands that have traditionally been used for ranching are beginning to grow their final crop: subdivisions.

In the Elk River valley northwest of Steamboat Springs, Jay Fetcher has led an effort to convince his fellow ranchers to voluntarily deed-restrict their hay meadows and bottomlands against such development with conservation easements. About 12,000 acres are now protected by the agreement among the ranchers, which was the first of its kind. As a consequence, the Elk River valley remains largely bucolic. Fetcher's efforts have been widely reported and emulated elsewhere, and led to the formation of a land trust specifically designed to help ranching families be able to afford to keep their lands in their families and in agriculture—which is becoming more difficult as urbanization pushes up land values throughout the Rocky Mountains.

FORGET-ME-NOT
(Myosotis scorpioides)

MOUNT ZIRKEL WILDERNESS

[Fig. 20] Mount Zirkel was one of the original wilderness areas created by the 1964 Wilderness Act. It has been expanded twice to its present 160,568 acres. Notably, it is one of the few Colorado wilderness areas to encompass contiguous lowland and upland terrain, making it valuable for species that migrate through different elevations at different times. This is particularly true on the northern (Encampment River) end. Mount Zirkel (12,180 feet) was named in 1874 for Ferdinand Zirkel, who established a common nomenclature for American and European rocks.

As is true in most of Colorado's northern ranges, the Park Range running through the core of the Mount Zirkel Wilderness was formed by an uplift of Precambrian granite, although there are other rocks here, too. Look for gneiss, easily identified by the swirling grey and white streaks in the rock, and schist, which contains flakes of mica. These are metamorphic rocks, formed in a semimelted state under intense heat and pressure. Around Rabbit Ears Pass, west of Steamboat Springs on US 40, these rocks are apparent. So too are the "rabbit ears" themselves—three small peaks eroded from the core of an ancient volcano.

The Elk River, which runs west of the Park Range and derives much of its water from these mountains, is the most productive in the state in terms of water yield; that is, the Elk River produces more water for each square foot in its drainage basin than any other river. Each year, the Elk drains a whopping 25 gallons for every square foot—testament to the vast quantities of precipitation, especially snow, that fall here.

TRAIL 1164 TO NORTH LAKE AND THE CONTINENTAL DIVIDE

[Fig. 20(2)] This trail climbs up moderate switchbacks to the open meadows and subalpine forest around North Lake, a small natural lake set amid spruce, then ascends 1 mile farther to the Continental Divide at 10,800 feet. The divide here is broad and partially timbered; from the intersection with the Continental Divide Trail you get excellent views up the broad spine to the flattened summit of Lost Ranger Peak (11,932 feet), 2 miles south.

Directions: Take US 40 (Lincoln Avenue) west from Steamboat Springs 1 mile to County Road 129 (to Clark). Follow this road about 20 miles up the Elk River valley to the hamlet of Glen Eden, then turn right (east) on County 64 (Forest Road 400). Go 12 miles to FR 443, a right; take this 6 miles to the trailhead. This route is passable by a two-wheel-drive vehicle in good weather.

Trail: 5 miles one-way.

Elevation: Change of 1,900 feet.

Degree of difficulty: Moderate

Surface and Blaze: Rough dirt and rocks; some stream crossings.

ROUTT DIVIDE BLOWDOWN AREAS

[Fig. 20(1)] In the early morning of October 25, 1997, winds of up to 120 miles per hour blew from the east over the Continental Divide, creating a vast blowdown of trees north of Steamboat Springs. Four million trees were flattened across an area 5 miles long and 30 miles wide. Most of the victims were spruce and fir, blown down in patches as large as 4,000 acres. From the air, the blowdown made the forest look like an incomplete jigsaw puzzle, and blowdown areas can be mistaken for logged-over land at a distance.

The blowdown is limited to the western side of the Continental Divide along the Park Range. Almost all the blown-down areas lie south of Gem Lake and north of the Dry Lake Campground in the Routt National Forest.

This event, while highly unusual, is also wholly natural. Within the Mount Zirkel

Wilderness, blown-down trees will be allowed to decompose naturally, although U.S. Forest Service trail crews worked through the summer of 1998 to reopen blocked trails. Outside the wilderness, some of the felled trees may be commercially logged.

The blowdown opened up large patches of forest. Over time, these areas will be colonized by successional species. Aspen or lodgepole pine may grow where Engelmann spruce and subalpine fir were felled. Forbs and grasses may create meadows, and "edge"—the ecotone between two types of forest—will develop, providing beneficial cover for animals.

Trees that fell into streams will provide cover for trout, but siltation resulting from soil disturbance may clog gravel bars where trout spawn, resulting in lowered fertility rates.

Cavity-nesters and woodpeckers will benefit; standing dead trees are expected to host spruce budworms, which provide food for birds but which may also spread into stands of living trees.

Directions: Blowdown areas are visible along many routes. Some of the most heavily hit terrain is north of the Slavonia trailhead. Take US 40 (Lincoln Avenue) west from Steamboat Springs 1 mile to County Road 129 (to Clark). Follow this road 20 miles up the Elk River valley to the hamlet of Glen Eden, then turn right (east) on County 64 (Forest Road 400). Follow this 15 miles to its end. Hike east and north on Trail 1162 (Mica Lake); the major blowdown areas are to the west of the trail. Alternatively, at Seedhouse Campground (10 miles east of Glen Eden on FR 400), take FR 433 north to the edge of this blowdown area, about 2 miles.

STEAMBOAT SPRINGS AREA HOT SPRINGS
STEAMBOAT SPRINGS HEALTH AND RECREATION

[Fig. 21(1)] On the eastern end of Elk Avenue, Steamboat Springs Health and Recreation runs a public set of pools and health club. The natural hot springs run at 103 degrees Fahrenheit. Five pools, treated with bromine and ozone, maintain temperatures between 80 and 103 degrees.

Directions: Located in downtown Steamboat Springs, on the north side of Elk Avenue, at its eastern end.

Facilities: Hot pools, locker rooms, full health club, tennis courts, massage, child-care facility.

Dates: Open year-round.

Fees: There is a fee to use the facilities.

For more information: Steamboat Springs Health and Recreation, PO Box 1211, Steamboat Springs, CO 80477. Phone (970) 879-1828.

STRAWBERRY PARK HOT SPRINGS

[Fig. 20(3)] In the foothills of the Park Range, Strawberry Park Hot Springs is a more rustic operation, set in the woods at 7,500 feet. Hot water comes out of the

At Strawberry Park Hot Springs, water comes out of the ground at a scalding 146 degrees Fahrenheit, but it is cooled in pools with temperatures from 105 to 85 degrees.

ground here at a scalding 146 degrees Fahrenheit; it is cooled with stream water and channeled into several masonry pools with temperatures from 105 to 85 degrees.

Directions: From Steamboat Springs, go north on Seventh Street. Follow signs for Strawberry Hot Springs (County 36 to Forest Road 323). The springs are 7 miles from town. The road is dirt and is not recommended in winter unless you have chains or snow tires and four-wheel drive. Strawberry Park Hot Springs can arrange transportation to and from town.

Facilities: Hot springs, rental cabins, canteen.

Dates: Open year-round.

Fees: There is a fee to use the springs.

Closest town: Steamboat Springs.

For more information: Strawberry Park Hot Springs, PO Box 77332, Steamboat Springs, CO 80477. Phone (970) 879-0342.

SARVIS CREEK WILDERNESS

[Fig. 21] Tributaries of the Yampa River—at 170 miles the longest undammed river in the state—form the core of this unusual protected area. Its uniqueness comes from what may seem to be its ordinary nature. Sarvis Creek Wilderness is simply an unbroken blanket of subalpine forest, cut by two sparkling trout streams, Service Creek (an early cartographer's misinterpretation of the correct name, Sarvis Creek) and Silver Creek. No trophy peaks, no big lakes. Just the hush of deep forest, and maybe the chance to see an elk or a mountain lion.

Directions: From Steamboat Springs, take US 40 South 4 miles to CO 131. Turn right (west) and proceed 5 miles to a T-intersection with County Road 18 (Lake Catamount). Take this south past Lake Catamount to a T; bear right (west) about 1 mile to another T; bear left (south) to the end of the road and the trailhead for Service Creek, a route that climbs up the forested side of the northern Gore Range.

Activities: Hiking, fishing, camping.

Closest town: Steamboat Springs, 10 miles north.

For more information: Yampa District, Routt National Forest, PO Box 7, Yampa, CO 80843. Phone (970) 879-1870.

STEAMBOAT LAKE STATE PARK

[Fig. 20] This spectacular state park is set at the foot of Hahn's Peak, the distinctive, nipple-shaped mountain at the northern end of the Elk River Valley. The 1,505-acre park is mostly water (the reservoir comprises 1,058 acres), but visitors are given stunning views of the Park Range to the east and Hahn's Peak to the north.

Directions: From Steamboat Springs, take US 40 (Lincoln Avenue) west 1 mile to County Road 129 (to Clark). Follow this road about 25 miles up the Elk River valley to the village of Hahn's Peak. Follow signs to the park on the left.

Activities: Camping, picnicking, self-guided nature trail, interpretive programs, fishing, water skiing (half the lake is zoned wakeless, however), horseback riding, snowmobiling, cross-country skiing, snowshoeing, ice fishing.

Facilities: 198 campsites, 35 picnic sites, marina, boat launching ramps, snack bar, visitor center, amphitheater.

Dates: Open year-round.

Fees: There is a fee to use the park.

Closest town: Steamboat Springs, 26 miles south.

For more information: Steamboat Lake State Park, PO Box 750, Clark, CO 80467. Phone (970) 879-3922.

STAGECOACH LAKES STATE RECREATION AREA

[Fig. 21] Stagecoach Lakes is an 866-acre park set in the sage and oak flatlands of the Yampa River south of Steamboat Springs. It provides a myriad of water sports, along with access to nearby Sarvis Creek Wilderness area.

Directions: From Steamboat Springs, drive south 4 miles on US 40 to CO 131; turn right (west), travel 9 miles to County Road 14, then follow signs 7 miles to the park.

Activities: Camping, picnicking, water skiing (limited to the northern half of the 780-acre lake), fishing (winter and summer), hiking, biking, and swimming.

Facilities: 100 campsites, 50 picnic sites, 2 boat ramps, marina, beach, showers, dump station, 5 miles of biking and hiking trails.

Dates: Open year-round.

Fees: There is an entry fee and a camping fee.

Closest town: Oak Creek, 11 miles west.

For more information: Stagecoach State Park, PO Box 98, Oak Creek, CO 80467. Phone (970) 736-2436.

SKIING IN STEAMBOAT SPRINGS

[Fig. 21(2)] Steamboat also has a deep connection to skiing. The sport came to the Yampa Valley in 1913—decades before Aspen, Winter Park, or other ski areas opened for business—when Carl Howelsen introduced skiing to the town's youngsters and taught them ski jumping off a small wooden platform. In 1917 the town honored Howelsen by naming the town's ski slope Howelsen Hill. The hill is located immediately south of the town center across the Yampa River, and is a major training center for U.S. Olympic athletes. Steamboat is home to 43 Olympians—more than any other U.S. town.

Steamboat Springs Resort is one of the busiest ski areas in the state. Each winter more than a million "skier days" are counted on its slopes (a skier day is a unit of measure: one skier or snowboarder using a lift ticket or ski pass for one day). The ski area, laid out on the slopes of Mount Werner east of Steamboat, encompasses 2,939 acres of trails. The ski area's westerly orientation means that late afternoon skiers can bask in the winter sun. The mountain's summit is at 10,568 feet—below tree line— and the runs drop 3,668 feet to the base.

Steamboat is famous for its snow, locally called "champagne powder"—a particularly light, fluffy snow that falls in the local hills and is sought after by skiers who like it deep. In an average year, 341 inches of it accumulates at the ski area.

Directions: From Steamboat Springs, drive south on US 40 approximately 2 miles to Steamboat Resort, on the left (east).

Activities: Skiing, snowboarding, lessons.

Facilities: On-mountain restaurants, base village.

Dates: Generally open Thanksgiving to Easter.

Fees: There is a fee to ride the lifts.

Closest town: Steamboat Springs, 3 miles northwest.

For more information: Steamboat Ski and Resort Corporation, 2305 Mount Werner Circle, Steamboat Springs, CO 80487. Phone (970) 879-8611.

Middle Park

Middle Park, like North Park, is edged by faults that separate it from the surrounding mountains. In fact, the same faults define both parks; the volcanic Rabbit Ears Range divided a larger single park into Middle and North parks. Middle Park is floored with Tertiary rocks, poorly consolidated sedimentary formations created by the eroded sands and gravels from surrounding mountain ranges. Although ubiquitous Mancos Shale typifies the geology of western Colorado, a little of the Pierre Shale found east of the Front Range pops up, as it does here, in the bluffs north of Kremmling. Both shales represent the ancient seabeds of vanished oceans that lapped around the ancestral Rocky Mountains.

Middle Park lies in a rain shadow, so that its low, rolling hills tend to be home to sagebrush and other species characteristic of semidesert shrublands.

For more information: Sulphur Ranger District, Arapaho National Forest, 9 Ten Mile Drive, PO Box 10, Granby, CO 80446. Phone (970) 353-5004.

GORE PASS LOOP TRAIL

[Fig. 21(3)] A lengthy but gentle bicycling loop through the forests of the northern Gore Range, this trail on the western edge of Middle Park follows logging and four-wheel-drive roads along the ridge that divides North Park from the Yampa

Valley south of Steamboat Springs.

Directions: From Kremmling, take US 40 north 7 miles to CO 134. Turn left (west) and proceed 10 miles to Gore Pass. Park on the right (north) side and begin riding north up Forest Road 185. This route works its way through an area that includes some active roads and logging, so there are many small side roads to explore or avoid, as your predilections dictate. Keep an eye peeled for other traffic. After 5 miles turn left on FR 100. After 2 more miles, go left on FR 250 (Farnham Creek Road). Follow this to FR 243 (a left). Go about 6 miles back to FR 185, then turn right to retrace the beginning of the trail to your car.

Trail: 18-mile loop.

Elevation: Change of 1,000 feet.

Degree of difficulty: Moderate.

Surface: Jeep roads and graded four-wheel-drive roads.

For more information: Hahns Peak/Bears Ears Ranger District, Routt National Forest, PO Box 771212, 57 10th Street, Steamboat Springs, CO 80477. Phone (970) 879-1870.

PTARMIGAN PEAK WILDERNESS AND WILLIAMS FORK HEADWATERS

[Fig. 22(3)] Because the City of Denver has designs on the headwaters of the Williams Fork River, this basin on the eastern side of the Williams Fork Mountains was excluded from the 13,175-acre Ptarmigan Peak Wilderness Area. The wilderness area itself runs along the western flank of the Williams Fork Mountains—the range running north from Interstate 70 at Silverthorne, which forms the eastern wall of the Blue River valley.

Despite this omission, however, the Williams Fork drainage remains largely untouched and an excellent place for a long, overnight loop hike through some of the Continental Divide's prime riparian areas.

For more information: Sulphur Ranger District, Arapaho National Forest, 62429 Highway 40, PO Box 10, Granby, CO 80446. Phone (970) 353-5004.

SOUTH WILLIAMS FORK AND BOBTAIL CREEK LOOP

[Fig. 22(4)] This loop climbs for 8 miles up the South Fork of the Williams Fork River, then turns east, passing over a 12,000-foot pass in the western shadow of several 13,000-foot peaks along the Continental Divide before dropping down into the Bobtail Creek drainage and meandering through riparian meadows and forests back to the trailhead.

Directions: From Hot Sulphur Springs, go 8 miles west on US 40 to Grand County 3, a left (if you reach

WHITE-TAILED
PTARMIGAN
(Lagopus leucurus)

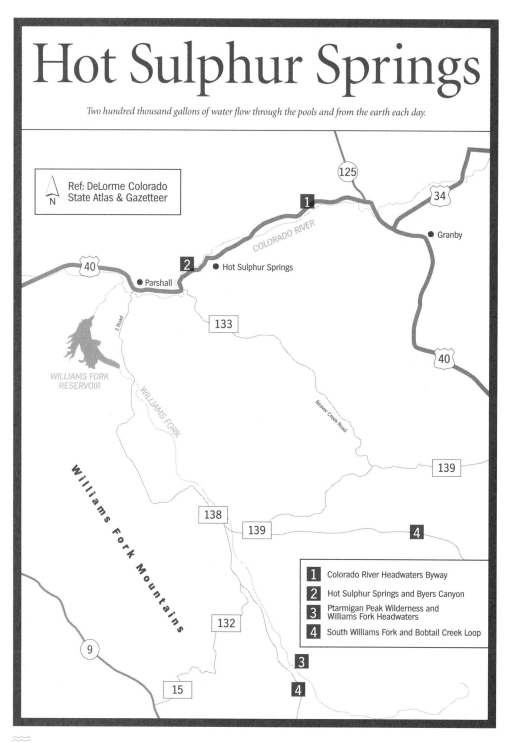

Hot Sulphur Springs

Two hundred thousand gallons of water flow through the pools and from the earth each day.

Ref: DeLorme Colorado
State Atlas & Gazetteer

N

125

34

1

COLORADO RIVER

Granby

40

2

Hot Sulphur Springs

Parshall

3 Road

133

40

WILLIAMS FORK
RESERVOIR

WILLIAMS FORK

Beaver Creek Road

139

Williams Fork Mountains

138

139

4

1 Colorado River Headwaters Byway

2 Hot Sulphur Springs and Byers Canyon

3 Ptarmigan Peak Wilderness and
Williams Fork Headwaters

4 South Williams Fork and Bobtail Creek Loop

132

9

3

15

4

Parshall you have passed the turn). Take County 3 south past Williams Fork Reservoir. The road eventually becomes Forest Road 138; stay on this to South Fork Campground (about 26 miles from Parshall).

Trail: 23 miles.

Elevation: Change of 2,800 feet.

Degree of difficulty: Strenuous.

Surface: Rocks and dirt intermixed with wetlands and multiple creek crossings (no bridges).

HOT SULPHUR SPRINGS AND BYERS CANYON

[Fig. 22(2)] Hot Sulphur Springs, like most hot springs in the state, is a place that has been used for centuries. The springs are the site of a modern spa and lodge, which offers hot tubs and pools filled with the naturally odoriferous water in a variety of temperatures. Two hundred thousand gallons of water flow daily from the earth and through the pools, the hottest of which is 112 degrees Fahrenheit.

The town was platted in 1860 by Cherry Creek real estate speculators who hoped to develop the hot springs and name the town Saratoga West, after Saratoga Springs, New York. It was more effectively promoted by William Byers in the 1870s. Editor of the *Rocky Mountain News*, Byers was an active real estate promoter. He is memorialized by the adjacent defile west of town, a 2-mile cut through a fault in the uplifted rock known as Byers Canyon.

The Colorado River—here a pleasant wading river a few dozen yards across—meanders through town and provides excellent trout fishing.

For more information: Hot Sulphur Springs Resort, PO Box 275, Hot Sulphur Springs, CO 80451. Phone (970) 725-3306.

The Flattops Mountains

One of Colorado's most remote regions, the Flattops massif is a transitional geologic form between the faulted anticline mountains to the east and the true sedimentary mesas to the west. Capped by basalt several hundred feet thick, the plateau sprawls from State Bridge on the east to Meeker on the west, Glenwood Springs at its southern limit and the hamlet of Pagoda on the north. The White and Yampa rivers spill from it, their tributaries incising deep, glaciated canyons through the caprock and the softer sediments below.

The Flattops were glaciated during the last Ice Age, but the results are not as dramatic as in other parts of Colorado. The hard basalt cap—deposited during the Tertiary Period by a slow, oozing igneous flow—resisted the ice, preventing the formation of the typical horns and arêtes of more classically glaciated peaks. Where glaciers did get a foothold, in the river courses, they carved small cirques and deep,

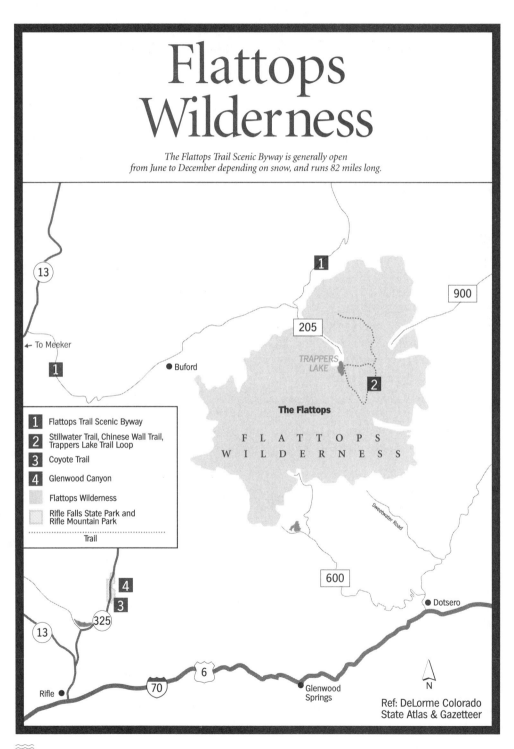

Flattops Wilderness

*The Flattops Trail Scenic Byway is generally open
from June to December depending on snow, and runs 82 miles long.*

13

900

205

← To Meeker

1

● Buford

TRAPPERS
LAKE

2

The Flattops

F L A T T O P S
W I L D E R N E S S

1 Flattops Trail Scenic Byway

2 Stillwater Trail, Chinese Wall Trail,
Trappers Lake Trail Loop

3 Coyote Trail

4 Glenwood Canyon

Flattops Wilderness

Rifle Falls State Park and
Rifle Mountain Park

Trail

Sweetwater Road

600

● Dotsero

4

3

325

13

6

70

Rifle ●

● Glenwood
Springs

N

Ref: DeLorme Colorado
State Atlas & Gazetteer

narrow valleys. Once the volcanic cap was broken, softer stone beneath it eroded, undermining the basalt, which then collapsed of its own weight.

The Flattops range in elevation between 10,500 and 12,000 feet; almost all of the terrain above the rims is open tundra or meadows. Only one road crosses the region east to west, linking Yampa and Meeker by way of Ripple Pass, and then only during the warm months (*see* Flattops Byway, page xx). The northern bulk of the region is encompassed in the Flattops Wilderness, and the tablelands here are not accessible except by foot or horseback. South of the wilderness area and north of Glenwood Springs the Flattops region is accessible by four-wheel drive roads.

Pika

The smaller of the two most noticeable mammals in high-altitude talus slopes, the pika (*Ochotona princeps*) makes up for its diminutive size with a sharp squeak when hikers approach. The larger yellow-bellied marmot emits a sharp, penetrating whistle. Although they are regularly heard by passers-by, these 0.5-pound, khaki-colored furballs are hard to discern among the rocks. Quiet observation, however, usually pays off. Pikas harvest and stockpile vegetation all summer, and remain active beneath the snow during winter, living off of their accumulated food.

FLATTOPS WILDERNESS AREA

[Fig. 23] Hikers or equestrians who climb to the vast, planar summit of the Flattops experience a feeling of having been lifted into the sky. Although distinct peaks can be found atop the tablelands, much of the highest country is tundra and bogs on which hikers can see for miles and walk almost anywhere they choose—a real change from most Colorado hiking, where visitors are constrained to valley trails or to ridgelines.

Views stretch back to the Gore Range on the east, down to the Elks on the south, and seemingly forever toward Utah and Wyoming across the mesas and rolling hills of the west and north.

This is a popular region during hunting season, but otherwise visitors are likely to encounter few others, and may be able to travel for days seeing no one. Home to a vast herd of elk and deer, the Flattops were contested by area ranchers for their grazing value as early as the late nineteenth century, when

PIKA
(Ochotona princeps)
Although this small mammal looks like a rodent with ratlike head and body, it is actually related to the rabbit.

sheep herders and cattlemen vied to control the summer grass of the high country. In 1891 President Benjamin Harrison decreed that the area be managed as part of the White River Timber Plateau Reserve, a precursor to the White River National Forest. When the U.S. Forest Service was created in 1905 as part of the U.S. Department of Agriculture, this region became part of the White River National Forest, one of 12 national forests in Colorado. The largest forest in the state, the White River encompasses 2.2 million acres.

While the tablelands of the Flattops can be enchanting, they can also be a challenge to travel upon. Many trails are lightly used or poorly marked. The ability to navigate by map and compass can be critical, particularly if a hiker is caught out in fog, storm, or darkness. In addition, shelter from afternoon thunderstorms can be sparse.

For more information: The Flattops are managed the three ranger districts in two national forests. For the portion north of Ripple Creek Pass Road: Yampa Ranger District, Routt National Forest, PO Box 7, Yampa, Colorado 80483. Phone (970) 879-1879. South of Ripple Creek Pass Road, on the western side: Blanco Ranger District, White River National Forest, 317 E. Market, Meeker, CO 81641. Phone (970) 878-4039. South of Ripple Creek Pass Road, on the eastern side: Eagle Ranger District, White River National Forest, PO Box 720, Eagle, CO 81631. Phone (970) 328-6388.

STILLWATER TRAIL-CHINESE WALL TRAIL-TRAPPERS LAKE TRAIL LOOP

[Fig. 23(2)] This loop trail begins and ends at the spectacular Trappers Lake trailhead. Hikers climb up a drainage past the Chinese Wall, a dramatic, west-facing cliff that runs for miles. Once up on the flat summit, the route runs south to a second drainage, descending a short glacial valley back to Trappers Lake. Numerous opportunities exist for more extended trips to the many lakes and tarns dotting the basalt crust and nestled into the cirques below the Flattops' steep faces.

Directions: From Trappers Lake Outlet trailhead (*see* page 140), pick up Forest Service Trail 1814 on the west side of the parking lot. Follow this around the east side of the lake to the intersection with Trail 1815 (Carhart Trail), at a private cabin; bear left (east) up the drainage on Trail 1814 (Stillwater Trail). The route climbs for 4 miles to an open saddle and trail intersection, where you can see down into the Yampa River valley. Turn right (south) on Trail 1803, the Chinese Wall Trail. This route, which disappears at times in the summer grass, continues south for 5 miles to an intersection with Trail 1842 (Island Lake Trail). Turn right (west) here for 0.25 mile to Trail 1816 (Trappers Lake Trail). Turn right again and descend into the Fraser Creek valley, passing Parvin Lake. After 3 miles you re-encounter Trail 1815 at the south end of Trappers Lake; follow this back to the parking lot.

Trail: 15-mile loop.

Elevation: Change of 1,800 feet.

Degree of difficulty: Moderate.

Surface and Blaze: Generally dirt and rock; trail disappears at times on tundra.

A favorite pastime of visitors and locals is fly-fishing on the Yampa River
flowing through Steamboat Springs.

TRAPPERS LAKE

[Fig. 23] Trappers Lake is, by many accounts, one of the most beautiful and dramatic waters in Colorado. Certainly, it has the best combination of size, remoteness, grandeur, natural beauty, and historical significance.

In 1919 the U.S. Forest Service's first landscape architect, Arthur H. Carhart, camped at the northern end of the lake. He had been assigned to survey the region as a likely site for private home development. Carhart did as he was told, but he returned to his office with an idea, too—a radical one. He suggested that the beauty of a place like Trappers Lake should not be enjoyed only by a few homeowners, but should be preserved for, and shared with, all Americans. The Forest Service agreed and halted plans to develop the lake shore. In 1932, the lake and its surroundings were designated the Flattops Primitive Area.

Carhart often is labelled the father of the American wilderness system. His ideas were considered radical at the time, but they gained currency. Other Forest Service employees who would grow famous as pioneering conservationists, including Aldo Leopold and Bob Marshall, championed the idea of wildernesses. Their thinking, and the Forest's Service's patchwork creation of primitive areas such as the Flattops, paved the way for the passage of the Wilderness Act in 1964, a federal bill that has set forth 9 million acres of designated wilderness in the United States—land where, as

COMMON RAVEN
(*Corvus corax*)

the law declares, "the earth and its community of life remain untrammeled by man, where man himself is a visitor who does not remain." Total designated wilderness acreage has increased significantly since then.

The concept of wilderness as something good and worth protecting, rather than something to be tamed and subjected, was a uniquely American one dating back to the foundation of Yellowstone National Park in 1872. No other country can begin to claim such a legacy of protection of its natural wonders, and even today, the concept of wilderness remains a political hot potato. America was founded, after all, on the premise of exploiting natural resources. But wilderness, in both the idea of the American frontier and the reality of national parks and monuments and designated wilderness areas, is part of the American character, too.

Today Trappers Lake has a public campground on its western side and a privately run lodge on its northern end. The lake is especially popular as a fishing area. Native cutthroat trout are captured here by the Colorado Division of Wildlife for purposes of harvesting their spawn to reintroduce the species elsewhere.

Directions: From Meeker, drive east 1 mile on CO 13, then turn right (south) onto Rio Blanco County 8. Follow this road (partly gravel and closed in winter) 40 miles to Forest Road 205, a right. Take FR 205 approximately 8 miles to Trappers Lake; signs here direct you to the private Trappers Lake Lodge, the Outlet Trailhead, and a Forest Service campground.

Activities: Hiking, camping, fishing, picnicking, hunting.

Facilities: Private lodge with cabins and general store; seasonal campground.

Dates: Open June through Oct.

Fees: There is a fee to camp.

Closest town: Meeker, 49 miles west.

For more information: Blanco Ranger District, White River National Forest, 317 E. Market, Meeker, CO 81641. Phone (970) 878-4039.

RIFLE FALLS STATE PARK AND RIFLE MOUNTAIN PARK

[Fig. 23] Only 48 acres in size, Rifle Falls State Park was created in 1966 to showcase the dramatic triple waterfall of East Rifle Creek, which drops across sharp limestone into a grotto. Contiguous, and immediately upstream, Rifle Mountain Park is managed by the City of Rifle as a sport-climbing area. Developed in the early 1990s, Rifle Mountain Park encompasses more than 100 bolted routes, none rated easier than 5.10. It is considered by many rock climbers to be the premier North American sport-climbing site.

Directions: From Rifle, take CO 13 approximately 2 miles north to CO 325; follow this north 10 miles (past Rifle Gap Reservoir) to Rifle Falls State Park. Rifle Mountain Park is immediately past the state fish hatchery on East Rifle Creek, where the road turns to dirt. Both parks are on the right.

Activities: At Rifle Falls State Park, camping, fishing, photography, picnicking, hiking. At Rifle Mountain Park, rock climbing and ice climbing (Dec. through Mar., depending upon conditions).

Facilities: 18 campsites, 9 picnic sites.

Dates: Open year-round.

Fees: There is a fee at both Rifle Falls and Rifle Mountain to enter the parks, and an additional fee for camping.

Closest town: Rifle, 13 miles south.

For more information: Rifle Falls State Park, 0050 Road 219, Rifle, CO 81650. Phone (970) 626-5822. Rifle Mountain Park: City of Rifle, PO Box 1908, CO 81650. Phone (970) 625-2121.

COYOTE TRAIL

[Fig. 23(3)] From the roundabout at the Rifle Falls picnic area, walk north across the footbridge below Rifle Falls. Continue up over the falls to a collection of natural caves in the limestone, the deepest of which is 90 feet. The trail loops back to the bridge.

Trail: 1 mile.

Elevation: Change of 80 feet.

Degree of difficulty: Easy.

Surface and Blaze: Packed dirt.

Water Ouzel

This bird is distinctive not for its color (slate), nor its shape (the size of a thrush, but with a bobbed tail). What makes *Cinclus mexicanus* so enjoyable to watch is its habitat and behavior. This small bird lives on, around, and literally under tumbling mountain streams during summer months. Also called a dipper, the water ouzel may be seen skimming inches above the water, weaving around boulders, and alighting in the spray of waterfalls. Most remarkably, the bird regularly pops underwater, running along the stream bed in search of bottom-dwelling insects.

Colorado National Monument

23-mile Rim Rock Drive connects the East and West Entrances of the monument and includes 10 overlooks into the canyons.

Ref: DeLorme Colorado
State Atlas & Gazetteer

N

70

COLORADO
RIVER

6

70

Devils Canyon

1

2

340

To
Grand
Junction

Redlands

Rim Rock Drive

1 Colorado National Monument
2 Monument Canyon Trail

Trail

Rim Rock Drive

Columbus Canyon

Colorado National Monument

[Fig. 24(1)] This monument—part of the National Park Service's holdings—showcases 32 square miles of peach and salmon-colored domes, towers, spires, canyons, and amphitheaters. It is the northeastern corner of the Colorado Plateau, a sprawling geological uplift that reaches across southeastern Utah into Arizona and includes Arches, Canyonlands, Bryce, Zion, Capitol Reef and Grand Canyon national parks, Glen Canyon National Recreation Area and Escalante National Monument.

Colorado National Monument is a place to experience a small piece of canyon country, a magical, high desert landscape of stone and silence. Rim Rock Drive, a 23-mile road connecting the East Entrance and West Entrance, traverses the length of the monument and includes 10 overlooks into the monument's canyons. Most of the monument's trails can be covered by day hikers, and backcountry campers can find solitude and serenity in the half-dozen canyons.

The monument lies quite close to the largest city in western Colorado, Grand Junction. Until 1921, the Colorado River was known as the Grand River from its headwaters in the Never Summer Range of Rocky Mountain National Park to its junction with the Green River in eastern Utah. Settlers who came hard on the heels of the displaced Ute Indians in the wake of the Meeker Massacre platted a town in 1882 in the wide valley where the Grand and Gunnison rivers joined. First they called it Ute, then West Denver, and finally, when they incorporated it, named the place Grand Junction, after the rivers that would help make this the heart of Colorado's fruit-growing region.

Today Grand Junction is a low, sprawling city of 100,000, but much of the arid valley is agricultural, and geology dominates everything. To the east, the Book Cliffs loom in a great wall, while the painted desert monocline of Colorado National Monument dominates the western horizon. The flat valley floor is formed by the region's omnipresent Mancos Shale.

The colored cliffs visible on the western valley wall from Grand Junction form the heart of the Colorado National Monument, part of the Uncompahgre Plateau, which is itself part of the larger Colorado Plateau. The Uncompahgre Plateau is uplifted west of a fault that runs along the western edge of the Grand Valley. It apparently was lifted more quickly during the Laramide Orogeny (about 65 million years ago) than the land to the east, which became the Grand Valley. This uplifting evidently turned the course of the Colorado River. Prior to the uplift, the river probably ran southwest through Unaweep Canyon, across the land that became the plateau (*see* Southwest Region and Long Trails, page 237). Now it turns north at Grand Junction and curls around the northern end of the plateau before resuming its southwestern journey to the Gulf of California.

Established in 1911, Colorado National Monument exists today largely due to the efforts of many in the Grand Valley who thought the area should be protected. They

Cryptobiotic Crust

Although the dirt between plants in Colorado National Monument may seem lifeless, it is not. Most undisturbed, sandy areas here are covered by cryptobiotic crust, a dark, crusty soil that appears to be a tiny formation of buildings and towers.

A symbiotic community of blue-green algae, lichens, microfungi, and soil bacteria, cryptobiotic soil stabilizes against soil erosion, stores water for other plants, and enriches the sparse desert soil. It is a fundamental building block in desert ecosystems, and an ancient one. Cryptobiotic soil was one of the primary forces that converted the earth's carbon dioxide-rich atmosphere to an oxygen-bearing one.

This soil is critical to the desert ecosystem, yet exceedingly fragile. Watch for it, and don't walk, drive, sit, or bike on it. Regeneration of the crust can take up to a century. This soil provides 80 percent of ground cover and, in many places, is not readily visible, so avoid walking off of trails.

were led by a single-minded cowboy, John Otto, who insisted the monument area should be protected. Otto orchestrated a letter-writing campaign in Grand Junction and built many trails in the region. When the monument was created, he was hired at the rate of $1 a month to serve as its caretaker, which he did for 16 years.

The monument was and is designed to showcase the region's striking geology, which ranges from Precambrian igneous and metamorphic rock to Triassic, Jurassic, and Cretaceous formations. Much of the monument's glory and geology is visible on the 23-mile Rim Rock Drive, a two-lane paved road that snakes along the upper edges of the monocline from Grand Junction to Fruita. The road itself, verging on precipitous drops, requires dedicated attention from drivers. Numerous pull-outs allow more relaxed viewing of the canyons and their geology.

The floor of the several canyons veining the monument is rough, Precambrian rock, the base of the ancient mountain range Uncompahgria, now entirely worn away. Immediately above this basement rock is the Chinle formation, the sediments of a vast river floodplain. Atop these sediments is one of the most striking formations, the Wingate formation. This smooth, vertical sandstone wall rises about 300 feet, forming beautiful, sheer canyon walls. The Wingate formation was once ancient desert dunes; look for the curving lines and fractures, known as cross-bedding, that show the ghostly illuminations of those ancient piles of sand.

The Chinle and Wingate formations are from the Triassic Period, 240 to 200 million years ago. Immediately above the Wingate is a lighter stone, the Kayenta formation. This Jurassic rock (200 to 135 million years old), a floodplain remnant laid down after seas reclaimed the desert, is harder than the Wingate below. It is a form of caprock, protecting the column beneath it. The towers and other formations of the monument depend on this helmet of harder rock to protect them from erosion.

Entrada Sandstone, a beautiful, salmon-colored rock, lies above the Kayenta. This is the same rock that forms the dramatic arches in Arches National Park, located in eastern Utah. Above this are the Wanakah, Morrison and Burro Canyon formations.

Across the Grand Valley to the east, Morrison Shale, Dakota Sandstone, Mancos Shale, and Mesaverde Sandstone are layered like a cake atop the Entrada formation. These rocks, from the Cretaceous and Jurassic periods (65 million to 200 million years ago), are younger than the Entrada, and once lay here on the monument, too. But uplift and erosion of the Uncompahgre Plateau eroded them away. Geologists comparing the alignment of the Entrada and other rocks in the Book Cliffs and the monument estimate that the monument region was uplifted 6,700 feet above the Book Cliffs. When this happened is a subject of some debate. Some scientists speculate that the uplift coincided with the disturbance that created the spine of the Rocky Mountains in the Front Range, about 65 million years ago; others think it was more recent, part of the Miocene-Pliocene uplift.

The monument's ecosystems are those of eastern Utah, characterized by sagebrush and four-wing saltbush at lower elevations, piñon and juniper forests higher up. This is country of little rain, but when it does arrive it often falls hard and fast and creates flash floods. Common plants include rabbitbrush, yucca (*Yucca harrimaniae*), and Mormon tea (*Ephedra*). These latter two species are good examples of adaption to desert environments. The yucca has tough, succulent leaves tipped by sharp spines, discouraging animals from eating it (deer, however, like the flowers that bloom on a tall, dramatic spike). Mormon tea has no leaves at all, only green stems. This adaptation reduces water loss through transpiration. The plant gets its common name from the pioneer practice of brewing the stems to create a laxative.

The monument is home to several dozen reptiles, although the only dangerous one is the midget faded rattlesnake, *Crotalus viridus concolor*, a rare species. Commonly seen species included the Eastern fence lizard (*Sceloporus undulatus*), a 6-inch brown lizard with blue side patches; the sagebrush lizard (*Sceloporus graciousus*), similar to the Eastern fence lizard but with light stripes along its back; and the yellow-headed collared lizard (*Crotaphytus collaris*), a yellow-and-green lizard that grows up to 14 inches in length.

Frogs or toads can often be heard in the stillness of the canyons, particularly after rain. The red-spotted toad, *Bofo punctatus*, is the most common amphibian in the monument and may even be seen along Rim Rock Drive following rain.

Common bird life includes scrub jays, mountain bluebirds (*Sialia curricoides*), and common ravens (*Corvus corax*), which seem omnipresent in the canyons. A bird more commonly heard than seen, but one that is emblematic of the canyon country in western Colorado and eastern Utah is the canyon wren (*Catherpes mexicanus*). Its clear, bell-like song, a descending cascade of "te-you, te-you, te-you, te-you," is distinctive and unmistakable. Peregrine falcons (*Falco peregrinus*) have successfully nested in the monument for much of the 1990s.

Directions: For the eastern entrance to the monument, take Exit 31 from I-70 to Horizon Drive and turn west at the stop sign toward the monument. Turn south at the intersection with 7th Street to Grand Avenue, then right (west). Grand Avenue becomes CO 340; take this across the Colorado River, then turn left on Rim Rock Drive to the monument's entrance station. For the western entrance, take Exit 19 at Fruita, turn west on CO 340, proceed 2 miles to the entrance station.

Activities: Hiking, photography, rock climbing, bicycling (on the Rim Rock Drive), camping, picnicking, scenic driving, backpacking, interpretive displays and talks.

Facilities: Visitors center, amphitheater, 1 campground with 80 sites, picnic areas.

Dates: Open year-round, but the visitors center is closed on Christmas Day.

Fees: There is a fee to enter the monument, and a fee to camp.

Closest town: Grand Junction is 4 miles east of the east entrance; Fruita is 2 miles east of the west entrance.

For more information: Colorado National Monument, Fruita, CO 81521. Phone (970) 858-3617.

MONUMENT CANYON TRAIL

[Fig. 24(2)] This trail descends from the Rim Rock Drive for 6 miles to CO 340, passing through the dramatic heart of the monument. If you have two vehicles you may leave one at each end of the trail. The eastern end quickly drops 600 feet to the canyon floor, descending in a series of switchbacks onto the Precambrian rock that covers the floor of Monument Canyon. Here, hikers may immerse themselves in the silence, sparse beauty, and towering rock of canyon country.

Monument Canyon, like most of the monument, faces roughly east. Consequently, shaded late afternoon hikes may be cooler than morning hikes. Although the region is desert, it is still roughly 1 mile high; carry plenty of water and sunscreen.

Directions: Park at Coke Ovens Trail, located 0.25 mile west of Coke Ovens Overlook on the Rim Rock Drive (the Coke Ovens Overlook is about 7 miles east of the visitor center). This trail quickly forks; bear left onto Monument Canyon Trail down into the canyon (the trail to the right proceeds about 200 yards to the Coke Ovens, a series of rock spires). To reach the western trailhead for Monument Canyon from CO 340, go east 4 miles from the west entrance to the monument; look for a sign marking the right-hand (west) turn to Monument Canyon Trail; the trailhead is a few hundred yards off CO 340.

Trail: 6 miles one-way.

Elevation: Change of 1,450 feet.

Degree of difficulty: Moderate.

Surface and Blaze: Sand and rock.

Scenic Drives

▓ FLATTOPS TRAIL SCENIC BYWAY

[Fig. 23(1)] The Flattops Trail Scenic Byway is generally open from June to November, depending on snow. It runs 82 miles—40 of them on gravel—from Meeker to Yampa, up the White River drainage and across the Flattops into the Yampa River valley. This byway travels though an untamed piece of Colorado, passing no towns and only a few outposts. Lacking ski areas, mining towns and 14,000-foot peaks, far from the Interstate system and the state's population centers, this route hints at what much of Colorado was like in the years immediately following World War II, before the world came calling.

The route begins in Meeker, a tiny town best known for the Meeker Sheepdog Trials, a national event that draws hundreds of competitors and thousands of spectators each year on the weekend following Labor Day. The White River, which runs through Meeker, eventually leads into the Green River in Utah. On the eastern side of the Flattops, the Yampa River, Colorado's longest free-flowing stream at 170 miles, also eventually feeds the Green. The Yampa and Green join in Dinosaur National Monument, in the northwestern corner of Colorado; the White joins up farther south, at Ouray, Utah.

Begin the byway 1 mile east of Meeker on CO 13, where County Road 8 branches off to the south (take this turn). A kiosk here offers information on the byway; at Mile 3, an interpretive display at a pull-out provides information on the surrounding region.

The White River bottomlands here are lush, providing excellent hay and grazing, in sharp contrast to some of the surrounding hillsides of Mancos Shale and Dakota Sandstone, which support patches of the Upper Sonoran ecosystem. Sagebrush, serviceberry, and four-wing saltbush are typical examples. They may also mix in with gambel oak.

Much of the byway passes through spruce and subalpine fir characteristic of the subalpine zone. Look for so-called "ghost forests." These are stands of dead, gray trees, killed by a spruce budworm infestation in the 1940s. Younger, healthy trees are now growing up among the dead timber, which was—and still is—coveted by logging companies that want to cut it. Much of the dead timber is in the Flattops Wilderness Area, and so not available for logging. Standing dead trees are enormously valuable for many species of wildlife, a fact now recognized by forest managers. These snags provide food (in the form of wood-eating insects) and nesting cavities for many species of birds. Fallen trees are often ripped apart by black bears (*Ursus americanus*) searching for grubs and beetles.

This route does not take you onto the tops of the Flattops Mountains; they lie within the Flattops Wilderness Area. Beginning around Mile 13, however, you can see the Flattops (commonly referred to in plural, but essentially a single, sprawling high plateau) to the south of the route.

At Mile 20 you pass the Buford store, the last chance for gas, bait, or anything else you might want in the region. The road follows the north fork of the White River (stay on County Road 8 at the several intersections along the way). The turn to

Trappers Lake, a major entry point to the Flattops Wilderness, and a site of some significance to the American wilderness movement (*see* Flattops Wilderness, page 139), is at Mile 40. Trappers Lake is about 8 miles up this road, a nice side trip.

A turnoff at Mile 44 (back on County 8) leads to an overlook identifying the nearby mountains. The route leads up into the basalt cap overlying the Mancos Shale, apparent beginning around Mile 44; Ripple Creek Pass, the high point at 10,400 feet, is 1 mile farther on. From here the road descends into the Yampa drainage, passing down through aspen forests and providing views east across the valley to the Gore Range. This portion of the Gores is less dramatic than the section northeast of Vail. Stay right at the junction with County Road 19, on the east fork of the Williams Fork River (Mile 56).

The route climbs again to Dunckley Pass at Mile 63. At Mile 73, Routt County Road 25 bears left toward Oak Creek; if you are headed north toward Steamboat Springs, this is a more direct route than continuing to Yampa. Similarly, at Mile 77, you may take a left on County 15 to Phippsburg, or follow the route across the agricultural valley floor to its termination at Yampa (Mile 82).

COLORADO RIVER HEADWATERS BYWAY

[Fig. 22(1)] This byway begins at Grand Lake, in the Arapaho National Recreation Area at the eastern terminus of Trail Ridge Road (*see* Rocky Mountain National Park, page 35). All or part of it can provide a scenic route for travelers who have crossed the park and are continuing west.

Begin the 69-mile route at the town of Grand Lake, which sits beside the largest natural lake in Colorado. The other two lakes here in Colorado's so-called Great Lakes Region are Shadow Mountain Lake and Lake Granby, both built in the 1950s as part of the grandiose Colorado-Big Thompson water project.

During the early and middle parts of the twentieth century, water engineers tended to think big in the American West. The idea of building two reservoirs, pumping water up 186 feet from Lake Granby to Shadow Mountain Reservoir and Grand Lake, and then running it all through a 9-foot-wide, 13-mile-long tunnel underneath the Continental Divide and Rocky Mountain National Park—well, that was progress. Colorado-Big Thompson was the most ambitious, but by no means the only, diversion to shift water from the relatively wet (and sparsely populated) Western Slope of the state to the thirsty farms and cities of the Front Range.

Follow CO 34 approximately 15 miles south past Shadow Mountain Reservoir and Lake Granby. The massive, dramatic range rising to the east above these reservoirs is the Indian Peaks, part of the Front Range. At the junction with US 40, turn right (west). At Mile 25 you enter the small town of Hot Sulphur Springs. In the process you have driven out of the Precambrian rock that is so central to the geology of the Front Range, and into the sedimentary rock produced by eons of erosion from the high mountains behind you.

Continue on US 40 into Byers Canyon, a short, steep-walled defile barely wide enough to accommodate the Colorado River, the highway, and the Union Pacific railway tracks. The river has cut through a fault between Precambrian rock on the north and Tertiary sediments on the south. As you enter Middle Park, you again drive out of this older rock and into younger, Tertiary sediments. The road parallels the Colorado River through dry, hilly terrain—Tertiary sediments—to Kremmling, which you enter at Mile 43.

Turn south (left) on CO 9 for 1 mile to a right on County Road 1, a gravel road that crosses the Blue River. The route skirts the northern limit of the higher peaks of the Gore Range (*see* West Central Mountain Region, page 153). This is remote, lonely country where slope aspect dictates vegetation, due to the relatively small amount of rainfall. Notice the forests of aspen and conifers on the wetter, cooler north-facing slopes, versus sagebrush on the south-facing, drier slopes.

At Mile 53, Inspiration Point gives views of Gore Canyon and its Precambrian rock jutting above the surrounding Tertiary sediments. The byway ends at State Bridge, which is just that—a bridge. Turn south (left) on CO 131 and follow this about 20 miles to reach I-70 at Wolcott (Exit 157).

CACHE LA POUDRE-NORTH PARK BYWAY

[Fig. 19] The eastern 72 miles of this 104-mile-long byway are described in the Northeast Mountains Region (*see* page 65). That section climbs the Cache La Poudre Canyon on CO 14 to Cameron Pass, which divides the Rawah Mountains to the north from the Never Summer Range to the south.

The route then descends, still on CO 14, from the 10,276-foot pass, dropping approximately 2,000 feet into the high valley of North Park. The extensive lodgepole pine forests around Mile 5 continue along the western flank of the Rawahs and form the predominant forest type in the Colorado National Forest, which flanks both sides of the road on the western side of Cameron Pass and extends 28 miles up the Rawahs.

The balance of the drive to Walden, the end of the byway at Mile 31 (as measured from Cameron Pass), runs northwest into the heart of the riparian meadows and grasslands of North Park. The Michigan River (crossed at Mile 11) is typical of the park's waterways: shallow, braided, and choked with willows and other vegetation. Much of the park, irrigated by waters from the Rawahs, the Rabbit Ears Range to the south, and the Park Range to the west, is cultivated for hay.

West Central Mountain Region

FIGURE NUMBERS

- 26 Vail Area
- 27 Leadville
- 28 Maroon Bells-Snowmass Wilderness
- 29 Hunter-Frying Pan Wilderness
- 30 Collegiate Peaks Wilderness
- 31 Skiing Aspen
- 32 Buffalo Peaks Wilderness
- 33 Continental Divide/Monarch Crest Trail
- 34 West Elk Wilderness
- 35 Raggeds Wilderness
- 36 Black Canyon National Monument
- 37 Curecanti National Recreation Area

West Central Mountain Region

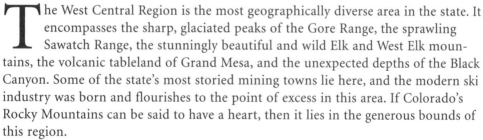

T he West Central Region is the most geographically diverse area in the state. It
encompasses the sharp, glaciated peaks of the Gore Range, the sprawling
Sawatch Range, the stunningly beautiful and wild Elk and West Elk mountains, the volcanic tableland of Grand Mesa, and the unexpected depths of the Black
Canyon. Some of the state's most storied mining towns lie here, and the modern ski
industry was born and flourishes to the point of excess in this area. If Colorado's
Rocky Mountains can be said to have a heart, then it lies in the generous bounds of
this region.

The northern boundary of the West Central Mountain Region begins at Silverthorne and runs north up CO 9, along the east side of the Gore Range. The border
turns through the Gores where they are divided by the Colorado River and runs
southwest to Wolcott, then follows I-70 west to Grand Junction. The western edge of

[*Above:* The ski area of Buttermilk with Pyramid Peak in the background] the region begins at Grand Junction and follows US 50 south to Montrose. The southern border runs east from Montrose on US 50 to CO 114, west of Gunnison. It turns southeast along CO 114 over North Pass to Saguache, in the northwest corner of the San Luis Valley. Here the border jogs northeast, following US 285 north over Poncha Pass. At Salida, in the Arkansas River valley, the boundary turns east on US 50 again at Poncha Springs to Cleona. The eastern edge picks up here and runs north along the summit ridge of the Tenmile and Mosquito ranges to Vail Pass, where it turns east on I-70 to Silverthorne.

A Geological Potpourri

The region's geology is not easily characterized, except to say that there's something for everyone. The eastern flank is dominated by the Sawatch (also spelled Saguache, and pronounced suh-WATCH) uplift, an anticline—that is, an upward bowing of rock—of the familiar Precambrian granite that shows up in most of the state's mountain ranges (rock that's about 1.7 billion years old). This anticline includes the Mosquito Range on the east side of the Arkansas River and the Sawatch and Collegiate ranges to the west; the whole formation is divided by the Arkansas, which has eroded the center of the anticline.

The head of the Arkansas Valley is truly the roof of the Rockies, a region sprinkled with big-shouldered, 14,000-foot peaks, and broad, alluvial valleys where towns were built at the rarefied altitude of 10,000 feet. The upper Arkansas Valley is geologically connected to the San Luis Valley, located on the south side of Poncha Pass. Both are part of the Rio Grande Rift, a down-dropping of the earth's crust that occurred as the mountains around rose in massive blocks; the rift valley extends into central New Mexico. At one time the Arkansas ran due south through the San Luis Valley, until more recent geologic disturbances (probably about 12 million years ago) altered its course to the east by throwing up a wall at Poncha Pass.

Farther west, the Holy Cross region south of Eagle is part of the Sawatch uplift. At the center of a tight cluster of peaks stands the Mount of the Holy Cross, a 14,005-foot peak photographed in 1873 by William H. Jackson. Jackson was part of the Hayden Survey, a federal government expedition that mapped Colorado's mountain regions and assessed their mineral potential. Mount of the Holy Cross's north face is bisected by a 1,200-foot-long, narrow couloir, or gully, that holds snow well into the summer. Across this runs a 400-foot-long ledge that also holds snow. The result was an image that electrified Americans when it was published immediately after the Hayden Survey. The fact that Jackson quietly touched up some of his photographs to make the natural cross look more like the Catholic church's cross didn't hurt.

As was the case in the mountains around the central and southern Front Range, the Sawatch and Mosquito Ranges were faulted—fractured—by upheavals of the earth's crust, then penetrated by volcanic solutions that brought vast quantities of minerals up toward the surface in dikes, veins, tubes, and outright eruptions. In places where the geology aligned itself favorably, such as California Gulch immediately east of Leadville, many of these ore-bearing formations were exposed and could be followed. Leadville was one of the richest mining towns in Colorado, and once vied with Denver to be the state's capital. Like Breckenridge and Fairplay to the east, Leadville, Holy Cross City, Independence, Aspen, Tin Cup, Ashcroft, and Crested Butte testified that the mineral belt extended in a broad, northeast-to-southwest carpet across the state.

Again and again through this region, formations to which geologists apply the catchall term "redbeds" appear in the rock. They are obvious at Vail Pass, again near Eagle, around Glenwood Springs, surrounding the eponymous town of Redstone, and most spectacularly in the Maroon Bells, two peaks south of Aspen. These red and maroon-colored rocks all derived from the same source: the ancient range Uncompahgria, which ran along the western quarter of today's Colorado, then eroded down to become a seabed during the Pennsylvanian and Permian periods (325 million to 240 million years ago). The eroded red sediments created the redbeds and formed the basis for many of this region's mountains—even though those mountains are not red. The heat and pressure of volcanic activity in the region metamorphosed some of the red rocks, creating quartzites and slates and turning red rocks gray.

Complexly faulted, the mountains in the Elk and West Elk ranges are seemingly all things: ancient granite, metamorphosed sediments, swirled gneiss and glittering schist, volcanic tuff and breccia, and the massive, intrusive, igneous bubbles known as stocks. Miners have found in these mountains—and in some cases, continue to extract—not only gold and silver but also molybdenum, lead, zinc, marble, and coal, testament to the panoply of geology in the West Central Mountains.

The western edges of the region are dominated by sedimentary and volcanic geology, with one notable exception. Grand Mesa and Basalt Mountain were once part of a large, flat-topped massif similar in geologic nature to the Flat Top Mountains north of I-70. All three peaks are comprised of sedimentary rocks from the Tertiary Period topped by a hard cap of basalt, a volcanic rock that oozed out and flowed along the sedimentary rock surface to form a protective, erosion-resistant layer. The Roaring Fork River cut through and separated Basalt Mountain from Grand Mesa, so the record of this volcanic event is jumbled and indistinct here. On its western end, however, Grand Mesa stands dramatically above the surrounding lands, protected by the harder basalt.

Tuff and welded tuff, the result of volcanic explosions in the West Elk and San Juan mountains, created picturesque, eroded palisades around Gunnison and Crawford. And just when you think you've seen everything on the region's geologic menu, there's the Black Canyon of the Gunnison. It's the equivalent of a knife-thin slice deep into Precambrian gneiss. At one point the canyon is 1,750 feet deep, only 40 feet wide at the base, and a mere 1,300 feet wide at the rim. At its deepest point the canyon drops 2,425 feet. There are deeper canyons in the world, but none so deep and so narrow.

Miners, Soldiers and Skiers

The West Central Region's human history is almost as varied as its geology. The Ute Indians who made it their home and hunting ground were pushed out here, as they had been elsewhere, as settlers and prospectors explored and then claimed the valleys during the second half of the nineteenth century. Treaties were written, broken, and rewritten during these years until the Utes were relegated to distant reservations (*see* Northwest Mountain Region, page 117). Mineral exploration that began in Denver and Central City rolled south and west through the mountains. Leadville became an enormously rich town in 1879. The town had been founded on a gold strike in 1860, and $5 million worth of gold was recovered. It was believed to be mined out and on the decline when someone decided to assay the area's sand, which was found to be rich in silver and became the basis for a city of 30,000 residents.

But as always, miners were looking in the next valley for the next strike. Aspen soon flourished, and so did nearby Ashcroft, but the former thrived and the latter died when railroads passed Ashcroft by. Crested Butte grew as a mining supply and coal town, and Redstone was built as a model, Utopian community for miners at a time when bitter strikes were the hallmark of the industry.

Carbondale, Delta, and Montrose arose as agricultural centers in the alluvial valleys at the edges of the mountain, supplying beef, grain, and produce to the mountain towns. Following the silver crash of 1893 (when the U.S. government repealed its guaranteed price on silver, and the market price plummeted), many mining towns vanished or went into a Rip Van Winkle—style slumber. The most significant development for the region in the twentieth century was the creation in 1939 of the 10th Mountain Division of the U.S. Army.

Troops were trained at Camp Hale, a 1,200-building outpost (removed after the war ended) on the north side of Tennessee Pass. In the wake of World War II, veterans who had skied and climbed in the region's mountains came back to build their lives—and to create the modern ski industry. By one estimate, 2,000 veterans of the 10th became involved in some aspect of the American ski industry. Aspen, then a town of 700, revived. Snowmass Village and Vail were created where nothing but ranches had existed. More than 50 years later, ski area development has become the most powerful economic engine in the region. People who visited to ski have come back to stay. Growth and development now threaten to overwhelm ski resorts and outlying towns, which struggle to maintain a balance between man and nature, trying not to kill that golden goose.

Aspen Forests

From the badlands east of Delta to the Continental Divide, the West Central Mountain Region encompasses many life zones. A drive across Kebler Pass, northwest of Crested Butte, takes a traveler through what some foresters say is the largest aspen forest in the world.

Aspen (*Populous tremuloides*) is the most widespread native tree in North America, growing from the eastern seaboard to Alaska. The common term "quaking aspen" denotes the way the leaves shimmer and flutter in the wind; this happens because the flattened stem of the aspen leaf is perpendicular to the leaf surface, so the leaf sways and twists in a figure-eight motion in the slightest breeze.

Although aspens are especially common between 8,000 and 10,000 feet in Colorado, they'll grow as low as 5,600 feet on cool, wet, north-facing sites, and as high as tree line (about 11,500 feet) in protected pockets. The tree reproduces both by seed and by rhizomes—roots that send up shoots. Like strawberry plants, aspen trees spring up from a common root system. Consequently, aspen groves do not contain many individual trees; they contain a single plant sharing the same root system that supports hundreds or thousands of trunks.

This fact is apparent in a large aspen forest, such as on the west side of Kebler Pass, at the change of seasons. Because each grove behaves as a single individual, all the trees in that grove will leaf out, or change color, or shed leaves at the same time. Where a group of trees has changed to yellow before its neighbors, there one can easily discern a single aspen colony.

Propagation via shoots, or suckers, allows aspen trees to colonize disturbed areas quickly. Suckers pop up from existing root systems and can grow 2 feet tall in a single season, shading out competing plants. Look for this phenomenon in avalanche slide paths. Slower-growing conifers can't effectively colonize avalanche zones because the conifers are broken off by the force of the sliding snow. But aspen trees will. If part of the aspen grove lies outside the slide path, younger suckers pop up in the wake of a devastating avalanche. In some places you may see several groves of variously aged aspen trees growing in parallel, vertical strips along a slide zone. Each tells the story of where a catastrophic avalanche did—or didn't—flow down the hill.

Like lodgepole pines, aspen trees are

QUAKING ASPEN
(Populus tremuloides)
Like other poplar trees, this is a pioneer tree which can be found in logged or burned-over areas.

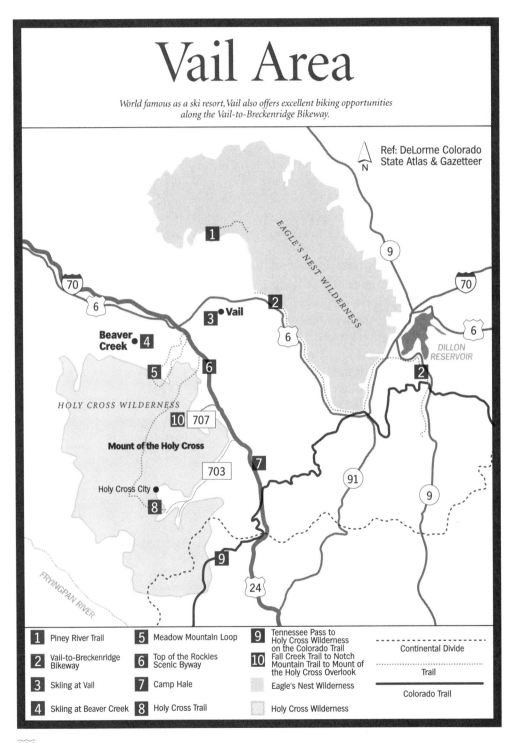

Vail Area

World famous as a ski resort, Vail also offers excellent biking opportunities along the Vail-to-Breckenridge Bikeway.

Ref: DeLorme Colorado
State Atlas & Gazetteer

N

1   EAGLE'S NEST WILDERNESS

9

70

6

2

3 Vail

6

Beaver Creek   4

5

6

DILLON RESERVOIR

2

HOLY CROSS WILDERNESS

10   707

Mount of the Holy Cross

703

7

91

Holy Cross City

8

9

9

24

FRYINGPAN RIVER

1 Piney River Trail	**5** Meadow Mountain Loop	**9** Tennessee Pass to Holy Cross Wilderness on the Colorado Trail
2 Vail-to-Breckenridge Bikeway	**6** Top of the Rockies Scenic Byway	**10** Fall Creek Trail to Notch Mountain Trail to Mount of the Holy Cross Overlook
3 Skiing at Vail	**7** Camp Hale	Eagle's Nest Wilderness
4 Skiing at Beaver Creek	**8** Holy Cross Trail	Holy Cross Wilderness

- - - - - Continental Divide

· · · · · · Trail

——— Colorado Trail

quick to colonize disturbed areas; unlike lodgepoles, aspens prefer a high water table. In places where there's too much water for conifers, aspens may grow unmolested, living as long as 200 years. In drier zones, conifers make up the climax forest, growing up from beneath the aspen trees and eventually shading them out. Ironically, aspens enrich the soil by lowering soil pH, adding nutrients, increasing invertebrate populations—and thus aiding the conifer seedlings that replace the aspen trees.

Cool and dappled with light, aspen forests are often remarkably open, in part because mature trees emit chemicals that discourage suckers from forming beneath them. Colorado columbine is commonly found in profusion beneath aspens, and in wetter areas, cow parsnip grows chest-high in their shade.

Many types of wildlife depend on aspen. Look for scars where black bears have climbed trees in search of early spring aspen buds. Elk commonly graze in winter upon aspen bark, sometimes scarring acres of trees. Fresh scars clearly show the marks of elk incisors scraped down the trunk. Aspen groves provide calving habitat for both elk and mule deer. Northern pocket gophers thrive in aspen forests; look for piles of dirt and long, serpentine dirt forms on the ground in early spring, evidence of the gophers' winter tunnelling. Beaver eat aspen trees when they cannot get enough willow or cottonwood.

Several species of woodpecker—red-naped sapsucker (*Sphyrapicus nuchalis*), hairy woodpecker, and northern flicker—nest in aspen forests. The cavities they create are used by other cavity-nesting birds, including house wrens (*Troglodyte aedon*), mountain bluebirds, and white-breasted nuthatches (*Sitta carolinensis*). Nuthatches can easily be identified among the various birds that hunt insects in tree bark because they tend to descend trees headfirst, picking at the bark. Woodpeckers (*Picidae*) stand head-up and peck at trees, while creepers (*Certhiidae*) ascend tree trunks in a hopping spiral.

Vail Area

[Fig. 26] World famous now as a ski resort, Vail was only a spread of sheep and cattle ranches in the rugged Eagle River valley until the first ski lifts opened in 1963. Today it is the anchor for extensive development along the Gore Creek and Eagle River valleys, which connect west of Vail and flow due west to join the Colorado River just east of Glenwood Canyon.

Vail lies in the narrow Gore Creek valley west of Vail Pass and southwest of the Gore Range. The Gores are a geologic continuation of the Tenmile Range to the south, but the Gores were more dramatically broken and sculpted by glaciers than their southern neighbors. Both ranges are upthrusts of Precambrian rock. Interstate 70 passes through the heart of this rock where it follows the Tenmile Canyon fault between Frisco and Copper Mountain.

At Mile 196 on the interstate, the fault surface is exposed; the eastern side of the canyon was polished by the two sides of the fault sliding against each other and has a slick, glassy look when the sunlight strikes at the right angle. Look for the swirling, banded gneiss of the Precambrian rock where it has been exposed along the western side of the fault and where the highway has cut through the rock. These patterns in the gneiss show how much the metamorphic rock has been twisted and contorted over time. The Tenmile Canyon fault continues south along US 24 at Copper Mountain, where I-70 turns northwest and crosses Vail Pass.

The interstate drops down on the western side of Vail Pass through extensive redbeds of Pennsylvanian and Permian rocks (325 million to 240 million years old). For more than 40 miles, I-70 West passes through redbeds and then brown shales and sandstones. Gypsum, west of Eagle, is a small town named for the prevalence of this mineral in the area. This deposit represents what was left when a small sea evaporated from the region 280 million years ago. Gypsum is where the concentrated salts and minerals were deposited when the last of the sea dried up.

The Sawatch Range, the largest in the state after the San Juans, extends west from Vail Pass as far as New York Mountain, south of Edwards. To the south it reaches to Mount Ouray, west of Poncha Pass at the northern extension of the San Luis Valley.

MOUNTAIN BIKING AT VAIL

Numerous mountain biking opportunities exist around the Vail region. A 35-mile paved bikeway stretches from Vail to Breckenridge, offering a chance for families to ride on pavement without fear of heavy automobile traffic. More experienced riders can find a challenge on this path, too; the elevation gain from Vail to Vail Pass is 2,430 feet in 14 miles.

Although the route is mostly free of vehicular traffic, it does run close to I-70 for much of its length. More remote and challenging trips include day rides or overnights on the 10th Mountain Hut system (*see* page 167), or exciting rides up (or down) Vail Mountain, which is open to mountain biking June through September. Bicycles may be transported for a fee up the mountain on the Lionshead Gondola or Vista Bahn chairlift.

Several wilderness areas flank the Vail region; bicycles are not allowed inside wilderness boundaries.

For more information: Holy Cross Ranger District, White River National Forest, PO Box 190, 401 Main, Minturn, CO 81645. Phone (970) 827-5715. Vail Chamber of Commerce, PO Box 7, Vail, CO 81658. Phone (800) 525-2257. Vail Resort Activities Desk Phone (970) 476-9090.

VAIL-TO-BRECKENRIDGE BIKEWAY

[Fig. 26(2)] This paved route generally separates bicyclists from motorists, but not entirely. For several miles the route runs on old US 6 on the west side of Vail Pass, which is open to cars; on the east side, at Copper Mountain, Frisco, and Breckenridge, the route crosses streets or runs along them for short sections.

This path is paved, 10 feet wide, and open to bicyclists, walkers, and in-line skaters. Be careful about oncoming traffic, particularly around corners with limited sight lines.

The route goes by different names in different towns. In Vail it is called the Vail Bikeway; at Copper Mountain it's the Ten Mile Canyon Recreation Trail; in Frisco, the Summit County Recreation Trail; and in Breckenridge, look for the Blue River Bikeway.

The trail is a suburban route, since it parallels CO 9 in the Blue River valley and I-70 from Frisco to Vail. But it does carry riders at a more leisurely pace than an automobile through the fault geology of Tenmile Canyon, and the high, riparian meadows of Vail Pass.

Biking in the Colorado mountains.

Directions: The path can be accessed in several places. In Vail, park at the Transportation Center (Exit 176 off I-70); at Copper Mountain, look for the trail at the west end of the resort, near Club Med; in Frisco, pick up the trail on the south side of town off Second or Seventh streets; in Breckenridge, find it at the intersection of Main and French streets. The Vail Pass rest stop on I-70 (Exit 190) also provides access.

Dates: Open June through September.

Closest town: There are 4 towns or resorts along the path: Breckenridge, Frisco, Copper Mountain, and Vail.

Trail: 35-mile bikeway.

Elevation: From Breckenridge to Vail Pass, change of 980 feet. From Vail to Vail Pass, change of 2,430 feet.

Degree of difficulty: Easy to moderate.

Surface: Paved, 10 feet wide.

For more information: Summit County Chamber of Commerce, PO Box 2010, Frisco, CO 80443. Phone (970) 262-2866. Vail Chamber of Commerce, PO Box 7, Vail, CO 81658. Phone (800) 525-2257.

TENNESSEE PASS TO HOLY CROSS WILDERNESS

[Fig. 26(9)] This out-and-back ride begins at 10,424-foot Tennessee Pass, south of Vail, where the Denver and Rio Grande Railroad once crossed the Continental Divide. The railroad was abandoned in the mid-1990s and may eventually be converted into a bicycle trail stretching from Pueblo to Gypsum. Also at Tennessee Pass is Ski Cooper, a small ski area created to help train U.S. soldiers at nearby Camp Hale during World War II, and still operational (although Camp Hale is long gone, *see* page 158).

BLACK BEAR
(Ursus americanus)

This trail cuts through lodgepole pine and across alpine wildflower meadows before entering the Holy Cross Wilderness, where bicycles are prohibited; riders must turn around and return as they came.

Directions: Take Exit 171 from I-70 and head south on US 24 for 23 miles to the top of Tennessee Pass. Park on the right (west) side of the road and pick up the signed Colorado Trail here, going southwest.

Dates: Open June through Oct.

Closest town: Leadville, 9 miles south.

Trail: 13 miles out and back.

Elevation: Change of 480 feet.

Degree of difficulty: Moderate.

Surface: Single track trail with some rocky and muddy spots that may require walking. The trail is marked with a stylized CT (Colorado Trail) on a white plastic blaze.

MEADOW MOUNTAIN LOOP

[Fig. 26(5)] This is a popular loop west of Vail on a broad, northeast-sloping mountain flank between Minturn and the ski area of Beaver Creek. Riders get views of the Gore, Sawatch and Tenmile ranges as the trail cuts through forests and meadows. During peak wildflower season in July, or when the aspen trees are turning in September, this can be an especially scenic ride.

Directions: Take Exit 171 from I-70, turn south on US 24. Go 0.25 mile to a U.S. Forest Service district office on the right-hand (west) side of the road. Park here and begin riding up the logging road.

Dates: June-Oct.

Closest town: Minturn, 1 mile south.

Trail: 12-mile loop, including 3 miles on US 24.

Elevation: Gain of 2,000 feet in the first 5 miles.

Degree of difficulty: Strenuous.

Surface: Dirt logging road, single track trail, and paved highway.

SKIING AT VAIL AND BEAVER CREEK

[Fig. 26(3)] Vail is the largest ski area in the United States, sprawling over 4,644 acres. In late 1998 the resort began work on an expansion to the south that will add several hundred acres of intermediate and expert terrain. Beaver Creek [Fig. 26(4)], located on the west side of the Eagle River and covering 1,625 acres, is one of the newest major ski areas in the United States. It was opened in 1981; except for Deer Valley, Utah, no major ski resort has been built since. Both Vail and Beaver Creek are

Black Bear

The only bear extant in Colorado is the black bear, *Ursus americanus*. About three-fourths of the state's black bears, however, are brown-hued. Black bears subsist principally on vegetation: 95 percent of their diet is vegetables, including acorns from gambel oak, chokecherries, serviceberries, grasses, and forbs. When these crops are sparse, the normally nocturnal and secretive black bear may venture into mountain towns in search of food—an act that often results in bears being killed by wildlife officers. Several Colorado towns have adopted ordinances regulating garbage storage, bird feeders, and barbecue grills, which can attract bears.

Black bears eat as many as 20,000 calories per day in the autumn, preparing for a unique hibernation that lasts until mid-April or May. Bears den in caves, thick brush or under logs. As winter closes in, a hibernating bear's metabolism changes. Its metabolic rate drops by as much as 50 percent, and its heart slows to 8 or 10 beats a minute. Yet the bear maintains the same body temperature as when awake. Throughout the winter the bear sleeps deeply; it will not wake, eat, drink, urinate or defecate.

Young are born in the den in late winter. At birth they are blind, hairless, and weigh less than 1 pound. Cubs quickly develop sharp claws; by the time the mother emerges from the den the cubs are able to climb trees, their best form of defense. They will spend a year with their mother before venturing out on their own.

Bears emerge from hibernation between mid-April and late May, awakened by a little-understood biological clock. For the first few days they eat little, but soon they are on the prowl for food. Mature males rove over areas as large as 200 square miles.

Black bears are most prevalent west of the Continental Divide in Colorado. Males average 220 to 350 pounds; females weigh between 150 and 215 pounds.

---

run by Vail Resorts, which also owns Keystone and Breckenridge, located east of Vail Pass in Summit County (*see* page 82).

The number of ski resorts in the United States has dropped by about one-half since 1970, to fewer than 700. The casualties generally have been small mom-and-pop operations in the Midwest and East. Yet major resorts, including many found in Colorado, have grown in those years; some, such as Beaver Creek and Vail, have grown spectacularly. The village of Beaver Creek now contains some of the most expensive real estate in North America.

Stringent environmental regulations and heavy capital requirements have precluded the opening of new ski resorts in recent years. Instead, the U.S. Forest Service (which owns the land on which most of Colorado's ski runs lie and leases it for a small fee to the ski areas) has encouraged ski resorts to expand if necessary. Expansion, however, has become a politically charged concept, for ski resorts have become magnets for real estate development, as a drive down the Eagle River valley illustrates.

Some community members fear too much development, and so try to limit resort expansion plans.

Nevertheless, Colorado remains the most popular state for skiers in the United States. About 10 million skier days, one-fifth of the nation's total, are tallied each year in Colorado (a skier day is a unit of measure: one skier or snowboarder using a lift ticket or ski pass for one day). Almost a quarter of those skier days are counted at Vail and Beaver Creek. Vail draws skiers because of its enormous size and its Back Bowls, huge, open expanses that can provide extraordinary powder skiing. Beaver Creek is an upscale resort known for its service and wide cruising runs.

Directions: For Vail: From Denver, take I-70 west to Exit 176, which is the middle of the three Vail exits. Turn south toward the ski mountain. Parking is available in several nearby covered parking garages.

For Beaver Creek: Take Exit 167 from I-70 and turn south through Avon. Cross the bridge and continue up to Beaver Creek Resort, about 3 miles south of Avon. Parking is available in covered garages.

Activities: Winter: skiing, snowboarding, guided backcountry snowcat skiing, guided snowshoeing, tubing. Summer: chairlift and gondola rides, mountain biking, hiking.

Facilities: At Vail Mountain: 4,644 acres of skiable terrain and a vertical drop of 3,335 feet. At Beaver Creek: 1,625 acres and a vertical drop of 4,040 feet. On-mountain restaurants.

Dates: The ski areas generally open in early or mid-Nov. and close on Easter weekend. Summer activities are available from June through Sept.

Fees: There is a fee for skiing, mountain biking and chairlift rides, and for parking.

For more information: Vail Resorts, PO Box 7, Vail, CO 81658. Phone (970) 476-5601. Vail Chamber of Commerce, PO Box 7, Vail, CO 81658. Phone (800) 525-2257.

EAGLE'S NEST WILDERNESS

[Fig. 26] Interstate 70 bends south at Dillon, carving a large arc past Copper Mountain and over Vail Pass. This route skirts the southern end of the Gore Range, which forms the heart of the Eagle's Nest Wilderness. During construction of Interstate 70 (prior to the wilderness area's designation), highway engineers wanted to go in a straight line west from Silverthorne to Vail, but this plan was abandoned for the gentler slopes of Vail Pass. Although it contains none of Colorado's 14,000-foot peaks, the Gore Range is strikingly vertical here, so much so that no trails cut across the range except at the northern and southern ends. The range extends up to Rabbit Ears Pass; the wilderness area contains the sharpest peaks, which lie in the southern half of the Gores, northeast of Vail and west of CO 9.

The Eagle's Nest Wilderness (133,688 acres) is readily accessible, since I-70 bounds its southern side and CO 9 runs along the east. The topography is particularly forbidding (and easily seen from atop adjacent Vail, Copper, and Beaver Creek ski areas), but Eagle's Nest contains a dozen alpine lakes in the steep clefts of alpine valleys, most accessible by a day hike.

Closest town: Several towns lie within a few miles of the wilderness area's borders: Silverthorne on the southeast corner, Vail on the western side, and Kremmling near the northeast border.

For more information: West side: Holy Cross Ranger District, White River National Forest, PO Box 190, 24747 US Highway 24, Minturn, CO 81645. Phone (970) 827-5715. East side: Dillon Ranger District, 680 River Parkway, PO Box 620, Silverthorne, CO 80498. Phone (970) 468-5400.

PINEY RIVER TRAIL

[Fig. 26(1)] Located on the western side of the Gore Range, this hike (a good overnight trip) dives into the heart of the mountains, climbing past a narrow waterfall and cutting behind a curling, crennellated wing of the mountain range into a hidden valley beneath dramatic avalanche chutes. Three lakes lie at the forked head of the valley.

Directions: Take Exit 176 from I-70 and follow the northern frontage road west for 1.25 miles to Red Sandstone Creek Road, a right. Follow this road up for several switchbacks; watch for a left turnoff onto a dirt road, Forest Road 700. Stay on FR 700 for 10 miles (ignore several turnoffs) to Piney River trailhead, which is at Piney Lake Ranch (located next to Piney Lake). Park in the lot to the right of the ranch gate and walk through the gate about 200 yards to the trail, which is readily apparent leading off the road and along the left side of the lake.

Trail: 5.5 miles to the first, unnamed lake, 7 miles to Upper Piney Lake, at the head of the valley.

Elevation: Change of 1,400 feet to the first, unnamed lake; 1,700 feet to Upper Piney Lake.

Degree of difficulty: Moderate.

Surface and Blaze: Packed dirt for the first mile, occasional mud, then dirt and rocks.

HOLY CROSS WILDERNESS

[Fig. 26] Holy Cross is one of Colorado's most popular wilderness areas, and with good reason. This 121,883-acre wilderness encompasses the Mount of the Holy Cross and is what many people think of when they conjure a vision of the Colorado mountains. The peaks are steep and forbidding, the valleys deeply forested and lush with wildflowers. Snow lingers late in the summer in the high cirques, and tumbling streams gain force as they fall from the high meadows through subalpine forest toward the Eagle River.

Just outside the southeast corner of the wilderness, at the rarefied altitude of 11,335 feet, lie the remains of Holy Cross City, a mining camp that in the early 1880s was home to 300 people, a hotel, a school, and a post office. Its remains—a few

Columbian Monkshood

Columbian Monkshood (*Aconitum columbianum*) is a highly poisonous plant that contains the alkaloid aconitine; a pound of the root will kill a horse. The plant has a long history as a traditional—if dangerous—medicine, and even as a poison set in bait for wolves.

cabins and rusting machinery—are visible to hikers willing to take a short detour from the Fall Creek Trail near its southern end.

Directions: To reach Holy Cross City, take Exit 171 from I-70 to US 24 South. Drive about 14 miles. Turn right (west) onto Homestake Road (Forest Road 703). Drive about 7 miles to Missouri Creek Road (FR 70r), another right. After about 2 miles turn right along the Homestake Collection Ditch Road. Continue for about 2 miles until you intersect the Holy Cross Jeep Road (FR 759). Turn left here. (This road may be impassable even in a four-wheel-drive vehicle, and is considered very difficult in the best of conditions. Hiking it is recommended.) Walk uphill (west). After 2 miles you will pass the Hunky Dory Trailhead, which is the southern end of the Fall Creek Trail. Do not take this trail; instead, bear left on the old jeep road to Holy Cross City, about a mile farther on.

For more information: Holy Cross Ranger District, White River National Forest, PO Box 190, 24747 US Highway 24, Minturn, CO 81645. Phone (970) 827-5715.

FALL CREEK TRAIL TO NOTCH MOUNTAIN TRAIL TO MOUNT OF THE HOLY CROSS OVERLOOK

[Fig. 26(10)] This popular hike leads climbers up a seemingly interminable set of 36 switchbacks to the location where William H. Jackson shot his famous picture of the northeastern side of the Mount of The Holy Cross. The site is marked by a dilapidated mountain hut (open to the public, but useful only for shelter in an emergency), and a small historic marker commemorating Jackson's photograph.

The trail cuts along the steep side of the Fall Creek valley for 3 miles, then turns west and begins the switchbacks, which continue for 2.5 miles to the broad saddle and the extraordinarily dramatic view. Mount of the Holy Cross is essentially ringed by lesser peaks, so it cannot be viewed unless one climbs the surrounding ridges. The effort is its own reward. Hikers get views of the Tenmile Range to the east, Gore Range to the north, and Collegiate Peaks to the south. The trail climbs from subalpine spruce-fir forest into alpine meadows thick at midsummer with Indian paintbrush, tall larkspur (*Delphinium glaucum*), and Columbian monkshood (*Aconitum columbianum*).

Directions: Take Exit 171 from I-70 and drive south on US 24 for 4.8 miles (passing through Minturn) to Forest Road 707 (Tigiwon Road), a right. Follow this 8.3 miles to the top of the road and the trailhead. This road is passable in a two-wheel-drive vehicle with moderate clearance, and some patience, if it is dry. Tigiwon Road climbs about 3,000 feet; allow 40 minutes to reach the trailhead from US 24.

Two trailheads depart here; take Fall Creek Trail, to the south of the parking lot.

Trail: 5.5 miles of well-built trail, including 3 dozen switchbacks on the second half.

Elevation: Change of 2,800 feet.

Degree of difficulty: Moderate.

Surface and Blaze: Dirt and rock; talus at higher elevations.

MOUNT OF THE HOLY CROSS

[Fig. 26] Here, in the very heart of the mountains, seemed to be proof that God endorsed the concept of "manifest destiny." The phrase was first coined in 1845 by John L. Sullivan, a magazine editor, when he prophesied "the fulfillment of our manifest destiny to overspread the continent allotted by Providence." The catchy term was quickly adopted by congressmen then arguing over the United States' expansion into the west via the annexation of Texas, the occupation of the Oregon Territory, and the coming war with Mexico (1846—1848). In subsequent decades the term "manifest destiny" became part of the public lexicon, shorthand for the belief that God had created the western lands for Anglo-Americans to control and exploit. Photographer William H. Jackson's discovery of what seemed to be a sign from God in the ceiling of the Rockies was taken as proof that the cause of western expansion was a just and good one.

10TH MOUNTAIN HUT SYSTEM

The 10th Mountain Hut System is the oldest and most extensive backcountry ski hut system in the United States. Run by a nonprofit organization, the system is a memorial to the soldiers who trained in the region and went on to glory in the Allied Italian campaign of 1945.

The first huts were opened in 1983; today, with a 300-mile skein of ski and biking trails, the system is nearly complete. The route stretches from Aspen, in the southwest corner of the system, north to Eagle; east from Aspen over the Continental Divide to Leadville; and north from there to Vail. A short, detached segment of the system stands on the northern side of I-70. The huts are set 6 to 12 miles apart; each is a solid day's travel from the next. Some skiers link huts together in multiday trips; others climb up a side trail from a roadhead for a quick overnight trip, then return to their car by the same route. In the late 1980s, many of the huts were opened for summer use by cyclists, hikers, and equestrians.

The idea for the hut system came from Fritz Benedict, an Aspen architect who trained during World War II with the U.S. Army's 10th Mountain Division at the now-vanished Camp Hale, north of Leadville on US 24. The ski troops were the 1939 brainchild of Minot Dole, a Connecticut skier who would go on to found the National Ski Patrol, and Robert Langley, then-president of the National Ski Association. The two men, having observed Finnish ski troops on maneuvers during the 1930s, believed the United States needed a similar fighting force and lobbied Washington to bring it into being.

The 10th was the first "invitation only" division in the U.S. military; would-be members had to be recommended by the United States Ski Patrol. Consequently, many of the men who came to Colorado, and eventually fought in the mountains during the Italian campaign, were accomplished mountaineers and skiers in their own right. Although the men of the 10th did not ski into battle, they did use their mountaineering skills in the brutal struggles for Riva Ridge and Mount Belvedere, and while pursuing the retreating German Army into the Alps. Nearly 1 in 10 men in the division was killed and almost half were wounded, a very high casualty rate. Many of the division's veterans went on after the war to found American ski resorts that have become household names today, including Aspen and Vail.

Among them was Benedict, who settled in Aspen after the war. Benedict admired the Haute Route, a series of mountain huts stretching on a classic, pre-war ski-touring route from Chamonix, France to Zermatt, Switzerland. To honor his war compatriots, he decided to create an American version of the European system.

The U.S. Forest Service, which owns the land where Benedict wanted to build ski huts, was skeptical. But the architect had the help of former Secretary of Defense Robert McNamara, who has a home in Snowmass Village and likes cross-country skiing. McNamara pressured the Forest Service to agree to allow the hut system to be constructed, which helps explain why the first two huts built were named for him and his wife, Margaret. The huts have grown steadily in popularity. In 1985 the nonprofit operation sold 2,625 "hut nights" (one person in one hut for one night). Ten years later that number had grown tenfold.

Hut systems are springing up all over the American West as backcountry skiing grows in popularity. Backcountry skiing never will eclipse downhilling or snowboarding, because it involves a lot of hard work in areas without ski lifts. But increasing numbers of skiers and mountaineers are looking forward by looking back. They are heading into untamed country to experience skiing the way it was 50 or 60 years ago, before ski patrollers and lift lines and moguls came to characterize modern skiing.

The system's 17 huts may be reached from trailheads throughout the region. Each hut is accessible in a day's skiing, bicycling, or hiking directly from the trailhead, or travelers may go directly from hut to hut, carrying food and clothing on their backs.

Activities: Cross-country skiing, summer biking and hiking.

Facilities: Unmanned huts fully equipped with cooking utensils, bedding, firewood, gas stoves, and solar-powered electric lights. Each hut sleeps 16 people.

Dates: Winter: Thanksgiving Day to Apr. 30. Summer: July 1 to Sept. 30.

Fees: There is a fee for use of the huts. Reservations are required; weekends and other popular times often book months in advance.

For more information: 10th Mountain Hut System, 1280 Ute Avenue, Aspen, CO 81611. Reservations and information: Phone (970) 925-5775. Several guide services are licensed to lead winter and summer trips to the huts; employing them is a good

The 10th Mountain Division

The 10th Mountain Division began as the 87th Mountain Regiment, created by the U.S. Army on November 15, 1941 and based at Fort Lewis, Washington. The 87th moved to Camp Hale in December 1942, after thousands of construction workers had leveled several miles of alpine valley floor at 10,300 feet on the north side of Tennessee Pass.

Twelve hundred buildings were constructed, and 14,00 men would eventually live at a place many called Camp Hell. Training was brutal. In addition to regular Army training, men learned rock climbing and ski mountaineering, practicing on the surrounding ridges in white winter suits while carrying 90-pound packs and wearing 7-foot skis.

In June 1944, the entire division was transferred to Texas for maneuvers. Morale, which had been bad at Camp Hale, didn't improve. Many of the soldiers were eager for battle but suspected they'd never see it before the war ended.

They were wrong. In January 1945, the 10th enterered World War II as part of the campaign to roll the German Army up the Italian peninsula. The men of the 10th scaled vertical cliffs (a feat considered impossible by the defending Germans) to take Campiano Peak via Riva Ridge, and then to dislodge the Germans from a mountaintop fortress called Mount Belvedere. The 10th continued to fight north and was the first division to cross the Po River in pursuit of the retreating Germans. One German commander who had faced them called them the best soldiers he had ever seen.

As the military downsized after World War II, the 10th Mountain Division was reduced and folded into other elements of the U.S. Army. Today the heirs to the 10th Mountain Division are members of the Green Berets, based in Germany and known as the 10th Special Forces Group (Airborne), 1st Special Forces.

idea for first-time hut visitors. 10th Mountain provides information on licensed guides. Travel to the huts requires backcountry skills, including the ability to navigate by map and compass in bad weather, cope with sudden storms, and conduct field repairs on broken equipment. Guides can be invaluable in these respects.

Trail: The 10th Mountain Trail system encompasses approximately 300 miles of trails. Routes to huts range from 5 to 12 miles in length.

Degree of difficulty: Moderate to strenuous.

Surface and Blaze: Routes are on dirt roads or hiking trails; in the winter these are obscured by snow, but they are marked intermittently with blue plastic diamonds.

CAMP HALE

[Fig. 26(7)] Almost nothing remains of the 1,200 buildings, Pando train depot, and training grounds where the 10th Mountain Division was headquartered. Summer hikers on the surrounding ridges occasionally discover World War II canteens, cartridge casings, or the faded outlines of machine gun emplacements built during the division's endless months of training. Still, this is a place heavy with history, and

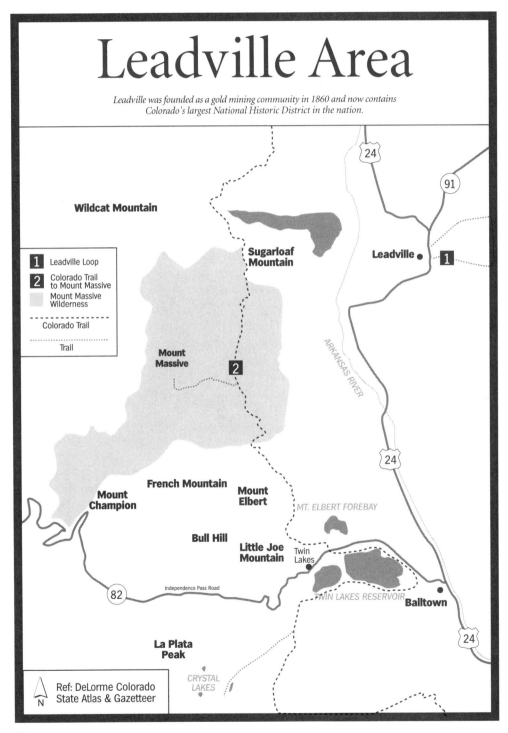

Leadville Area

*Leadville was founded as a gold mining community in 1860 and now contains
Colorado's largest National Historic District in the nation.*

24

91

Wildcat Mountain

1 Leadville Loop
2 Colorado Trail
to Mount Massive
Mount Massive
Wilderness

- - - Colorado Trail

.... Trail

**Sugarloaf
Mountain**

Leadville ● **1**

**Mount
Massive**

2

ARKANSAS RIVER

24

French Mountain

**Mount
Champion**

**Mount
Elbert**

MT. ELBERT FOREBAY

Bull Hill

**Little Joe
Mountain**

Twin
Lakes

82

Independence Pass Road

TWIN LAKES RESERVOIR

Balltown

24

**La Plata
Peak**

*CRYSTAL
LAKES*

N

Ref: DeLorme Colorado
State Atlas & Gazetteer

with import—not only because of the military history here, but because this place introduced ski pioneers (including Pete Siebert, who founded Vail) to these mountains, setting the stage for the creation of Colorado's ski industry.

Directions: From I-70, take Exit 171 to US 24 south; proceed 17 miles to the Camp Hale pull-out.

Facilities: Interpretive signs, a few building foundations.

Dates: Open year-round.

Fees: None.

Closest town: Leadville, 13 miles south.

For more information: Holy Cross Ranger District, White River National Forest, PO Box 190, 401 Main, Minturn, CO 81645. Phone (970) 827-5715.

Leadville Area

[Fig. 27] There may be no more fabled mining town in Colorado than the city of Leadville, set on a windswept plateau at the head of the Arkansas Valley. At 10,152 feet, Leadville is the highest incorporated city in the nation.

Among all of Colorado's mining towns, none can claim to be as rich, as dangerous, or as storied as Leadville. None had the combination of extraordinary wealth, famous names, and debauchery as this city, which at one point was home to 30,000 people (almost all men). Leadville was founded as a gold-mining community in 1860 when gold was discovered around what is now the townsite. For five years, gold mining was profitable, and 5,000 miners were scattered through Oro City (renamed Leadville in 1878) and settlements in the surrounding gulches.

But heavy black sand made mining in the area difficult, and the gold began to play out. In 1875 a pair of curious miners had the sand assayed and learned that it contained 15 ounces of silver per ton. They kept their discovery secret for two years, but word eventually leaked out and the second boom was on. By 1879 Leadville—until then little more than a cluster of log buildings—claimed 19 hotels, 82 saloons, 10 lumber yards, three undertakers, 21 gambling houses, and 36 brothels. That was just the beginning.

Leadville produced tens of millions of dollars of silver and gold and launched the careers of men whose names became famous around the nation and the world. Meyer Guggenheim and his seven sons all became millionaires from the mines in Leadville. David May began the May line of department stores with a single shop in Leadville.

The sensation of the day was Horace Tabor's wild ride from rags to riches and back to rags. Tabor, who ran a general store, fronted two miners with $17 worth of supplies and $47 worth of tools in 1878, in exchange for a one-third interest in their claim. Their discovery of the Little Pittsburg mine made Tabor a millionaire. He earned more millions in other mines, divorced his wife Augusta, and married Elizabeth

McCourt "Baby" Doe, a beautiful divorcee, at a lavish wedding attended by President Chester Arthur.

From that point on, the pair spent Tabor's millions as fast as he could make them. When the federal government repealed the Sherman Silver Act in 1893, eliminating a minimum market price for the metal, Tabor was broken. He lost his fortune in the crash, and died in 1899. Baby Doe lived on in poverty on the site of Tabor's most famous mine, The Matchless. Tabor's rumored last words to his wife were, "Hold on to the Matchless." However, the historian who reported that "fact" confessed that she had, in truth, invented the phrase.

Leadville was a remarkably dangerous place, where a man could be shot for any reason, or no reason at all. Walking the streets at night, even with a loaded pistol in hand, was very risky. Agreeing to be a marshal was a good way to get killed. Lynchings and vigilante justice were the primary forms of law enforcement during the boom years, but the city had more than its share of culture. English writer Oscar Wilde performed at the Tabor Opera House and then got drunk with a number of local miners. Harry Houdini appeared (and disappeared) here as well. Susan B. Anthony came through on a campaign for women's suffrage.

Unlike many mining towns, Leadville never died. Today it is home to more than 3,000 people, many of whom commute over Fremont or Tennessee passes to jobs in the ski resorts along I-70. The town retains its Victorian flavor and several notable public buildings from the late nineteenth century. Leadville contains Colorado's largest National Historic District, encompassing 70 blocks of the city.

The Mosquito Range runs behind the city on its eastern edge. Across the broad Arkansas River valley, the Sawatch Range rolls south from Tennessee Pass, unfolding in gentle undulations along a ridge that includes Mount Massive and Mount Elbert, the state's two highest peaks. The Colorado and Continental Divide trails pass nearby, and several huts in the 10th Mountain Trail hut system are situated on ridges to the north and west.

For more information: Leadville Ranger District, San Isabel National Forest, 2015 N. Poplar, Leadville, CO 80461. Phone (719) 486-0749. Leadville Chamber of Commerce, 809 Harrison Avenue, Leadville, CO 80461. Phone (719) 486-3900 or (800) 933-3901.

LEADVILLE LOOP

[Fig. 27(1)] This 10-mile mountain bike ride curls through the hills and gulches east of Leadville, following dirt roads through part of the mining district that made the city famous. The massive effort that went into mining is readily apparent. Some mine headframes still stand over shafts that once made men rich and famous. The remains of several small communities are also here amid endless mine tailings piles and decaying stumps in an open, awe-inspiring landscape.

It is important to stay on-route here. Although they appear abandoned, the mine sites are privately owned. Mines can also be exceedingly dangerous. Do not enter open tunnels or shafts, even a few feet. Dangerous gases may have accumulated and deprived the mine of oxygen. Hazards ranging from falling rocks to rusty nails are many and not always obvious, so enjoy the mine sites from a safe distance.

Directions: Begin in Leadville. Pedal east on Seventh Avenue, which leads out of town and up into the hills. After 3 miles, at the ruins of Evansville, bear left on the main road. At about 4.5 miles, the road forks toward Mosquito Pass (left), the old stage route to Fairplay. Stay to the right. Stay on the main road across a creek; a short steep section here is the only hard part of the ride, and can be ridden or walked. After 6.5 miles the road merges with another and begins the 3.5-mile descent back to Leadville.

Trail: 10-mile loop.

Elevation: Change of 1,300 feet.

Degree of difficulty: Easy, although bear in mind this route is situated entirely above 10,000 feet.

Surface and Blaze: Dirt road and paved road.

Coyotes

Its name comes from the Aztec word for barking dog, *coyotl*. Prevalent throughout North American mythology, the coyote (*Canis latrans*) is one of the very few predators that seems to thrive in man's presence.

Research indicates that the harder coyotes are hunted, trapped, and poisoned, the more reproductively prolific they become. Wildlife managers believe coyotes are more abundant today in Colorado than when the state was settled by Anglo-Americans. Coyotes have extended their range over much of the United States.

They are reviled by many livestock ranchers and often shot on sight. Yet coyotes thrive in all environments, from Denver's suburbs to alpine tundra, eating everything from fruit to carrion to deer trapped in deep snow.

The coyote has been called "God's dog." Like the deity, he seems to be everywhere, although more often heard giving his characteristic evening yips and howls, than seen.

▓ MOUNT MASSIVE WILDERNESS

[Fig. 27] This wilderness area sits on the high point of the Continental Divide, not simply in Colorado but between the Arctic Ocean and the country of Panama. Mount Massive and nearby Mount Elbert, La Plata Peak, and Mount Harvard are four of the five highest Fourteeners in the state, and make up the highest region on the Continental Divide.

This 30,540-acre wilderness is contiguous with the Hunter-Frying Pan Wilderness on the western side of the Continental Divide. This area was supposed to be an addition to the Hunter-Frying Pan Wilderness, but a mistake in the legislation created a separate wilderness area. Because the hikes to the peaks here are relatively easy, although long, the trails up Mount Massive are quite popular.

Black-billed Magpie

Magpies are as common in the West as crows in the East—and are, in fact, a member of the crow family, Corvidae. The black-billed magpie (*Pica pica*) is easily identified by its size (17 to 22 inches in length), and its distinctive black and white plumage, which flashes on its wings during flight. The magpie's long tail is an iridescent green-blue in the sun.

Magpies are widely distributed through Colorado and are commonly seen along roadsides, for they eat carrion.

For more information: Leadville Ranger District, San Isabel National Forest, 2015 North Poplar, Leadville, CO 80461. Phone (719) 486-0749.

COLORADO TRAIL TO MOUNT MASSIVE

[Fig. 27] This is a long day hike up the state's second highest peak (14,421 feet). The upper sections of the route are exposed in a large, east-facing bowl, and the ridge walk to the summit, although gentle, is very exposed to weather, which generally approaches from the west. Mount Massive actually includes four lesser summits, all above 14,000 feet, but for record-keeping purposes is counted as a single Fourteener.

The first 3 miles of trail follow the Colorado Trail through lodgepole pine forest, which is quite extensive on the east-facing slopes of the Sawatch Range in the upper Arkansas River valley. Then the trail climbs into a massive bowl that provides views to the east across the Mosquito Range. Once on the summit ridge, hikers can look west into the Hunter-Frying Pan Wilderness, which encompasses much of the western flank of the Sawatch Mountains here. The Collegiate Peaks (part of the Sawatch Range) run to the south. Mount Elbert, the highest peak in the state at 14,433 feet, is the next peak south from Mount Massive.

Directions: From Leadville, drive south on US 24 approximately 4 miles to CO 300, a right-hand (west) turn, located immediately after US 24 turns 90 degrees left and heads south. Go approximately 0.8 mile on CO 300, then turn left onto Forest Road 110 to Halfmoon Campground, approximately 4 miles farther on. Drive through the campground and across Halfmoon Creek 1 mile farther on. Park at the trailhead here.

Trail: Dirt and rock, some narrow ridge walking for the last 0.5 mile.

Elevation: Change of 4,220 feet.

Degree of difficulty: Strenuous.

Surface and Blaze: Packed dirt and rock.

FISHING

UPPER ARKANSAS RIVER

[Fig. 27] The upper Arkansas River above Twin Lakes is not particularly good trout habitat because toxic runoff from mine wastes in the Leadville area limits insect life and spawning success. Below Twin Lakes, where CO 24 parallels the river, access is quite good and water from Twin Lakes improves the river habitat substantially. As with rivers everywhere, be sure to check for access permission if ownership is not clearly public. The Arkansas is primarily a brown trout river, although some rainbow trout may be caught.

Directions: US 24 closely follows the Arkansas River between Malta, 1 mile west of Leadville, and Granite, 16 miles south of Malta.

Activities: Fishing.

Facilities: None.

Dates: Open year-round.

Fees: None.

Closest town: Leadville is located 17 miles north of Granite, a hamlet containing few commercial services. Twin Lakes is 5 miles west of US 24 on CO 82.

For more information: Colorado Division of Wildlife, 6060 Broadway, Denver, CO 80216. Phone (303) 297-1192.

TURQUOISE LAKE

[Fig. 27] This is a 1,500-acre reservoir on the east side of Hagerman Pass that offers good boat fishing for brown trout and lake trout.

Directions: From Leadville, go south on US 24 (Harrison Avenue) 1 mile from the only stoplight in town. Turn right (north) on McWethy Drive (County Road 4) and follow the signs for 3.5 miles to Turquoise Lake.

Activities: Camping, fishing, boating, scenic drive, picnic areas.

Facilities: Six campgrounds containing 175 campsites; 3 picnic areas; 3 boat ramps.

Dates: Campgrounds are open from Memorial day to Labor Day.

Fees: There is a fee to camp.

Closest town: Leadville, 4 miles east.

TWIN LAKES

[Fig. 27] Like Turquoise Lake, Twin Lakes is a stocked, man-made impoundment (actually an enlargement of natural lakes). The lake is popular with boat fishermen who troll for lake trout that run up to 20 pounds in size, as well as cutthroat and rainbow trout.

Directions: From Leadville, travel south on US 24 approximately 15 miles to CO 82 west, a right-hand turn. Turn here and travel approximately 2 miles along the shores of Twin Lakes to the boat ramp, on the left.

Activities: Fishing, boating, camping.

Facilities: Three campgrounds containing 149

BLACK-BILLED COMMON MAGPIE
(Pica pica)
The magpie's black and white pattern, which is seen while in flight, contrasts with its long, metallic green tail.

campsites; 1 boat ramp.

Dates: Campgrounds are open from Memorial Day to the end of September.

Fees: There is a fee to camp.

Closest town: Twin Lakes, 1 mile west of the reservoir.

CRYSTAL LAKES

[Fig. 27] Located adjacent to US 24, these two small lakes are stocked with trout and managed by the U.S. Forest Service. Given the easy access and open shores, this is a good place to fish with children. Small boats are allowed and can get you out to deeper water, where trout up to 20 inches long have been caught.

Directions: From Leadville, travel south on US 24 approximately 2 miles. Look for the sign for "Colorado's Highest Peaks." Turn right (west) here and follow signs for "Fishing Access" to a parking area south of the western lake, about 0.25 mile.

Activities: Fishing.

Facilities: Parking area.

Dates: The reservoir is open to the public year-round, but freezes over in winter. Campgrounds and other facilities

Fees: None.

Closest town: Leadville, 2 miles north on US 24.

Aspen Area

Aspen was the site of a massive silver strike in 1879, and like Central City and Leadville before it, the mining tent camp quickly became a boom town. Yet during its first winter Aspen's residents formed a literary society, setting the tone for all that would follow. Natural beauty, wealth, and culture combine in Aspen today as they have for 125 years.

Aspen's geology is different from that of the Front Range. The rocks exposed around the town are not the Precambrian basement rocks, but younger, Paleozoic rocks dating from 600 million to 300 million years ago. These rocks were cracked and faulted during the lifting process of the Laramide Orogeny; the faults allowed mineral-rich solutions to impregnate the rock. However, Precambrian granite isn't far away; the fault line between the granite and the Paleozoic rock runs north to south only a few yards east of the Aspen Mountain ski area. East of this fault, no mining to speak of was conducted. A drive east on CO 82, toward Independence Pass, goes through the older, metamorphic rock of the Sawatch Range.

Immediately west of Aspen the redbeds common to the western side of Frontrangia appear. The small, humped red peak on the northwest corner of town, Red Butte, is a chunk or Mesozoic-era sedimentary rock with a twist; it has been completely inverted by movement here along a fault. The youngest Cretaceous shale lies at the bottom of Red Butte, while older, red, Triassic sediments are near the top.

The Roaring Fork River and CO 82 meander northwest past the Elk Mountains. The most visible of these is Mount Sopris (12,953 feet), south of Carbondale. This peak was formed as a volcanic stock very similar to the Spanish Peaks in southeastern Colorado (*see* page 108). It was created when a large mass of lava bulged toward the surface, pushing up against overlying Cretaceous shales. The lava cooled slowly in place, forming feldspar and quartz. The softer Cretaceous layers eroded, leaving the harder core of the mountain in place.

Aspen Highlands Ski area with Pyramid Peak on the left and the Maroon Bells on the right.

Aspen sits astride the center of the mineral belt that runs from the Front Range to the San Juan Mountains. Prospectors from Leadville discovered gold at Independence, 5 miles west of Independence Pass, on July 4, 1879. Other miners exploring down the valley made a strike beside the flat bench between Aspen and Smuggler mountains, and the rush was on.

Early access to Aspen was via Leadville, but the route was circuitous and difficult. Miners trekked south from Leadville to Buena Vista, west up the Taylor River over Taylor Pass, north down Castle Creek, and then east around West Aspen (now Shadow) Mountain. The town of Ashcroft was founded that same year on a silver strike near the confluence of Express Creek and Castle Creek, and lay on the Aspen-Leadville route. Yet when the first rail line reached Aspen in 1887 by climbing the Roaring Fork Valley, it signalled the doom of Ashcroft, which had been home to about 2,000 people.

Aspen was first named Ute City by Henry Gillespie, one of the initial prospectors, but he left for the winter in the fall of 1879. B. Clark Wheeler stayed the winter and renamed the town Aspen.

The mines were numerous and extraordinarily rich. Both Smuggler Mountain and Aspen Mountain contained incredible wealth. The Smuggler Mine, still visible near the base of Smuggler Mountain on the northeast side of town, extended up and down inside the mountain over more than 30 levels covering 3,000 vertical feet. The largest silver nugget ever found, bigger than a man and weighing approximately 1 ton, was pulled from the Smuggler. Mining tunnels extended beneath Aspen and connected to the miles of tunnels honeycombing Aspen Mountain.

By 1880 Aspen was producing $3.5 million worth of ore annually. By 1889 production was up to $10 million annually, and Aspen had eclipsed Leadville as the state's greatest mining town. Enormous stamping works were built at the base of Smuggler Mountain, and an ore concentrating plant was erected along Castle Creek. Aspen was a major industrial city; with a population of 12,000, it was the state's third

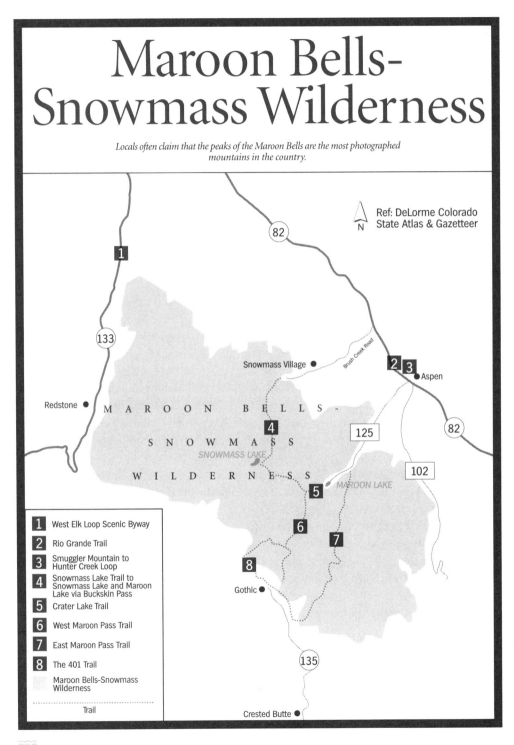

Maroon Bells-Snowmass Wilderness

Locals often claim that the peaks of the Maroon Bells are the most photographed mountains in the country.

Ref: DeLorme Colorado State Atlas & Gazetteer

1 West Elk Loop Scenic Byway

2 Rio Grande Trail

3 Smuggler Mountain to Hunter Creek Loop

4 Snowmass Lake Trail to Snowmass Lake and Maroon Lake via Buckskin Pass

5 Crater Lake Trail

6 West Maroon Pass Trail

7 East Maroon Pass Trail

8 The 401 Trail

Maroon Bells-Snowmass Wilderness

Trail

largest metropolis after Denver and Leadville.

The 1893 silver crash, however, hit Aspen especially hard. Other communities such as Leadville and Telluride limped along on gold mining or other minerals, but Aspen, the Silver Queen, had no such fallback. All the mines closed within a month of the crash, and the population plummeted.

The old mining town became a Victorian time capsule until it was discovered by Walter Paepcke at the end of World War II. Paepcke, the chairman of Chicago-based Container Corporation of America, saw possibilities in Aspen.

His vision included both skiing and great intellectual pursuits. In the late 1940s, he set out to revive Aspen (then a city of 700) as a retreat for the complete man. He founded many of the institutions that would bring the former mining town international success as a resort, including The Aspen Institute (a think-tank), and the summer-long Aspen Music Festival. He founded the Aspen Skiing Company, which today runs four ski areas: Aspen, Snowmass, Buttermilk, and Aspen Highlands.

For more information: Aspen Chamber Resort Association, 425 Rio Grande Place, Aspen, CO 81611. Phone (970) 925-1940.

▨ MAROON BELLS-SNOWMASS WILDERNESS

[Fig. 28] The late Morris Udall, an Arizona congressman who wrote the 1964 Wilderness Act, is said to have visited the Maroon Bells for the first time in the 1970s and commented that, had he known how spectacular the area is, he would have had the central Elk Mountains designated as a national park, rather than as a federal wilderness.

Such a designation might have honored the region, but it would certainly have drawn even more people to what is already one of the most popular mountain locales in the nation. Each summer, several hundred thousand visitors travel the two-lane road from Aspen to Maroon Lake at the foot of North and South Maroon peaks, a twinned sedimentary formation known as the Maroon Bells for its color and shape.

Locals often claim that the Bells are the most photographed mountains in the country. Certainly, they are among the most dramatic and accessible in Colorado. The image of the Bells, in all seasons, shows up again and again on calendars, in coffee table books, and in advertisements around the world. During the 1980s the Bells were even appropriated by an advertising agency to illustrate the mountain beauty of Utah, a faux pas that caused a good deal of amusement in Colorado.

The Bells and adjacent Pyramid Peak (the dramatic, triangular peak visible to the south of CO 82 from Aspen's western edge) were formed by complex geologic events. The ancestral Rockies, Uncompahgria and Frontrangia, rose about 300 million years ago, then eroded into red, sedimentary depositions. These rocks were then uplifted twice; the original sandstone and quartzite of the Permian redbeds metamorphosed under the heat of pressure of those uplifts into shale and slate.

Then, the Elk Mountains were glaciated. The combination of water and ice working on Pyramid and the Maroon Bells cut them, and all the Elk Mountains, into

Dominguez and Escalante Expedition of 1776

In the year of the American Revolution, Fray Francisco Atanasio Dominguez and Fray Silvestre Vélez Escalante departed the Spanish provincial capital of Santa Fe on a bold and daring mission. They planned to march 1,000 miles overland to the Spanish mission at Monterey, California. Their journey would chart an overland route between the two settlements and help the Spanish consolidate their hold on the region.

Their mission was a venture into *terra incognita*. It was ultimately unsuccessful; the group was turned back by bad weather in Utah. However, Dominguez and Escalante and their band became the first Anglo-Americans to explore western Colorado and eastern Utah. Their route of exploration took them around the Sangre de Cristo Mountains into the Gunnison River valley, up the North Fork of the Gunnison, over Grand Mesa to the Grand Valley, through northwestern Colorado into Utah's Unitah Mountains, and across the Colorado River at previously undiscovered Glen Canyon.

Today their route is remembered in place names of Dominguez and Escalante, which are common in western Colorado and eastern Utah.

the jagged teeth and fins that characterize them today. The sedimentary layers of the original redbeds are still clearly visible along the slopes of the Bells. The slates and shales lie loosely on the Bells and Pyramid Peak and seem to tumble from them constantly, making climbing these peaks especially hazardous.

The entire Maroon Bells-Snowmass Wilderness is spectacular, encompassing nine passes over 12,000 feet, six peaks above 14,000 feet, and countless lush, alpine valleys. Trails in the southwest portion of this wilderness area are discussed in the Crested Butte section of the book (*see* page 206.)

Four of the high area's high peaks (Pyramid, North Maroon, South Maroon, and Capitol) are among the most difficult and dangerous Fourteeners in the state. Capitol Peak, located in the western half of the 180,962-acre wilderness area, rears out of the head of the valley like a shark's tooth. Its forbidding north face plunges a vertical 0.5 mile into Capitol Lake. That face has been climbed only a few times.

The Maroon Bells-Snowmass Wilderness is, like Colorado itself, a pageant of natural beauty that never seems to quit. Every bend in the trail, every pass, every peak is more breathtaking than what came before. Portions of the wilderness that draw heavy traffic include East and West Maroon Creek trails, Cathedral Lake, Snowmass Lake, Capitol Lake, and Buckskin Pass. Visit these locales during the week to avoid the crowds.

The West Maroon Creek valley, between the Maroon Bells and adjacent Pyramid Peak, is the most heavily visited site of all. The trip up Maroon Creek Road has become so popular that vehicle access is limited during the summer months. Automobiles generally are not permitted on the road from Memorial Day to late September, with some exceptions. Visitors are transported directly to Maroon Lake, and the trailheads there, by bus from Ruby Park, the bus terminal in downtown Aspen. The road is open in late spring and early autumn, but closed during the winter.

For more information: For bus schedules to the Bells, call the Roaring Fork Transit Agency. Phone (970) 925-8484. For other information: Aspen Ranger District, White River National Forest, 806 West Hallam, Aspen, CO 81611. Phone (970) 925-3445.

SNOWMASS LAKE TRAIL TO SNOWMASS LAKE AND MAROON LAKE VIA BUCKSKIN PASS

[Fig. 28(4)] This is a one- or two-night backpacking trip through the heart of the wilderness area. It does require a vehicle shuttle to complete. Because the route finishes at Maroon Lake, you will be able to catch a bus from there back to downtown Aspen. Cars are not permitted in the Upper Maroon Creek Valley during the summer, so you cannot leave your second car there. Instead, take the bus to Aspen, then drive from there and retrieve your first vehicle from the Snowmass Lake trailhead after you complete your hike. If you only have one car, consider taking an overnight trip to Snowmass Lake and hiking back out the same way, which can be equally rewarding.

The route winds up through dark alpine forests and open meadows and along the splashing streams of Snowmass Creek valley to Snowmass Lake, a large natural lake set beneath 14,092-foot Snowmass Mountain. Many people camp near the lake, which is about 8 miles from the trailhead. From the lake the trail backtracks slightly, then climbs steadily to Buckskin Pass, set at 12,500 feet along the northern shoulder of North Maroon Peak. The route then descends into the Maroon Creek valley and down to Maroon Lake, where hikers may catch a bus back to Aspen.

The entire route is very popular, so consider undertaking it at off-peak times, such as midweek or in the early autumn.

Directions: From Aspen, drive west on CO 82 approximately 17 miles to Snowmass Creek Road (do not take the turn for Snowmass Village), at the Old Snowmass Conoco station. Turn left (south) and proceed for 2 miles to a T-intersection. Turn left (east) and drive for approximately 10 miles (the road will turn to graded dirt). Immediately after crossing a culvert over Snowmass Creek, at a T-intersection, turn right. Go 0.5 mile to the Snowmass Creek trailhead and park.

Closest town: Snowmass Village, 3 miles up a rough dirt road opposite the trailhead. This road is possible in a two-wheel-drive vehicle if conditions are dry.

Trail: 16 miles point-to-point.

Elevation: Change of 4,100 feet from the Snowmass Lake trailhead to Buckskin Pass; change of 2,880 from Buckskin Pass to Maroon Lake.

Degree of difficulty: Moderate.

Surface and Blaze: Narrow trail through forest and tundra. Some creek crossings which may be impossible or difficult in high water.

CRATER LAKE TRAIL

[Fig. 28(5)] This is a very popular, and very rewarding, 2-mile walk from the end

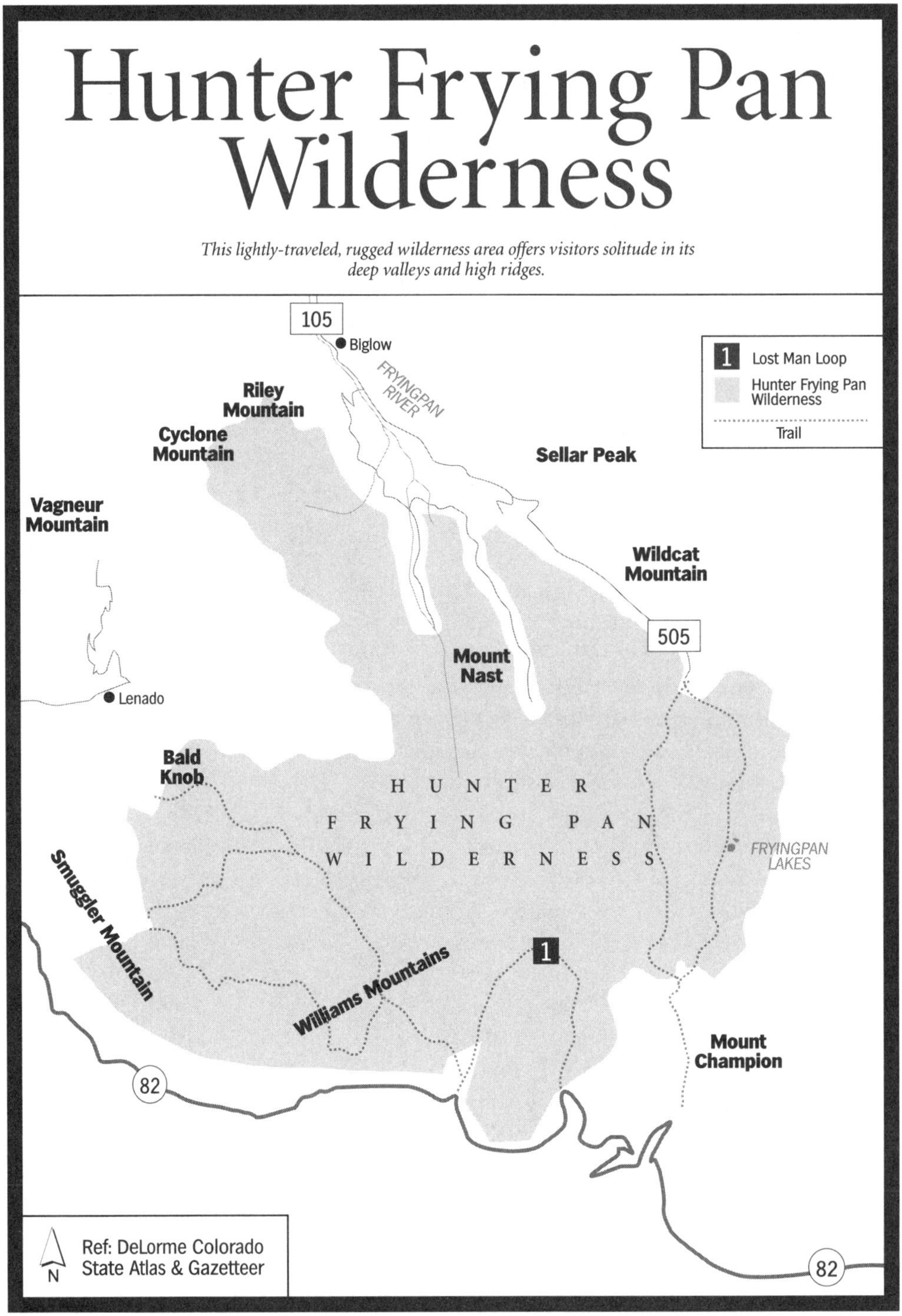

Hunter Frying Pan Wilderness

This lightly-traveled, rugged wilderness area offers visitors solitude in its deep valleys and high ridges.

105

● Biglow

FRYINGPAN RIVER

Riley Mountain

Cyclone Mountain

Sellar Peak

Vagneur Mountain

Wildcat Mountain

505

● Lenado

Mount Nast

Bald Knob

H U N T E R

F R Y I N G   P A N

W I L D E R N E S S

● FRYINGPAN LAKES

Smuggler Mountain

Williams Mountains

Mount Champion

82

82

1	Lost Man Loop
	Hunter Frying Pan Wilderness
⋯	Trail

△
N

Ref: DeLorme Colorado
State Atlas & Gazetteer

of Maroon Creek Road, past Maroon Lake to Crater Lake, which sits partway up the valley between the Maroon Bells and Pyramid Peak. This is a good walk for kids who like to hike, and Crater Lake offers picnicking along its open shores. The lake itself is not in a crater at all, but was formed by a small rock slide, which blocked the flow of West Maroon Creek. Late in the summer the lake level may drop significantly.

Directions: From the bus drop-off point at the end of Maroon Creek Road, walk south, toward the Bells, along Maroon Lake and up the valley. Crater Lake is the turnaround point for this walk, although the West Maroon Creek trail continues south up the West Maroon Creek valley and eventually over West Maroon Pass, about 4 miles farther on (for a description of the longer hike, see the West Maroon Pass-East Maroon Pass Loop, page xx). The Minnehaha Gulch Trail climbs to the right (west) toward Buckskin Pass, 3 miles away.

Note: The Maroon Bells look temptingly close and relatively easy to climb from the vantage point of Crater Lake. Do not be deceived. These peaks are known as "the deadly Bells" among local mountaineers and have taken the lives of many experienced climbers. Climbing them requires preparation, a predawn start, and significant mountaineering skills.

Trail: 4 miles round-trip to Crater Lake.

Elevation: Change of 500 feet.

Degree of difficulty: Easy.

Surface and Blaze: Wide dirt and rock trail.

HUNTER-FRYING PAN WILDERNESS

[Fig. 29] The rugged Williams Mountains at the heart of the 82,729-acre Hunter-Frying Pan Wilderness encircle the head of Hunter Creek and offer a hidden reward for hikers in the region. Their serrated, 13,000-foot peaks are almost completely invisible from surrounding roadways. Without Fourteeners and containing few lakes, the Hunter-Frying Pan is a lightly-traveled, rugged wilderness with relatively few trails. It offers visitors solitude in deep, forested valleys and on high, nameless ridges.

The Hunter-Frying Pan is overshadowed by the high peaks of the Sawatch and Elk mountains. It contains the headwaters of Hunter Creek and the Frying Pan River, two tributaries to the Roaring Fork River, and lies contiguously with the Mount Massive wilderness on the eastern side of the Continental Divide.

Much of the northern portion of the wilderness is deep timber on long ridges and in remote valleys, the kind of country favored by elk, black bear, and pine martens. Although the Canada lynx (*Felis lynx*) appears to have been extirpated from this region by trapping

SNOWSHOE HARE
(*Lepus americanus*)

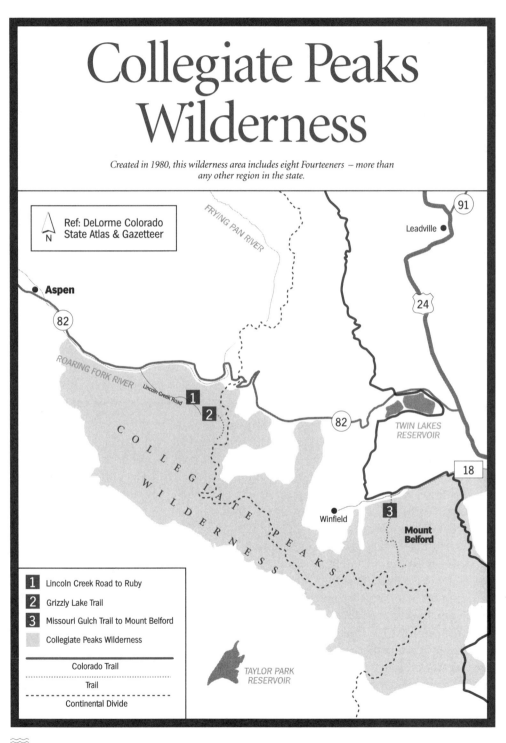

Collegiate Peaks Wilderness

Created in 1980, this wilderness area includes eight Fourteeners – more than any other region in the state.

Ref: DeLorme Colorado State Atlas & Gazetteer

N

FRYING PAN RIVER

91

Leadville

Aspen

82

24

ROARING FORK RIVER

Lincoln Creek Road

1

2

82

TWIN LAKES RESERVOIR

C O L L E G I A T E

W I L D E R N E S S

18

Winfield

3

Mount Belford

P E A K S

1 Lincoln Creek Road to Ruby

2 Grizzly Lake Trail

3 Missouri Gulch Trail to Mount Belford

Collegiate Peaks Wilderness

Colorado Trail

Trail

Continental Divide

TAYLOR PARK RESERVOIR

and development pressure, such old-growth forests are prime habitat for this animal, a bobcatlike predator that hunts snowshoe hares.

Activities: Backpacking, day hiking, camping, fishing.

Closest town: Aspen lies at the southwestern corner of the Hunter-Frying Pan, about 5 miles from the wilderness boundary. Most access is from here, along Highway 82 to the east or up Hunter Creek.

For more information: Aspen Ranger District, White River National Forest, 806 West Hallam, Aspen, CO 81611. Phone: (970) 925-3445.

LOST MAN LOOP

[Fig. 29(1)] This popular hike is a spectacular walk, almost entirely in the open, through two valleys fringing the Continental Divide at the headwaters of the 60-mile-long Roaring Fork River. The valleys are joined by an easy pass that lies between two jewel-like alpine lakes.

From the upper trailhead, follow the trail up the valley for 2 miles to Independence Lake, the source of the Roaring Fork River. Climb over Lost Man Pass (12,800 feet) into Lost Man Creek, pass Lost Man Lake, and stay on this trail through open alpine meadows until you arrive at the Lost Man lower trailhead.

The trail is not a true loop but an arc; both ends touch CO 82. Thus, this hike requires two cars. If you prefer to hike downhill rather than up (all the grades here are relatively gentle), start at the upper trailhead, as described below.

Directions: From Aspen, drive east on CO 82 approximately 16 miles to the Upper Lost Man upper trailhead. You will pass Lost Man Campground (on the right) after about 13 miles; the Lower Lost Man lower trailhead is situated at the parking lot opposite the campground across the highway. Drop a vehicle here if you plan to hike the full length of the trail and then shuttle back to your starting point.

The Lost Man upper trailhead is located at the outside bend of the last hairpin turn before CO 82 passes over the Continental Divide at Independence Pass. The final 2 miles of road to the summit are easily visible as you approach the hairpin from below.

Closest town: Aspen, 16 miles west.

Trail: 10 miles one-way.

Elevation: Gain of 900 feet, then descent of 2,300 feet.

Degree of difficulty: Moderate.

Surface and Blaze: Narrow footpath through alpine tundra and meadows.

COLLEGIATE PEAKS WILDERNESS

[Fig. 30] Created in 1980, this wilderness area encompasses 167,994 acres of the southern Sawatch Range and includes more Fourteeners—eight—than any other wilderness region in the state. All of these peaks (Huron, La Plata, Missouri Mountain, Mount Belford, Mount Columbia, Mount Harvard, Mount Oxford, and Mount Yale), and many lesser mountains draw alpinists. Roads penetrate to the edge of the wilderness from several directions, so access to peaks is quite easy. Consequently, on summer weekends a relatively straightforward Fourteener such as Mount Huron may be host to 70 people climbing to its summit.

The Continental Divide wanders among these peaks. Along with the Mount Massive Wilderness to the north, this stretch of Colorado's Continental Divide is the highest portion in the Northern Hemisphere. Because it sprawls across the state's spine, the wilderness area can be reached from the Arkansas, Roaring Fork, and Gunnison river valleys, and is managed accordingly. This wilderness area is also discussed in the Buena Vista section of the book (*see* page 196).

Activities: Hiking, backpacking, camping, fishing, mountaineering.

Closest town: Aspen is about 10 miles from the trailheads in the northern portion of the Collegiate Peaks Wilderness (around the Lincoln Creek Valley). Gunnison is 40 miles from the southwestern section, around Taylor Reservoir. Buena Vista lies 10 miles east of the eastern wilderness area boundary.

For more information: Northwest sections: Aspen Ranger District, White River National Forest, 806 West Hallam, Aspen, CO 81611. Phone (970) 925-3445. Eastern sections: Leadville Ranger District, San Isabel National Forest, 2015 N. Poplar, Leadville, CO 80461. Phone (719) 486-0749. Southwest sections: Cebolla/Taylor River Ranger District, Gunnison National Forest, 216 N. Colorado, Gunnison, CO 81230. Phone (970) 641-0471.

GRIZZLY LAKE TRAIL

[Fig. 30(2)] This is a popular out-and-back day hike to a small, deep lake set at the foot of 13,988-foot Grizzly Peak, a former volcano and the highest non-Four-teener in the state. The walk leads through a deep, alpine valley lush with wildflowers such as alpine bistort, Indian paintbrush, and asters.

Directions: From Aspen, drive east on CO 82 approximately 8 miles to Lincoln Creek Road (Forest Road 106). Turn right (south) and drive 6 miles to Grizzly Reservoir, part of a water diversion project to transfer water through a tunnel be-neath the Continental Divide and into the Arkansas River drainage for use by Pueblo. This route is a dirt road but generally passable by two-wheel-drive vehicles with moderate clearance.

Park at the reservoir and follow the road on the eastern side. The trailhead is about 100 yards up on the left.

Closest town: Aspen, 14 miles west.

Dates: CO 82 is closed between Aspen and Twin Lakes during the winter, begin-ning with the first heavy snows in Oct. It generally reopens on Memorial Day. Lincoln Creek Road may be closed until early summer.

Trail: 4 miles one-way.

Elevation: Gain of 2,000 feet.

Degree of difficulty: Moderate.

Surface: Dirt and rock.

FISHING

Two rivers in the Aspen area, the Roaring Fork and the tributary Frying Pan, have been designated Gold Medal waters by the Colorado Division of Wildlife. This designation acknowledges that these are some of the best fisheries in the state. Fishing is limited to flies and lures only and for much of the length of both rivers all fishing is catch-and-release, so check local regulations and signs.

Fly-fishing has become very popular nationally in the last decade, a fact apparent on these two rivers. Particularly along the Frying Pan, access increasingly has been limited by private landowners and fishing clubs, and on busy summer weekends the fishing experience is anything but solitary. Anglers seeking quiet and solitude should try to fish during the week and at off-hours.

Independence Pass

By 1881 Aspen was a booming silver town, but access from Leadville was difficult. A group of adventuresome bakers in Leadville decided they could do well in the new mining town if they could get a large baking oven over 12,095-foot Independence Pass.

They set out in March, dragging the oven uphill on a mule-powered sled, widening the existing trail in places where they had to. The trip was so slow they spent a cold night sleeping inside their oven. Eventually, freight traffic backed up for 1 mile on the narrow route behind the slow-moving oven.

The bakers made it to Aspen, but the monumental traffic jam they created underlined the demand for a real road, which was built that summer by 75 laborers and opened on November 6, 1881. The new route—largely followed today by CO 82—shortened the trip from Leadville to Aspen via the Cottonwood and Taylor pass roads by 40 miles.

For more information: Basalt Chamber of Commerce, 105 Midland Avenue, Basalt, CO 81611. Phone (970) 927-4031. Colorado Division of Wildlife, 50633 US Highway 6 and 24, Glenwood Springs, CO 80601. Phone (970) 945-7228.

ROARING FORK RIVER

[Fig. 30] This stream begins at the Continental Divide and tumbles 20 miles toward Aspen. East of town, in the Northstar Nature Preserve, access is available for catch-and-release fishing where the river meanders through wet meadows. The river can be reached at several places where it wanders through Aspen, but one of the most popular places to begin wading is at the bottom of Cemetery Lane. Fishermen can walk upstream and downstream on the old Rio Grande Railroad roadbed.

Downstream from Cemetery Lane the river runs through Woody Creek Canyon. Trout up to 18 inches long, principally rainbows, are not uncommon here. The lower end of the canyon can be reached via the Woody Creek Bridge. From the village of Woody Creek to Basalt there are several means of access through Snowmass Canyon; look for turnouts on CO 82, which parallels the river. Below Basalt public access is largely prohibited.

Directions: To reach the river via Cemetery Lane, take CO 82 (Main Street) west out of Aspen to the first stop light. Turn right (north) on Cemetery Lane; drive approximately 1 mile until you cross the river. Park in the parking lot on the left. To reach the river at the Woody Creek Bridge, stay on CO 82 approximately 4 miles to the right-hand (north) turn to Upper River Road. The bridge is 0.25 mile down the road; cross the bridge and park in the lot to the right.

FRYING PAN RIVER

[Fig. 30] The Frying Pan may offer Colorado's best combination of scenery, access, and good fishing, which helps explain why it has become quite crowded in recent years. The 14-mile stretch of this river running east from Basalt to the Reudi Reservoir dam cuts through a narrow canyon of cottonwood trees and horse farms. The geology is that of the ancient, eroded Permian rocks, the redbeds that crumbled from the ancestral Rockies to form the Maroon Formation on the western side of the Continental Divide and the Fountain Formation on the east.

The Frying Pan is a small, cozy river of pools and riffles. Steady flow from Reudi (pronounced ROO-die) Reservoir keeps the temperature a cool 39 to 50 degrees Fahrenheit year-round, and silt flow is minimal. The result is a remarkably prolific fishery for brown and rainbow trout. In the 0.5-mile stretch of river below the dam some trout are so big that local anglers call them "footballs." Their size and wariness has led to extensive fishing pressure on the river, which is entirely catch-and-release.

Several guiding services in Basalt, Carbondale, and Aspen take fishermen on the Roaring Fork and Frying Pan rivers.

MOUNTAIN BIKING

A glance at the map might suggest that mountain biking activities around Aspen are limited, given the prevalence of wilderness designations. Yet Aspen played a supporting role in the development of mountain biking when cyclists from Crested Butte rode from that town to Aspen in 1976 on prototype mountain bikes (*see* page 215).

Extensive mountain bike trails exist on Smuggler Mountain, in the lower Hunter Creek Valley, and on Red Mountain, all along the northern side of Aspen. To the south, ambitious riders can pedal up the ski area and ride 10 miles south to Taylor Pass. Several passes lead through the Elk Mountains to Crested Butte. Trails also exist in and around Snowmass Village and on Buttermilk, Aspen Highlands, and Snowmass ski areas. Some trails are closed in early summer to protect elk calving habitat; check with Forest Service offices for details.

For more information: Aspen Ranger District, White River National Forest, 806 West Hallam, Aspen, CO 81611. Phone (970) 925-3445.

LINCOLN CREEK ROAD TO RUBY

[Fig. 30(1)] On this ride bicyclists can get a taste of a high mountain valley without having to work especially hard to get there, thanks to the relatively high-altitude starting point. The first 7 miles of the ride are on a dirt road that sees a fair bit of vehicular traffic and includes a couple of short, steep climbs. The route ascends through lodgepole pine forest and passes close to narrow grottos where Lincoln Creek has cut a deep, narrow gorge into the bedrock.

After passing Grizzly Reservoir the route becomes a little rockier as it traverses open wet meadows. The old mining camp of Ruby, at the head of the valley, contains several private homes, so stay on the road. At its peak in the late 1890s, Ruby was home to about 300 miners. The task of moving gold and silver ore from the remote camp was very difficult, however. Before the Lincoln Creek Road was built, ore was packed by burro over the red-tinged hill on the eastern side of the valley to smelters near Leadville. Look for faint signs of the old burro trail near the base of the peak, which gets its coloration from iron ore in the rock.

Directions: From Aspen, drive east on CO 82 approximately 8 miles to Lincoln Creek Road (Forest Road 106). You may begin to ride here, or drive 7 miles to Grizzly Reservoir and ride from there.

Closest town: Aspen, 8 miles west.

Dates: The Lincoln Creek Road may be closed to motorized traffic until early summer, but it can be bicycled then. CO 82 is closed 4 miles east of Aspen from the first snows of Oct. until Memorial Day.

Trail: 22 miles round-trip.

Elevation: Change of 1,840 feet.

Degree of difficulty: Moderate.

Surface: Roughly graded Forest Service road to Grizzly Reservoir; rough double-track from there to Ruby.

SMUGGLER MOUNTAIN TO HUNTER CREEK LOOP

[Fig. 28(3)] Smuggler Mountain is Aspen's year-round Stairmaster. Hikers, bikers, and dog walkers flock to the south-facing Smuggler Mountain Road for exercise even in the dead of winter. The climb up the face of this ridge on the northeastern edge of town is arduous, but it earns a cyclist entry into the hanging valley of Hunter Creek and the many single- and double-track trails there.

Directions: Smuggler Mountain Road begins on Park Circle, at the northeastern edge of town. Ride up the road, which immediately turns to dirt, for 1 mile. The road switchbacks to the right into a small grove of aspen trees and arrives at a multiple intersection. Take the first left. Follow this down into the Hunter Creek valley and continue upstream along the valley floor for 1 mile to an old wooden bridge across Hunter Creek.

The Hunter-Frying Pan Wilderness boundary is about 0.5 mile upstream from this bridge. At the bridge you may take a sharp left onto a single-track trail, or cross Hunter Creek and pick up a double-track on the north side of the stream. If you cross, follow the double-track for 1 mile past several collapsing buildings, then turn left toward the 10th Mountain Bridge. Cross the creek again and reconnect with the single-track. Turn right and follow the trail along the south side of the creek down

Skiing Aspen

Aspen offers excellent skiing opportunities with four ski mountains situated closely together. Aspen Mountain, Aspen Highlands, and Snowmass average 300 inches of snowfall per year, while Buttermilk averages around 200 inches.

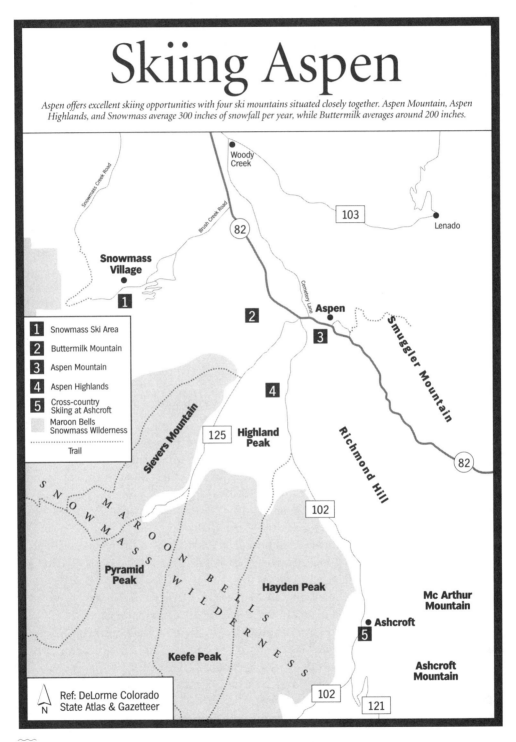

Woody Creek

103

Lenado

Snowmass Creek Road

Brush Creek Road

82

Snowmass Village

1

Cemetery Lane

Aspen

2

3

Smuggler Mountain

Legend:
1 Snowmass Ski Area
2 Buttermilk Mountain
3 Aspen Mountain
4 Aspen Highlands
5 Cross-country Skiing at Ashcroft
  Maroon Bells Snowmass Wilderness
  Trail

4

Sievers Mountain

125 Highland Peak

Richmond Hill

82

102

SNOWMASS MAROON BELLS WILDERNESS

Pyramid Peak

Hayden Peak

Mc Arthur Mountain

Ashcroft

5

Keefe Peak

Ashcroft Mountain

102

121

N Ref: DeLorme Colorado State Atlas & Gazetteer

across a second footbridge. After another 75 yards you will arrive at Hunter Creek Road. Turn left, downhill, and follow this to a stop sign. Turn left again on Red Mountain Road. Follow this back to town.

Trail: 4.5-mile loop.

Elevation: Change of 900 feet.

Degree of difficulty: Strenuous.

Surface: Graded road, single-track and double-track trail, some difficult rocky sections, paved road.

RIO GRANDE TRAIL

[Fig. 28(2)] This is a great ride for beginning bicyclists or people riding with small children. This trail, paved for the first 1.5 miles, follows the old railroad bed of the Denver and Rio Grande along the Roaring Fork River. It is popular with walkers and in-line skaters as well as cyclists, so beware of traffic, particularly on blind corners.

Directions: From downtown Aspen, go downhill (north) on Mill Street to Puppy Smith Street (a left-hand turn at the stop sign below the Hotel Jerome). Turn left; after 25 yards look for the paved Rio Grand Trail angling off to the right.

Trail: 1.5 miles to Cemetery Lane; 5 miles to the Upper Woody Creek Bridge on Upper River Road, where the trail ends.

Elevation: Descent of 600 feet from Aspen to the Upper Woody Creek Bridge.

Degree of difficulty: Easy.

Surface: Paved and 10 feet wide for the first 1.5 miles. After the trail crosses Cemetery Lane it is wide dirt. The last several hundred yards to Upper River Road are a descent on a loose single-track.

SKIING ASPEN

[Fig. 31] Years after encountering Aspen, Frield Pfeiffer, an Austrian who founded the Aspen Ski School in 1947, recalled, "It was love at first sight. I was convinced that Aspen was made with skiers in mind, and that something should be done about it."

Aspen is one of the world's storied ski areas, its name recognition on par with Gstaad, St. Moritz, and Chamonix. Skiing began in the region in the mid-1930s; early pioneers envisioned building a ski area not at Aspen, but 10 miles south, on the flanks of Hayden Peak above Ashcroft.

Before World War II, Olympic bobsled champion Billy Fiske teamed up with two partners to open the 16-bed Highland Bavarian Lodge at the northern toe of 13,561-foot Hayden Peak, the first development in a European-style ski village conceived for the remote Castle Creek Valley south of Aspen. The lodge owners summoned Italian mountaineer Gunther Lange and Swiss skier Andre Roch to spend the winter of 1936 skiing the region and planning the resort.

Roch proposed lodging for 2,000 skiers and a two-stage tram rising 3,300 feet. But war intervened. Fiske was killed, and by 1947 the rival Aspen Skiing Corporation (now the Aspen Skiing Company) had installed its first lifts on Aspen Mountain. The momentum for building on Hayden faded, and in 1964 the peak was included in the Maroon Bells-Snowmass Wilderness Area, precluding any development.

Aspen's ski areas were part of a broader vision of Walter Paepcke. Nowhere else in Colorado are four ski mountains situated so close to each other. Summit County, home to Keystone, Breckenridge, Arapahoe Basin, and Copper Mountain, is the only other region with similar offerings. Aspen, because of its greater distance from Denver, attracts few Front Range skiers, who prefer to visit resorts closer to home. Instead, Aspen and Snowmass appeal to out-of-state and international visitors.

All of the ski areas average about 300 inches of natural snowfall annually, except for Buttermilk, which gets about 200 inches.

For more information: Aspen Skiing Company, Box 1248, Aspen, CO 81612. Phone (970) 925-1220.

ASPEN MOUNTAIN

[Fig. 31(3)] Called "Ajax" by locals, after a silver mine located near the top, Aspen Mountain is riddled with the relics of the silver boom. Much of the inside of the mountain was hollowed out by miners; at one point approximately 2,000 people lived in Tourtelotte Park, now an open bowl near the summit.

The ski area is not particularly large—only 675 acres—but it is challenging. There are no "green," or easiest, slopes on Aspen Mountain. Veteran skiers know many hidden lines and powder shots in the trees. Snowcat skiing is available on wild, ungroomed slopes south of the summit.

Aspen Mountain's vertical drop is 3,267 feet; the timbered summit is at 11,212 feet.

Directions: Aspen Mountain lies immediately south of the town of Aspen. Walk to the Silver Queen gondola at the intersection of Hunter and Durant Streets, or to Lift 1A, at the southern end of Monarch Street.

Activities: Skiing and ski lessons only; snowboarding is prohibited. Foot passengers are permitted on the gondola, which terminates at the Sundeck restaurant.

Facilities: On-mountain restaurants.

Dates: Generally open from Thanksgiving to Easter.

Fees: There is a fee to ride the lifts and a fee to park.

Closest town: Aspen.

For more information: Aspen Skiing Company, Box 1248, Aspen, CO 81612. Phone (970) 925-1220.

ASPEN HIGHLANDS

[Fig. 31(4)] Highlands is draped like a blanket along the south-running spine of the Highlands Peak. Steep, expert trails fall off to the east and west, while intermediate blue runs are concentrated along the spine itself.

The enormous Highlands Bowl is situated to the south of the main ski area. Ski area officials have begun to open portions of the bowl to expert skiers who don't mind hiking for 15 or 20 minutes. Like all expert terrain, however, these trails may be closed by avalanche hazards.

Highlands contains 651 acres of skiable terrain. The Loge Peak summit is at 11,675 feet, and the vertical drop totals 3,635 feet.

Directions: From Aspen, drive west on CO 82 0.5 mile to the second stoplight. Turn left (south) on Maroon Creek Road. Drive 1 mile to Aspen Highlands, located on the left. Because parking is limited, skiers and snowboarders are encouraged to take the free bus from Ruby Park bus station, on Durant Avenue in downtown Aspen.

Activities: Skiing, snowboarding, lessons.

Facilities: On-mountain restaurants, base village.

Dates: Generally early Dec. to early Apr.

Fees: There is a fee to use the lifts and a fee to park.

Closest town: Aspen, 2 miles northwest.

For more information: Aspen Skiing Company, Box 1248, Aspen, CO 81612. Phone (970) 925-1220.

BUTTERMILK

[Fig. 31(2)] The smallest of the four ski areas, Buttermilk is the most laid back. It's a place where beginners congregate, practicing their downhill, telemark, and snowboard technique on the open, gentle slopes of West Buttermilk and Main Buttermilk. Tiehack, the eastern flank, is steeper and more challenging.

Buttermilk encompasses 410 acres of terrain, 74 percent of which is rated "easiest" (green) or "more difficult" (blue). The vertical drop is 2,030 feet.

Directions: From Aspen, drive west on CO 82 to the Buttermilk parking lot, a left-hand (south) turn. Skiers and snowboarders are encouraged to take the free bus from Ruby Park bus station, on Durant Avenue in downtown Aspen.

Activities: Skiing, snowboarding, lessons.

Facilities: On-mountain restaurant and base lodge.

Dates: Generally early Dec. to early Apr.

Fees: There is a fee to use the lifts.

Closest town: Aspen, 3 miles east.

For more information: Aspen Skiing Company, Box 1248, Aspen, CO 81612. Phone (970) 925-1220.

SNOWMASS

[Fig. 31(1)] The second largest ski area in Colorado (after Vail), Snowmass sprawls across 3,010 acres. It can feel like five ski areas, rather than one. On the eastern edge is the Elk Camp area, with the most gentle slopes. Big Burn and Sam's Knob, in the middle of the mountain, are intermediate and expert areas with steep, groomed slopes and fast chairs. To the far west is Campground, a remote region with few crowds and long, deep bump runs. The newest addition, the Cirque, reaches up onto the alpine tundra at the very top of the ski area; with its wide-open, ungroomed terrain it feels like a little piece of Europe.

Snowmass has the greatest lift-served vertical drop of any ski area in the country, dropping 4,406 feet from the 12,510-foot summit to the base.

Directions: From Aspen, take CO 82 west 4 miles to Brush Creek Road, a left-hand (south) turn at a stoplight. Turn onto Brush Creek Road and drive 5 miles to Snowmass Village. During the winter, free parking and shuttle bus service is available at the Rodeo Intercept parking lot, 2 miles from the village on Brush Creek Road. Skiers and snowboarders are encouraged to take the free bus from Ruby Park bus station, on Durant Avenue in downtown Aspen. This bus goes directly from Aspen to the north end of the Snowmass Village Mall.

Activities: Skiing, snowboarding, lessons.

Facilities: On-mountain restaurants, base village.

Dates: Generally Thanksgiving to Easter.

Fees: There is a fee to use the lifts and a fee to park in Snowmass Village.

Closest town: Snowmass Village, located at the base of the ski area.

For more information: Aspen Skiing Company, Box 1248, Aspen, CO 81612. Phone (970) 925-1220.

CROSS-COUNTRY SKIING AT ASHCROFT

[Fig. 31(5)] Around the old mining town of Ashcroft, 38 kilometers of groomed cross-country ski trails amble through aspen forests, along the spruce-shaded banks of Castle Creek, and across broad, open meadows, all below the towering summit of the Elk Mountains. The skiing is dramatic and beautiful.

Ashcroft is a colder, more wintery place than Aspen. It gets snow sooner, holds it longer, and carries a bit more bite in the air, given its elevation of 9,600 feet. Skiing here conveys a sense of being in the heart of the mountains, a point emphasized by the jagged, 13,000-foot peaks rising to the south and the avalanche paths sweeping across the surrounding ridges.

Two rustic, unmanned cabins along the trails are open to Ashcroft skiers. Ski area staff keep fires burning in the woodstoves and make sure the cabins are stocked with free hot drinks. Arrival at such a place, nestled in the snowy woods, can feel like something out of a fairy tale.

A popular lunch and dinner restaurant, the Pine Creek Cookhouse, is located in the middle of the ski area and accessible only on skis or by a horse-drawn sleigh operated by the Cookhouse. Reservations are necessary and should be made well in advance.

Although the ski area is privately operated and charges a fee, the unplowed portion of Castle Creek Road through the ski area toward Pearl Pass and Taylor Pass is open to the public at no charge. Avalanche danger may close portions of the road and ski area.

Directions: From Aspen, drive west on CO 82 to the second stoplight (Maroon Creek Road). Turn left (south), then immediately turn left (east) again, onto Castle Creek Road. Drive 10 miles to the parking lot at Ashcroft. Ski area tickets may be purchased at the King Cabin, on the left at the end of the plowed portion of the road.

Activities: Cross-country skiing, sleigh rides and guided evening ski tours to the Pine Creek Cookhouse.

Facilities: 38 kilometers of groomed tracks, ski and boot rental, two warming huts, Pine Creek Cookhouse.

Dates: Open Thanksgiving to Easter, weather permitting.

Fees: There is a fee to ski, and an additional fee for a guided evening tour to the Cookhouse or to take the sleigh to the Cookhouse.

Closest town: Aspen, 11 miles north.

For more information: Ashcroft Ski Touring, 312-H Aspen Airport Business Center, Aspen, CO 81612. Phone (970) 925-1971. For reservations at Pine Creek Cookhouse, phone (970) 925-1044.

10TH MOUNTAIN AND BRAUN HUT SYSTEMS

Aspen anchors the southwestern corner of the 10th Mountain Trail hut system, a legacy of the 10th Mountain Division of the United States Army, which trained during World War II at Camp Hale north of Leadville (*see* page xx for details on the hut system and the 10th Mountain Division).

An older line of huts dating back to the 1950s and 1960s, the Braun hut system, stretches south through the Elk Mountains to Crested Butte. The trip to Crested Butte across 12,700-foot Pearl Pass generally takes two to three days.

Smaller and more rustic than the huts on the 10th Mountain Trail, the Braun huts demand more of skiers. The half-dozen Braun huts are located in hazardous terrain; routes to and from them cross avalanches' paths and should not be attempted without a guide or strong backcountry winter mountaineering skills.

The huts vary in size, sleeping between 6 and 14 people. They come equipped with wood and gas stoves and fuel, cooking supplies, mattresses, and pillows. Skiers carry their own food and sleeping bags.

Huts on the Braun system are rented on a reservation basis in their entirety to a single group. On the 10th Mountain Trail, skiers may rent individual beds. There are no hut keepers on either hut system.

Dates: Generally open from the end of Nov. to the beginning of May, weather permitting.

Fees: There is a fee to rent the huts.

Closest town: Aspen on the northern end of the system, 15 miles from the trailhead; Crested Butte on the southern end, 6 miles from the trailhead.

For more information: 10th Mountain Trail Association, 1080 Ute Avenue, Aspen, CO 81611. Phone (970) 925-5775.

King Bolete Mushrooms

Many edible varieties of mushrooms are found in Colorado's forests, including puffballs (*Lycoperdaceae*), morels (*Morchellaceae*), chanterelles (*Cantharellaceae*), and boletes (*Boletus*). Mushroom hunters know their secret spots and guard them carefully.

The king bolete (*Boletus edulis*) is among the most prized. This fat, fleshy mushroom is common in gourmet restaurants: It is the same fungus as Italy's *porcini* mushroom, and France's *cepe*. Many varieties of *Boletus* grow in Colorado's forests, generally in the subalpine and montane region, typically in aspen or conifer forests.

Although boletes are fairly easy to recognize, never harvest or eat wild mushrooms without the guidance of an experienced picker.

Buena Vista Area

The midvalley town of Buena Vista was, like Salida to the south, an outgrowth of development at Leadville. Buena Vista, lying on the Denver and Rio Grande railway route to the mining boom town at the head of the Arkansas River, was not incorporated until 1879, after Leadville's major silver rush was well underway.

Salida literally was created by the Denver and Rio Grande, which had formed Durango and Alamosa the same way—by purchasing settlers' lands along the tracks and platting a town site. The D&RG arrived in Leadville in 1880, putting an end to enormous profiteering. Up to the time of the train's arrival, freight rates to carry goods between Denver and Leadville had been as high as those from New York to San Francisco around Cape Horn.

Buena Vista (which means "good view" in Spanish and it is purposely mispronounced by locals as Be-yoon-ah Vista) is built on the eroded Miocene-Pliocene sediments (deposited during the erosion associated with that regional uplift) and Pleistocene gravel deposits from the surrounding, glaciated peaks. Old Precambrian granite and volcanic debris are interspersed among the hills east of town, across the Arkansas River.

KING BOLETE MUSHROOM
(Boletus edulis)

Rail service continued up the Arkansas Valley from Cañon City and over Tennessee Pass to Gypsum until the early 1990s. Buena Vista and Salida are now being discovered by urban refugees and outdoor enthusiasts who like the banana-belt climate of the dry, middle Arkansas Valley and the close proximity of the Collegiate Peaks and Mosquito Range. Despite new development, much of the middle valley remains bucolic, full of hay meadows, cattle, and horses.

MISSOURI GULCH TO MOUNT BELFORD

[Fig. 30(3)] The 14,000-foot peaks in the Collegiate Peaks Wilderness (*see* page 184) are wide and relatively gentle, which means their summits generally can be reached on nontechnical routes. They're good peaks for beginners or families who want to tackle the high summits. This route up 14,197-foot Mount Belford has an intermediate achievement at 13,200 feet, Elkhead Pass, for those who want a goal but aren't inclined to seek the summit.

The trail climbs south from Clear Creek, a valley that hosted hundreds of mining claims and four mining towns during the 1880s: Vicksburg, Rockdale, Winfield, and Turret. Remains of all four can still be found along the creek.

This route climbs steeply up 10 switchbacks into a high, hanging valley between Missouri Mountain (14,067 feet) and Mount Belford. Elkhead Pass lies between these two peaks. Atop the switchbacks the trail grade eases as the route ascends through a grove of aspen trees. After a total distance of about 1.5 miles, a stream comes in from the left, draining off a gulch on the north side of Mount Belford. Continue up the valley, which is open and full of alpine wildflowers during the summer. Where the trail forks south toward Missouri Mountain, bear east to Elkhead Pass 0.5 mile to the southeast. If you wish to continue to the summit of Belford, climb east, then north up the ridge. The summit is about 1 mile from the pass.

Mount Belford is named for James B. Belford, Colorado's first U.S. congressman following the state's admission to the Union in 1876. Red-haired and a fiery orator, Belford argued vigorously for miners' interests. The peak named in his honor has a reddish outcropping near its summit, which may be why it was chosen. Miners worked throughout the Missouri Gulch valley and up to the summits of the surrounding peaks; look for their old prospects, exploratory mines that are marked by the lighter, fan-shaped tailings piles below their mouths.

Directions: Two miles south of Granite on US 24, turn west on Forest Road 390 (Clear Creek Canyon Road). After 8 miles, look for a sign marking "Missouri Trail Parking" on the south side of the road. Park here, cross the creek, and begin climbing the trail.

Trail: 9 miles round-trip to Elkhead Pass; 11 miles round-trip to Mount Belford.

Summer Skiing

Around Memorial Day, motorists on US 40 or CO 82 might be surprised to find people hitchhiking while carrying skis on their shoulders. Skiing into June is possible most years at many high altitude locations. Popular road-accessed areas include Independence Pass and Berthoud Pass. Skiers park in the early morning at the pass summits, hike out the ridges to a preferred bowl, ski to the road and hitchhike up. Sun usually warms the snow to the point where avalanches are a hazard by mid- to late morning, making this a sport for early risers.

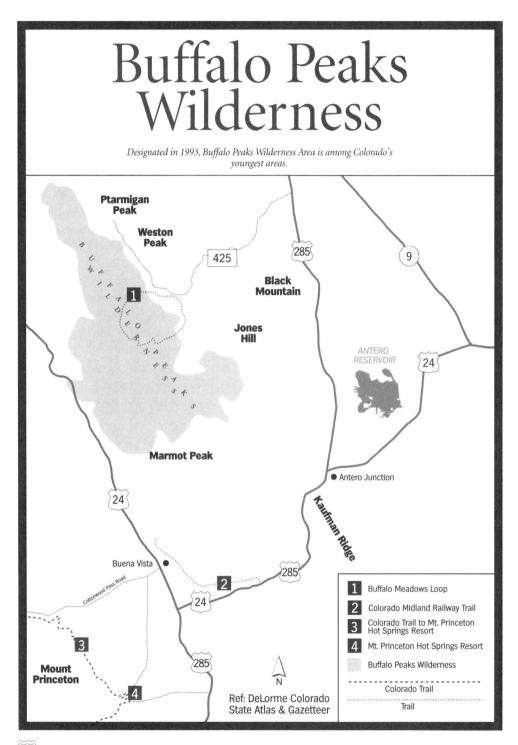

Buffalo Peaks Wilderness

Designated in 1993, Buffalo Peaks Wilderness Area is among Colorado's youngest areas.

Ptarmigan Peak

Weston Peak

425

285

9

Black Mountain

B U F F A L O R N P E A K S

1

Jones Hill

ANTERO RESERVOIR

24

Marmot Peak

Antero Junction

24

Kaufman Ridge

Buena Vista

Cottonwood Pass Road

2

285

24

3

285

Mount Princeton

4

N

Ref: DeLorme Colorado State Atlas & Gazetteer

1	Buffalo Meadows Loop
2	Colorado Midland Railway Trail
3	Colorado Trail to Mt. Princeton Hot Springs Resort
4	Mt. Princeton Hot Springs Resort
	Buffalo Peaks Wilderness
- - - -	Colorado Trail
. . . .	Trail

Elevation: Change of 3,600 feet to Elkhead Pass; change of 4,500 feet to Mount Belford.

Degree of difficulty: Moderate to Elkhead Pass, strenuous to Mount Belford.

Surface: Dirt trail; tundra and rocks above Elkhead Pass.

BUFFALO PEAKS WILDERNESS

[Fig. 32] Lacking Fourteeners, glaciated valleys, and significant lakes, Buffalo Peaks Wilderness (43,410 acres) is a relatively lightly trodden wilderness area where visitors can find not only solitude, but also a substantial resident bighorn sheep herd, as well as deer and elk in the headwaters of the South Platte River. The southwestern slopes of the wilderness area host a piñon-pine ecosystem; as you climb into the wilderness you encounter montane and aspen forests, numerous large, open alpine meadows, extensive beaver dams and ponds, and, near timberline on the southern slopes of the peaks, stands of bristlecone pine.

Buffalo Peaks is among Colorado's youngest wilderness areas, designated in 1993. It encompasses East Buffalo and West Buffalo peaks; these are the southernmost summits of the Mosquito Range, which divides the Upper Arkansas Valley on the west from South Park on the east. Hikers who scramble to the summits (there are no defined trails on the open peaks) earn views of South Park to the east, the Arkansas Valley and Collegiate Peaks to the west, the Sangre de Cristo Mountains to the south, and the rest of the Mosquito Range running up to the north.

Activities: Hiking, fishing, backpacking, mountaineering.

Closest town: Buena Vista is 8 miles south of the southwest corner of the wilderness area. Fairplay is about 20 miles northeast. Several trailheads can be reached from either side.

For more information: For the western side, contact: Leadville Ranger District, San Isabel National Forest, 2015 North Poplar, Leadville, CO 80461. Phone (719) 486-0749. For the eastern side: South Park Ranger District, Pike National Forest, P.O. Box 219, Fairplay, CO 80440. Phone (719) 836-2031.

BUFFALO MEADOWS LOOP

[Fig. 32(1)] This loop trail, which traverses along two creeks and through long, ranging meadows and conifer stands, can be undertaken as a long day hike or an overnight backpacking trip. The terrain is gentle and rolling. The Buffalo Meadows lie halfway along the loop. Many camping opportunities exist here, and the adventurous can find their way up the open slopes of 13,326-foot West Buffalo Peak from the meadows.

Directions: From Buena Vista, drive south 2 miles on US 24 to the junction with US 285; turn left (east) on US 285. Drive approximately 20 miles east over Trout Creek Pass to Antero Junction; bear left here on US 285. Drive north about 30 miles to Weston Pass Road (Park County Road 5). Turn left, west, on Weston Pass Road. After 7 miles, bear right at a fork; in approximately 3 miles, cross a cattle guard marking the Pike National Forest Boundary. Park immediately past the cattle guard on the left at the sign for the South Fork of the South Platte River.

If you wish to hike the loop, you may proceed right up Rich Creek or left up Rough and Tumbling Creek.

Trail: 12-mile loop.
Elevation: Change of 1,500 feet.
Degree of difficulty: Easy.
Surface: Dirt.

MOUNTAIN BIKING

Buena Vista and the middle Arkansas Valley are gaining recognition as an up-and-coming mountain biking region in Colorado. The Arkansas Valley, which lies in the rain shadow of the Collegiate Peaks, is relatively snow-free for much of the year. Consequently, trails in the valley and at lower elevations among the hills may be ridden when neighboring valleys (such as the Gunnison Valley around Crested Butte) are still snowed in.

COLORADO MIDLAND RAILWAY TRAIL

[Fig. 32(2)] The former Midland Railway roadbed immediately east of Buena Vista is a rails-to-trails conversion that has produced a 5-mile path. There are four challenging but short detours on the route where the trail crosses sandy gullies that were once spanned by railroad trestles.

The route passes through a dry, piñon-juniper and ponderosa landscape from west to east. On the return ride you're rewarded with a fast downhill grade and spectacular views across the irrigated fields of the Arkansas Valley to the big-chested summits of six Fourteeners: Mount Harvard (14,420 feet), Mount Columbia (14,073 feet), Mount Yale (14,196 feet), Mount Princeton (14,197 feet), Mount Antero (14,269 feet), and Mount Shavano (14,229 feet). Notice the classic, U-shaped, glaciated tributary valleys that drain into the Arkansas Valley. Erosion from the Sawatch Range carried massive quantities of rock into the Arkansas (the northern extension of the Rio Grande Rift), filling it and giving it today's flat floor. Although glaciers extended into and across the Arkansas Valley from the surrounding mountains, the valley itself was not glaciated.

Along this route look for narrow-leaved yucca (*Yucca glauca*), which is common on dry, desert-like slopes in the foothills of the Rockies from Alberta to New Mexico. Another species you may see here, and on dry slopes along the Arkansas, is Rocky Mountain bee-plant, also called spider flower (*Cleome serrulata*). This is a showy, leggy flower that grows on dry, sandy, often disturbed sites. It is easily picked out because its small, reddish-fuchsia flowers grow in long, fist-like clusters that wave in the breeze. It is similar in appearance to fireweed (*Epilobium angustifolium*), which also has great, showy pink or purplish blooms. Fireweed, which springs from rhizomes, is a rapid colonizer of disturbed areas and is often apparent along roadsides or in recently burned areas. Fireweed flowers grow in tall, somewhat pointed racemes (clusters), with the lowest flowers blooming first.

The old railroad bed runs along, and sometimes through, crumbly Precambrian granite, the core of the Mosquito Range, which is the eastern half of the faulted anticline that includes the Sawatch Range.

Directions: On US 24, turn east at the downtown stoplight into Buena Vista's old downtown. Follow the main street east about 0.5 mile to Buena Vista River Park, beside the Arkansas River. Park beside the public toilets. Ride across the footbridge to the Whipple Trail. Bear right at a fork and follow the winding trail up onto the plateau above the river, a moderate climb of approximately 200 feet. The Whipple Trail joins the old railroad bed where the Buena Vista depot stood; the location is marked by an interpretive plaque.

Ride south (right) on Chaffee County Road 304 for 2 miles to another parking area and trail sign. Cross the road and continue on the railway grade to the intersection with Shields Gulch Road (Chaffee County Road 315). Turn around and return the same way.

Trail: Graded road, old railroad bed, and some single-track.

Elevation: Gain of 400 feet.

Degree of difficulty: Easy.

Surface: Dirt, sand, some loose rock.

COLORADO TRAIL TO MOUNT PRINCETON HOT SPRINGS RESORT

[Fig. 32(3)] This ride can be undertaken as a challenging out-and-back, or as a longer loop that includes about 10 miles of dirt and paved roads. The reward, of course, is a dip in the Mount Princeton Hot Springs Resort after a grinding ascent and then a rolling ride along the Colorado Trail.

The route climbs 1,300 feet in the first 3 miles, which is the primary reason this trail is rated strenuous; the climbing is a sustained effort.

After about 2 miles you will reach a fork; bear right here. After another 1 mile, notice radio towers on your right. The correct route leads into the woods; watch for small wooden signs marking the Colorado Trail on the left where the main road turns to the right. Take the turnoff toward the Colorado Trail and climb until you intersect the trail, about 0.25 mile from the road. At the Colorado Trail, turn left (south). Follow this for 5.5 miles to Chaffee County 322, a dirt road, which leads downhill to Chaffee County 321, a paved road. Follow this to the Mount Princeton Hot Springs Resort.

Directions: From Buena Vista, drive west on Cottonwood Pass Road (Chaffee County Road 306). After 5.5 miles, turn left (south) onto Chaffee County 342 and then almost immediately right onto Chaffee County 345. Park here and begin riding up Chaffee County 345, a moderately rough jeep road.

If you wish, return the way you came. Or, follow Chaffee County 321 downhill to Cottonwood Pass Road, then ride up this road back to your car to close the loop.

Continental Divide/Monarch Crest Trail

Monarch Crest trail is a popular route for serious bicyclists. The route is 34 miles long and takes 6 to 10 hours to complete.

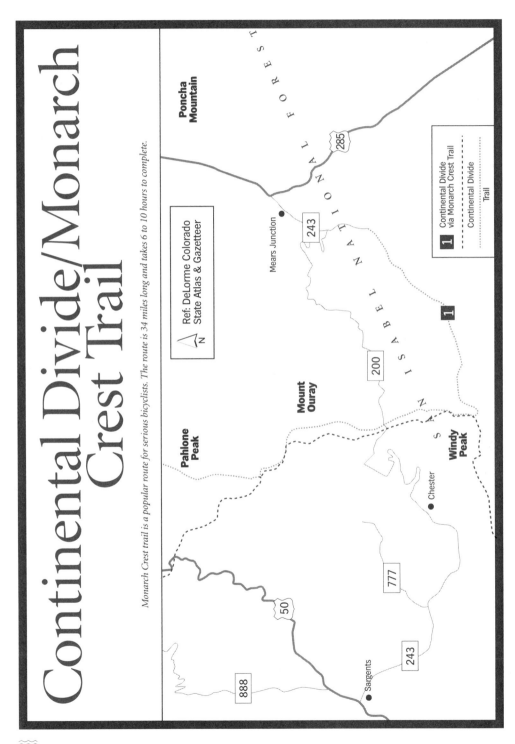

Ref: DeLorme Colorado
State Atlas & Gazetteer

N

Poncha Mountain

Mears Junction

285

243

200

1

Pahlone Peak

Mount Ouray

Windy Peak

Chester

Sargents

888

50

777

243

ISABEL NATIONAL FOREST

1 Continental Divide
via Monarch Crest Trail

- - - Continental Divide

········· Continental Divide
Trail

Trail: 17 miles out-and-back or 21 miles as a loop.

Elevation: Gain of 1,760 feet.

Degree of difficulty: Strenuous.

Surface: Jeep road and single-track. Paved sections if you take the longer loop.

MOUNT PRINCETON HOT SPRINGS RESORT

[Fig. 32(4)] The hot springs on the eastern flank of Mount Princeton at 10,160 feet, are the result of hot water rising along the fault separating the Arkansas Valley from the uplifted core of the Sawatch Range. These springs, which run at a very hot 132 degrees Fahrenheit, carry a mineral called kaolinite. Chalk Creek, south and east of Mount Princeton, gets its name from this deposit, although it is a misnomer, since chalk is a very different mineral from kaolinite. Several natural springs can be found along Chalk Creek.

Directions: From US 285 at Nathrop, turn west on CO 162 and drive 5 miles.

Activities: Swimming and soaking in hot springs, hiking nearby trails.

Facilities: Public pools, restaurant, phone, locker rooms, picnic area.

Dates: Open year-round.

Fees: There is a fee to use the springs.

Closest town: Buena Vista, 18 miles northeast.

For more information: Mount Princeton Hot Springs Resort, County Road 162, Nathrop, CO 81236. Phone (719) 395-2561.

CONTINENTAL DIVIDE VIA MONARCH CREST TRAIL

[Fig. 33] Monarch Crest is considered by some bicyclists to be one of the classic high single-track routes in Colorado. This ride entails a long and demanding day and requires either two vehicles (for a shuttle), or hiring someone to drop you off.

The route is 34 miles long and takes 6 to 10 hours to complete. Portions of the route are on the Colorado and Continental Divide trails. The first 9 miles are very open and exposed, so this is not a trip to try if the weather looks questionable. Also, snow can linger into midsummer, depending on the severity of the previous winter. For all that, however, Monarch Crest is literally a ride along the Continental Divide in the Sawatch Range. Meadows of wildflowers, sweeping vistas, and endless pedaling characterize this very memorable journey.

On the Continental Divide Trail, climb for about 1 mile to a sign that reads "North Fooses Trail/South Arkansas River 7 Miles." Stay to the right on a jeep road and ride toward Marshall Pass. After 0.5 mile, turn right onto a single track where there's a CDT sign and the notation "Marshall Pass — 9 miles."

In 2 miles you reach the trail's high point of 12,145 feet on the southern side of 12,218-foot Mount Peck. In another 2 miles you will come to a sign for "South Fooses Creek Trail." This is the Colorado Trail, which joins the CDT here. Stay to the right. Two miles farther along you pass Green Creek Trail to your left; again, stay right. In another mile the Little Cochetopa Trail turns down to the left; avoid it, too. Farther down the Colorado Trail, the Agate Creek Trail leads west toward Sargents.

Doc Holliday

John Henry Holliday died of tuberculosis in Glenwood Springs after a long and storied career as a gambler and gunman. He had become a sometime companion of lawman Wyatt Earp in Dodge City, Kansas, evidently by saving Earp's life. As a consequence, Holliday seemed to work both sides of the law.

Born in Griffin, Georgia in 1851, Doc traveled around Colorado and New Mexico in the late 1870s and 1880s, repeatedly getting into trouble. He is known to have shot at least seven men and been suspected in several stage robberies, but he was always acquitted or freed, often with Earp's help. Holliday's most famous shootout was at the O.K. Corral in Tombstone, Arizona Territory, in 1881, where he helped Wyatt and Virgil Earp (the town marshal) in a gun battle with Ike and Billy Clanton and Tom and Frank McLaury, cattle rustlers. Holliday killed Tom McLaury, while the Earps did in Billy Clanton and Frank McLaury.

Holliday is portrayed by historians as wild and fearless in battle, perhaps because he would have preferred to have died by the gun than from tuberculosis. In the end, however, it was the disease that killed him, at the age of 36 in 1887. He is buried in Glenwood Springs.

Stay on the Colorado Trail.

The descent along the Colorado Trail from the Green Creek Trail turnoff is about 3.5 miles. At Marshall Pass you will encounter County Road 200, which is the old Denver and Rio Grande railroad bed over the pass. You may turn left here and descend to US 285 at this point, shortening the trip by about 8 miles. Otherwise, stay on the Colorado Trail for another 2.5 miles to the junction with the Rainbow Trail, a double-track. Turn left (east). The route becomes a single-track that crosses an old rockslide (you may choose to dismount for this).

The trail leads into Forest Road 201 (Silver Creek Road). Follow this to Shirley (from the junction of the CDT and the Rainbow Trail the total distance to Shirley is about 12 miles). At Shirley (a junction of several trails) follow Forest Road 243 down Poncha Creek to US 285. Cross the road and coast downhill to Poncha Springs.

Directions: Start in Poncha Springs. Leave one car here and drive west on US 50 to Monarch Pass, about 17 miles. Park in the Aerial Tramway and Monarch Crest parking lot. Ride up the jeep trail behind the tram building. Look for a Crest Trail sign bearing a Continental Divide Trail (CDT) emblem immediately on your right. You are now on the Continental Divide Trail.

For more information: Vehicle shuttles may be arranged with some local bicycle shops. Contact the Salida Chamber of Commerce, 406 West Highway 50, Salida, CO 81201. Phone (719) 539-2068.

Trail: 34-mile loop requiring vehicle shuttle.

Elevation: Gain of about 1,300 feet; loss of about 4,900 feet.

Degree of difficulty: Strenuous.

Surface: Single track, jeep road, paved road.

Bristlecone and Limber Pine

Bristlecone pine (*Pinus aristata*) and limber pine (*Pinus flexilis*) are often confused. They are quite distinctive in appearance from other pines in Colorado. Both species grow as short, gnarled trees, live as long as a 1,000 years but don't rise above a maximum height of 50 feet, and prefer rocky knobs and outcroppings along ridges and at timberline. Little else grows around the widely spaced trees except lichens; three-fourths of the surrounding terrain typically is exposed rock.

Limber pines can be identified by their longer needles (2 to 3 inches, versus 1 to 1.5 inches for bristlecone), and by their cones. Bristlecones have a sharp, upward-pointing spine at the end of each cone scale.

Limber and bristlecone pines are found most abundantly in the northern and eastern quadrant of Colorado's mountains, especially in the Front Range. However, colonies are located on the east side of Independence Pass in the Collegiate Peaks and the eastern side of the Sangre de Cristo Mountains, as well as in the Mosquito Range.

Although the two species look similar and prefer the same habitat, they are propagated in very different ways. Limber pines produce heavy nuts that are generally carried to new sites by Clark's nutcrackers and other birds. Bristlecones produce small, papery seeds disseminated upon the wind.

RAFTING AND KAYAKING THE ARKANSAS RIVER

The 148-mile Arkansas Headwaters Recreation Area stretches from Leadville to Pueblo. The portion between Granite and Salida is the most exciting, and most popular river rafting and kayaking resource in Colorado. Numerous outfitters offer day trips on the river, particularly between Buena Vista and Salida. Depending upon flow levels, rapids in this area range in rating from Class II to Class V (intermediate to expert).

Upstream of Buena Vista, in the section of river downstream from Granite, a set of rapids called Pine Creek and The Numbers are rated Class IV to Class VI, meaning they are for expert kayakers and rafters only. Boaters come from around the state and country to pit themselves against the river here.

Commercial day trips run south from Buena Vista through Brown's Canyon, a hot, dry gorge of ancient pink granite, ponderosa pine, and Rocky Mountain bee flower. This can be an extremely popular trip; outfitters will, at times, nearly cover the river with rafts full of paying clients. Consider running the river on a weekday to avoid the biggest crowds.

Much of the Arkansas is bordered by private land, but several public put-ins are maintained here. Locations include Granite, Buena Vista, Fisherman's Bridge, Ruby Mountain, Hecla Junction, Stone Bridge, Big Bend, and Salida.

The Arkansas Headwaters Recreation Area is jointly managed by the U.S. Bureau of Land Management, U.S. Bureau of Reclamation, U.S. Forest Service, Colorado State Parks, and Colorado Division of Wildlife.

For more information: Arkansas Headwaters Recreation Area, PO Box 126, Salida, CO 81201. Phone (719) 536-7789.

Crested Butte Area

[Fig. 34] Like so many other towns in the mountains, Crested Butte got its start in mining. Yet while it looks like the boom towns of Silverton, Aspen, and Telluride, Crested Butte's history has more in common with that of Redstone, Paonia, and Marble, for its fortunes were principally tied not to gold or silver, but to coal.

The town's name came early, when surveyor Ferdinand Hayden climbed Teocali Peak at the head of the East River valley in 1873 and described Gothic Peak and Crested Butte Peak as "crested buttes." A butte is an isolated hill or mountain, usually with steep sides and a flat top, not as wide as a mesa. The "crest" in Mount Crested Butte is the horn, or peak, atop this particular mountain. The only problem with Hayden's terminology is that, in fact, the mountain is not a true butte, which is eroded from sedimentary rock. Both Gothic Peak and Crested Butte are laccoliths—volcanic intrusions between layers of rock that domed the rocks above.

Early placer miners who had worked the surrounding gulches reported the valleys seemed to hold significant coal deposits. This news attracted Howard F. Smith from Leadville, who in 1878 bought all the land at the confluence of Coal Creek and the Slate River. Over time, several large coal mines would be developed in the hills around Crested Butte, producing tens of millions of tons of coal and coke for the hungry smelters of an expanding, mineral-rich state.

But Crested Butte's first buildings were erected to supply the surrounding silver-mining camps of Irwin, Gothic, Pittsburgh, Elko, and several more over the mountain passes, including Schofield, Crystal, Ashcroft, and Aspen, which lie to the north. Aspen was first reached from Leadville not via today's route on CO 82 over Independence Pass. Instead, early settlers and merchants traveled into the Roaring Fork valley from the south. They climbed up the Taylor River and Slate River drainages and over the Elk Mountains, including Taylor Pass, Pearl Pass, and East Maroon Pass, all

DOUGLAS FIR
(Pseudotsuga menziesii)
Named after a 19th century explorer, David Douglas, this tall, straight tree is found from the coast to the mountains.

Spruce-Fir Ecosystems

The mountains surrounding Crested Butte are deeply forested on their flanks. These deep, dark, almost medieval forests are broadly distributed through Colorado's mountains at elevations from 9,000 feet to tree line. They thrive at 10,000 to 11,000 feet and run in nearly undisturbed blankets for miles in the colder, wetter mountains of the central and southwestern portions of the state.

The two dominant tree species, which intermix very well, are Engelmann spruce (*Picea engelmannii*) and subalpine fir (*Abies bifolia*). A simple rule of thumb for identifying the trees is "sharp, spiky spruce" and "flat, friendly fir." These alliterative phrases refer to the feel of the needles. Both trees have needles about 1 inch long, attached singly to the twig. Engelmann spruce needles are square in cross section and relatively sharp and prickly; the subalpine fir's needles are flatter and softer to the touch.

Mature Engelmann spruce have a distinctively reddish bark that sheds thin flakes. Fir bark is generally smooth, with a silvery cast, except on the oldest trees. Both spruce and fir can grow for three or four centuries, albeit very slowly, given their preferred altitude. A tree with a 36-inch diameter at chest height may be 400 years old.

These trees are marvelously adapted to snow. Their spirelike shape and downward-sloping branches allow them to shed enormous snowloads. Spruce-fir forests are sometimes called snow forests because of the way they capture and hold winter snowfall. Snow that blows from open tundra falls again in the upper reaches of spruce-fir forests. The cool, dark floor of these forests holds snow for weeks or months after open areas have melted dry.

Spruce-fir forests create and sustain their own cool, moist ecoystems. This is starkly illustrated by what happens when a high-elevation forest is disturbed, as by a fire. Burned areas near timberline may be invaded by tundra ecosystems. Spruce and fir seedlings cannot gain a toehold in the drier, windier conditions of tundra and may not reclaim the area for a century or more.

Look for heart-leaved arnica (*Arnica angustifolia*), sickle-top lousewort (*Pedicularis racemos*), and the occasional Venus slipper (*Calypso bulbosa*) in the moist, soft humus floor. Mushrooms and other fungi thrive in the dark, wet environment of spruce-fir forests.

Because these forests are prime targets for spruce beetles, they are also hosts to woodpeckers of several species, including flickers and three-toed woodpeckers (*Picoides tridactylus*). These ecosystems are also favored by the Canada lynx, a species endangered in Colorado, which hunts snowshoe hares and small rodents.

of which lie near Crested Butte.

Crested Butte incorporated in 1880 with 250 citizens and a diversified economy that kept it going even after other towns around it died in the silver crash of 1893 and the subsequent national economic depression. It functioned primarily as a

Sego Lily

Sego lily (*Calochortus nuttalli*) is one of several varieties of *Calochortus* found in the western mountains. This distinctive, tuliplike perennial is found in open or partly shaded dry areas from the edges of the high desert up to montane regions. The lily has three wide, whitish petals held vertically on a stem, forming a large, cuplike flower. A deep purple spot marks the interior base of each petal.

Sego lilies grow from edible bulbs that provided food to Indians and settlers.

coal-mining town, surviving despite several disastrous downtown fires, a mining explosion that killed 52 workers, and bitter and violent coal strikes. The last coal mine closed in 1952; the entire downtown was designated a National Historic District in 1972. Most of the town's streets were not paved until the early 1980s.

The presence of coal and silver together in the region speaks to the fact that the geology of the West Elks is quite complex. West of McClure Pass, in the Muddy Creek region, along the North Fork Valley of the Gunnison, and in the valleys around Crested Butte, Mesozoic-era Mesaverde Sandstones and Mancos Shale represent the shoreline and floor, respectively, of a vanished sea. Coal is found in the Mesaverde formations, which are about 240 million years old.

The West Elk peaks are part of a vast batholith, or upwelling, of molten rock. Although this upwelling did not reach the surface in most places, it did at West Elk Peak, located north of Gunnison, about 25 million years ago. The resulting eruptions created vast, breccia mudslides, which reveal themselves as brown cliffs and spires west of Gunnison and near Blue Mesa Reservoir, along the southern edge of the West Elk Range. Breccia is a conglomerate-type rock that was blown out of volcanoes or otherwise violently broken and then welded together by volcanic heat and pressure.

Volcanic intrusions created formations such as The Dyke, a sharp wall of rock located just west of Kebler Pass on the flanks of Ruby Peak, and Needle Rock, southeast of Crawford.

The flatter mesas and tablelands around the southern and western foothills of the West Elk exist because of eruptions that blew out great clouds of hot ash, which solidified into a form of rock known as welded tuff. This harder rock protected the softer mudflows beneath from erosion. Geologists believe some of the welded tuff in the West Elks is made of ash blown from volcanoes in the San Juan Mountains to the southwest.

MAROON BELLS-SNOWMASS WILDERNESS

[Fig. 28] This wilderness area sprawls between Aspen, Marble and Crested Butte. A general description and specific trails in the northern three-fourths of the wilderness are described in the Aspen section of the book (*see* page 176). A very popular summer trip involves hiking over West Maroon Pass to the road at Schofield Pass, spending the night in Crested Butte, and then hiking back the same way, or via East Maroon Pass. This is an uncommon, European-style hike that allows you to spend the day in the high country and the night in a small, alpine town. The best season for the hike is from mid-July through September. There are several significant stream crossings on both pass routes that may not be passable earlier in the year, due to high runoff.

The trip described here is from Aspen to Crested Butte, but, of course, it can be walked the opposite direction.

WEST MAROON PASS-EAST MAROON PASS LOOP

[Fig. 28(6), Fig. 28(7)] The southern flanks of the Maroon Bells-Snowmass Wilderness reach down to Gothic and Schofield Pass, 15 miles north of Crested Butte.

The West Maroon Pass route, 8 miles long, begins at the Maroon Lake Trailhead. Private vehicle traffic is prohibited on Maroon Creek Road during the summer months; take the bus from Ruby Park bus station, in downtown Aspen, to this trailhead, and begin hiking south up the West Maroon Creek Trail. On the return trip, you can flag the bus down at the East Maroon Creek trailhead for a ride back to Aspen.

After 2 miles, Pass Crater Lake. The Maroon Bells loom up the west; Pyramid Peak towers to the east. The upper two-thirds of this valley to 12,600-foot West Maroon Pass is a vast, open bowl of wildflowers and yet the bowl on the southern side of the pass is often even more dramatic and flower-filled. The trail climbs 5 miles to the pass and descends 3 miles down the East Fork of the Crystal River to a trailhead near Schofield Pass. Many hikers hire a taxi in Crested Butte (call to make arrangements ahead of time) for the 12-mile ride to town for the night.

The return trip over East Maroon Pass begins at the trailhead at Gothic, 5 miles from Crested Butte (take the taxi to the trailhead in the morning). The trail, a nineteenth-century wagon route between Gothic and Aspen, climbs 5 miles to 11,800-foot East Maroon Pass, then descends 7 miles down East Maroon Creek, on the east side of Pyramid Peak, to the East Maroon Portal on Maroon Creek Road. Copper Lake, named for its distinctively greenish hue, lies on the south side of the pass. Flag down a passing bus on Maroon Creek Road for a ride back to town. The route can be done in either direction.

For more information: For bus schedules to and from Maroon Lake and the West Maroon Creek Trail, call the Roaring Fork Transit Agency at (970) 925-8484. For trailhead pickup and dropoff reservations (and, often, the best information on trail conditions on this loop), contact Crested Butte Town Taxi. Phone (970) 349-5543.

SEGO LILY
(Calochortus nuttallii)
This lily is the state flower of Utah, named as such because of their edible bulbs' role in keeping pioneer Mormons from starving.

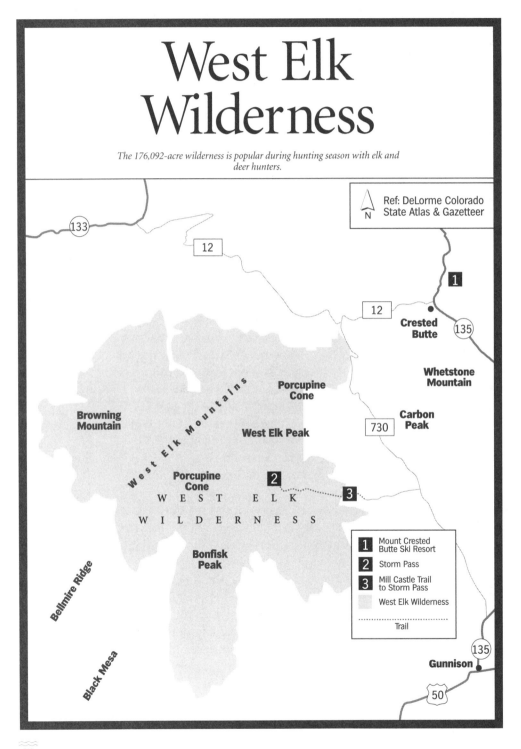

West Elk Wilderness

The 176,092-acre wilderness is popular during hunting season with elk and deer hunters.

Ref: DeLorme Colorado State Atlas & Gazetteer

N

133

12

12

1

Crested Butte

135

Whetstone Mountain

Porcupine Cone

Carbon Peak

Browning Mountain

730

West Elk Mountains

West Elk Peak

Porcupine Cone

2

3

WEST ELK WILDERNESS

Bonfisk Peak

Bellmire Ridge

1   Mount Crested Butte Ski Resort

2   Storm Pass

3   Mill Castle Trail to Storm Pass

West Elk Wilderness

Trail

135

Gunnison

50

Black Mesa

For other information: Aspen Ranger District, White River National Forest, 806 West Hallam, Aspen, CO 81611. Phone (970) 925-3445.

Fees: There is a fee for the bus and the taxi ride at either end of the hike.

Trail: West Maroon Pass: 8 miles one-way. East Maroon Pass: 12 miles one-way.

Elevation: Climb of 3,000 feet, descent of 1,600 feet, from north to south on West Maroon Pass. Going south to north via East Maroon Pass, climb of 2,300 feet, descent of 3,000 feet.

Degree of difficulty: Moderate.

Surface: West Maroon: Clearly marked trail through tundra, two stream crossings. East Maroon: Old roadbed, now principally a horse trail, and three stream crossings.

WEST ELK WILDERNESS

[Fig. 34] The 176,092-acre West Elk Wilderness was one of Colorado's original five wildernesses, designated by Congress in 1964 and expanded several times since. It encompasses the violently formed, volcanic heart of the West Elks. Despite its size, this region attracts few visitors, except during hunting season, when it is very popular with elk and deer hunters. It contains no major lakes or Fourteeners.

Directions: The West Elk Wilderness is situated west of Crested Butte, northwest of Gunnison, and east of Crawford. There are many access points into the wilderness area. From Crested Butte, drive west up Coal Creek (Gunnison County Road 12) toward Kebler Pass. At the pass, turn south onto Forest Road 730 (Ohio Creek Road) or continue west on County Road 12; both pass several marked trailheads.

Activities: Day hiking, backpacking, fishing.

Closest town: Crested Butte is 10 miles from the northeastern corner of the wilderness. Gunnison is 10 miles from the southeastern corner; Paonia and Crawford are each about 10 miles from the western boundary.

For more information: For the eastern half: Taylor Ranger District, Gunnison National Forest, 216 North Colorado, Gunnison, CO 81230. Phone (970) 641-0471. For the western half: Paonia Ranger District, Gunnison National Forest, North Rio Grande Street, Paonia, CO 81428. Phone (970) 527-4131.

MILL CASTLE TRAIL TO STORM PASS

[Fig. 34(3)] The Mill Castle Trail brings hikers to dramatic views of the Castles, which are eroded spires and pinnacles of volcanic rock that tower like small cities. The trail to Storm Pass is about 8 miles long and strenuous. It can be done either as a long day hike or an overnight trip.

The route parallels Mill Creek to treeline at Mill Basin. Follow cairns through Mill Basin (the trail can be indistinct here) to the base of Storm Pass, where several switchbacks climb to the 12,460-foot summit. The Castles are visible 1 mile to the north. West Elk Peak (at 13,025 feet, it's the highest in the range) is to the northwest along the ridge.

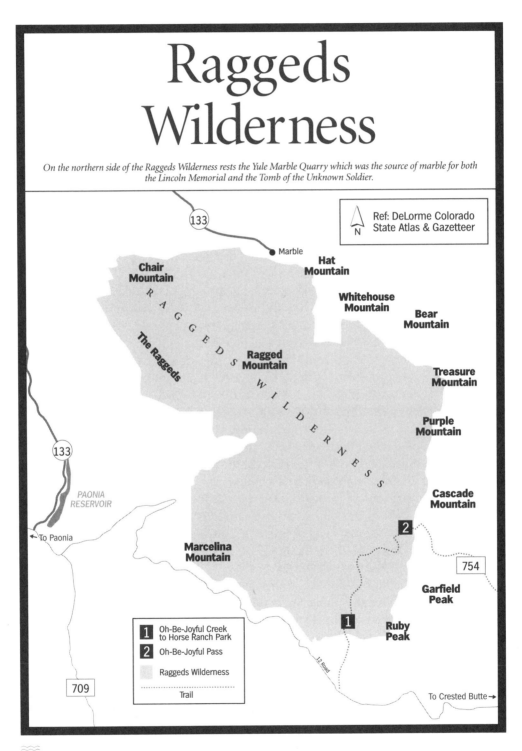

Raggeds Wilderness

On the northern side of the Raggeds Wilderness rests the Yule Marble Quarry which was the source of marble for both the Lincoln Memorial and the Tomb of the Unknown Soldier.

133

Ref: DeLorme Colorado
State Atlas & Gazetteer
N

Marble

Chair
Mountain

Hat
Mountain

Whitehouse
Mountain

Bear
Mountain

The Raggeds

R A G G E D S

Ragged
Mountain

Treasure
Mountain

W I L D E R N E S S

Purple
Mountain

133

PAONIA
RESERVOIR

Cascade
Mountain

2

To Paonia

Marcelina
Mountain

754

Garfield
Peak

1

Ruby
Peak

12 Road

1 Oh-Be-Joyful Creek
   to Horse Ranch Park

2 Oh-Be-Joyful Pass

   Raggeds Wilderness

709

.... Trail

To Crested Butte →

Directions: From Kebler Pass (about 7 miles west of Crested Butte), travel south on Forest Road 730 (Ohio Creek Road) about 11 miles to Forest Road 727 (Mill Creek Road). Drive as far as you can (depending on conditions, a two-wheel-drive car may not make it all the way to the locked gate at the 4-mile point).

Hike past the locked gate; the old road eventually becomes the trail.

Trail: 8 miles one-way.

Elevation: Gain of 3,500 feet.

Degree of difficulty: Strenuous.

Surface: Dirt and tundra.

For more information: Cebolla/Taylor Ranger District, Gunnison National Forest, 216 North Colorado, Gunnison, CO 81230. Phone (970) 641-0471.

RAGGEDS WILDERNESS

[Fig. 35] The Raggeds Mountain Range, sandwiched between the West Elk Wilderness and the Maroon Bells-Snowmass Wilderness, stretches southeast from the head of the Crystal River valley to the outskirts of Crested Butte.

The northern side of the Raggeds Wilderness wraps around Yule Creek, site of the Yule Marble Quarry. The quarry is the source of a creamy, white stone that has been likened to Italian Carerra marble. The marble of both the Lincoln Memorial and the Tomb of the Unknown Soldier in Washington, DC and Arlington, Virginia, respectively, was quarried here. The quarry was reopened in the 1990s after being closed for several decades.

The Raggeds Wilderness includes strikingly vertical peaks, although no Fourteeners. Chair Mountain (12,721 feet) rests like a throne east of McClure Pass; 11,348-foot Marcellina Mountain dominates the western approaches to Kebler Pass.

Directions: Several trailheads lead into the wilderness along the north side of Kebler Pass Road (Gunnison County Road 12), which runs west out of downtown Crested Butte.

Activities: Hiking, backpacking, mountaineering.

For more information: For the eastern portion of the wilderness: Taylor River Ranger District, Gunnison National Forest, 216 North Colorado, Gunnison, CO 81230. Phone (970) 641-0471. For the western portion: Paonia Ranger District, Gunnison National Forest, North Rio Grande Street, Paonia, CO 81428. Phone (970) 527-4131.

OH-BE-JOYFUL CREEK TO HORSE RANCH PARK

[Fig. 35(1)] The route described here is a point-to-point, overnight trip that requires dropping a vehicle at one end and shuttling around to the other. If you can't do that, consider a one-way trip up Oh-Be-Joyful Creek to Oh-Be-Joyful Pass.

The Oh-Be-Joyful Valley reveals the sedimentary and metamorphic nature of this portion of the region's mountains. The red and grey shale and slate are metamorphized remnants of the redbeds deposited by erosion from the ancient Uncompahgria

Range. This route makes a semicircle through the red-tinted Ruby Range immediately west of Crested Butte.

The trail climbs 7 miles up Oh-Be-Joyful Creek to Oh-Be-Joyful Pass, then descends 8 miles on the west side of the Ruby Range, where you get expansive views across the largest continuous aspen forest in Colorado.

Directions: To drop a car at Horse Ranch Park, drive west over Kebler Pass on Country 12 (Kebler Pass Road) for 12 miles to the signed Horse Ranch Park trailhead and parking area on the right-hand side of the road. To begin the route at Oh-Be-Joyful, return to Crested Butte, drive east through town on Elk Avenue (the main street, one block north of where Kebler Pass Road comes into Crested Butte) and then turn left (north), at the foot of Elk Avenue onto Gothic Road (toward Mount Crested Butte). Cross the Slate River and, approximately 1 mile from town, turn left (west) onto Forest Road 734, up the Slate River. Drive approximately 4 miles to Forest Road 754, a left, at Oh-Be-Joyful Creek. You must cross the Slate River at the beginning of the trail, which at this point is a four-wheel-drive road. Don't try this if the water is high.

If you choose to hike the road, the wilderness boundary is 1.5 miles up the road from the river crossing.

For more information: Cebolla/Taylor Ranger District, Gunnison National Forest, 216 North Colorado, Gunnison, CO 81230. Phone (970) 641-0471.

Closest town: Crested Butte, approximately 6 miles southwest of the trailhead.

Trail: 21 miles one-way.

Elevation: Gain of 2,700 feet from Oh-Be-Joyful trailhead to Oh-Be-Joyful Pass, then a descent of 2,900 feet to Horse Ranch Park.

Degree of difficulty: Strenuous.

Surface: Single-track trail.

NORTH AMERICAN PORCUPINE

(Erethizon dorsatum)
When threatened, the porcupine strikes with its tail, leaving some of its 30,000 barbed quills embedded in its enemy; the quills are actually modified hairs loosely attached to the porcupine's skin.

Rocky Mountain Biological Laboratory

Rocky Mountain Biological Laboratory is the nation's foremost high-altitude biological field station, where scientists and students from around the world study the natural environment. About 60 researchers, many of them graduate students, study the natural world in the meadows and on the hillsides around Gothic. The biological laboratory was founded in 1928 by Dr. John Johnson, a dean at Western State College in Gunnison. Johnson bought much of the townsite of Gothic, a short-lived silver boom town that was founded in 1879 yet began to die within two years due to a shortage of quality ore.

Gothic today still looks much like an abandoned ghost town, but a few newer buildings, and the prevalence of staked plots and scientific measuring equipment in adjacent meadows, hint at the nature of the research work being conducted here on the alpine environment. Examples of research projects include: avian and mammalian adaptations to high elevation; animal behavior; plant-pollinator interactions; butterfly population ecology; stream ecology; acid precipitation; stressed ecosystems; flowering phenology of alpine wildflowers; and insect predator-prey systems. Many research projects are of twenty to thirty years' duration.

The laboratory is not open to the public, but does provide summer-long classes to small groups of graduate and undergraduate students.

For more information: Rocky Mountain Biological Laboratory, PO Box 519, Crested Butte, CO 81224. Phone (970) 349-723.

MOUNTAIN BIKING

Crested Butte claims, along with Marin County, California, to be the birthplace of the mountain bike. The evolution of this toy seems to have occurred simultaneously at both locations. In the early 1970s, Crested Butticians (as residents are called) began modifying fat-tired, one-speed bikes for use on all types of terrain. Crested Butte's volunteer firefighters were particularly innovative on this front.

In 1976, a group of Aspenites (whose name isn't as interesting as that of their neighbors in Basalt, known as Basaltines) rode motorcycles over rugged 12,705-foot Pearl Pass to Crested Butte. They proclaimed in the local bars that their motorized feat could not be topped. As an answer, the Crested Butticians rode to Aspen on their newly created mountain bikes, parked them in front of the Hotel Jerome, and proceeded to get good and drunk and proclaim their superiority over the local motorcyclists.

Their bicycles were crafted by trial and error. Multiple gears, drum brakes, balloon tires, and outsized handlebars were used to modify newsboy bicycles. The finished products weighed close to 50 pounds. Even today, with state-of-the-art equipment weighing less than half that much, cyclists who attempt the 39-mile trip to Aspen find themselves pushing their bikes at least half the distance for the last

Stinging Nettle

Colorado has little poison ivy or poison oak, and these plants are nonexistent at higher altitudes. But one innocuous plant, stinging nettle, found along trails and in disturbed soils along roadsides from the plains up to high mountain valleys, can cause plenty of discomfort.

Urtico dioica is an erect, perennial herb that grows to heights of several feet. Identify it by its leaves. Narrowly lance- to heart-shaped with saw-toothed edges, the leaves are 4 to 15 centimeters long and set in opposite pairs along the four-sided stem. Flowers are tiny, greenish, and inconspicuous, set in clusters near the tops of the plants.

Stinging nettle is covered with tiny, hollow, quill-like hairs. Brush against these hairs and a tiny droplet of formic acid, held in a sac at the base of each hair, is injected into your skin. The result is a painful itch that lasts for a few minutes, or even a few days, but will eventually subside.

3 miles to the pass, a jeep "road" that closely resembles a boulderfield. During the late1970s, the trip to Aspen took two days and was supported by vehicles carrying food and beer.

Since that time Crested Butte has been considered Colorado's mountain biking Mecca, although that title is being challenged by other communities that are aggressively developing mountain bike trails.

THE 401 LOOP

[Fig. 28(8)] One of the most spectacular single-track rides in the state, this classic is not for the faint of heart. It is physically and technically demanding but remarkably rewarding. Don't try it before late June; snow on the trail takes awhile to melt out.

The first 3 miles of trail cling to the grassy, steep sides of Bellview Mountain. Staying on the trail requires concentration—if you want to take in the views, stop first. After 3 miles, the trail leaves the steep mountainside and descends into Rustler Gulch. You may ride to the right on a dirt road back to the Schofield Pass Road, or continue down the 401 Trail, which offers all the roots, rocks, bogs, and steep ups and downs a cyclist could want. Nine miles from the pass, the trail pops out at a parking lot located slightly upstream from Gothic.

Directions: Beginning at the old mining town site of Gothic (8 miles north of Crested Butte), ride up the dirt road to Schofield Pass. At the very top of the pass (about 7 miles), look for a single-track trail leading steeply uphill (it may or may not have a sign). Shoulder your bike and start hiking until you reach a meadow; follow cairns across the meadow until you reach Forest Service Trail 401, which heads south down the valley back toward Gothic (don't expect to find a sign here). Start riding to the right.

Trail: 16-mile loop.

Elevation: Climb of 1,200 feet to Schofield Pass, then hike-a-bike carry of 400 feet to the 401 Trail. Descent of 1,600 feet.

Degree of difficulty: Strenuous.

Surface: Dirt road, exposed single-track, mud, rocks, roots.

For more information: Cebolla/Taylor Ranger District, Gunnison National Forest, 216 North Colorado, Gunnison, CO 81230. Phone (970) 641-0471.

SKIING CRESTED BUTTE

Skiing has a venerable and well-documented history in Crested Butte. As was true in other mountainous mining regions, miners in the 1870s and 1880s learned to build basic wooden skis with leather bindings in order to traverse from camp to camp, or down to town for supplies. There wasn't a lot of finesse to the experience. Skiers (called snowshoers) could turn by using a modified stem or telemark turn, if they were skillful. Most regulated their speed and direction with the help of a stout stick, which they dragged behind like a rudder.

A tough breed of skiing mailmen delivered mail to outlying camps from Crested Butte. The most locally famous of these was Al Johnson, who regularly traversed the avalanche-riddled route over Schofield Pass to Crystal City, on the headwaters of the Crystal River.

Skiing became a competitive sport around Crested Butte in the 1880s. One race, near Irwin, offered $25 in prize money to the first skier to complete a 0.25-mile course into town. Most crashed before the finish line.

The biggest early ski race in Crested Butte came on February 22, 1886, commemorating Washington's birthday. Spectators came from as far as Gunnison to watch skiers compete for the title of Champion Skier of the Rocky Mountains on a 525-yard course that began with a 35-degree pitch and finished with 250 feet on the flats. The title, and the $20 prize, was won in a neck-and-neck final by Al Johnson, the skiing mailman, who is reported to have hit a speed of 60 miles per hour.

MOUNT CRESTED BUTTE SKI RESORT

[Fig. 34(1)] Modern skiing didn't come to Crested Butte until the ski area on Mount Crested Butte's northern slopes was opened in 1960. Today Crested Butte has a reputation as one of the toughest small mountains in the country. Skiers flock to it for its very challenging Headwall and North Face, which have in recent years been the site of the ESPN Winter X-Games and the U.S. Extreme Free Skiing Championships. Crested Butte also is home to many accomplished telemark skiers. Telemark equipment and technique are older than that of downhill skiers, and can be both trickier and more versatile to use. Telemark ski boots attach to the skis only at the toe; telemarkers must ski with their heels free, or unattached. Consequently, the skiing technique is different than that used by downhill skiers, who clamp toe and heel firmly to ski.

The ski area offers 1,160 acres of skiing with 2,775 feet of vertical drop. Of that terrain, a large portion—550 acres—is ungroomed, double-black diamond terrain rated for experts only. The summit reaches 12,162 feet above sea level.

Black Canyon National Monument

South Rim Drive offers a 12-mile winding route to view this almost frighteningly narrow gorge.

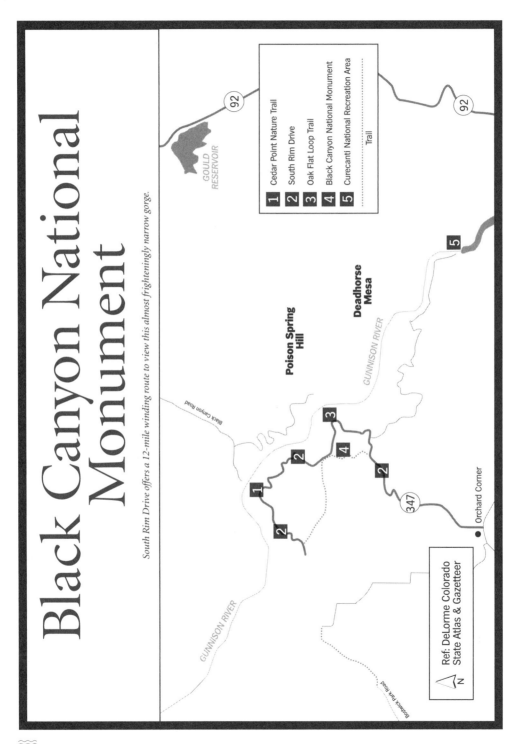

1	Cedar Point Nature Trail
2	South Rim Drive
3	Oak Flat Loop Trail
4	Black Canyon National Monument
5	Curecanti National Recreation Area
....	Trail

GOULD RESERVOIR

Poison Spring Hill

Deadhorse Mesa

GUNNISON RIVER

Black Canyon Road

GUNNISON RIVER

Orchard Corner

Bostwick Park Road

Ref: DeLorme Colorado State Atlas & Gazetteer

N

Directions: From Crested Butte, 3 miles north on Gothic Road.

Activities: Skiing and snowboarding on the mountain; nordic center near the town of Crested Butte; 45 kilometers of dedicated snowshoeing and cross-country skiing trails.

Facilities: Base village, on-mountain restaurants.

Dates: Ski season generally runs from Thanksgiving to Easter.

Fees: There is a fee to ski or snowboard.

Closest town: Crested Butte, 3 miles south.

For more information: Crested Butte Mountain Resort, PO Box A, Mount Crested Butte, CO 81225. Phone (888) 463-6713.

Black Canyon National Monument & Curecanti National Recreation Area

▨ BLACK CANYON NATIONAL MONUMENT

[Fig. 36(4)] The Black Canyon of the Gunnison is usually described as awesome, gorgeous, and terrifying, and it is all of these things. Yet such descriptions do not begin to convey the reality of this strange, unnerving, and sublime Colorado anomaly, a great gorge that unexpectedly divides a mountain. Visitors come to peer into its narrow depths, to scramble to the canyon floor thousands of feet below the rim, or simply to marvel at how a river has laid open a great slice of the earth.

Other canyons in the world are deeper, but there is no canyon as deep and as narrow as the Black Canyon. At its narrowest the canyon is 1,750 feet deep, only 40 feet wide from wall to wall beside the river, and a mere 1,300 feet wide at the rim. The deepest point in the canyon lies 2,425 feet below the rim.

"The Black Canyon of the Gunnison is one of the most spectacular gorges of the United States," wrote National Park Service representative Roger Toll in a 1932 report to his superiors. The Park Service agreed, and in 1933 the monument was created by President Herbert Hoover, who set aside 12 of the canyon's 53 miles in a 33-square-mile preserve. Legislation introduced in Congress in 1999 would add 10,000 acres to the Park Service's holdings there and upgrade the status of the Black Canyon from national monument to national park. The Clinton administration and Colorado's Congressional delegation support the changes, and the Black Canyon could become a national park before the year 2000.

The canyon itself is the result of "an interplay of coincidences," in the words of geologist Wallace Hansen. The first stage in the canyon's development came during the Laramide orogeny, 65 million years ago, when a fault block of 1.7 billion-year-old gneiss and schist arose southwest of today's West Elk Mountains. During the succeeding

35 million years the top of this uplift eroded down to the valley floor as if the top of a pyramid had been bevelled down. Then, 25 million years ago, volcanoes in the West Elk and San Juan mountains erupted.

The eruptions had two effects. First, they covered the Gunnison and Uncompahgre valley floors with a layer of softer volcanic rock. Second, the volcanic creation of the West Elks pushed the Gunnison River southwest, so that it arced around the new mountains. The Gunnison proceeded to carve a young canyon through the newer, soft volcanic rock, underlying sedimentary rock, and finally down to the older, harder surface of the Gunnison uplift—which was the bevelled top of the pyramid. Now the Gunnison was trapped in the canyon it had carved through the volcanic debris. Unable to go around the harder rock, it began to erode the gneiss and schist.

That job was facilitated by the river's very steep gradient. The Gunnison drops 2,150 feet in 50 miles, and averages 95 feet per mile through the monument—a very steep drop that generates a lot of power and erosive strength. Before dams were built in the eastern portions of the canyon, outside the monument, the river flowed at levels as high as 12,000 cubic feet per second (cfs), a flow rate that carried vast quantities of sand, gravel, and whole boulders—abrasive material that cut deeply into the bedrock. Today, peak flows rarely reach 4,000 cfs, and the debris once washed downstream is trapped in the reservoirs of Curecanti National Recreation Area [Fig. 36].

PEREGRINE FALCON
(*Falco peregrinus*)

The river cut through the Precambrian core of the Gunnison uplift at a rate of about 1 inch per century, or the width of a human hair per year, for the past 2 million years. Meanwhile the softer, volcanic rock elsewhere in the Uncompahgre valley floor, to the west and north, also eroded. This erosion exposed the more durable sides of the Precambrian fault block, the pyramid that had once been buried under softer rock. As the softer rock of the valley floor eroded away, the fault block of hard gneiss rose up out of it.

All the while, the Gunnison River was trapped in a canyon of its own making and continued to grind down through the gneiss, splitting it like a knife drawn through an orange. The result is a river that flows along a relatively flat, broad valley to the east of the Black Canyon, cleaves the hard rock uplift in its path, and emerges out of the canyon into a broad, flat valley. Although it seems as if the mass of the hard rock walls of the canyon rose up from the valley floor around the river, in truth, the valley floor washed away from the shoulders of the Precambrian rock.

The result is a strange canyon, one that obliges a visitor to drive up from the lower, Uncompahgre Valley floor in order to reach the canyon rims, so that he or she may then look down into the canyon.

These high rims are one reason the Black Canyon is so narrow. Tributary streams help widen canyons, but streams near the Black Canyon tend to flow downhill and away from it, rather than into it, so that there are no significant tributaries to open up the narrow canyon. Also, the rock of the canyon

COMMON JUNIPER (Juniperus communis) Also called dwarf juniper, this produces blue berries that are used in flavoring gin.

itself is very strong. The dark schist and gneiss of the canyon walls is braided with a light-colored net of pegmatite, a very hard igneous intrusion that veins the canyon walls. Like reinforcing bar in concrete, pegmatite gives the walls of the canyon structural strength to stand vertically for enormous heights. Painted Wall, near the western end of the canyon, is the highest cliff in the state, dropping 2,250 feet from rim to river.

The canyon was one of the last places in Colorado to feel the footsteps of Anglo-Americans. It was not successfully traversed until 1901, when William Torrence and Abraham Lincoln Fellows took nine days to cover 36 miles of the canyon, hiking, swimming, and scrambling through it. Their survey paved the way for one of the first projects of the United States Reclamation Service (now the Bureau of Reclamation): a 5.9-mile-long tunnel beneath Vernal Mesa to carry Gunnison River water northwest into the Uncompaghre Valley. Completed in 1909, the tunnel begins just below Crystal Dam at the East Portal and irrigates 80,000 acres of the Uncompahgre River valley to the west.

The canyon is home to the endangered peregrine falcon (*Falco peregrinus*), which nests on its vertical walls. A much more common bird is the violet-green swallow (*Tachycineta thalassina*), which hunts insects near the canyon rims. Down in the canyon, water ouzels, yellow-rumped warblers (*Dendroica coronata*), and canyon wrens may be seen and heard.

The canyon has a somewhat inverted set of ecosystems. The rim, at 8,000 feet, hosts scrub communities of gambel oak, mountain mahogany, and piñon pine. In the lower

**AMERICAN
GOLDFINCH**
(Carduelis tristis)

slopes of the canyon, Douglas fir and aspen ecoystems can be found, especially on north-facing aspects. These are species that typically grow above the rim ecosystems; here they grow lower, because of the shade, moisture, and coolness afforded by the canyon walls. Down along the river, riparian ecosystems are formed by willow, narrowleaf cottonwoods and box elder (*Acer negundo*) trees. Box elder, despite its name, is actually a maple, as evidenced by the "keys" its seeds form.

Directions: From Montrose, drive east on US 50 approximately 5 miles to CO 347. Turn left (north) and drive approximately 7 miles to the entrance station. The visitor center is approximately 2 miles inside the monument.

Activities: Scenic drives, hiking, camping, backpacking, fishing, nature trails.

Facilities: The visitor center is situated on the South Rim Road. A dozen overlooks, some by the road, some involving several hundred yards of walking, are located along the South Rim Road. North Rim Road is a dirt road with 7 overlooks. Picnic areas are located at East Portal, High Point, and Sunset View.

There are 102 sites in the South Rim Campground and 13 in the North Rim Campground. The East Portal Campground, with 8 campsites in the canyon by the river, is located in the Curecanti National Recreation Area but is reached via the south rim (this route is closed in winter). The road is paved but extremely steep; vehicles longer than 22 feet are prohibited.

In addition to the campgrounds at East Portal and on the north and south rims, several backcountry sites are located along the river. Everything below the canyon rims is managed as wilderness, however, and the routes to the campsites are so steep they are not even considered trails, but are more appropriately described as scrambles. Three routes from the south rim and three from the north rim descend between 1,800 and 2,660 feet in distances from 1 to 2.5 miles. Nineteen campsites are scattered at the bases of these trails. The routes are considered extremely strenuous and are exposed in places. Permits are required for any activity below the canyon rims. They are available free of charge from the visitor center or North Rim Ranger Station.

Dates: The monument is open year-round, but the North Rim Road and North Rim Campground are closed in winter.

Fees: There is a fee to enter the Monument, and another fee to camp.

Closest town: Montrose, 13 miles southwest.

For more information: Black Canyon National Monument, 102 Elk Creek, Gunnison, CO 81230. Phone (970) 641-2337.

SOUTH RIM ROAD DRIVE

[Fig. 36(2)] About 12 miles long, this winding route stops along a dozen overlook points. Allow a couple of hours to complete the out-and-back trip, which begins at Tomichi Piont, 0.5 mile south of the visitor center. At each overlook, listen to the remote roar of the distant river and gain a different perspective on the profound, almost frightening canyon, which is a complex interplay of rock walls and spires, light, and shadow.

Directions: Follow the main road at the south side entrance station. Pull-outs and overlooks are clearly marked.

HIKING IN BLACK CANYON NATIONAL MONUMENT

Because of the vertical nature of the monument, and the constriction of the canyon floor, most hiking is limited to the canyon rims.

OAK FLAT LOOP TRAIL

[Fig. 36(3)] This loop allows visitors to experience the environment below the canyon rim without hiking all the way to the river.

Directions: From the visitor center, follow the trail marked Oak Flat/River Access, bearing right. At a signed junction, turn left onto the Oak Flat Loop Trail, which wanders along the rim and then back to the visitor center.

Trail: 2.5-mile loop.

Elevation: Change of 400 feet.

Degree of difficulty: Strenuous.

Surface: Dirt and rock with some steep slope traverses.

CEDAR POINT NATURE TRAIL

[Fig. 36(1)] This trail leads out to an overlook of the Painted Wall, the highest cliff in Colorado. Plant species along the route are marked with interpretive signs.

Directions: Drive north on the South Rim Road about 9 miles from the visitor center to the Cedar Point parking area.

Trail: Round trip of 0.7 mile.

Elevation: Change of 20 feet.

Degree of difficulty: Easy.

Surface: Dirt and gravel.

PHOEBUS PARNASSIAN
(Parnassius phoebus)
Flying in colder temperatures than many other butterflies, the phoebus is identified by gray markings and red spots on the white male and transparent female.

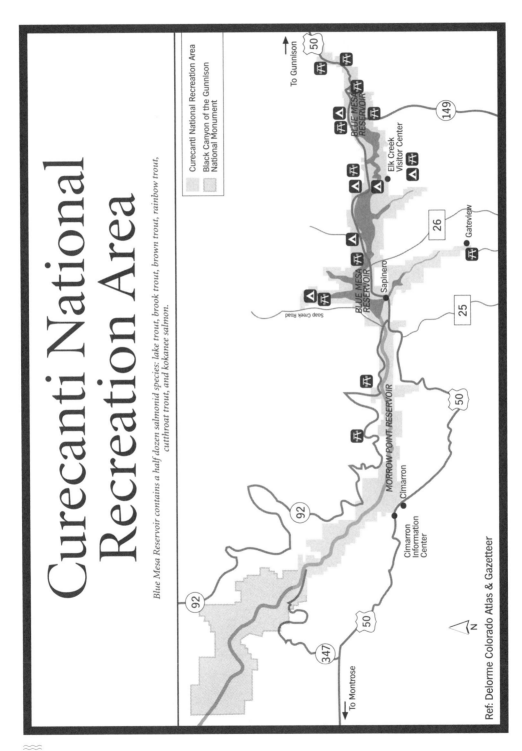

Curecanti National Recreation Area

Blue Mesa Reservoir contains a half dozen salmonid species: lake trout, brook trout, brown trout, rainbow trout, cutthroat trout, and kokanee salmon.

Curecanti National Recreation Area

Black Canyon of the Gunnison National Monument

To Gunnison

BLUE MESA RESERVOIR

Elk Creek Visitor Center

Gateview

Sapinero

Soap Creek Road

BLUE MESA RESERVOIR

MORROW POINT RESERVOIR

Cimarron

Cimarron Information Center

To Montrose

Ref: Delorme Colorado Atlas & Gazetteer

CURECANTI NATIONAL RECREATION AREA

[Fig. 37, Fig. 36(5)] Curecanti is comprised of three lakes immediately upstream of and contiguous with the Black Canyon National Monument: Crystal Lake, Morrow Point Reservoir, and Blue Mesa Reservoir. The three lakes were created as part of the 1956 Colorado River Storage Project, an enormous water development scheme that was principally responsible for making the Colorado River (of which the Gunnison is a tributary) the most dammed and regulated in the world.

The three dams, built in the 1960s and 1970s, are managed in concert. Blue Mesa is used for water storage, Morrow Point Dam is operated for power generation, and Crystal Dam mediates the surges of water from Morrow Point to allow for a smoother, more consistent downstream flow.

The three lakes are a magnet for water sports enthusiasts, and attract 1 million visitors annually to fish, sail, windsurf, and water ski. By far the largest of the three lakes, Blue Mesa cover 9,000 acres and has 96 miles of shoreline when it is full. Drawdowns can reduce reservoir levels as much as 70 feet.

In winter, elk and deer herds can be seen grazing in or near the reservoirs. Bald eagles, which subsist largely on fish, winter over in Curecanti. Recent January counts have found two dozen of the birds in residence, as well as golden eagles.

FISHING

The biggest attraction to the area may be its fishing. Blue Mesa Reservoir contains a half dozen salmonid species: lake trout, brook trout, brown trout, rainbow trout, cutthroat trout, and kokanee salmon (a landlocked version of sockeye salmon, of the genus *Oncorhynchus*). Many of these fish have found their way into Morrow Point and Crystal reservoirs as well. The vast majority of the fish caught are kokanee salmon or rainbow trout.

Below Crystal Dam in the Black Canyon of the Gunnison National Monument, the Gunnison River is one of Colorado's designated Gold Medal waters. This appellation implies some of the best trophy trout fishing in the state. Fishing is limited to flies and lures only and bag limits are tightly regulated to preserve the quality of the fishing. Access is difficult; except for the road down to East Portal, all other access to the canyon involves strenuous hiking from the rim. Access to East Portal is free and open to anyone; the road is closed to trailers and vehicles longer than 22 feet, and is closed during winter. All other access into the canyon requires a permit, available from the Black Canyon visitor center.

Directions: Curecanti National Recreation Area stretches 30 miles west of Gunnison. From Gunnison, drive west on US 50. The Elk Creek Visitor Center is about 15 miles west, on the left (south). Boat launching ramps, campsites, picnic areas, and interpretive exhibits for Blue Mesa Reservoir are scattered along US 50 West to Blue Mesa Dam, and along Colorado 92, which runs along the north side of Morrow Point Reservoir and Crystal Reservoir.

Both Morrow Point Reservoir and Crystal Reservoir are situated inside the eastern

Mountain Men

Romanticized in movies and literature, mountain men—trappers pursuing beaver—lived a lonely and perilous life. But they were the first Anglo-Americans to regularly visit Colorado's mountains, exploring drainages throughout the region as they trapped beaver nearly to extinction in one area and had to move on to new drainages. As early as 1810, groups of trappers were working the mountains of southern Colorado, although conflicts with Mexican authorities limited their activities until Mexican independence in 1821. Trappers working out of Taos and Santa Fe, New Mexico spread out over southern Colorado's mountain valleys, while the Hudson's Bay Company and American Fur Company reached deep into the Rockies from Saint Louis and Vancouver.

Trappers either brought beaver pelts to trading posts such as Taos or to an annual "rendezvous," a bazaar and gathering held at a different locale in the mountains each fall. Rendezvous were very popular with mountain men, who lived an ascetic life most of the trapping season. By the 1830s beaver prices began to decline as beaver felt went out of fashion in Europe. Prices dropped from $4 a skin to $1, and many trappers turned their attention to hunting buffalo for commercial markets.

portion of the Black Canyon, making access difficult. Morrow Point Reservoir can be reached by boaters via the Pine Creek Trail, about 5 miles west of Blue Mesa Dam on US 50. There are 234 steps on the trail, but it is possible to carry a small boat to the lake.

Crystal Reservoir can be accessed only via the Mesa Creek Trail at Morrow Point Dam. To reach this, continue west on US 50 from Blue Mesa Dam to Cimarron, approximately 20 miles. Turn right (north) at the Cimarron Information Center to Morrow Point Dam, about 2 miles.

Activities: Power boating, sailing, fishing, hiking, cross-country skiing, ice fishing, windsurfing, water skiing. Interpretive boat tour on Morrow Point Reservoir during the summer.

Facilities: The Elk Creek Visitor Center is located on the north shore of Blue Mesa Reservoir. The Lake Fork Information Center is on the south side of the same reservoir, just upstream from Blue Mesa Dam. The Cimarron Information Center is located on US 50 at Cimarron. The East Portal Ranger Station is at the bottom of East Portal Road and is reached via Black Canyon National Monument.

There are 10 campgrounds along the lake shores containing 410 campsites. In addition, there are several backcountry sites along the shores and tributary streams that may be reached on foot or by boat, and are available on a first-come, first-served basis. There are 19 picnic areas, 2 marinas, and 1 boat launching ramp.

Dates: Curecanti is open year round; however, Lake Fork and Cimarron visitor centers are closed from Labor Day to Memorial Day. Elk Creek visitor center is open intermittently (depending on staffing, it may be closed for lunch or at other times) from the end of Sept. to mid-May, then is open every day during the summer.

Fees: There is no fee to use the national recreation area, but there is a fee if you put a boat in the water.

Closest town: Gunnison, about 15 miles east of the Elk Creek Visitor Center.

For more information: Curecanti National Recreation Area, 102 Elk Creek, Gunnison, CO 81230. Phone (970) 641-2337. For information and reservations regarding the Morrow Point Reservoir tour, contact Elk Creek Marina. Phone (970) 641-0402.

Scenic Drives

▓ TOP OF THE ROCKIES SCENIC BYWAY

[Fig. 26(6)] A Y-shaped byway tracing the headwaters of three rivers (the Eagle, Arkansas, and Tenmile Creek), the Top of The Rockies is the highest scenic byway in Colorado. Most of the 76-mile route lies above 9,000 feet. This byway crosses the Continental Divide twice and wends its way through a landscape drastically altered by nature (glaciers), and man (miners).

The route is anchored on its northern legs by Copper Mountain Ski Area and Minturn, and on the south by the hamlet of Twin Lakes. Beginning at Twin Lakes, at the base of Mount Elbert (14,433 feet), drive east on CO 82 past the lakes, which were formed naturally by a glacial terminal moraine from Lake Creek (the valley west of Twin Lakes), and enlarged in 1897. Today they are part of the Arkansas-Frying Pan water diversion project, which shifts water from the Western Slope to Colorado's Front Range.

At Mile 6 you pass through large piles of rock, the waste from placer mining. Much of the Arkansas Valley from this point north to Tennessee Pass is comprised of lateral and terminal moraines, and glacial outwash, from the tongues of ice that extended down from the Sawatch Range to the west and Mosquito Range to the east.

Turn north (left) on US 24. North of Mount Elbert, Mount Massive (14,421 feet, second highest in the state) is the large peak dominating the western skyline. At Mile 17 the road bears sharply right toward Leadville.

WESTERN HEMLOCK
(Tsuga heterophylla)
This hemlock has long cones, flat needles that are dark green above and whitish below, and are found on cool, moist slopes.

This is the site of Malta, one of the outlying mining villages that cropped up around Leadville, but which have now vanished. From this point into Leadville proper you pass old slag piles, the waste from the smelters that produced millions of dollars of wealth from Leadville's mines.

Follow the main road through Leadville. At Mile 23, bear left to stay on US 24 over Tennessee Pass. Many of the hills around this region are swathed in lodgepole pine forests. This is a successional species that grew up after the climax spruce and fir forests of the region were logged by miners working the many mines east of Leadville. Prior to the arrival of the Denver and Rio Grande Railroad in Leadville in 1880, there was little coal available for all the industrial activity, so Leadville's residents denuded the surrounding hills, turning the forests into charcoal for fuel.

Around Mile 25 you enter a high, open plain, Tennessee Park. This is a wetland ecosystem, typified by willows, bog birch (*Betula nana*), and grasses that tolerate high water tables.

Tennessee Pass is at Mile 32. Ski Cooper, on the eastern side of the pass, was originally constructed as a training ground for the 10th Mountain Division (*see* page 167). A memorial to the nearly 1,000 men of the 10th who were killed in action is mounted at the pass's summit. The remains of Camp Hale, the 10th's training base, are at Mile 35.

The route now follows the Eagle River, which carves a deep canyon to the north. At Mile 42 a steel span crosses Turkey Creek, a tributary of the Eagle. The small mining town of Red Cliff is located 1 mile east up Turkey Creek. The road clings to the flanks of Battle Mountain and passes above the abandoned town of Gilman at Mile 47. Gilman was a company town, founded in 1886. The mines here were among the last nineteenth century workings to close in Colorado, which now has very few active mines in the mountains. Gilman was shuttered in 1984, after producing 300,000 ounces of gold, 50 million ounces of silver, 90,000 tons of copper, 35,000 tons of lead, and 250,000 tons of zinc.

The northwestern leg of the byway ends at Mile 54, in Minturn. The northeastern leg runs from Leadville over Fremont Pass to Copper Mountain. The most striking element of this 22-mile leg (on CO 91) is the Climax molybdenum mine at the top of Fremont Pass. Molybdenum is used to produce stainless steel. Roughly half of Bartlett Mountain, on the eastern side of the pass, has been removed, processed, and the waste rock deposited in two valleys on the western side of the pass, almost filling them. At peak operation, in 1970, the mine employed 3,000 workers and produced 50,000 tons of ore per day. The mine was closed in 1984, but little effort has been made to remediate its environmental impact.

The northeastern end of the byway ends at Copper Mountain Ski Area, beside I-70.

Facilities: Commercial services are available in Leadville, at the center of the byway, and at the towns at each end.

Dates: The byway is open year-round, although winter weather can make the route treacherous, particularly over Tennessee and Fremont passes.

Fees: None.

Closest town: Minturn on the northwestern end of the byway; Leadville in the center.

For more information: Leadville Chamber of Commerce, 809 Harrison Avenue, Leadville, CO 80461. Phone (719) 486-3900.

ASPEN TO TWIN LAKES

Colorado Highway 82 is not a state-designated scenic byway, but the 40-mile drive east from Aspen to US 24 near Twin Lakes is a spectacular trip across the Continental Divide. It is open only during the warm months; the first major snows of October close the road (the closures are set 4 miles east of Aspen and about 6 miles west of Twin Lakes). The route across Independence Pass generally is reopened for Memorial Day weekend. Vehicles over 35 feet in length are prohibited.

If you begin in Aspen, head east out of town on Cooper Avenue (CO 82). Immediately on your right you will pass the Northstar Nature Preserve, a swath of wet meadows and the meandering Roaring Fork River managed by the Aspen Center for Environmental Studies. This is a traditional wintering area for elk herds that spend their summers on Smuggler Mountain and in the upper reachers of the Hunter Creek valley. Look for these animals early on winter mornings on the far side of the valley, near the base of Aspen Mountain.

Northstar Preserve is set on glacial outwash; note the loose, rounded rocks and gravel in the road cuts, deposited by the glacier that filled this valley 12,000 years ago and at places ran several thousand feet thick.

At Mile 3 the road begins to climb, stairstepping up the northern side of the valley. Around Mile 7 the road is literally blasted out of the granite, part of the core rock of the Sawatch Range. This smooth, solid rock is popular with rock climbers who have blazed dozens of sport climbing routes on the walls and cliffs immediately adjacent to the highway, from Mile 4 to Mile 10.

Above the turn to Lincoln Creek (Mile 8), the valley flattens out and the road passes through lodgepole pine. Sweeping avalanches have cleared wide slopes, particularly on the southern side of the valley, in glacial cirques. Snow bridges form each spring at the foot of these slopes across the Roaring Fork River. These are caused when avalanches slide down into the valley and block the stream. The river soon tunnels through the snow, which, like snow that has been piled up with a plow, is much harder and denser than snow that has not slid. Consequently, large snow bridges may last until midsummer.

Two kinds of old rocks can be seen in the cliffs around the highway. Wavy, folded gneiss and glittery schist were formed more than 1 billion years ago. A cleaner, whitish granite is a younger intrusion, yet still dates from the Precambrian Era more than 600 million years ago.

Around Mile 15 the road climbs into a nearly treeless valley, the old townsite of Independence. Gold was found here on July 4, 1879, the same summer when strikes were made at what would become Aspen. The gold and silver found around here apparently were deposited by an Oligocene volcanic intrusion to the south, which has eroded into 13,988-foot Grizzly Peak.

In the early 1880s the population of Independence peaked at round 2,000 people. Some records indicate that at this time skiing was introduced to the region by Norwegian and Swedish miners who steamed and bent 12-foot-long skis out of long boards to make the winter trek from Independence to Aspen or Leadville. Independence lay along a toll road between Twin Lakes and Aspen (today's CO 82). When train service came to Aspen in 1887, and as the Independence mines began to play out, the town faded. Today it is maintained by the Aspen Historical Society.

The summit at Independence Pass (12,095 feet), at Mile 18, is one of the highest paved passes in the United States. Mount Elbert's 14,433-foot summit (Colorado's highest) can be discerned due east; the round summit of Mount Massive (14,421 feet) lies to Elbert's north. La Plata Peak (14,336 feet) is fully visible immediately south of the pass. Its summit is Precambrian granite, but its lower slopes are younger rock, the result of a batholith from the Laramide orogeny that intruded into and lifted the older granite. A batholith is a volcanic intrusion like a stock, only larger, covering 40 square miles or more. Mount Huron (14,005 feet) is part of the same batholith.

CO 82 drops quickly to the east into the glaciated Lake Creek valley. La Plata Peak rises to the south, while the flanks of Mount Elbert comprise the steep, northern side of the valley. Around Mile 37 the valley opens out near the town of Twin Lakes. These lakes were formed by terminal moraines of the glaciers in the Lake Creek valley, which extended to, but did not fill, the Arkansas Valley. At Twin Lakes, the Collegiate Peaks lie to the south; the Mosquito Range is across the valley to the east.

Facilities: Full facilities at Aspen; gas, phone, general store on the eastern end of the route, at Twin Lakes.

Dates: Generally Memorial Day until mid-Oct.

Fees: None.

Closest town: Aspen, on the western end of the route.

For more information: Aspen Chamber Resort Association, 425 Rio Grande Place, Aspen, CO 81611. Phone (970) 925-1940.

WEST ELK LOOP SCENIC BYWAY

[Fig. 28(1)] Draped like a lariat around the West Elk Mountains, this 207-mile byway offers as much scenery and variety as any in Colorado. Beginning in the Roaring Fork Valley, the byway runs south through the joint where the southern end of the Grand Hogback contacts the granitic intrusion of Mount Sopris, in the Elk Mountains. It crosses McClure Pass into the Mancos Shale country of Muddy Creek and the North Fork of the Gunnison River, a relatively warm region of coal mines and fruit trees.

The route skirts the western flanks of the West Elks and the northern edge of the Black Canyon, passing through piñon pine and gambel oak ecosystems. Some of the pines in this area of the Black Canyon National Monument are more than 700 years old. From Gunnison the byway circles north to the historic town of Crested Butte, then climbs over Kebler Pass and descends through extensive aspen forests to rejoin itself at Paonia Reservoir.

Begin at Carbondale and take CO 133 south, up the Crystal River drainage. Around Mile 9, notice the rock glacier near the foot of the large, north-facing couloir (gully) on 12,953-foot Mount Sopris, which rises to the left (east). This glacier is composed of rock and ice; fed by winter snows, it is grinding slowly down the mountain.

At Mile 17, coke ovens line the highway on the western side. The town of Redstone, a National Historic District, is to the east, across the Crystal. Founded by John C. Osgood, Redstone was a model mining town in the late nineteenth century, a far cry from the mean and dirty mining towns typical of the era. Osgood built homes for workers, a hotel for single men (now the Redstone Inn), and his own mansion, Cleveholm Manor, 1 mile south of town, visible to the east across the river around Mile 18. The coal mines themselves were located several miles up Coal Creek to the west. They were operated until the early 1990s.

The large peak at the head of the valley is 12,721-foot Chair Mountain, the westernmost of the Ragged Mountains. The route climbs up McClure Pass (8,755 feet) to the west of Chair Mountain. From the pass the road descends into the Muddy Creek region, typified by Mesaverde Sandstones and Mancos Shale. Paonia Reservoir, at Mile 40, was authorized in 1956 as part of the Colorado River Storage Project; it holds water for downstream irrigators, principally fruit growers. At the base of Paonia Dam, at Mile 43, Gunnison County Road 12 comes in from the east; this is where the byway closes the loop. You can take this road during the summer over Kebler Pass to Crested Butte (it is mostly gravel and is closed in winter).

GIANT RED PAINTBRUSH
(Castilleja miniata)
Growing up to 3 feet tall, this flower produces red bracts atop straight stems from May until September.

Coal mines mark the North Fork of the Gunnison Valley from Paonia Dam to the town of Hotchkiss. This is also fruit-growing country, notable for its peaches, pears, and cherries. At Hotchkiss, Mile 69, turn south (left) onto Colorado 92. The large, conical mountain almost directly in front to the southeast, Landsend Peak (10,806 feet) is the westernmost extension of Colorado's central mountains.

At Mile 80 you enter the small town of Crawford. Continue south on CO 92 across the Smith Fork of the Gunnison. The route follows the foothills of the West Elks here, through ranch country and into the piñon pine and gambel oak environment of the Black Canyon rims. At Mile 87 Castle Rock projects up from the hills to your left (east). This is a weathered volcanic remnant of the West Elk eruptions. The road winds along the mesa above the north shore of Morrow Point Lake. The San Juan Mountains are visible to the south and southwest across Blue Mesa and the upper Uncompahgre Valley. At Mile 116 there is a pulloff with a good view of the Curecanti Needle, a formation of eroded volcanic breccia.

At Mile 121 the route crosses Blue Mesa Dam. Turn left (east) on US 50. At mile 126 there are good views of the Dillon Pinnacles, another weathered breccia formation, on the shores of Blue Mesa Reservoir. Stay on US 50 into Gunnison. At the junction with CO 135 (Main Street), turn left (north). Follow this through Gunnison and up the Gunnison River valley. At Mile 157 the Slate and Taylor rivers join to form the Gunnison.

The route climbs slowly up the riparian valley for 26 miles to Crested Butte. Many of the old ranches in the valley are being developed as more people move to the resort town or build second homes there. At Mile 173, turn left (west) onto Crested Butte's main street, Elk Avenue. Follow this through town and onto Gunnison County Road 12, a dirt road. At Mile 183 you have reached 10,007-foot Kebler Pass. The former mining town of Irwin is located 1 mile to the east; its graveyard is marked here at the pass.

At Mile 186 you pass The Dyke, a volcanic intrusion similar to those found around the Spanish Peaks in southeastern Colorado (*see* page108). This is the southernmost extension of the Ruby Range. East Beckwith Mountain (12,432 feet) and West Beckwith Mountain (12,185 feet) lie to the southwest. As the route winds down to the west, Marcellina Mountain (11,348 feet) looms up to the north.

The byway ends at Mile 207, at the base of Paonia Dam.

Facilities: Several towns along the route—Carbondale, Redstone, Paonia, Hotchkiss, Crawford, Gunnison, and Crested Butte—provide all services.

Dates: Open year-round, with the exception of the Crested Butte-Paonia Dam leg over Kebler Pass, which is closed in the winter.

Fees: None.

For more information: Carbondale Chamber of Commerce, 590 Highway 133, Carbondale, CO 81623. Phone (970) 963-1890. Gunnison Chamber of Commerce, 500 East Tomichi Avenue, Gunnison, CO 81230. Phone (970) 641-1501. Crested

Butte Chamber of Commerce, 601 Elk Avenue, Crested Butte, CO 81224. Phone (970) 349-6430.

GRAND MESA SCENIC BYWAY

This short (22-mile) scenic byway crosses the basalt-topped summit of Grand Mesa, a 10,500-foot plateau dotted with hundreds of small lakes. Along this route drivers climb quickly from Sonoran desert ecosystems characterized by juniper and saltbush, up to subalpine forest, then descend again to a high desert environment.

Both Grand Mesa and its lakes are the product of volcanic activity. The hard basalt covering the Grand Mesa, and protecting it from erosion, was laid down in a slow, oozing flow. The result is a flat-topped mountain that has withstood erosion more effectively than the surrounding desert lands and stands like an island in the sky above the sere landscape below. From the western tip of the mesa visitors can see the La Sal Mountains in Utah, the San Juan Mountains in southwestern Colorado, and the full span of the Uncompaghre and Grand valleys.

The mesa is geologically similar to the Flattops region to the northeast. Like the Flattops, Grand Mesa exists because oozing volcanoes spread a hard, protective cap of basalt over the sedimentary Green River and Wasatch formations that covered much of western Colorado. As surrounding lands eroded into valleys, both Grand Mesa and the Flattops remained relatively undisturbed, as did Basalt Mountain (above Basalt), once the easternmost extension of the Grand Mesa massif.

Grand Mesa's flat summit—about 10,500 feet high—holds more than 300 lakes, ponds, and puddles in depressions in the basalt. That basalt tops a geologic column that tells of a complex marine history in the region. Beginning in the Cretaceous Period, roughly 100 million years ago, sediments up to 5,000 feet deep accumulated at the bottom of a shallow sea. This became the ubiquitous Mancos Shale of western Colorado. As the sea receded from western Colorado, the Mesaverde group sandstones, shales, and coal formations were laid down in the swamps and coastlines that now covered the old seabed. Beginning 65 million years ago, up to 4,800 feet of Wasatch Formation rock was deposited in the early Tertiary Period. The Wasatch was made from eroded rock carried off the surrounding uplifts created during the Laramide orogeny.

Where the sea had once been, an enormous freshwater lake formed over western Colorado, eastern Utah, and southeastern Wyoming atop the Wasatch Formation. Lake bed deposits created the Green River Formation, the top of the sedimentary geology of this region. The topmost lava depositions came approximately 10 million years ago.

Consequently, the valleys you see today have been formed around Grand Mesa since that relatively recent geologic date. Glaciation, in the form of an ice cap on the flat mesa, ground out the depressions that became today's lakes.

Begin the byway route at Exit 49 on I-70, which leads directly onto CO 65 south.

AMERICAN KESTREL

(Falco sparverius)
This tiny bird can be seen hunting along parkways and fields, diving from above for other birds, insects or small mammals as prey.

The official byway begins about 10 miles on, at the junction with CO 330. Continue south on CO 65 from this junction. The route climbs up from a gambel oak and sage environment through aspen and into the subalpine spruce-fir ecoystem at the top of the mesa, around Mile 12. On the way up, notice the way the mesa erodes. Softer sedimentary rocks slip out from beneath the edges of the basaltic cap, undermining the cap rock and causing it to break off of its own weight at the edges and collapse downslope.

At Mile 20, turn right onto Lands End Road (gravel). At Mile 25, if the weather is clear, you may see the La Sal Mountains, a snowy cordillera located in eastern Utah, near Moab. Continue out to the western edge of the mesa at Mile 32. Return to CO 65 and reset your odometer; continue south (right) on CO 65.

At Mile 5 the road starts to switchback down the south side of the mesa. Here the gambel oak ecosystem extends almost up to the lip of the mesa, since the southern aspect of the mesa is much warmer and drier than the northern side. The byway ends at Mile 22, in Cedaredge, a town that has made a name for itself as an apple-growing district.

Facilities: There are no facilities along the byway.
Dates: Open year-round.
Fees: None.
Closest town: Cedaredge, on the southern end of the byway.
For more information: Cedaredge Chamber of Commerce, 208 West Main, Cedaredge, CO 81413. Phone (970) 856-6961.

GLENWOOD CANYON

[Fig. 23(4)] This 17-mile section of I-70 offers a spectacular illustration of geology. The Colorado River has cut down through the rock at a fault where harder Mississipian limestone meets softer Pennsylvanian shale. Today the river and highway share a narrow gorge 1,500 feet deep.

Sedimentary layers angle down to the east and west from the middle of the canyon, which bisects an anticline. Approaching from the east, look for Mississipian limestone near the top of the canyon walls. This is a gray rock between 200 and 300 feet thick. Beneath it lies Devonian limestone, then Ordovician dolomite. The Devonian rock creates green-gray cliffs; Ordovician cliffs are browner. Near the base of the cliffs, Cambrian quartzite up to 600 feet thick rests on Precambrian granite, which is not visible throughout most of the canyon but can be seen briefly at Mile 128. Then the anticline angles down to the west, and the rock sequence is reversed as you drive toward Glenwood Springs.

The highway through the canyon was one of the last stretches of Interstate 70 to be built; it was completed in the late 1980s, replacing two-lane US 6.

Several rafting companies in Glenwood Springs offer half-day and full-day float trips through the lower portion of the canyon.

Facilities: Paved bike path through canyon adjacent to Interstate 70.

Dates: Open year-round.

Fees: None.

Closest town: Glenwood Springs at Exit 116.

For more information: Glenwood Springs Chamber of Commerce, 1102 Grand Avenue, Glenwood Springs, CO 80601. Phone (970) 945-6589.

STRIPED SKUNK
(Mephitis mephitis)
Look for the striped skunk's white facial stripe, neck patch, and V on its back.

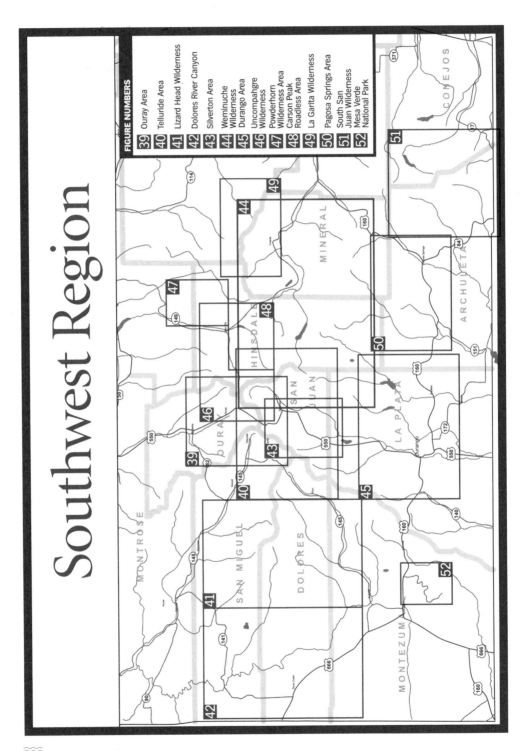

Southwest Region

FIGURE NUMBERS

39 Ouray Area
40 Telluride Area
41 Lizard Head Wilderness
42 Dolores River Canyon
43 Silverton Area
44 Weminuche Wilderness
45 Durango Area
46 Uncompahgre Wilderness
47 Powderhorn Wilderness Area
48 Carson Peak Roadless Area
49 La Garita Wilderness
50 Pagosa Springs Area
51 South San Juan Wilderness
52 Mesa Verde National Park

Southwest Region and Long Trails

T he San Juan mountain range is Colorado's largest, covering 10,000 square miles—an area the size of Delaware and New Jersey, combined. This is volcano country; the San Juans are peaks of a complex volcanic origin that makes for confusing geology, spectacular scenery, and extraordinary mineral wealth. The San Juans are the state's youngest mountains, only about 35 million years old at their oldest. That's roughly half the age of the peaks created by the Laramide uplift in northern and central Colorado.

The mountains of southwestern Colorado lie far from a major city. They are arguably bigger, wilder, more remote, and less developed than any in the state. They encompass Colorado's best-preserved mountain mining towns, some of its most challenging peaks, and its largest wilderness area.

Foot or horseback travel into the wilderness of the San Juan Mountains brings

[*Above:* The Needle Mountains and Animas River near Durango]

visitors into deep, forested valleys favored by bobcats, Canada lynx, black bears and mountain lions. There are even rumors of a few, hidden grizzly bears. Long volcanic and sedimentary plateaus skirting the high peaks invite backpackers to strike out across country.

Because humans love—and need—to name things, the San Juan region's mountains go by many names. Within the sprawling mass of mountains that make up the San Juans are the Grenadier Mountains, the Needles and West Needles and Turret Needles, the La Plata Mountains, the San Miguels, the Sneffels Range, and yes, the San Juans and South San Juans.

The Alpine Loop Scenic Byway affords jeepers, dirt bikers and mountain bikers a historic, unique route between Ouray, Lake City, and Silverton. The high country here has not only dramatic geology and geography; but also lush meadows filled with alpine bistort, mountain bog gentian (*Gentiana calycosa*), harebell (*Campanula rotundifolia*), and the towering green spires of monument plant (*Frasera speciosa*).

The Southwestern Mountain Region is defined by a line running from the Utah border due east to the village of Whitewater, then south along US 50 to Montrose. At Montrose the border turns east on US 50 and runs to Gunnison, skirting south of Curecanti National Monument (included in the West Central Mountain Region, *see* page 153) along the way. At Gunnison the border turns southeast along CO 114 to Saguache, where it turns south, running along the western edge of the San Luis Valley to the New Mexico border.

This region encompasses the ancient ruins of Mesa Verde National Park and the redrock canyons of the Uncompaghre Plateau, places that seem more like Utah than Colorado. It includes the headwaters of the Rio Grande River, which flows to the Gulf of Mexico, and of the San Juan River, which carves beautiful canyons across Utah on its way to the Colorado River and the Gulf of California.

Principally, though, the Southwest Mountain Region encompasses a vast, contiguous massif that stretches from Dolores to Del Norte, from Chromo to Ridgway. These mountains are the result of 30 million years of volcanic activity that began 35 million years ago in the Oligocene Epoch of the Tertiary Period and continued, in three waves, into the Pliocene Epoch, which began about 10 million years ago.

Volcanic activity takes many forms. Molten magma may push up against overlying layers of rock, but not break through. Cooling in place, this magma creates hard stocks that form mountains like Mount Sopris, near Carbondale, and the Spanish Peaks, near La Veta. These mountains were revealed only after the softer overburden of sedimentary rock had eroded away and left the hard core standing above the surrounding landscape. Magma may flow out of the ground in a slow, liquid ooze, spreading across the landscape—exactly what happened to cap the Flattops and Grande Mesa in northwestern Colorado.

Or volcanoes may explode. Their explosive potential is determined by the magma's chemical composition and the amount of dissolved gas in the molten rock.

During the late Tertiary Period in the San Juan region, explosive, cataclysmic events occurred regularly. Eruptions were sometimes so violent that the spent volcanoes collapsed on themselves, creating dished and fractured calderas. In the San Juans, 15 calderas have been identified,, ranging in size from 5 miles to 20 miles in diameter and often overlapping like craters on the moon.

Volcanic activity created three commonly found types of rock: lava flows such as basalt; ash-based tuff; and breccia, formed when rock was broken in explosions or collapses, then welded together again by heat and pressure.

The collapsing calderas produced arcurate fractures around their rims. As is the case throughout Colorado, such fractures were a pathway for later intrusions of super-heated liquid solutions to bring mineral-carrying solutions up into the overlying rock. Often minerals such as silver or gold, or compounds of them, would precipitate out of the hot solutions along the contact line between an igneous intrusion and overlying rocks. An example includes the Leadville Limestone found around Ouray, where the seeds were sown for rich, nineteenth century mines.

The three phases of the San Juans' volcanology played out roughly as follows:

About 35 million years ago a field of volcanic debris estimated to be 100 miles across and 0.8 mile thick was deposited during a period of 5 million years. This debris, much of it in the form of heavy ash layers, probably came from eruptions in the San Juan region and the West Elk Mountains. The ash formed a rock known as San Juan Tuff.

More volcanic activity erupted around present-day Silverton, adding new lava, ash, and breccia. Erosion then removed most of this first-phase rock and ash.

The second phase of eruptions began 29 million years ago. At least eight distinct eruptions have been identified in the ash layers from this period. After 3.5 million years, volcanic activity essentially ceased and the Miocene-Pliocene regional uplift began, lifting the San Juan region, and all of Colorado, 1 mile into the air.

About 25 million years ago, while the uplift was underway, the third volcanic phase began. This was less explosive than the previous phases; sheets of basalt spread over the eastern San Juans. Pleistocene-era glaciers then polished up the mountains, carving the classic deep valleys, horns, and ridges typical of glaciated regions. Their work is particularly apparent in the west San Juans west of Lake City, and along the northern front of the massif. Because these mountains are so young, relatively little erosion has taken place, so they remain steep and particularly dramatic.

For all the volcanic activity, the mountains here are not exclusively igneous. There are sedimentary rocks here, particularly apparent around Ouray, Telluride, Molas Divide, and Coal Bank Pass. Some are Precambrian sediments, more than 300 million years old. Others are younger, thrust up by the lifting and faulting of this remarkably active, young, mountain range.

Prospectors quickly recognized the potential of the region. As early as 1860, only a year after the Colorado Territory's first major ore strike in Gregory Gulch, site of

Central City, prospectors were panning gold at Baker's Park, which would become the site of Silverton. But protests by Ute Indians, who laid claim to the area under treaties with the federal government, plus the onset of the Civil War and the great inaccessibility of many of the most promising sites meant that real exploration and discovery would not begin until 1873.

In 1868 the Utes agreed to relocate to terrain west of the 107th meridian, a north-south line just west of Gunnison. But this was not a sufficient concession for settlers who wanted the mineral and agricultural wealth of these lands. They trespassed onto Ute lands, particularly in the San Juans. In 1873 Chief Ouray (relying heavily on the advice of his wife, Chipeta) negotiated the Brunot Agreement. This treaty opened the mountaintops of the San Juans to miners while reserving the valleys for Utes—an unworkable arrangement that quickly resulted in more pressure on the Utes to leave land coveted by settlers from the east.

In the treaty Chief Ouray was officially designated the spokesman for the entire Ute tribe. He may have been venerated by Anglos because he spoke English, but the truth was he had little control over the entire tribe. He would, however, help bring a peaceful settlement in the aftermath of the Meeker massacre in 1879, an event which resulted in the Utes being driven onto small reservations in Utah and southwestern Colorado. He died before his people were expelled from their traditional lands.

Following the Brunot Agreement the San Juan region boomed and kept booming. Two types of development, mining and railroads, produced the communities of today's San Juan Mountains. Telluride, Creede, Lake City, Silverton, Ophir, and Ouray were places built atop rich mineral wealth. Durango, Dolores, South Fork, and Ridgway were communities founded by or for the railroads, which burrowed into the mountains to reach those mining towns.

The mountain towns in the western San Juans—Silverton, Lake City, Ouray, Telluride, and Ophir—lie quite close as the crow flies, but driving among them can take the better part of a day. For instance, mining tunnels connect the old mining camp of Red Mountain to Pandora, a mine site just upstream from Telluride in the San Miguel Valley. Yet to drive the circuitous roads from one site to the other takes at least two hours.

This sense of separateness and isolation gives each of these communities distinct characteristics. Their residents have preserved the architecture, the history, and much of the spirit of the mining era. They are populated by people who love the mountains first and foremost. These towns seem to be far removed from the outside world; even today, traveling to them on the narrow, steep, and twisting mountain roads of the San Juans is an achievement measured by time and difficulty, not simply mileage.

Extraordinary engineering—much of it conducted by Otto Mears, a Russian Jewish immigrant who planned and built seemingly impossible toll roads and railway lines—eased one of the biggest problems for settlers, transportation. But nobody familiar with the San Juan Mountains would say they have been tamed.

Avalanches and blizzards regularly close Highway 550, sometimes cutting Silverton off from the outside world for days at a time. Thunderstorms still occasionally flood Creede, Telluride, and Ouray. In a geological instant, the enormous, creeping earthflow of Slumgullion Slide will slither into Lake City—no one can stop it. And the vast heart of the San Juans is buried deep in the Weminuche Wilderness, nearly 800 square miles of wildness.

The Sherman Act of 1890 added a great deal of wealth to the mining communities of the San Juans, for it guaranteed a government purchase price of $1.06 an ounce for all the silver the mines could produce. When the act was repealed in 1893 (politicians argued the purchasers were bankrupting the country, which was in a deep recession), many of Colorado's mining towns failed. Some of the San Juan towns, however, hung on, because they found in their mines copper, lead, and—especially— gold. Industrial mining ended in the region in 1991, with the closure of the Sunnyside Mine near Silverton.

Silverton today is the northern terminus of the Durango and Silverton Narrow Gauge Railroad, a spectacular, summer steam train ride up the Animas Canyon.

Douglas Fir Ecosystems

Douglas fir (*Psuedotsuga menzeisii*) may grow to enormous heights in the Pacific Northwest; in Colorado, limited by colder weather and shorter growing seasons, it seldom rises above 100 feet. Douglas fir is widely spread through the state's mountains. It creates a dark, cool, moist forest at elevations from 5,600 to 9,000 feet.

In some areas Douglas fir is found adjacent to ponderosa pine. The ponderosas grow on the warmer, sunnier south-facing slopes, while the firs shelter in the cooler, wetter northern exposures.

The best way to identify Douglas fir is by the cones. It is the only Colorado conifer that has a three-pronged bract, like a snake's tongue, extending from between the scales of its cones, which hang down from branches throughout the tree (subalpine fir and white fir [*Abies concolor*] have cones that point up, and are distributed principally in the top of the tree).

Douglas fir needles are flat and soft to the touch and are laid out along the twig in a rough spiral formation that may look more like two flat rows. Mature trees have a thick, corky, almost black bark. The bark of younger trees is silver and filled with sap blisters.

Douglas fir was some of the best timber to be found in Colorado in the nineteenth century; much of it was logged for bridge trestles, mine timbers, and other uses.

Birds and animals that frequent subalpine coniferous forests of Engelmann spruce, subalpine fir, and lodgepole pine are common in Douglas fir ecosystems, too.

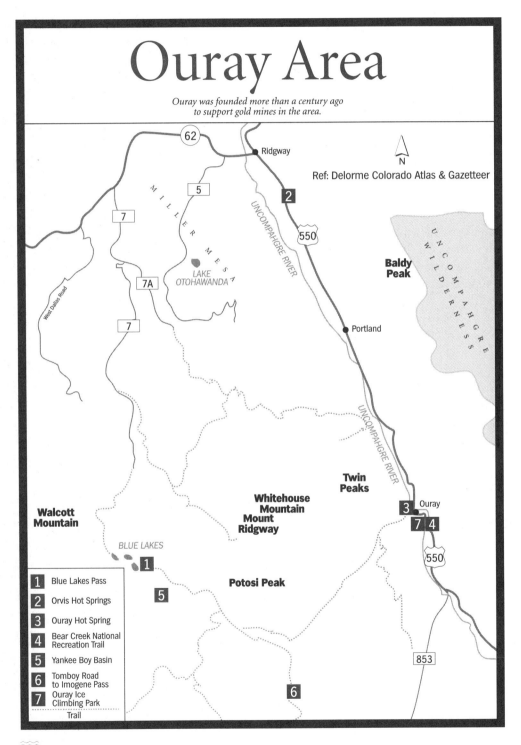

Ouray Area

*Ouray was founded more than a century ago
to support gold mines in the area.*

Ref: Delorme Colorado Atlas & Gazetteer

1 Blue Lakes Pass
2 Orvis Hot Springs
3 Ouray Hot Spring
4 Bear Creek National
  Recreation Trail
5 Yankee Boy Basin
6 Tomboy Road
  to Imogene Pass
7 Ouray Ice
  Climbing Park
⋯⋯ Trail

The ground squirrel, or chickaree (*Tamiasciurus hudsonicus*) is common to all these areas. This squirrel is easily identified by the vociferous chiding it gives intruders. Other common rodents are the golden-mantled ground squirrel (*Spermophilus lateralis*) and Colorado chipmunk (*Tamias quadrivittatus*).

Common bird species include the dark-eyed junco (*Junco hyemalis*), a small, gray bird identified by a dorsal rust-colored patch between its wings, and the ruby-crowned kinglet (*Regulus calendula*). The male of this small (4-inch-long) olive-drab species has a small, red crown, but it is generally hidden beneath other feathers. Look for two white wing bars, and a dark black bar beneath them, to identify this species.

The forest floor in a grove of Douglas firs is shady and damp. Relatively few plant species thrive in this environment. A very common one, however, is kinnikinnik, or common bearberry (*Arctostaphylos ova-ursi*). This plant grows only a few inches tall in mats of small, spoon-shaped, light green leaves that sprawl along the forest floor like a thin green carpet.

Look also for false Solomon's seal (*Maianthemum racemosum*, also known as *Smilacina racemosa*), which likes damp, shady sites. It grows up to 2 feet tall, bearing a stalk of broad, alternate leaves about 3 inches long and 1 inch wide. A small pyramid of tiny flowers sits atop the stalk. The plant flowers from May to July.

Ouray Area

[Fig. 39] Stuffed into a crevice of Colorado's soaring San Juan Mountains, Ouray (pronounced you-ray) was founded a century ago to support gold mines amid the surrounding peaks. The town was originally named Uncompahgre; that appellation was later changed to honor Chief Ouray.

The town now bills itself as The Switzerland of America. The surrounding San Juan Mountains, which spring like wings from the valley of the Uncompahgre River, may be the most dramatically vertical in the state. They are characterized by narrow canyons and vertiginous peaks. An enormous natural amphitheater rises to the east of town; the small but dramatic Box Canyon defines the western edge of the community.

Ouray was the site of some spectacular road-building by Otto Mears, the engineer who almost singlehandedly brought roads and railroads to the towns and camps buried deep in the inaccessible San Juans.

In 1883 Mears began work on a project considered impossible: building a road 12 miles south from Ouray up to the mining camp of Red Mountain, where a very rich silver strike had been made the year before. Borrowing a technique he used to lay the Denver and Rio Grande Railroad line into the eastern end of the Black Canyon of the Gunnison, Mears lowered drillers down canyon walls on ropes. There they drilled and set dynamite charges with long fuses, then were raised to safety before the blast. Mears had his "impossible" road roughed out in three months. Today US 550 traces over it.

GRAY JAY
(*Perisoreus canadensis*)

Camp Bird Road, leading to the fabulous Camp Bird, Yankee Boy, and Sneffels mines, took Mears a little longer. Winter interrupted work, and he didn't get that 5-mile bit of engineering done until 1884. That same summer he was hired to build a road to provide the businesses of Silverton with a piece of the action at the high mines of Red Mountain. A road meant trade.

By November, Mears had completed that route, too, connecting Ouray and Silverton on what would later be celebrated—and lamented—as the "Million Dollar Highway." It was celebrated as a great engineering achievement, but lamented because it turned out that Mears had used valuable mine tailings, with a high mineral content, to surface the road.

For more information: Ouray Chamber of Commerce, 1222 Main Street, Ouray, CO 81427. Phone (970) 325-4746.

BEAR CREEK NATIONAL RECREATION TRAIL

[Fig. 39(4)] Nearly all the hikes and roads around Ouray connect the traveler to the mining history of the region, and this route is no exception. It is impossible to hike this trail, once a roadway to several mines, and not be awed in the extreme by the engineering feats and simple bravado associated with wresting minerals from the precipitous mountains of this region.

This trail is exposed to steep drops in several locations. Consequently it is not for children, dogs, the faint of heart, or those with fear of heights.

The trail climbs steeply up 13 switchbacks above the V-shaped gorge of the Uncompahgre River, passing through Douglas fir and up into a world that quickly illustrates the varied geology of the region. On the lower switchbacks, dark, tinkling slate of the Uncompahgre Formation rattles underfoot like broken glass; higher up, the trail cuts — literally — through volcanic tuff and veins of quartz and pyrite.

The route climbs about 1,000 feet in the first mile, then winds precariously around the corner of the Bear Creek valley and along the cliff wall above the creek. As you enter the canyon here, look to the south. Wavy lines on vertical rock above the creek are the fossilized remains of prehistoric mud flats uplifted from ancient sediments. Farther south is the prominently hued Red Mountain, site of a major mining town during the late nineteenth and early twentieth centuries.

The trail was once a wagon road, blasted out of the rock and supported by wood and stone cribs. Sloughing has narrowed it considerably in some places. The route levels out somewhat after about 2 miles. At the 2.5-mile mark you pass the machinery and old buildings of the Grizzly Bear Mine, and shortly after, an open mine portal on the left side of the trail. Do not enter mines; they are exceedingly dangerous places. Even a few feet inside a mine tunnel, dangerous gases may have accumulated, displacing oxygen.

The route continues up through meadows, aspen groves, and subalpine spruce-fir forest to a fork at the 4-mile mark, where the Yellowjacket Mine is located. An old bunkhouse still stands, and much heavy machinery from a stamping mill (used to concentrate metal ores) has been left here. This is the end of the Bear Creek National Recreation Trail; overnight hikes can be undertaken from here north into the Uncompahgre Wilderness or south toward Engineer Pass, a four-wheel-drive road leading to Lake City (*see* the Alpine Loop Scenic Byway, page 320).

Look back to the west from Bear Creek to see Mount Sneffels, the nipple-tipped peak on the northern edge of Yankee Boy Basin. Like Engineer Mountain to the south of Silverton, and some of the San Miguel Mountains northwest of Telluride, Sneffels (a third-phase volcanic intrusion through other volcanic depositions) was probably a nunatak— that is, a peak that protruded through the ice cap during the Pleistocene Epoch and so was not eroded the way surrounding terrain was.

Directions: Drive south from Ouray on US 550 for 2 miles, passing through a tunnel cut through the rock. Immediately after exiting the tunnel, park on the left (east). To reach the trailhead, cross the highway and begin climbing at the west side of the tunnel portal; the route traverses over the tunnel and continues up the mountain.

Closest town: Ouray, 2 miles north.

For more information: Ouray Ranger District, Uncompahgre National Forest, 2505 South Townsend, Montrose, CO 81401. Phone (970) 240-5300.

Trail: 4 miles one-way.

Elevation: Change of 2,800 feet.

Degree of difficulty: Strenuous.

Surface: Loose rock, scree, dirt.

Gray Jay

The gray jay (*Perisoreus canadensis*) goes by many names: Canada jay, camp robber, whiskyjack. The gray jay is easily identified in coniferous forests because, unlike most wildlife, this bird is attracted to humans. In the gray jay's world, people mean food.

Gray jays are aggressive and will actively try to steal food from a picnic or camp site. However, feeding these birds is bad for them, as it is for all wildlife. Animals that are fed become dependent on people. Such birds and animals may seem tame, but they are not. When conflicts occur with people, animals lose.

The gray jay lives year-round in high conifer forests. It nests at altitudes as high as 11,300 feet and survives the long winters on caches of food. An omnivore, the gray jay eats small birds and mammals, insects, and seeds.

YANKEE BOY BASIN

[Fig. 39(5)] Yankee Boy Basin, situated on the southern side of Mount Sneffels between Ouray and Telluride, was home to some of Colorado's richest mines. An estimated $27 million worth of ore was extracted from the high basin, which tops out at Blue Lake Pass at 13,000 feet. (The Tomboy mines on the far side of Imogene Pass were equally wealthy.) The basin is a riot of summer wildflowers and impressive volcanic geology. Thanks to Otto Mears's road, it can be reached by car during the summer.

This region of the San Juans produced both silver and gold, although much of the gold was found deep in the mines. This was not the case at Camp Bird. An Irish carpenter, Thomas Walsh, discovered gold here on the surface and bought up 100 claims in 1896. Soon he was producing $1 million a year in gold, second in Colorado production only to the Portland Mine at Cripple Creek. As many as 400 miners lived in luxury in his boarding houses at the mine, where they dined on fancy meals off of china plates and enjoyed steam heat and marble bathrooms.

The Camp Bird Mine produced $2.5 million in gold for Walsh, who then sold the property for $5.2 million—after which it produced another $22 million. Altogether, the mines around Ouray generated $125 million in mineral wealth.

Camp Bird Road, which leads to Camp Bird, Upper Camp Bird, Imogene Pass, and Yankee Boy Basin, was a busy, dangerous road when the mines were active. It is now closed in winter and is swept regularly by avalanches, but it remains a popular road during summer.

The route over Imogene Pass, to the southwest from Yankee Boy Basin, may be driven only by experienced four-wheelers with high-clearance vehicles. Passenger cars, however, generally can make it as far as Lower Camp Bird, 4.5 miles up the road, with no trouble in summer; higher clearance two-wheel-drive vehicles can generally reach the town site of Sneffels, 1 mile farther on.

Wherever you park, the surroundings are spectacular. Towering, ragged peaks, picturesque and impressive mining ruins, and sweeping bowls of wildflowers surround you. This is a popular area, however. Be sure to drive and park only on bare

MULE DEER
(Odocoileus hemionus)
Named for its large, mulelike ears, this deer browses the foothills in winter and moves to higher elevations in spring.

ground, to respect private property around the mines, and to leave the place better than you found it.

Directions: Take US 550 south from Ouray to the first switchback, about 0.25 mile. Turn right onto Camp Bird Road; bear left immediately after the turn and take the higher bridge across the Box Canyon. Follow this road 4.5 miles to Camp Bird.

For more information: Ouray Chamber of Commerce, 1222 Main Street, Ouray, CO 81427. Phone (970) 325-4746. Or Ouray Ranger District, Uncompahgre National Forest, 2505 South Townsend, Montrose, CO 81401. Phone (970) 240-5300.

HIKING BLUE LAKES PASS

[Fig. 39(1)] From Blue Lakes Pass at the northwestern edge of Camp Bird basin you look down into the 16,505-acre Mount Sneffels Wilderness, which barely includes 14,105-foot Mount Sneffels, located north of the pass. The views are spectacular to the north across Hasting Mesa toward Dallas Divide and the long, broad back of the Uncompahgre Plateau, and down into the spruce and aspen forests along the northern side of the east-west running Sneffels Range. When aspen trees turn golden in early autumn, and the mountains are dusted with snow, the scenery here is sublime. On clear days the La Sal Mountains, located in eastern Utah, are easily visible northwest of the Uncompahgre Plateau.

Mule Deer

The mule deer (*Odcoileus hemionus*) is the most common large mammal in Colorado. Approximately 600,000 mule deer live in the state. They prefer brushy terrain and adapt well to human habitation.

Mule deer molt twice annually, shifting between a reddish-brown summer coat and a dull gray winter coat. The animal is a browser with a multi chambered stomach capable of digesting many different plants.

During the early summer, bucks follow the melting snow to summer range above timberline. Does give birth in timber and then follow the bucks once their spotted fawns are able to move.

Although food and range are widely available in summer, winter is a critical time for mule deer, which must find forage in areas that hold relatively little snow cover—14 inches or less. In an average year 10 to 20 percent of the state's mule deer do not survive winter. Residential, golf, and ski area development of traditional winter range in mountain valleys has limited available forage. Animals are forced to cross highways in search of food; an average of 3,000 deer are killed on highways each year.

Directions: From Camp Bird, follow the road uphill, either on foot or by vehicle. After 2.2 miles the turnoff to Governor Basin branches to the left; bear right. Above this point the route can be driven only in high-clearance four-wheel-drive. Another 1.3 miles brings you to a trail (a left) where the road begins to switchback. Either the trail or the jeep road will take you to the pass, about 2 miles ahead.

For more information: Ouray Ranger District, Uncompahgre National Forest,

2505 South Townsend, Montrose, CO 81401. Phone (970) 240-5300.

Closest town: Ouray, 7 miles east.

Trail: 6.6 miles round-trip from the turnoff to Governor Basin.

Elevation: Change of 2,200 feet.

Degree of difficulty: Strenuous.

Surface: Jeep road, rocky trail.

﷽ OURAY ICE CLIMBING PARK

[Fig. 39(7)] Until the mid-1990s, Ouray pretty much closed up for the winter. That changed with the creation of the Ouray Ice Climbing Park on the western edge of the town. The park is the most established, and most elaborate, organized ice-climbing facility in the United States, and the only park created solely for ice climbing. Spectators can get a good view of climbers from a nearby bridge.

An old reservoir system above the town leaks water down the cliffs of the Box Canyon, forming long, blue ice falls, some as high as 140 feet, along the western edge of town. Local and visiting climbers tackle these and dozens of more remote ice climbs in the valleys and clefts of the surrounding San Juans. As recently as 1991, Box Canyon was off limits to climbers; the Ouray Electric Power and Light Company owns the land and prohibited trespassing. But then Eric Jacobsen bought Ouray Electric. Sympathetic to climbers, he worked with local authorities and The Access Fund, a climbers' group, to open the gorge to the public.

Local climbers have built the ice park. Ouray Electric runs a small hydropower plant at the base of the gorge, funneling water through a penstock—a 44-inch steel pipe that draws from a small dam upstream and carries water 1.5 miles under pressure along the gorge. Jacobsen allowed climbers to draw water off the penstock and build ice falls. Sixty-five taps have been set in place, sprinkling a fine spray of cold water that's filled 0.5 mile of the canyon wall with ice. The natural climbs are a deep, misty indigo, while those fed by the penstock sport a rusty hue from the iron oxide that drains into the Uncompahgre River from the area's old mines.

Directions: Drive south on US 550 approximately 0.25 mile to the right-hand turn marked Box Canyon, a dirt road. Take this turn; bear left at the first fork, after about 50 yards. Cross the bridge over the canyon after about 300 yards; park on the left-hand side of the road. Climbers may be observed from the bridge; do not enter the canyon unless you are equipped to climb and to protect yourself from falling ice and other hazards.

Dates: Ice climbing is dependent upon the weather and generally coincides with ski season, roughly from Nov. to Apr.

Fees: None.

Closest town: Ouray, 1 mile north.

For more information: Do not attempt ice climbing, and do not enter the park, without proper equipment and training, or unless you are under the supervision of a guide. For information on climbing guides, contact Ouray Mountain Sports (970) 325-4284, or The Ouray Victorian Inn (970) 325-7222. For general information, contact the Ouray Chamber of Commerce, 1222 Main Street, Ouray, CO 81427. Phone (970) 325-4746.

HOT SPRINGS
OURAY HOT SPRINGS
[Fig. 39(3)] Several hot springs have been developed in and near Ouray. Five private hotels have tapped into the local hot water, as has the municipal pool. The natural springs were used by Ute Indians at least as early as the fourteenth century, and probably earlier. The public hot springs pool on the northern edge of Ouray was constructed in 1926 by volunteers; the bathhouse was built the following year, and the whole operation turned over to the city in 1930.

Mineral water flows out of the ground here at about 150 degrees Fahrenheit; it is cooled to temperatures ranging from 80 degrees to 105 degrees in several large pools. The largest is a 150-foot by 250-foot lap pool.

Directions: The hot springs are located on the northern edge of Ouray directly beside US 550, the main street through town.

Facilities: Lockers, showers, fitness center, soaking pools, lap pool, playground.

Dates: Open year-round.

Fees: There is a fee.

For more information: Ouray Hot Springs, PO Box 468, Ouray, Colorado 81427. Phone (970) 325-468.

ORVIS HOT SPRINGS
[Fig. 39(2)] The rustic Orvis Hot Springs are situated beside hay meadows in the Uncompahgre Valley between Ouray and Ridgway. Mineral water here runs from the ground at temperatures from 112 to 127 degrees Fahrenheit. One of the unusual features for a commercial hot springs is the outdoor soaking pond, which is an enlarged, natural spring. Water flows naturally up from the unlined mud bottom. Temperatures here run about 103 to 105 degrees. In the other pools, temperatures are maintained at levels from 102 to 110 degrees.

Directions: From Ridgway, drive south 2 miles on US 550 to Ouray County Road 3; turn right (west) to the hot springs, located just off the highway.

Facilities: Hot pools and pond, lodge rooms, private pools.

Dates: Open year-round.

Fees: There is a fee.

Closest town: Ridgway, 2 miles north.

For more information: Orvis Hot Springs, 1585 County Road 3, Ridgway, CO 81432. Phone (970) 626-5324.

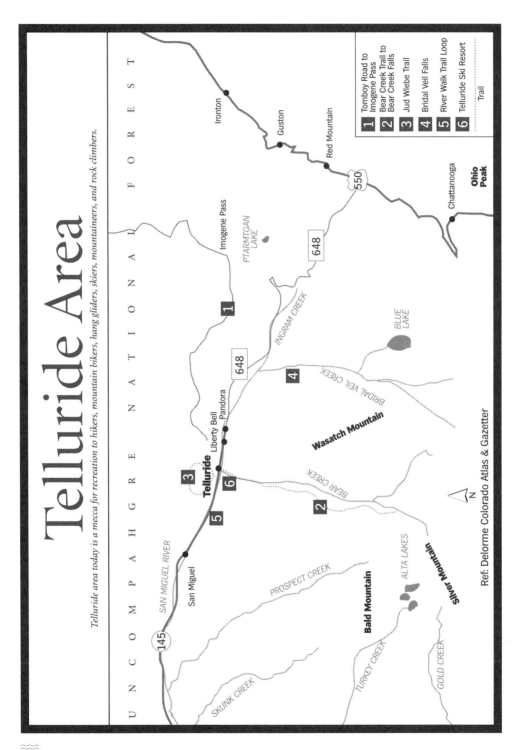

Telluride Area

Telluride area today is a mecca for recreation to hikers, mountain bikers, hang gliders, skiers, mountaineers, and rock climbers.

UNCOMPAHGRE NATIONAL FOREST

1. Tomboy Road to Imogene Pass
2. Bear Creek Trail to Bear Creek Falls
3. Jud Wiebe Trail
4. Bridal Veil Falls
5. River Walk Trail Loop
6. Telluride Ski Resort
- - - Trail

Ref: Delorme Colorado Atlas & Gazetter

Telluride Area

[Fig. 40] Telluride's name is often said to be an approximation of the phrase, "to hell you ride," although the valley is anything but hellish and the community promoted itself in the nineteenth century under the slogan "The Town Without A Bellyache." The phrase "to hell you ride" was probably derived from a conductor's pronunciation as he announced the Telluride station on the Rio Grande Southern Railway, which helped bring prosperity to the stunningly beautiful San Miguel Valley and its high, rich mines when it arrived in 1890.

The more likely origin of the town's name is geological; gold was found here in a tellurium compound called telluride. Gold caused a lot of activity in the upper San Miguel Valley; 350 miles worth of mine tunnels were dug through the surrounding hills, including one that went 7 miles east to the mines on Red Mountain Pass. Some veins were followed vertically for 3,000 feet.

Telluride sits in a flat valley floor, the middle step in a stair-stepped, glaciated valley. A box canyon to the east marks the upper valley, from which Bridal Veil Falls cascades 365 feet through the air. To the west, at Keystone Hill, a glacial moraine blocked the middle valley where Telluride now rests. This portion backfilled with eroded alluvial material, which piled 500 feet deep to form the smooth valley floor. West of the moraine the San Miguel River drops down into a narrow canyon of redbeds.

Look along the walls of the valley around Telluride for what geologists call an angular unconformity. Tilted layers of Mesozoic-Era rock (240 million to 65 million years old) were beveled flat by erosion, then overlaid by a purplish, horizontal layer up to 250 feet thick known as Telluride Conglomerate. Above this is San Juan Tuff, deposited during the first volcanic phase in the region, about 35 million years ago. This tuff runs 1,500 to 2,000 feet thick. Younger second- and third-phase volcanic debris, dikes, stocks, and veins intrude into and protrude through this tuff. Examples of these intrusions include Mount Sneffels to the north and the Ophir Needles, a towering, crenellated cliff located about 5 miles south of Telluride on CO 145. The San Miguel mountain range, a free-standing massif lying west of Telluride, is another intrusion.

Telluride served as a mining supply town; the big mines were up in the Savage and Marshall basins, located 10 miles east of Telluride on the rough, high road that leads to Ouray over Imogene Pass. The first strike was made there in 1875, and the town boomed steadily until the end of the century.

Telluride was clearly divided into the "sunny side," located north of Colorado Avenue, and the "shady side," to the south. Saloons (26 at one time), bordellos, and cribs—prostitutes' quarters—were located on the shady side and drew a steady clientele. Several historic Telluride buildings still contain secret passages through which the town's more upstanding men could sneak out to the red light district. Women of the "respectable" classes made sure never to be seen south of Colorado Avenue, where 175 prostitutes worked.

Like most mining communities, Telluride was a potpourri of workers from many parts of the world, in particular Sweden, Finland and Cornwall. It was also a notably lawless place; the town marshall was shot down by a sniper one night, to no one's particular concern.

Two violent events are particularly remembered here: On June 24, 1889, Butch Cassidy (Robert Leroy Parker) robbed his first bank when he held up the San Miguel Valley Bank in broad daylight. Cassidy and his companions had practiced their holdup several times by galloping down Colorado Avenue and causing a ruckus; when they took off that morning with the bank's money, bystanders thought the event was only more hijinks, not a real robbery. Cassidy's successful heist marked the beginning of a career of cattle and train robberies that purportedly ended in a shootout in Bolivia around 1909—although some researchers maintain that Butch Cassidy actually lived until 1957 under a new identity in New Mexico.

The second event was more protracted and complicated. In May 1901, the Western Federation of Miners went out on strike against the Smuggler-Union Mine, demanding $3 for an eight-hour day. This precipitated three years of violence and bloodshed; during much of this time Telluride lived under a state of martial law, occupied by the Colorado National Guard. In the end, the strike and the union were broken.

Telluride today is a Mecca for recreation. Hikers, mountain bikers, hang gliders, skiers, mountaineers, rock climbers, and even mushroom pickers flock to the town, which was designated a National Historic District in 1964. Summer festivals celebrate some of these pastimes; weekends consequently can be very crowded. But surrounding trails and jeep roads lead quickly away from the crowds into the alpine country of the San Juans.

For more information: Telluride Visitors Services, 700 West Colorado Avenue, Telluride, CO 81435. Phone (970) 728-3041 or (888) 783-0257.

HIKING BEAR CREEK TRAIL TO BEAR CREEK FALLS

[Fig. 40(2)] The vertical terrain surrounding Telluride suggests that gentle hikes are nonexistent. This is almost true, but not entirely. The 2-mile hike to Bear Creek Falls climbs only 1,000 feet—a gentle hike by San Juan Mountain standards, anyway.

The Bear Creek valley floor, located immediately southeast of Telluride and east of the Telluride Ski Area, is owned by the San Miguel Conservation Fund, which purchased it to prevent development of this spectacular cleft. (This is a different Bear Creek from that traversed by the Bear Creek National Recreation Trail near Ouray— see page 242.) The Bear Creek Trail to Bear Creek Falls is an old mining road, is a very popular route for hikers, bikers, and dog walkers. The walk terminates at the cascading Bear Creek Falls.

Avalanches rake down the steep mountains and carry across the narrow valley from both sides in the winter. In the early spring, when snow conditions are judged to be safe enough, hardy back country skiers climb up from Ophir, located south of the Bear Creek valley, over the pass at the head of the valley and ski down to Telluride.

Directions: The Bear Creek Trail leads directly out of Telluride to the southeast from the southern end of Pine Street. There is no parking. The trailhead is a five-minute walk from the San Miguel County courthouse at the center of town, on Colorado Avenue.

Closest town: Telluride, at the foot of the trail.

For more information: Town of Telluride, 113 West Columbia Avenue, Telluride, CO 81435. Phone (970) 728-3071. Or Norwood Ranger District, Uncompahgre National Forest, 1760 East Grand Avenue, Norwood, CO 81423. Phone (970) 327-4261.

Trail: 4 miles round-trip.

Elevation: Change of 1,000 feet.

Degree of difficulty: Easy

Surface: Packed dirt, old jeep road.

HIKE TO BRIDAL VEIL FALLS

[Fig. 40(4)] Four spectacular waterfalls bracket Telluride: Cornet Creek Falls, a few hundred yards up the red canyon at the north end of Aspen Street; Bear Creek Falls, 2 miles up the Bear Creek Trail (*see* page 250); and Ingram Falls and Bridal Veil Falls, near Ajax Peak and Ingram Peak. Ajax Peak is the conical mountain dominating the head of the valley above Telluride. It is a peak with two summits: 12,785 feet for the western summit and 13,230 feet for the eastern. Its upper faces are barren; in the winter they gather enormous volumes of snow that slide down the several avalanche chutes between the rocky buttresses on the mountain's western side. Known as the Finnboy Slides, these deadly avalanches can careen all the way across the head of Telluride's box canyon. Consequently, this hike is not a good idea in the winter.

South of Ajax is Ingram Peak, 12,552 feet high. Ingram Falls lies between the two; south of Ingram Peak is Bridal Veil Falls, which is visible from the hillside immediately north of downtown Telluride, and from the approach to town on CO 145.

Three hundred and sixty-five feet high, Bridal Veil is the longest free-falling waterfall in Colorado. The improbable building perched at the lip of the falls is a hydroelectric generating station built in 1907 to generate electricity for the Smuggler Union Mine, located to the north in the Marshall Basin. It operated until 1953. In the early 1990s it was renovated by entrepreneur Eric Jacobsen and again generates electricity. It is, however, private property.

This hike begins at the old mill site of Pandora, east of Telluride, and progresses up a switchbacking jeep road to the base, and then the top, of the falls. The trail continues farther up the valley behind the falls, if you wish to explore.

Directions: Drive east from Telluride on Colorado Avenue (the main street, which turns to dirt) for about 2 miles. Park at the parking area where the road begins to climb the head of the canyon, and walk up the road.

Closest town: Telluride, 2 miles west.

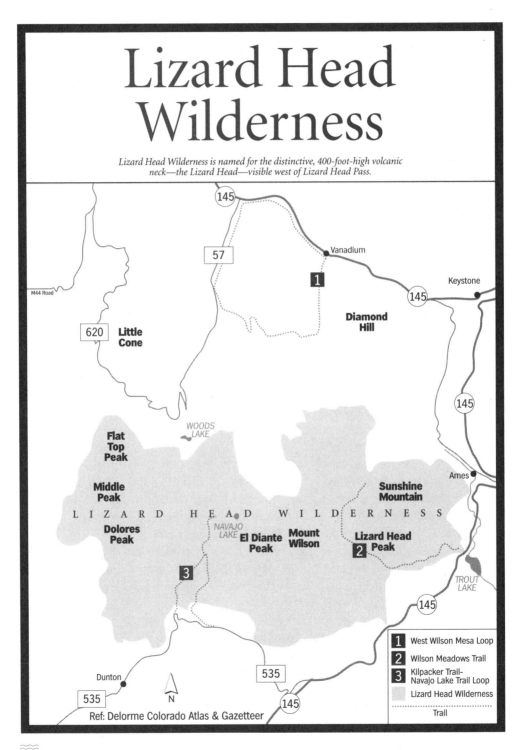

Lizard Head Wilderness

Lizard Head Wilderness is named for the distinctive, 400-foot-high volcanic neck—the Lizard Head—visible west of Lizard Head Pass.

145

57

Vanadium

1

145   Keystone

M44 Road

Diamond
Hill

620   Little
Cone

145

WOODS
LAKE

Flat
Top
Peak

Middle
Peak

Sunshine
Mountain

Ames

L I Z A R D   H E A D   W I L D E R N E S S

Dolores
Peak

NAVAJO
LAKE   El Diante   Mount
Peak   Wilson

Lizard Head
Peak
2

3

TROUT
LAKE

145

1	West Wilson Mesa Loop
2	Wilson Meadows Trail
3	Kilpacker Trail- Navajo Lake Trail Loop

Lizard Head Wilderness

Dunton

535

N

535

145

Trail

Ref: Delorme Colorado Atlas & Gazetteer

For more information: Telluride Visitor Services, 700 West Colorado Avenue, Telluride, CO 81435. Phone (970) 728-3041. Or Norwood Ranger District, Uncompahgre National Forest, 1760 East Grand Avenue, Norwood, CO 81423. Phone (970) 327-4261.

Trail: About 2 miles to the top of the falls.

Elevation: Change of 1,200 feet.

Degree of difficulty: Moderate.

Surface: Four-wheel-drive road.

JUD WIEBE TRAIL

[Fig. 40(3)] Like the Bear Creek Trail to Bear Creek Falls, this is a popular hike, often used for a quick workout by local residents. Unlike Bear Creek, however, it's moderately difficult. It climbs up the side of the valley, affording views of the Telluride ski area, Bridal Veil Falls, and, to the far west, the La Sal Mountains, 100 miles away in Utah.

The trail is named for the late U.S. Forest Service ranger who designed the trail in 1986. (It's pronounced Jud Wee-bee.)

Directions: The trailhead may be found at the top (northern) end of Aspen Street, about a five-minute walk from Colorado Avenue. There is no parking here. Cross the footbridge at the beginning of the trail and bear left. (If you would like to see Cornet Falls, don't cross the bridge; scramble about 400 yards up the narrow footpath along Cornet Creek to the base of the falls. This is a strenuous side hike that gains about 400 feet in elevation.)

After about 1 mile, and three major switchbacks, the Jud Wiebe Trail encounters the Deep Creek Trail; bear right, east, here. In another mile, at Liberty Bell Flats, bear the old road to the Liberty Bell Mine. The trail switchbacks sharply back Telluride, exiting onto the Tomboy Road just above town. Bear right

immediately south of the trailhead.

ride Visitor Services, 700 West Colorado Avenue,

28-3041. Or Norwood Ranger District, Un-

Grand Avenue, Norwood, CO 81423. Phone

rea encompasses Colorado's

Wilson (14,246 feet), and

Belted Kingfisher

The belted kingfisher (*Ceryle alcyon*) is most common in Colorado in winter, when migrating birds come south from their summer range. It lives near open water at elevations from the plains up to timberline.

The belted kingfisher can be seen perched near water. It is distinctive with its big head, heavy bill, large, dark crest, and dark "belt" across its chest. The bird is 11 inches to 15 inches in length and marvelously adapted to hunting fish underwater. An oily coating on its eyes helps it peer through glare and see beneath the surface.

Kingfishers dive after small fish, which the birds then swallow whole. The birds nest in deep tunnels in mud banks. Immature kingfishers must practice their hunting as well as their flying; some adults have been observed dropping a caught fish back in the water so that a juvenile may catch and kill it.

Wilson Peak (14,017 feet). These are difficult and exposed climbs, and not for the faint of heart. The beauty and attraction of the area lies in the way this abrupt, classic massif rises so close to the arid desert of the Colorado Plateau, only a few miles away to the west. The juxtaposition in Colorado of 14,000-foot alpine peaks and redrock deserts is unique to this corner of the state.

Lizard Head Wilderness is named for the distinctive, 400-foot-high volcanic neck—the Lizard Head— visible west of Lizard Head Pass. This 13,113-foot spire is described by some climbing authorities as the most difficult technical climb in the state, in part due to its rotten rock.

Besides the three Fourteeners, this distinctive massif of the San Miguel Mountains (a subrange of the San Juan Mountains) contains 15 peaks above 13,000 feet. Yet it's also a wilderness of rolling meadows and aspen-draped mesas.

WILSON MEADOWS TRAIL

[Fig. 41(2)] This is an easy hike to a south-facing bowl at the base of 12,930-foot Sunshine Peak and 11,861-foot San Bernardo Mountain. The route passes through meadows filled with wildflowers at the peak of summer. In the wetter areas look for false hellebore (*Veratrum viride*), a vigorous plant with big, lance-shaped leaves that grows waist-high; larkspur; and, in early fall, bog gentian (*Gentiana calycosa*).

Gentians like open ground. They flower in late summer and early autumn, when the tundra and bogs around them are turning russet and tan. They bear tulip-like flowers, usually a deep blue or purple, that flare at the lip like a miniature vase. The plants rarely grow higher than 6 inches. A white-and-blue version of the flower, arctic gentian (*Gentiana algida*), may mix with bog gentian.

Directions: From Telluride, drive west out of town 2 miles to CO 145; turn left (south) on CO 145 for about 13 miles to Lizard Head Pass. Park on the right (west) side of the road; pick up the Lizard Head Trail (Forest Service Trail 505) at the interpretive sign beside the parking area, follow this to the Wilson Meadows Trail

(Forest Service Trail 512), and then on to Wilson Meadows.

Closest town: Rico, 12 miles south; Telluride, 15 miles north.

For more information: Norwood Ranger District, Uncompahgre National Forest, 1760 East Grand Avenue, Norwood, CO 81423. Phone (970) 327-4261.

Trail: 6 miles round-trip.

Elevation: Change of 1,000 feet.

Degree of difficulty: Easy.

Surface: Single track; boggy in some areas.

KILPACKER TRAIL-NAVAJO LAKE TRAIL LOOP

[Fig. 41(3)] This loop—really an inverted Y—leads into the San Miguel Mountains from the south, curving around El Diente Peak into the Navajo Basin, an alpine valley surrounded by El Diente, Mount Wilson, and Wilson Peak, which hold snow on their northern faces all year long. Navajo Lake is set at 11,100 feet in a high basin just above treeline. Campfires are prohibited in the basin.

Directions: From Telluride, drive south on CO 145 to Dunton Road (Forest Road 535), a right-hand (west) turn about 6 miles south of Lizard Head Pass and 21 miles from Telluride. Drive about 5 miles up to a fork; the Kilpacker trailhead is to the right, 0.25 mile up FR 535. If you want to go to the Navajo Lake trailhead, continue on FR 535 another 1.5 miles to a sharp left turn where the road encounters the West Fork of the Dolores River; the trailhead is to the right after the turn.

Begin at either trailhead; the trails converge after about 2.5 miles and continue up the West Fork of the Dolores River to Navajo Lake. To complete the Y, return to the trail junction and take whichever trail you didn't start on. When you reach Dunton Road, walk from that trailhead along Dunton Road back to your car. The trailheads are 1.5 miles apart.

Closest town: Rico, about 12 miles from the Kilpacker trailhead, south on CO 145.

For more information: Mancos-Dolores Ranger District, San Juan National Forest, PO Box 210, Dolores, CO 81323. Phone (970) 882-7296. Or Norwood Ranger District, Uncompahgre National Forest, 1760 East Grand Avenue, Norwood, CO 81423. Phone (970) 327-4261.

Trail: 9.5 miles from trailhead-to-trailhead, plus 1.5 miles of hiking on the road

BELTED KINGFISHER
(Ceryle alcyon)
Identified by its blue-gray breast band (an additional chestnut band is on the female), the kingfisher can be seen near water where it swoops close to the surface before plunging in after its prey.

to get back to your starting point.

Elevation: Change of 1,000 feet. Sixty percent of this elevation change is on the Dunton Road; it's necessary to walk about 1.5 miles between the Navajo and Kilpacker trailheads. If you'd like to walk uphill at the end of your hike, start at Navajo; if you'd like to walk downhill, start at Kilpacker.

Degree of difficulty: Moderate. If you choose simply to hike out and back on the Navajo Trail, and not make the Y along the Kilpacker Trail, the route earns an easy rating.

Surface: Single track and revegetated wagon road, with some creek crossings on logs. Forest Service road connects the two trailheads.

MOUNTAIN BIKING

Mountain bikers face an obvious obstacle in the Telluride area: very steep mountains. Most rides tend to involve some heavy-duty climbing, but cyclists are usually rewarded with easier riding after the initial push, especially on the mesas northwest and southwest of Telluride.

Those advanced cyclists who want high-altitude challenge can find plenty of it east and south of Telluride. Although bikes are banned from the Lizard Head and Mount Sneffels wilderness areas, as they are from all designated wilderness areas, plenty of high country has been left open for riders, particularly between Telluride, Ophir, and Ouray.

The terrain around Telluride can mean demanding riding, but the scenic rewards are extraordinary. A short drive to the west, cyclists can cruise along the canyons of the Dolores River at lower elevations when snow still lies deep on the trails of the San Juans.

RIVER WALK TRAIL LOOP

[Fig. 40(5)] This flat loop ride circles the alluvial San Miguel Valley west of Telluride. It's a good ride to undertake with kids or beginners. It winds through the willows along the San Miguel River and then follows a paved bike path back into town.

Directions: Begin at the south end of Pine Street; turn right here on the River Walk Trail. Follow this to the western edge of Telluride, then follow the trail across a bridge and continue downstream on the trail, now on the southern side of the river. After 2 miles you encounter Highway 145 near Society Turn. Turn right here for about 200 yards along the highway until you pick up the bike path that parallels the highway spur back to Telluride. Turn right onto this path and follow it into town.

Closest town: Telluride, at the beginning and end of the trail.

For more information: Telluride Visitors Services, 700 West Colorado Avenue, Telluride, CO 81435. Phone (970) 728-3041.

Trail: 4.5-mile loop.

Elevation: Change of 180 feet.

Degree of difficulty: Easy.

Surface: Gravel, single track and paved bike path.

WEST WILSON MESA LOOP

[Fig. 41(1)] This loop traverses the broad mesa north of the San Miguel Mountains and south of the San Miguel River valley. Most of the uphill climbing is in the first third of the ride, which then cuts through rolling meadows and stands of aspen below Wilson Peak.

Directions: From Telluride, drive north on CO 145 to Silver Pick Road (Forest Road 622), about 8 miles from Telluride. Turn left (south) onto Silver Pick Road and park by the river. Ride south up the creek (Big Bear Creek, not to be confused with the Bear Creek east of Telluride) for about 3 miles until you nearly crest the mesa and come to a four-way intersection. Turn right (northwest). Follow this road, which makes a large hairpin over the course of about 6 miles. As the road begins to descend you will come to a T intersection; turn right. After about 1 mile, turn right once more; you are now headed northwest. Travel down to Fall Creek Road (FR 616). Follow Fall Creek Road to CO 145; turn right and ride up the highway 1 mile to Sawpit. At Sawpit bear right onto the dirt road visible along the river, and follow this 4 miles back to Silver Pick Road. This dirt road parallels the highway but is more pleasant to ride.

Closest town: Sawpit, 1 mile east of Fall Creek Road on CO 145.

For more information: Norwood Ranger District, Uncompahgre National Forest, 1760 East Grand Avenue, Norwood, CO 81423. Phone (970) 327-4261.

Trail: 15-mile loop.

Elevation: Gain of 1,500 feet.

Degree of difficulty: Moderate.

Surface: Dirt road, plus several miles on paved CO 145.

TOMBOY ROAD TO IMOGENE PASS

[Fig. 40(1)] This demanding route follows the old road to Savage Basin, home of the enormous and lucrative Tomboy, Columbia, Japan, and Smuggler-Union mines, and leads on to the top of 13,114-foot Imogene Pass. This ride gives modern athletes a sense of the hardiness and fortitude of the miners who lived and worked in the 12,000-foot-high basin year-round. Ore was transported by aerial tramlines south down the precipitous slope to the millworks at Pandora, located in the valley floor east of Telluride. Despite the threat of winter avalanches, miners regularly made the trip up and down Tomboy Road to partake of the illicit delights of Telluride's red light district.

Today Tomboy Road is the course for the annual Imogene Pass Run, an 18-mile foot race between Telluride and Ouray. The race route continues east down Imogene Basin to Camp Bird and Ouray (the race itself is run in the opposite direction, from Ouray to Telluride).

The road clings to the southern side of the San Miguel Valley, crosses two streams,

Dolores River Canyon

The Dolores River Canyon cuts 2,000 feet into the sedimentary rocks of the Colorado Plateau, which stretches from the Uncompahgre region southwest to the Grand Canyon.

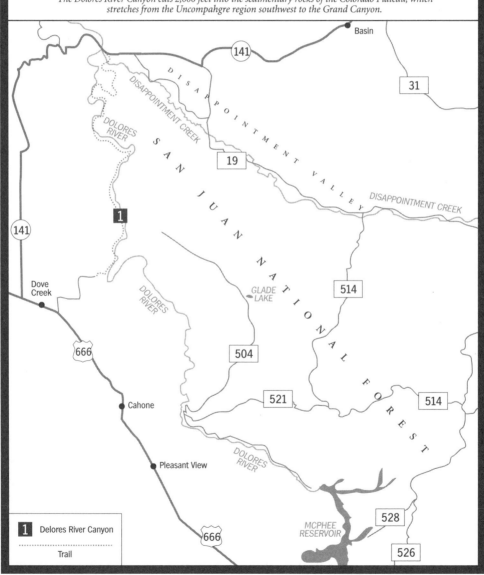

and passes through a tunnel. As you rise up out of the valley the surrounding peaks and alpine basins reveal themselves, while the houses in the valley below diminish almost to nothing. The old mining camp of Tomboy is a good intermediate stop for those who may not want to push on to the pass; above Tomboy the route is steeper, and the rock looser.

This route is very exposed to weather; start early, be prepared for afternoon thunderstorms, and don't push your luck if lightning is threatening.

Directions: From downtown Telluride, ride north up Oak Street to the top of the street. Turn right onto the dirt road climbing up the side of the valley; this is Tomboy Road.

Closest town: Telluride, 7 miles west of Imogene Pass.

For more information: Norwood Ranger District, Uncompahgre National Forest, 1760 East Grand Avenue, Norwood, CO 81423. Phone (970) 327-4261. Or Ouray Ranger District, Uncompahgre National Forest, 2505 South Townsend, Montrose, CO 81401. Phone (970) 240-5300.

Trail: 7 miles one-way; 5 miles one-way to Tomboy.

Elevation: Change of 4,400 feet.

Degree of difficulty: Strenuous.

Surface: Old jeep road, loose rock; technical riding on rock for the last 0.5 mile.

DOLORES RIVER CANYON

[Fig. 42] This ride is located northwest of Telluride on the Uncompahgre Plateau. It offers a very different experience than the high-altitude trails of the San Juans and their adjacent mesas. The canyon cuts 2,000 feet into the sedimentary rocks of the Colorado Plateau, which stretches from the Uncompahgre region southwest to the Grand Canyon and covers 130,000 square miles. The sedimentary rocks laid down in flat layers here of red, white, and pink are the same rocks that typify the entire plateau (*see* Colorado National Monument, page 145).

The ride is relatively flat for the most part, although there are a few short, steep sections. It traces the Dolores River, a waterway named in the eighteenth century by Spanish explorers from New Mexico as *El Rio de Nuestra Señora de las Dolores*, The River of Our Lady of Sorrows. Look for canyon wrens and violet-green swallows coursing through the clear air between the canyon walls.

Look also for tamarisk, a weedy invasive plant from the Middle East, which is taking over riverbanks on the Dolores as it is throughout the West. The plant, which may grow 20 feet high, can be identified by its feathery, needle-like leaves.

Tamarisk (*Tamarix ramosissima*) was introduced by nineteenth century settlers who hoped it would aid in streambank stabilization. Its long racemes of pink flowers are popular with honeybees, and the tamarisk provides shelter for mourning doves.

Like most exotic species, however, it turned out to do more harm than good. Tamarisk thrives on riverbanks to the detriment of other vegetation. It grows in dense, impenetrable thickets along thousands of miles of riverbank in the western

United States. These thickets prevent humans and wildlife alike from moving easily between the surrounding desert and the river.

The desert subspecies of the bighorn sheep (*Ovis canadensis*) has lost much of its range because of tamarisk. The animals can't or won't pass through the heavy thickets; as a consequence, large stretches of desert river are not available to the sheep as a water source, so the sheep no longer populate much of their traditional range.

Tamarisk consumes enormous quantities of water and is almost impossible to kill. The plant is remarkably adaptable to the saline waters of the American West. Tamarisk excretes excess salt through its leaves and twigs, creating salty deposits on their surfaces and leading to the plant's common name, salt cedar.

This bike ride can be undertaken as an out-and-back ride, or a one-way if you leave a vehicle at each end. The full trip is 52 miles out and back. For an easier version, turn around at the 11-mile mark; the trail is slightly more challenging after this point.

Directions: Begin northwest of Dove Creek. From Telluride, drive west on CO 145 to Dolores, about 65 miles. About 2 miles past Dolores, turn north on CO 184. Go 8 miles to the intersection with US 666. Turn right (north) and drive about 18 miles to County Road 10, a right. Take this and drive 2 miles, following the road around a sharp left, and then take a right (still on County 10). From this turn, drive 3 miles northeast to the start of the trail, in the Dolores River Canyon.

If you wish to leave a car at the northern end of the trail, continue north on US 666 to CO 141 North, a right just north of Dove Creek. Follow this road north past the village of Slick Rock, about 22 miles. County Road 13R—the end of the ride through the Dolores River Canyon—joins CO 141 about 4 miles east of Slick Rock, just past the landing strip on the left (north) side of the road.

Begin riding north down the canyon from the access near Dove Creek. The trail, a rough dirt road, follows the river for 10 miles, then climbs over a saddle that short-cuts an oxbow, and returns to the river. This climb is a good place for a

OSPREY
(Pandion haliaetus)
Also known as the fish hawk, the osprey hovers over water before plunging in feetfirst to grasp the fish with its talons.

turnaround if you don't want to ride the full length of the canyon. Four miles past this point it is necessary to ford the river. Do not attempt this at high water. Three miles after the ford the route climbs two small hills, then climbs southeast out of the canyon. Near the top, turn left on County Road 16R; 1 mile farther on, turn left on County Road 13R. Follow this to CO 141.

Closest town: Dove Creek, 10 miles west of the trailhead.

For more information: Bureau of Land Management, San Juan Resource Area, 701 Camino Del Rio, Durango, CO 81301. Phone (970) 247-4874.

Trail: 26 miles one-way.

Elevation: Loss of 500 feet start to finish, with several short, steep uphills in between.

Degree of difficulty: Moderate.

Surface: Dirt and loose rock.

FISHING

SAN MIGUEL RIVER

[Fig. 40] Since it lacks upstream reservoirs, the San Miguel is a river of wide flow fluctuations. At high water in June the river may flow at levels as high as 2,000 cubic feet per second (cfs). At low water in late August that rate may drop to 60 cfs. Nevertheless, the river is a good fishery.

From the confluence of the South Fork of the San Miguel and the river's main stem, located about 3 miles west of Telluride along CO 145, north to Placerville, the river is populated with brown trout, generally in the 10- to 14-inch range. North of Placerville to the Norwood Bridge, rainbow trout mix in with the browns, in roughly the same size categories.

Directions: The river parallels CO 145 from the base of Keystone Hill (3 miles west of Telluride) to the Norwood Bridge, about 20 miles. Public access along the river is generally good and includes about 1 mile of streambank owned by The Nature Conservancy northwest of Placerville.

For more information: Colorado Division of Wildlife, 2300 South Townsend Avenue, Montrose, CO 81401. Phone (970) 249-3431.

DOLORES RIVER AND MCPHEE RESERVOIR

[Fig. 42] The Dolores rises west of Lizard Head Pass and flows west, then north. From Lizard Head to McPhee Reservoir, located 1 mile west of the town of Dolores, the river contains brown and rainbow trout in the 10- to 12-inch range. Land ownership along the river is a checkerboard pattern of public and private; be sure to ask permission for access if you are not sure of public ownership.

McPhee Reservoir has rainbow trout, kokanee salmon, and smallmouth bass, as well as populations of yellow perch and black crappie. The reservoir is becoming known for its smallmouth bass fishery; all fish smaller than 15 inches must be released. Trout and salmon run 10- to 14-inches, on average.

Elephant Head

The common name for *Pedicularis groenlandica* is an apt one. Each of the tiny flowers on the upright stems looks like the head, ears, and trunk of a pink elephant.

Elephant head prefers wet, open sites in high alpine environments. The plant grows low to the ground, with only the flower stems extending upward. The stems rarely grow as high as 1 foot.

As the latin name suggests, this plant was first identified in Greenland. It is common throughout Arctic and Northern Hemisphere alpine regions.

A boat is almost a necessity to fish McPhee, which has 110 miles of shoreline but very little vehicular access.

Downstream of McPhee, 12 miles of the Dolores River are managed jointly by the U.S. Forest Service and Colorado Division of Wildlife as the Lone Dome State Wildlife Area. A dirt road parallels the river here. This is catch-and-release water; anglers may use flies or lures only. Most of the trout here are browns, with a few rainbows. Fish sizes range from 10 inches up to the rare 24-inch prize. Below this point the water is generally too warm to sustain a trout fishery.

Directions: CO 145 generally follows the Dolores River east of the town of Dolores. McPhee Reservoir is located 1 mile west of Dolores. To reach the reservoir, take CO 145 west to CO 184 north, and follow signs to the boat ramps.

To reach the Lone Dome State Wildlife Area and the Dolores River below McPhee Reservoir, continue north on CO 184 for 8 miles to the intersection with US 666. Turn right (north) and drive about 15 miles to County Road R, a crossroads at Cahone. Turn east (right) on County Road R, then turn right at a T intersection onto County Road 16. After 1.25 miles, turn left on County Road S. Follow this down and across the river to an intersection with Forest Road 504. Turn right (south) on FR 504 to follow the river.

For more information: Colorado Division of Wildlife, 151 East 16th Street, Durango, CO 81301. Phone (970) 247-0855.

SKIING AT TELLURIDE

[Fig. 40(6)] Telluride Ski Resort opened in 1972, overlapping the mining era by several years (the last mine near town shut down in 1978). The ski mountain lies between the historic town of Telluride and the new resort of Mountain Village, incorporated as Colorado's youngest town in 1987. The two communities are joined by a free public gondola, which carries skiers up onto the slopes and allows visitors and commuters to travel between them in 13 minutes—about half the amount of time necessary to drive from one to the other. The gondola is the only public transportation system of its kind in the United States.

The ski area is known for its long, steep mogul runs on the front (north-facing) side. These are narrow trails that drop directly to Telluride. The west-facing sections above Mountain Village feature wide, groomed intermediate and beginner slopes—plus an experts-only area called Gold Hill. Here ungroomed trails draw expert skiers who hike to in-bounds terrain that drops through cliff bands and avalanche chutes.

From the top of the ski area (11,890 feet at the top of Lift 9; 12,247 if you hike to the top of Gold Hill), numerous mountains are visible. The rugged ridge immediately south is Palmyra Peak (13,319 feet); to the east, across Bear Creek, are (north to south) Ballard Mountain (12,804 feet), La Junta Peak (13,472 feet), and Wasatch Ridge (13,555 feet). North of Telluride, the rugged Saint Sophia Ridge rises to a high point of 13,581 feet at Mount Emma, on its northwest corner. Due north of Telluride, Mount Sneffels tops out at 14,150 feet.

The San Miguel Mountains are visible in the middle distance to the southwest; look for Little Cone (11,981 feet) and Lone Cone (12,613), the nearer and farther pyramidal volcanoes that stand alone to the northwest of the San Miguels. On the distant western horizon, the La Sal Mountains of Utah are apparent.

Directions: Three lifts to the ski area are situated on the southern edge of Telluride. To drive to Mountain Village, take CO 145 west out of Telluride to the intersection at Society Turn (2 miles). Turn left (south) for 1 mile; turn left into Mountain Village. Free parking is available at the entry station, where the gondola connects to Mountain Village, the ski area, and Telluride.

Activities: Skiing, snowboarding, lessons.

Facilities: On-mountain restaurants, base village.

Dates: Generally open from Thanksgiving to mid-Apr.

Fees: There is a fee to ski or snowboard. However, the gondola connecting Mountain Village and Telluride is free.

Closest town: Telluride is located at the northern base of the mountain, Mountain Village at the western base.

For more information: Telluride Ski and Golf Company, PO Box 11155, Telluride, CO 81435. Phone (970) 728-6900.

SAN JUAN HUT SYSTEM

Two separate backcountry hut systems operate in the Telluride region: one for winter, one for summer.

The five huts of the San Juan Hut System link Telluride to Ouray via a route that runs northwest from Telluride around the western corner of the Sneffels Range, then east along the north face of that range to Ouray. The route roughly traces the northern boundary of the Mount Sneffels Wilderness. This hut system gives backcountry skiers an opportunity to spend the night in comfort near endless north-facing bowls and ridges, which provide great backcountry skiing for those willing to climb for their turns.

The wooden huts contain eight padded bunks each, propane cook stoves and lamps, and a wood stove for heat. The system can be skied as a 31-mile trek between

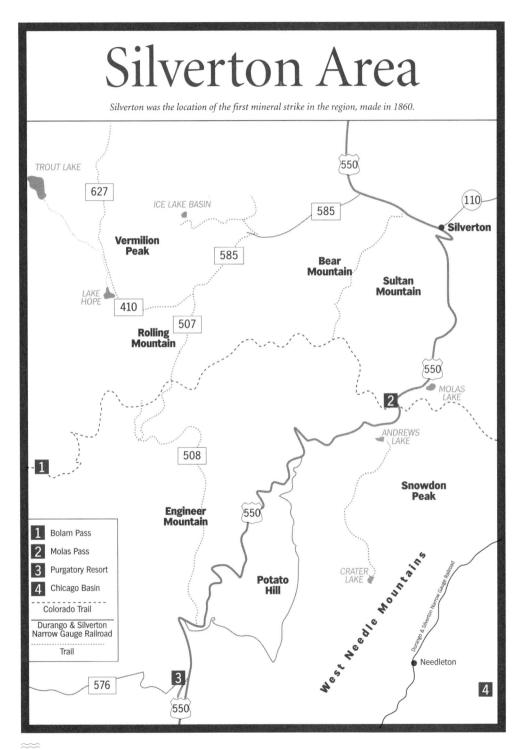

Silverton Area

Silverton was the location of the first mineral strike in the region, made in 1860.

TROUT LAKE

627

ICE LAKE BASIN

550

585

110

Silverton

Vermilion
Peak

585

Bear
Mountain

Sultan
Mountain

LAKE
HOPE

410

507

Rolling
Mountain

550

MOLAS
LAKE

2

ANDREWS
LAKE

Snowdon
Peak

1

508

Engineer
Mountain

550

1 Bolam Pass
2 Molas Pass
3 Purgatory Resort
4 Chicago Basin

- - - Colorado Trail

Durango & Silverton
Narrow Gauge Railroad

········· Trail

Potato
Hill

CRATER
LAKE

West Needle Mountains

Durango & Silverton Narrow Gauge Railroad

Needleton

576

3

4

550

the two towns (huts are set between 4 and 7 miles apart), or each hut may be accessed via a trailhead.

The summer hut system connects Telluride to Moab, Utah over a 206-mile route that runs the length of the Uncompahgre Plateau. That route takes mountain bike riders from the Sneffels Range northwest into the piñon-juniper country of the Uncompahgre Plateau, then west through the canyons of the Colorado River and around the La Sal Mountains to Moab, Utah. The result is an unparalleled trip through contrasting geology and geography of western Colorado and eastern Utah.

At its high point, this route takes cyclists to an elevation of 11,000 feet; in Moab, the low point, the ride finishes at 4,000 feet.

The system encompasses six huts and takes seven days to ride. Unlike the winter hut system, this route is designed to be ridden from start to finish, so it requires a full week. No motorized vehicles are allowed on the trails system or at the huts. The San Juan Hut System stocks all summer huts with mattresses, sleeping bags, cooking equipment, food, and water, which are included in the hut fee. Cyclists carry tools, clothing, and personal gear only.

Activities: Backcountry skiing and mountain biking.

Facilities: Five winter huts, six summer huts. Each sleeps eight people and is equipped with gas and wood stoves and cooking equipment. Summer huts also are stocked with food, water, and sleeping bags.

Dates: Winter huts: Generally open Nov. to Apr. Summer huts: Open June 1 to Oct. 1.

Fees: There is a fee to use the huts. Reservations are required.

Closest town: Telluride and Ouray anchor the western and eastern ends of the winter hut system. On the summer system, Telluride lies on the eastern end, Moab on the western end. There are no towns in between.

For more information: San Juan Hut System, PO Box 1663, Telluride, CO 81435. Phone (970) 728-6935.

Winter Trail: Backcountry skiing trail requiring alpine touring or telemark skis.

Summer Trail: Dirt roads and single-track.

Degree of difficulty: Strenuous.

Silverton Area

[Fig. 43] The mountain towns of the San Juans often seem deeply isolated from the rest of the state, but none is so isolated as Silverton. Two things keep this vintage town going: the fact that it is the county seat for San Juan County, and the summer operation of the Durango and Silverton Narrow Gauge Railroad (*see* page 266), which brings as many as 2,000 daily visitors to Silverton from May to October.

Once the railroad line closes for winter (shorter train trips run year-round near

BOBCAT
(Lynx rufus)

Durango), Silverton goes into a deep slumber. San Juan County is home to fewer than 500 people, most of whom live in Silverton. Adjacent Hinsdale County counts even fewer residents, most in Lake City.

It wasn't always so. Silverton was one of the wildest, rowdiest mining towns in Colorado. Silverton's town site was the location of the first mineral strike in the region, made in 1860. The fact that the land was deep in Ute Indian territory, and the Civil War, delayed serious development of the region until a decade later, when the Little Giant Mine opened near Silverton. Even then, miners were jumping the gun. The Brunot Agreement with the Ute Indians, which legalized high country mining in the San Juans, did not go into effect until 1874. By then Silverton was well on its way to becoming a town.

Most of the mine development lay in a vast district that ran northeast from Silverton up the Animas River for 15 miles, rolling up and over the shoulders of the mountains flanking the river. Silverton did not truly boom until the Denver and Rio Grande Railroad's tracks reached the town in 1882 (those tracks are used today by the Durango and Silverton Narrow Gauge Railroad).

The price of shipping mineral ore and supplies dropped dramatically with the arrival of the railroad, and development took off. East of Silverton's main avenue, Greene Street, bordellos, dance halls, and saloons rocked day and night. Wyatt Earp, an occasional lawman already famous for his role in the 1881 shootout at the O.K. Corral in Tombstone, Arizona, found work briefly in Silverton as a card dealer. Gunfights were common, and 2 tenants in the local jail were lynched by angry crowds.

Mining was the region's mainstay. Silverton was the railhead town for the communities of Mineral Point, Howardsville, Eureka, and Animas Forks, all farther up the Animas River, and the town of Red Mountain, located up Mineral Creek on Red Mountain Pass. In 1896, Otto Mears built the Silverton-Northern Railroad, which extended rail service 12 miles up the Animas Valley to Eureka. Eureka was the site of the Sunnyside Mine, which operated almost continuously from 1873 to 1991. At times as many as 2,000 people lived in Eureka. The tracks above Silverton were removed in 1942.

AVALANCHE CONTROL ON RED MOUNTAIN PASS AND MOLAS DIVIDE

Avalanches are a natural event in Colorado's mountains, thanks to a deep and fragile snowpack and glacier-steepened slopes that have not been beveled down by erosion. Avalanches can be especially common in the San Juan Mountains; people who live among these peaks, and especially those who live in Silverton, accept avalanches as part of life.

At times avalanche danger dictates how residents go about their quotidian lives. The portion of US 550 from Coal Bank Pass to Ouray is overhung by 133 identified avalanche paths. Seventy-seven of those slides have the potential to hit the highway. The result, according to one avalanche forecaster, is "the hairiest avalanche road in the United States."

Avalanches are deadly; between 1950 and 1993, 58 vehicles were hit by slides on US 550, and six people were killed in their vehicles. Because US 550 is the only north-south route through the San Juan Mountains, the Colorado Department of Transportation tries to keep it open year-round. Since 1993, forecasters from the Colorado Avalanche Information Center have worked with the Colorado Department of Transportation to try to predict avalanches and to close the highway temporarily when necessary.

When the risk is high, highway gates are closed on the road leading to Red Mountain Pass, which lies between Silverton and Ouray, and to Molas Divide and Coal Bank Pass, between Silverton and Durango. In a typical winter the road may be closed a half dozen times. If the road is closed in both directions, Silverton is cut off from the outside world. Closures may last as long as a week, but generally are shorter than 24 hours. During closures avalanche controllers try to trigger threatening avalanches. This is accomplished by the use of concussive explosives detonated in the avalanche starting zones at the top of a slide path.

The explosives are either delivered like artillery shells by a truck-mounted cannon or dropped by hand from a helicopter. Once avalanche hazard has been diminished and plows have cleared the debris from the road, the highway is reopened. Winter travelers may find themselves driving between snowbanks of avalanche debris 10 or 20 feet high on US 550.

Avalanches are the reason US 550 has relatively few guardrails, despite its narrowness and the precipitous drops only a few feet from the pavement. Avalanches running across the road would rip out any guardrails that were installed beneath their slide paths. In addition, snowplows must be able to push enormous quantities of snow and avalanche debris off the road.

SAN MIGUEL PEAK ROADLESS AREA

San Miguel Peak Roadless Area is the sort of dramatic, mountainous place that typifies a Colorado wilderness area. This 60,000-acre region lying west of US 550 is a spectacular collection of near-Fourteener peaks, dark spruce-fir forests, colorful aspens, and meadows filled with summer wildflowers. It has not been designated a federal wilderness because it contains mining claims that preclude such protection, and does contain some closed roads.

COLORADO TRAIL FROM MOLAS PASS TO BOLAM PASS

[Fig. 43(1), Fig. 43(2)] Several trails lead into and across the San Miguel Roadless Area, including 20 miles of the Colorado Trail. This portion of the trail, which traverses southwest from Molas Divide to Bolam Pass, makes for a good, two-day backpacking trip. The route crosses an area near Molas Divide that was burned in the Lime Creek fire a century ago. Tundra has taken over where subalpine forest stood before the burn. Even after a century, trees have not been able to regain much of a toehold in this high, windy environment. Observant travelers may spot lodgepole pines around the Molas Pass area; these trees were planted by volunteers, beginning in the early 1930s, in an attempt to revegetate the burned areas. Lodgepole pine (*Pinus contorta*) is not an indigenous species in the San Juans.

The trail is situated between 10,800 and 12,500 feet. It traverses large, open meadows and tundra. On the eastern end of the route hikers get views deep into the Weminuche Wilderness Area. To the east lie the Grenadier and Needle mountains, two ranges located south of Silverton. The La Plata range is visible northwest of Durango. Farther west, the trail affords views of the San Miguel Mountains, including Lizard Head Peak.

The high alpine terrain is filled with flowers at midsummer. One common denizen is mountain buttercup (*Ranunculus eschscholtzii*), which flowers from June to August. Another flower common throughout Colorado's high country is lupine. Silky lupine (*Lupinus sericeus*) grows at lower elevations (up into the montane zone). Silvery lupine (*Lupinus argenteus*) grows up into the subalpine zone. Both like moderately dry sites and will tolerate some shade, although they prefer sun. Identifying individual lupine species isn't easy; approximately 600 lupine varieties grow in North America.

Directions: It is necessary to shuttle a four-wheel-drive vehicle to Bolam Pass. To do this, drive south from Silverton on US 550 approximately 15 miles to Purgatory Ski Area. At the northern parking area, turn right (west) onto Forest Road 578. After several switchbacks, go left at a fork. Follow the road across Hermosa Creek (a ford), then bear right and go 7 miles to Celebration Lake. Park here; the Colorado Trail passes the lake along its southern side. The driving distance from Purgatory Ski Area is about 15 miles.

To begin the trail at Molas Divide, drive north from Molas Pass 1 mile on US 550 to the Molas Trail parking area, on the right. The trail begins on the left (south) side of the highway. In 0.2 mile it will connect with the Colorado Trail; follow the trail west 20 miles to Bolam Pass.

Closest town: Silverton, 5 miles north of Molas Pass trailhead.

For more information: Columbine Ranger District, San Juan National Forest,

110 West 11th Street, Durango, CO 81301. Phone (970) 247-4874. This district has a second office: 367 South Pearl. PO Box 439, Bayfield, CO 81322. Phone (970) 884-2512.

Trail: 20 miles one-way.

Elevation: Rolling terrain, with a change of 1,700 feet between the lowest and highest points.

Degree of difficulty: Moderate.

Surface: Single-track, some of it poorly marked, through tundra, meadows, and forest.

ICE LAKE BASIN

[Fig. 43] This hike leads past several waterfalls and mining-era ruins to a beautiful cluster of alpine lakes. The high (12,000-foot) Ice Lake Basin holds snow almost all summer in its shadier, north-facing pockets. The hike to the basin passes through meadows full of midsummer wildflowers.

Several lakes dot the basin and nearby cirques. The best camping is around Lower Ice Lake, about halfway to Ice Lake itself, which is very high and exposed. The adventurous visitor can scramble up the rocky, treeless drainage north of Lower Ice Lake to Island Lake, situated in a tributary cirque to the north.

US Grant Peak (13,767 feet) is north of Island Lake; Pilot Knob (13,738 feet) rises west of Ice Lake; and Golden Horn (13,765 feet) is immediately south of Pilot Knob. Farther south down the ridge, the next high point is Vermillion Peak (13,894 feet), then Fuller Peak (13,761 feet).

Regardless of where you camp, be sure to do so at least 200 feet from any water, and to use a gas cookstove rather than build a fire.

Directions: From Silverton, drive north on US 550 approximately 2 miles to Forest Road 585, a left (west) turn. Drive approximately 4 miles to South Mineral Campground. The trailhead is directly across from the campground, on the right.

Closest town: Silverton, 6 miles southeast.

For more information: Columbine Ranger District, San Juan National Forest, 110 West 11th Street, Durango, CO 81301. Phone (970) 247-4874. Or Columbine Ranger District, San Juan National Forest, 367 South Pearl. PO Box 439, Bayfield, CO 81322. Phone (970) 884-2512.

Trail: 9 miles round-trip.

Elevation: Change of 2,400 feet.

Degree of difficulty: Strenuous.

Surface: Single track trail, some creek crossings.

Great Mullein

This tall, spiky plant is commonly found in open meadows and hot, dry, disturbed sites from the plains to the subalpine zone. *Verbascum thapsus* is not a North American native, but a Eurasian exotic that has spread across the continent.

Sometimes called wooly mullein, the plant is easily identified by its height—up to 8 feet—its single stalk of small yellow flowers, and its fuzzy basal and lower-stalk leaves.

Weminuche Wilderness

The Weminuche Wilderness is 790 square miles, which is twice the size of the next largest Colorado wilderness area, the Flattops.

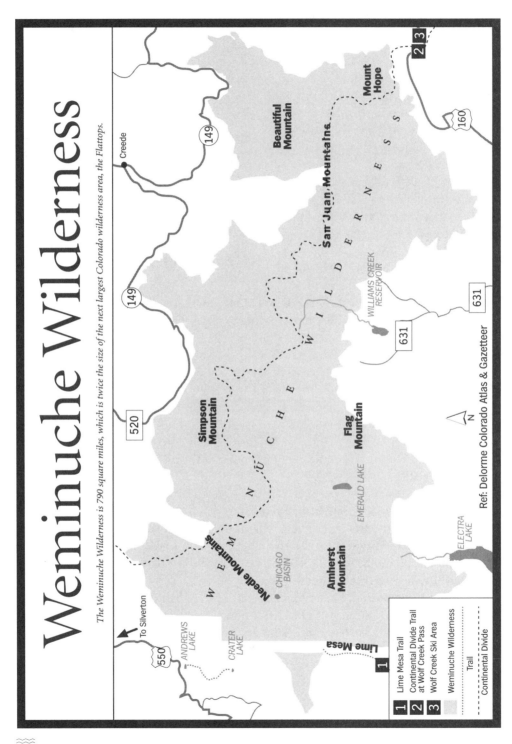

Ref: Delorme Colorado Atlas & Gazetteer

1	Lime Mesa Trail
2	Continental Divide Trail at Wolf Creek Pass
3	Wolf Creek Ski Area
	Weminuche Wilderness
	Trail
	Continental Divide

▨ WEMINUCHE WILDERNESS AREA

[Fig. 44] The Weminuche (pronounced WEH-min-ooch) is Colorado's vastest wilderness. At 790 square miles it is three-fourths the size of the state of Rhode Island. It is more than twice the size of the next largest Colorado wilderness area, the Flattops.

Stretching from Wolf Creek Pass to Creede, from Coal Bank Pass to South Fork, the Weminuche encompasses deep, forested canyons, broad limestone plateaus, towering, volcanic peaks, and vast acreages of silence. Because the wilderness area covers so much ground it is discussed in the Silverton, Durango, and Pagosa Springs portions of this book. Relative to Silverton, the Weminuche lies to the south and east.

The western portions of the Weminuche Wilderness Area are more geologically dramatic than the eastern. This part of the San Juans, including the mountains northwest of the Weminuche around Ouray, Silverton, and Telluride, was punctuated by powerful secondary and tertiary phase volcanoes that left striking mountains. The Needle, West Needle, and Grenadier mountains all crowd into the western half of the Weminuche.

Marine sediments are visible in these mountains in many areas, particularly along the western, northern, and southern edges and along US 550. These are very old Paleozoic rocks (240 million to 600 million years old) uplifted along fault lines and hefted toward the sky by the Precambrian core that remains from the ancestral Rockies of this region.

These Paleozoic sedimentary layers lie like skirts around some of the Weminuche's higher peaks, creating uncommon, undulating tablelands southwest of the Needle Mountains. Similar formations are found in the South San Juan Wilderness, which is located west of the Conejos River and southeast of the Weminuche Wilderness. Both wilderness areas are contained within the San Juan massif.

Hiking, camping, climbing, and fishing opportunities in the Weminuche are almost limitless. Twenty-one miles of the Colorado Trail cross the northwest corner of the Weminuche; 80 miles of the Continental Divide Trail are encompassed in its borders. The divide runs east-west along the wilderness area's length. Dozens of other trails vein the valleys and mesas. Portions of the Weminuche are heavily traveled, especially Chicago Basin at the upper end of Needle Creek, the access point for the three Fourteeners in the wilderness area. Nevertheless, hikers seeking solitude can quickly leave the beaten path and find their way to an isolated valley or nameless tarn.

For more information: The Weminuche Wilderness

OLIVE-SIDED FLYCATCHER

(Contopus borealis)
The flycatcher's call is pip-whee-beer or, when alarmed, pip-pip-pip-pip.

Area lies in two national forests and several ranger districts. For the northeastern portion contact: Creede Ranger District, Rio Grande National Forest, 3rd Street and Creede Avenue, Creede, CO 81130. Phone (719) 658-2556 (this district office is open only May through Nov.). For the southeastern corner, or for the northeastern portion from Dec. to Apr.: Divide Ranger District, Rio Grande National Forest, 13308 West Highway 160, Del Norte, CO 81132. Phone (719) 657-3321. For the east-central portion: Pagosa Ranger District, San Juan National Forest, PO Box 310, Pagosa Springs, CO 81147. Phone (970) 264-2268. For the west central and western portion: Columbine Ranger District, San Juan National Forest, 110 West 11th Street, Durango, CO 81301. Phone (970) 247-4874. Or Columbine Ranger District, San Juan National Forest, 367 South Pearl. PO Box 439, Bayfield, CO 81322. Phone (970) 884-2512.

CHICAGO BASIN

[Fig. 43(4)] The hike into Chicago Basin on the Needle Creek Trail is unlike any other you will experience in Colorado because the trip to the trailhead is made on a steam train. The Durango and Silverton Narrow Gauge Railroad, a scenic steam line that runs several times daily between the two namesake towns, cuts through the dramatic Animas River canyon en route. Hikers ride the train north from Durango about 30 miles to Needleton, a brief train stop deep in the heart of the canyon (the wilderness area does not encompass the train tracks, but lies on both sides of it through the gorge).

Disembark at Needleton. Be sure the conductor knows you plan to get off there, and that you know how and when to flag down a train when you want to catch a ride at the end of your hike. Find the trail on the far side of the Needleton Bridge. The route climbs up the narrow valley of Needle Creek into Chicago Basin, set at 11,000 feet. A half dozen jagged, volcanic peaks surround the head of the valley: Mount Eolus (14,084 feet) lies to the northwest, Sunlight Peak (14,059 feet) to the north, Windom Peak (14,087 feet) to the northeast, Jupiter Mountain (13,830 feet) to the east, Aztec Mountain (13,310 feet) to the south, and Mount Kennedy (13,125 feet) to the southwest. A city of lesser, unnamed spires and ridges is scattered among these big summits.

The Needle Creek Trail is the standard approach for peak-baggers seeking to climb the three Fourteeners in the massif here. Consequently, this is a popular trail; camping is prohibited in the upper basin around the two lakes that make up the headwaters of Needle Creek. Camp instead down near tree line. A gas campstove is a necessity because wood fires are prohibited.

Directions: Catch the Durango and Silverton train at the station in Durango, at the southern end of Main Avenue, or in Silverton, south of Greene Street. Disembark at Needleton. Reservations are advisable.

Facilities: There are no facilities at Needleton or in the wilderness.

Dates: The train runs from early May to the end of Oct. Expect the trail to Chicago Basin to be at least partially snow-covered into June, and again by the end of September.

Fees: There is a fee to ride the train.

Closest town: Silverton is 20 miles north of Needleton on the train; Durango is 30 miles south on the train.

For more information: For reservations and information on the train, contact the Durango and Silverton Narrow Gauge Railroad. Phone (970) 247-2733. For information on the wilderness area: Columbine Ranger District, San Juan National Forest, 110 West 11th Street, Durango, CO 81301. Phone (970) 247-4874. Or Columbine Ranger District, San Juan National Forest, 367 South Pearl. PO Box 439, Bayfield, CO 81322. Phone (970) 884-2512.

Trail: 16 miles round-trip.

Elevation: Change of 1,900 feet.

Degree of difficulty: Moderate.

Surface: Single-track trail with some creek crossings.

ANDREWS LAKE

[Fig. 43] Andrews Lake is located at the end of a paved road and is managed for the physically disabled. The lake is set in a high, open meadow near Molas Divide, with excellent views to the north and south.

Activities: Handicapped fishing access at Andrews Lake.

Directions: Drive south from Molas Divide on US 550 approximately 0.25 mile to the left turn (east) to Andrews Lake (the turn is marked by a sign). Drive 0.25 mile and park in the parking lot above the lake.

Facilities: Parking area, restrooms and handicapped access. Development at Andrews Lake is designed to accommodate the physically disabled. Vehicles may be driven directly to the lake, which covers several acres; wheelchair access is available along portions of the lakeshore. Camping is prohibited at Andrews Lake.

Fees: None.

Closest town: Silverton, 6 miles north on US 550.

For more information: Columbine Ranger District, San Juan National Forest, 110 West 11th Street, Durango, CO 81301. Phone (970) 247-4874.

Trail: Wooden walkway around the southern portion.

Elevation: Change of 40 feet to Andrews Lake from the overnight parking lot; no change from the day-use parking lot.

Degree of difficulty: Easy.

Surface: The trail to Andrews Lake from the overnight parking lot is paved and wheelchair accessible. A wooden walkway traces the southern edge of the lake and is directly accessible from the day-use parking area.

CRATER LAKE

[Fig. 43] The trail to Crater Lake departs from Andrews Lake. Follow signs from the parking lot to the trailhead. This trail (a long day hike or good overnight backpacking trip) angles south along the western edge of the West Needle Mountains.

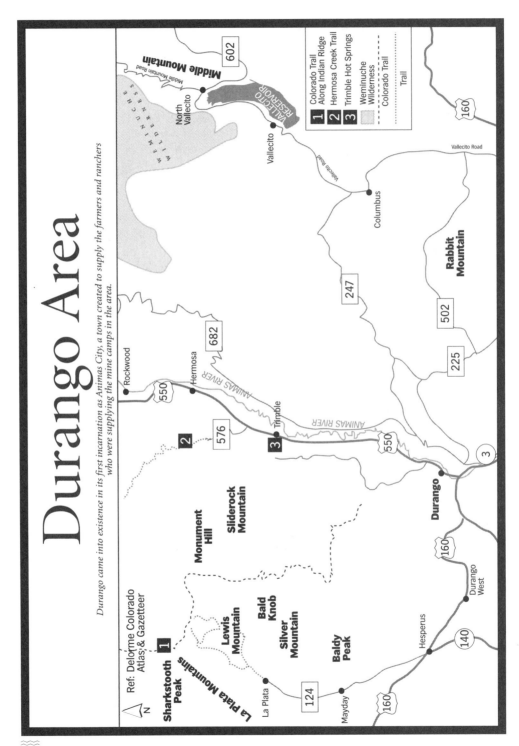

Durango Area

Durango came into existence in its first incarnation as Animas City, a town created to supply the farmers and ranchers who were supplying the mine camps in the area.

Ref: Delorme Colorado Atlas; & Gazetteer

Short trips into the Weminuche Wilderness Area tend to whet the appetite for more extended trips; after a day of hiking to Crater Lake, you may discern by a glance at the map that you have hardly nicked the western edge of the Weminuche.

Because the trailhead is located near Molas Divide, this route involves relatively little climbing. The trail passes through open meadows and subalpine forests before terminating at a small, pocket-sized lake tucked amid spruce trees beneath the rocky ridge of Twilight Peak (13,158 feet). Along the way the trail gives excellent views of Engineer Mountain (12,968 feet), the La Plata Mountains, located to the southwest, and down Lime Creek Valley, which runs south from Molas Divide.

The trail runs through several wet meadows. High meadows here, and in much of Colorado, are often covered in mountain marsh marigold, also called elkslip or elk spinach (*Caltha leptosepal*). The plant bears a white and yellow flower that appears even when old snow lies on the ground. Elk browse on the species, and astute observers may find matted, bathtub-shaped depressions where the animals recently have bedded down in it.

Directions: Drive south from Molas Divide on US 550 approximately 0.25 mile to the left turn (east) to Andrews Lake (the turn is marked by a sign). Drive 0.25 mile and park in the parking lot above the lake.

Closest town: Silverton, 6 miles north on US 550 from the trailhead.

For more information: Columbine Ranger District, San Juan National Forest, 110 West 11th Street, Durango, CO 81301. Phone (970) 247-4874. Or Columbine Ranger District, San Juan National Forest, 367 South Pearl. PO Box 439, Bayfield, CO 81322. Phone (970) 884-2512.

Trail: 12 miles round-trip.

Elevation: Gain of 800 feet.

Degree of difficulty: Moderate.

Surface: Single-track dirt and rock.

Durango Area

[Fig. 45] Durango was a construct of trains, hungry miners, and geography. Miners in the high camps needed to be fed and supplied during the boom years of the 1870s and 1880s. Durango consequently came into existence in its first incarnation as Animas City, a town created to supply the farmers and ranchers who were supplying the mine camps. Agricultural lands were being brought into production in the bottomlands of the Animas Valley to the north and on the open mesas to the south and west.

In 1880 the Denver and Rio Grande Railroad purchased land south of Animas City and platted a new town near the tracks, which became Durango when the train first arrived in 1881. Animas City was folded into the new town as the northern portion of Durango. Situated at an elevation of 6,600 feet at a wide spot in the Animas River valley, Durango soon became a major depot, a supply town for miners, loggers and ranchers. Smelters here processed ores coming from the high mining camps.

Durango is surrounded by cliffs of Cretaceous rock. The town sits in a valley of Mancos Shale; to the north is Dakota Sandstone, and to the south the mesas of the Mesaverde Group, a formation that thickens and widens as you travel west from Pagosa Springs toward Mesa Verde National Park. The park, and the Anasazi ruins it protects, are set on this Mesaverde Sandstone (*see* page 310).

Along the southern flank of the San Juans from Durango to Pagosa Springs, the geology is typified by uplifted and eroded sedimentary layers, principally Mesaverde Group Sandstone, Mancos Shale, and Dakota Sandstone. These layers were displaced by the rise of the San Juan Mountains to the north; to the south, the sedimentary rocks lie in the flat mesas and tablelands typical of northern New Mexico and Arizona and southern Utah.

DURANGO AND SILVERTON NARROW GAUGE RAILROAD

[Fig. 43] This steam-powered train may be the most spectacular scenic train line in the nation. Durango was founded in 1880 by the Denver and Rio Grande Railroad, which laid out the town site as it built tracks west along the southern flank of the San Juan Mountains (it had done the same thing to create Alamosa in the San Luis Valley, which lies to the east).

One hundred and one years later, in 1981, steam trains began running again between Durango and Silverton, a town the railway had first reached in 1882. Now, however, the trains carry tourists, not mining supplies and mineral ore.

The train's route follows the Animas Valley north from Durango. It diverges from US 550 near the hamlet of Hermosa and winds its way up the narrow, wild valley of the Animas River. The Weminuche Wilderness Area lies on either side of the tracks along this canyon. Fifty miles from Durango, the steam train pulls into Silverton, set at an elevation of 9,300 feet in an alpine park. Riders generally travel both directions on the train, but may choose to return via bus over US 550. Advance arrangements should be made for the bus leg at the time you purchase your ticket.

Each Memorial Day, approximately 1,000 cyclists race the train from Durango to Silverton, following US 550, in a race called the Iron Horse Classic. The train has never won.

Directions: The Durango train station is located at the southern end of Main Avenue. Tickets may be purchased here. Reservations are recommended.

Activities: Scenic train ride to Silverton, with a layover of several hours in Silverton.

Facilities: Both Durango and Silverton have all facilities. There are railway museums at each station.

Dates: Between two and four daily trains run round trips to Silverton from early May to the end of Oct. Between Nov. and May, shorter excursions are run from Durango to Cascade Canyon, just north of Hermosa.

Fees: There is a fee to ride the train. There is a fee to enter the railway museums, but if you are riding the train this is included in the price of your ticket.

Closest town: Durango on the southern end of the route; Silverton on the northern end. There are no towns in between.

For more information: Durango and Silverton Narrow Gauge Railroad, 479 Main Avenue, Durango, CO 81301. Phone (970) 247-2733 or (888) 872-4607.

TRIMBLE HOT SPRINGS

[Fig. 45(3)] A century ago the Trimble Hot Springs were the site of a Second Empire hotel, now long gone. The springs today include an Olympic-size swimming pool (maintained at 82 degrees Fahrenheit), and two spacious soaking pools, maintained at 102 degrees and 108 degrees. All the facilities are outdoors and offer great views of the surrounding mountains.

Directions: From Durango, drive north on US 550 approximately 7 miles to Trimble Lane. Turn left (west) here and drive 100 yards to the Trimble Hot Springs.

Activities: Swimming, soaking in natural hot springs.

Facilities: Changing rooms, snack bar, picnic area, massage rooms.

Dates: Open year-round.

Fees: There is a fee.

Closest town: Durango, 7 miles south.

Otto Mears

The Russian-born son of Jewish parents, Otto Mears is celebrated as the great road builder of the San Juan Mountains. He started his engineering career in 1867 when, as a veteran of the Union Army, he became a shopkeeper and wheat farmer in Saguache. Mears grew frustrated by the local roads. He wanted to ship supplies over Poncha Pass to the mines at Oro City (which would soon be renamed Leadville), but despaired at the road's condition and determined to build his own.

A coincidental visit at that time by former Colorado Territorial Governor William Gilpin helped Mears gain a charter from the Territorial legislature for a toll road. Thus began Mears' career as a builder of toll roads and later railroads. At one time he operated 300 miles of toll roads.

Mears built roads that seemed to be impossible. He built the Denver and Rio Grande Southern Railroad, which linked Durango, Dolores, Rico, Telluride, Ouray and Ridgway. He engineered the Denver and Rio Grande Railroad's route through the eastern end of the Black Canyon. And he built the Silverton-Northern Railroad, which extended up the Animas Valley to the rich mines east of Silverton.

For more information: Trimble Hot Springs, 6475 County Road 203, Durango, CO 81301. Phone (970) 247-0111.

HERMOSA ROADLESS AREA

[Fig. 45] The Hermosa Area is managed as if it were wilderness, although it does not have official wilderness protection. It encompasses the 90,000-acre core of the La Plata Mountains, the southwestern corner of the San Juan Mountain massif. The La Platas stand as a punctuation mark at the southwestern corner of Colorado's mountains. To the west, broad tablelands of the Colorado Plateau are cut by the canyons of southeastern Utah. To the south are the mesas of Mesa Verde.

The La Plata Mountains were formed when igneous sills (horizontal intrusions of magma between layers of sedimentary rock), dikes, and other intrusions pushed up into Permian redbeds. Today the peaks, as high as 12,300 feet, are a combination of igneous, sedimentary, and metamorphic rock.

The Hermosa Area contains, by one count, 17 defined ecosystems, from riparian zones to ponderosa pine forest to alpine tundra. Because it is not legally protected as wilderness, much of the region is accessible by mechanized means, especially mountain bikes. The Hermosa Creek drainage has become a popular mountain biking area, and is considered by many riders to be one of the most scenic routes in the Durango area.

COLORADO TRAIL ALONG INDIAN RIDGE

[Fig. 45(1)] This route is a portion of the Colorado Trail that follows a spectacular ridgeline walk north through the La Plata Mountains. During the summer, the Colorado Trail along Indian Ridge is a 5-mile walk amid spectacular meadows of wildflowers. From the ridge, hikers can see the surrounding La Plata Mountains, the San Miguel Mountains to the northwest, and the Needle Mountains to the northeast.

This hike should not be attempted if the weather is less than perfect, for the ridge is an exposed and dangerous place to be during a thunderstorm. Take this hike early in the day and, since you must return the way you came, keep a close eye on the weather. Because of its height (12,258 feet at the high point), expect to find patches of snow well into summer.

Directions: From Durango, drive west on US 160 approximately 12 miles to County Road 124, a right (north) turn. This road is located approximately 0.5 mile west of the crossroads of Hesperus, marked as La Plata Canyon. Drive 14 miles north on County 124. The last 2 miles of this road are passable only in a four-wheel-drive vehicle. The road may hold snow until late June. At the intersection with the Colorado Trail (at the end of the road, on the northern side of Cumberland Mountain), begin hiking uphill to the left (west).

Closest town: Durango, approximately 26 miles southeast.

For more information: Columbine Ranger District, San Juan National Forest, 110 West 11th Street, Durango, CO 81301. Phone (970) 247-4874. Or Columbine Ranger District, San Juan National Forest, 367 South Pearl. PO Box 439, Bayfield, CO

81322. Phone (970) 884-2512.

Trail: An out-and-back trail, as long as 5 miles one-way.

Elevation: Gain of as much as 660 feet.

Degree of difficulty: Moderate.

Surface: Single track trail and ridgeline walk, with some exposed areas of steep drops on the ridge.

MOUNTAIN BIKING
HERMOSA CREEK TRAIL

[Fig. 45(2)] The Hermosa Creek Trail is considered one of the finest mountain biking trails in the region, a long descent through a tree-filled canyon along a tributary to the Animas River.

Although the trail has a net drop of 2,100 feet from north to south, there is 1,500 feet worth of climbing up several hills along the route. Consequently, it's a mountain bike trail that requires a modicum of endurance. Note that this area is open to multiple types of uses; off-road motorcycles, hikers and equestrians may be encountered here.

Because the trail is so popular—not only with cyclists but also with hikers—try to ride it during weekdays, when traffic is lighter.

Directions: The best way to ride the trail is north to south after dropping a vehicle at the southern end. From Durango, drive north 10 miles on US 550 to Hermosa, an unincorporated settlement. The Durango and Silverton Narrow Gauge Railroad tracks cross the highway here; immediately south of the tracks, take a dirt road that goes left (west). After 30 yards this road intersects Forest Road 576. FR 576 climbs 1,100 feet to the north (right) to the Hermosa Creek trailhead, 4 miles north. You may park here and ride your bike down to this point from the trailhead at the end of the ride, or drive up to the trailhead and park there.

To reach the northern end of the trail, continue north from Hermosa on US 550 to Purgatory Ski Area, about 28 miles north of Durango. Turn left (west) onto Forest Road 578 (Hermosa Park Road) toward Sig Campground. About 2 miles past the campground, and 8 miles from US 550, look for trailhead parking on the left after crossing East Hermosa Creek. The first 0.75 mile of trail is across private land.

Closest town: Durango is 36 miles southeast from the trailhead and 10 miles south from the car drop-off point at Hermosa.

For more information: Columbine Ranger District, San Juan National Forest, 110 West 11th Street, Durango, CO 81301. Phone (970) 247-4874.

Trail: 16 miles one-way, plus 4 miles of graded and paved road back to Hermosa from the southern trailhead.

Elevation: Net loss of 1,000 feet to the southern trailhead, plus another 1,100 feet of descent on FR 576 to Hermosa.

Degree of difficulty: Strenuous.

Surface: Single-track.

WEMINUCHE WILDERNESS AREA

[Fig. 44, Fig. 45] The southwestern corner of the Weminuche Wilderness Area is about 18 miles from Durango. This portion of the wilderness is characterized by high, limestone mesas fringing the volcanic peaks around Chicago Basin. (For a full description of this wilderness area, *see* page 273.)

LIME MESA TRAIL

[Fig. 44(1)] This is a moderately difficult hike that leads up onto a broad table-land of alpine tundra. The trail ends at an overlook on Mountain View Crest, the northern edge of Lime Mesa. The overlook is 500 feet above a small tarn, Ruby Lake. There are panoramic views from here of the West Needle Mountains, 8 miles to the northwest across the Animas River canyon, and the three Fourteeners in the Weminuche, Mount Eolus, Windom Peak, and Sunlight Peak, 5 miles to the northeast.

Directions: From Durango, drive 7 miles north on US 550 to the crossroads of Trimble. Turn right (east) here onto County 252 and cross the Animas River and turn left (north) at a T intersection. Go 4 miles on this road (County 250) to a fork and bear right on Forest Road 682. From this point the road climbs through numerous switchbacks. Stay on FR 682 until Henderson Lake, about 20 miles. Turn right here onto Forest Road 81. The Lime Mesa trailhead is 5 miles up FR 81, at the end of the road. The last 2 miles of this road are passable only by high-clearance, four-wheel-drive vehicles, and the Forest Service may close this portion of the road to vehicles altogether in the near future.

Closest town: Durango, about 30 miles south.

For more information: Columbine Ranger District, San Juan National Forest, 110 West 11th Street, Durango, CO 81301. Phone (970) 247-4874.

Trail: 8 miles round-trip to Mountain View Crest.

Elevation: Change of 1,000 feet.

Degree of difficulty: Moderate.

Surface: Single-track.

FISHING

ANIMAS RIVER

[Fig. 45] The upper portions of the Animas River contain few fish, but the lower sections are a trophy trout stream.

The Animas heads northeast of Silverton in one of the most heavily mineralized regions of Colorado. This area was extensively mined in the nineteenth and twentieth centuries. Mining produces dilute acid solutions that flow from mine tunnels and into nearby waterways. These acids leach naturally occurring heavy metals from the surrounding rock. The net effect of this pollution is to sterilize streams. Some reclamation work is underway in the upper Animas basin, but the river remains largely lifeless above Hermosa.

Public access is very limited until the river enters the town limits of Durango.

Enormous brown trout have been caught in the city limits. The portion from Lightner Creek (at the intersection of US 160 and US 550) south for 2.5 miles to Purple Cliffs is a designated Gold Medal trout fishery. This is the highest designation for a state trout fishery. It reflects the ability of the river to produce significant numbers of large fish.

Public access is readily available along this section of the river, which runs close to the highway. South of the Gold Medal portion, the river passes through private land, then enters the Southern Ute Indian Reservation. Anglers must purchase a tribal fishing permit to fish within the boundaries of the reservation. Permits are available at sporting goods stores in Durango and at tribal headquarters in Ignacio.

For more information: Colorado Division of Wildlife, 151 East 16th Street, Durango, CO 81301. Phone (970) 247-0855.

VALLECITO LAKE

[Fig. 45] This reservoir is located 22 miles northeast of Durango. The lake is stocked with rainbow trout and kokanee salmon. Record northern pike and German brown trout have been caught here.

Fishing access is good along the 21 miles of Vallecito's shoreline, but most fishing is done by boat. Boats may be rented from marinas on the lake, and there is a public boat launching ramp.

Directions: From Durango, drive north on Main Avenue to 15th Street, located immediately south of the Animas River. Turn right on 15th Street and go two blocks, then veer left onto Florida Road, also known as County Road 240. Follow it 22 miles to Vallecito Lake.

Facilities: Boat ramp, public and private campgrounds, marinas.

Dates: Campgrounds tend to be open from Memorial Day to Labor Day.

Fees: There is a fee to camp.

Closest town: Bayfield, 15 miles south.

For more information: Colorado Division of Wildlife, 151 East 16th Street, Durango, CO 81301. Phone (970) 247-0855. Vallecito Lake Chamber of Commerce, PO Box 804, Bayfield, CO 8122. Phone (970) 884-9782.

RAFTING THE ANIMAS RIVER

Commercial rafting takes place on two sections of the Animas River. Trips on the lower Animas from 6 to 16 miles in length run from the northern edge of Durango through town and continue as far as the Southern Ute Reservation.

The river here is typified by Class II and Class III rapids. Water levels vary significantly; high water can be as high as 6,000 cubic feet per second (cfs), although anything over 2,500 cfs is considered high. High flows usually peak sometime between late May and early July. In late summer, flows drop as low as 300 cfs.

Rafting on the upper Animas River begins in Silverton and follows the river through the Animas Canyon, which divides the Weminuche Wilderness Area. Several commercial outfitters make this trip, an overnight, 24-mile-long expedition between

Rafting on the upper Animas is more difficult than running the rapids on the lower portion of the river.

14,000-foot-high peaks.

The rapids in the upper Animas are significantly rougher. The river is almost continuous Class III through the canyon, with intermittent Class IV and Class V rapids—expert-only water. It is considered one of the most difficult regularly run commercial trips in the country. Rafters on the upper Animas, even those who use a guide service, are advised to be physically fit and have previous whitewater experience.

High water on the upper Animas flows at 2,500 cfs to 4,000 cfs. Low water is 500 cfs to 200 cfs.

Dates: Rafting season runs from May through Sept. on the lower Animas, mid-May to mid-Aug. on the upper Animas.

Fees: There is no fee to raft without a guide. Commercial rafters, of course, charge a fee.

For more information: Durango Chamber of Commerce, PO Box 2587, Durango, CO 81302. Phone (800) 525-8855.

PURGATORY RESORT

[Fig. 43(3)] Opened in 1965, Purgatory Resort is known for its deep snow and mild temperatures. An average of 240 inches of snow falls annually at the ski area, yet four out of five winter days are sunny and clear.

The river connecting Durango and Silverton was named *El Rio de las Animas Perdidas*, or The River of Lost Souls, by eighteenth century Spanish explorers who first encountered it. A nineteenth century wag decided to name a tributary Purgatory Creek. Purgatory's trail crew followed the tradition by referring to Dante's *The Divine Comedy* in their search for trail names. The result was ski trails christened Styx, Upper Hades, Demon, Paradise and Limbo.

The ski area is situated 28 miles north of Durango. Its summit, atop the Hermosa Cliffs, is set at 10,822 feet. Total vertical drop is 2,029 feet. There are 1,200 skiable acres.

Directions: From Durango, drive 28 miles north on US 550 to Purgatory Resort, on the left (west).

Activities: Skiing, snowboarding, lessons.

Facilities: Base village.

Dates: Generally open Thanksgiving to Easter.

Fees: There is a fee to use the lifts.

Closest town: Durango, 28 miles south.

For more information: Purgatory Resort, No. 1 Skier Place, Durango, CO 81301. Phone (970) 247-9000.

Lake City Area

[Fig. 46] Lake City lies at the northeastern edge of an overlapping pair of collapsed volcanic calderas. The rim of these calderas is marked by the high peaks northwest of Lake City (Uncompahgre, Matterhorn, Wetterhorn), the north-south divide running between Lake City and Silverton (site of Engineer Pass and Cinnamon Pass), and the Continental Divide, which runs through the Carson Peak Roadless Area south of Lake San Cristobal.

In the center of these calderas Red Cloud Peak (14,034 feet) and Sunshine Peak (14,001 feet) are part of a third-phase volcanic uplift, or dome, that occurred in the volcanic core after the older caldera collapsed. Some of the peaks along the north rim of the caldera are probably also third phase.

Such calderas are common in the San Juans: 15 have been identified by geologists. They are often associated with rich mining areas, and this region is no exception. A half dozen mining towns sprang up in the drainages around the inside the ancient volcanic basins.

Lake City sits downstream of Lake San Cristobal, a very new addition to the earth. The lake is only about 730 years old. It was created by the Slumgullion earthflow, a massive, thirteenth century landslide (*see* page 291).

Lake City was founded in the early 1870s and soon became a supply town for the mines located up the Lake Fork of the Gunnison and up Henson Creek. When the Denver and Rio Grande Railroad arrived in Lake City in 1889 (coming up from the north along the Lake Fork), Lake City became a railhead for supplies and shipment of ores.

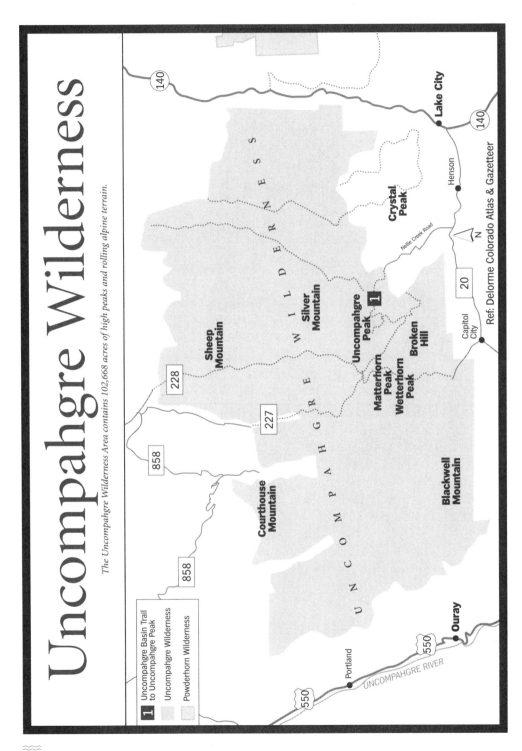

Uncompahgre Wilderness

The Uncompahgre Wilderness Area contains 102,668 acres of high peaks and rolling alpine terrain.

Uncompahgre Basin Trail to Uncompahgre Peak

Uncompahgre Wilderness

Powderhorn Wilderness

Ref: Delorme Colorado Atlas & Gazetteer

Lake City

Henson

Crystal Peak

Nellie Creek Road

Silver Mountain

Uncompahgre Peak

Capitol City

Sheep Mountain

Matterhorn Peak

Wetterhorn Peak

Broken Hill

Courthouse Mountain

Blackwell Mountain

Portland

Ouray

UNCOMPAHGRE RIVER

The town had a raucous red light district, Hell's Acre, that is today a downtown park where children play. During the 1880s and 1890s, Lake City was so busy that boardwalks along the streets were literally worn out and replaced on a regular basis. Lake City still has boardwalks. It is the only incorporated town in Hinsdale County, one of the least populous counties in Colorado. Much of the southern half of the county lies in the Weminuche Wilderness Area.

For more information: Ouray Ranger District, Uncompahgre National Forest, 2505 South Townsend, Montrose, CO 81401. Phone (970) 240-5300 or Taylor River/ Cebolla Ranger District, Gunnison National Forest, Lake City Office, Lake City, CO 81235. Phone (970) 944-2500.

UNCOMPAHGRE WILDERNESS AREA

[Fig. 46] The Uncompahgre Wilderness Area encompasses the northern front of the San Juan Mountains between Ouray and Lake City. This is a dramatic ridgeline of improbably steep and abrupt mountains reminiscent of Wyoming's Teton Range. From the Uncompahgre Valley north of the San Juans these mountains rake the horizon like a frozen city: Matterhorn Peak (13,590 feet), Wetterhorn Peak (14,015 feet), Uncompahgre Peak (14,309 feet), Precipice Peak (13,144 feet), Coxcomb Peak (13,656 feet).

Rising a mile or more from the nearby valley floor, these mountains appear nearly impregnable. Uncompahgre Peak, for instance, is a flat-topped mountain with sheer flanks on three sides. (The route to its summit climbs the gentler south side.)

The Uncompahgre Wilderness Area, first protected in 1930, contains 102,668 acres of high peaks and rolling alpine terrain. Much of its higher-elevation terrain is tundra, dotted with nodding heads of Colorado columbine (*Aquilegia coerulea*) and common harebell (*Campanula rotundifolia*). In the shade of subalpine forests and in sheltered bogs look for sickletop lousewort (*Pedicularis racemosa*) and bluebells (*Mertensia paniculata*).

Yellow-bellied marmots (*Marmota flaviventris*) frequent the rock piles of the high country. At higher elevations in the Uncompahgre's forests you may find the grey fox (*Urocyon cinereoargenteus*); the more common red fox (*Vulpes vulpes*) prefers montane terrain.

From the flanks of Uncompahgre Peak, a hiker looks into a thicket of uncountable mountain peaks and ridges, the heart of the San Juan Mountains, stretching to the far western and southern horizons.

Directions: Trailheads into the Uncompahgre Wilderness Area can be found on all sides. On the west, several trails lead out of Ouray or off of CO 550. To the south, Henson Creek Road, which leads west from Lake City, provides access. CO 149 skirts the eastern side of the region; on the north, several trails lead from around Silver Jack Reservoir.

For more information: Taylor River-Cebolla Ranger District, Gunnison National

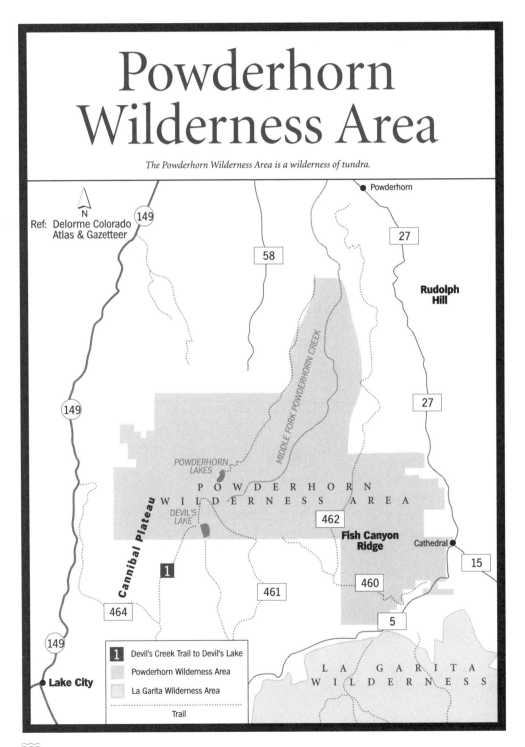

Powderhorn Wilderness Area

The Powderhorn Wilderness Area is a wilderness of tundra.

Ref: Delorme Colorado Atlas & Gazetteer

Powderhorn

Rudolph Hill

MIDDLE FORK POWDERHORN CREEK

POWDERHORN LAKES

P O W D E R H O R N
W I L D E R N E S S   A R E A

DEVIL'S LAKE

Cannibal Plateau

Fish Canyon Ridge

Cathedral

Lake City

L A   G A R I T A
W I L D E R N E S S

Legend:

1 — Devil's Creek Trail to Devil's Lake
— Powderhorn Wilderness Area
— La Garita Wilderness Area
········· Trail

Forest, Lake City Office, PO Box 89, Lake City, CO 81235. Phone (970) 944-2500.

UNCOMPAGHRE BASIN TRAIL TO UNCOMPAHGRE PEAK

[Fig. 46(1)] This hike leads quickly into an open alpine basin and then onto the steep shoulder of Uncompahgre Peak. The climb to the summit is not particularly difficult, although the last 1,000 feet are strenuous. Almost all of this hike is above timberline; get an early start and keep a close eye on the weather to avoid afternoon thunderstorms. These daily summer events usually threaten by noon.

Directions: From Lake City, drive to the southwestern corner of town and follow County Road 20 (Henson Creek) west on the Alpine Loop Scenic Byway, which is clearly signed. Drive about 7 miles to the Nellie Creek Road, a right (north) turn. Take this right. This is a four-wheel-drive road. Drive north on Nellie Creek Road 4 miles to the Uncompahgre Peak trailhead.

Facilities: Restrooms at the trailhead.

Dates: Generally open late June to Sept. County Road 20 is not plowed past Henson, 4 miles west of Lake City.

Closest town: Lake City, 11 miles southwest.

Trail: 6 miles round-trip.

Elevation: Change of 2,700 feet.

Degree of difficulty: Strenuous.

Surface: Dirt and loose rock, some scrambling near the summit.

▓ POWDERHORN WILDERNESS AREA

[Fig. 47] The Powderhorn Wilderness Area is a wilderness of tundra. The 12,000-foot Cannibal Plateau (named for Alferd Packer, *see* page 290) and Calf Creek Plateau are believed to encompass the largest unbroken stretch of alpine tundra in the lower 48 states. Devil's Lake and the Powderhorn Lakes make good destinations for hikers who want to stride across these sprawling meadows. In every direction there are mountains: the La Garita Peaks to the southeast, the Uncompahgre massif of the northern San Juan front to the southwest, and the West Elk Mountains to the north.

This is good country in which to spot elk and mule deer, particularly at dawn and dusk along the edges of the surrounding forests. These ungulates are relatively common in the Powderhorn Wilderness Area. Elk often spend their summers in high, open terrain, bedding down in nearby timber during the day and feeding in the wet meadows of high valleys and plateaus. Beaver are common in the willow-choked streams draining the plateaus of the Powderhorn.

In drier tundra areas here common plant species include alpine pussytoes (*Antennaria alpina*), alpine milk vetch (*Astragalus alpinus*), and cinquefoil (*Potentilla*). Matts of moss campion (*Silene acaulis*) and clumps of roseroot (*Sedum integrifolium*) add flashes of magenta and red to the complex carpet of tundra. Roseroot looks very similar to rosecrown (*Sedum rhodanthum*), also called queenscrown. Roseroot, however, grows only about 15 centimeters tall; rosecrown may rise to twice that

Alferd Packer, Cannibal

The story of Alferd Packer (who apparently couldn't spell his own name) is one of the best-known in the annals of American cannibalism, second in notoriety only to California's Donner Party.

Packer, an erstwhile mountain guide, left a Ute Indian camp near today's Montrose, Colorado with five clients in February 1874, bound for the Los Pinos Indian Agency, which was located southeast of Gunnison in the headwaters of the Gunnison River.

The group apparently made a wrong turn. Packer led his clients south up the Lake Fork of the Gunnison, toward Lake City, rather than east, up the main stem of the Gunnison. The group became lost in deep snows. On April 16, Packer showed up alone at Los Pinos Indian Agency. There he confessed to killing one man and eating part of him in desperation.

Packer was jailed at Saguache, but escaped. His story quickly captured the public imagination, in part because the remains of his victims had been discovered coincidentally by John A. Randolph, a sketch artist on assignment in the Rocky Mountains for his employer, *Harper's Weekly Magazine.*

Packer did not surface again until 1883, when he revealed his identity to a friend at Fort Fetterman, in the Wyoming Territory, where Packer was living under an alias. Packer was returned to Lake City, convicted on Friday, the 13th of April, 1883, and sentenced to be hanged. A Lake City barfly, James Dolan, attended the trial and rushed to the nearest watering hole to report Judge M.B. Gerry's verdict. Although it is probably not entirely accurate, this version of the verdict has survived as a favored rendition:

"Stand up, ye son-of-a-bitch, and receive your sentence. You voracious, man-eating son-of-a-bitch, there were only six Democrats in Hinsdale County and you et five of them. I'm going to hang you on Friday and this should teach you a lesson not to reduce the Democratic population of this state."

Packer never was hanged. His conviction was reversed on a technicality. He was convicted again in Gunnison in August 1886 and sentenced to 40 years in prison. He was pardoned by Governor Charles S. Thomas—a Democrat—in 1901, and died in 1907.

Packer is remembered in many ways. Perhaps none, however, is so delicious as this: The student cafeteria at the University of Colorado in Boulder is named after him.

height. Both plants are succulents that generally grow in clumps and carry dark red clusters of flowers set on a single head.

Directions: Several roads skirt the Powderhorn Wilderness. From Slumgullion Pass, located 15 miles east of Lake City on CO 149, Forest Road 788 passes between the northeastern side of the La Garita Wilderness and the southeastern side of the Powderhorn Wilderness. Several trailheads depart into both wilderness areas along this road, which is closed in winter. The Devil's Creek Trail leads into the Powderhorn Wilderness from the Lake Fork of the Gunnison, on the west side of the wilderness area.

For more information: Taylor River-Cebolla Ranger District, Gunnison National Forest, Lake City Office, PO Box 89, Lake City, CO 81235. Phone (970) 944-2500.

DEVIL'S CREEK TRAIL TO DEVIL'S LAKE

[Fig. 47(1)] This trail leads hikers up onto the highlands east of the Lake Fork of the Gunnison, into the same territory where Alferd Packer and his ill-fated companions were trapped by snow in the late winter of 1874. The trail climbs through aspen and spruce forests onto the open escarpment of the plateau. Devil's Lake is situated in a slight depression between Cannibal Plateau and Calf Creek Plateau, surrounded for several miles on all sides by open tundra.

In rocky areas here and elsewhere in the alpine zone look for sky pilot (*Polemonium viscosum*), a plant whose flower stalks are covered with small, violet-like flowers. Sky pilot grows up to 16 inches, but is usually much shorter. Its leaves and stems are covered by sticky hairs that exude a skunky scent.

Directions: Drive north from Lake City about 7 miles on CO 149 to the Devil's Creek Trailhead, on the right (east) side of the highway.

Trail: 13 miles round-trip.

Elevation: Gain of 3,400 feet.

Degree of difficulty: Strenuous.

Surface: Dirt and rock; tundra at upper elevations.

SLUMGULLION SLIDE

[Fig. 48(1)] West of Slumgullion Pass on CO 149 is a dramatic illustration of geology at work. Approximately 700 years ago (best estimates put the event at A.D. 1270), a vast portion of nearby Mesa Seco slid into the Lake Fork Valley of the Gunnison River.

This earthflow—named for the miner's concoction slumgullion stew, which it resembles—was caused by water saturating the volcanic tuff and ash that make up Mesa Seco. The slide was 4.5 miles long and up to 2,000 feet wide. More than 3 billion cubic yards of earth collapsed from the western rim of the mesa, which was 11,500 feet high, toward the valley, set at 8,500 feet. The earthflow dammed the Lake Fork and created Lake San Cristobal, the second largest natural lake in Colorado after Grand Lake.

Approximately 300 years ago, a second earthflow began. This second earthflow has overridden about 2.5 miles of the original slide and it continues to move. The flow has been measured moving downhill at rates ranging from 2 feet to 20 feet per year.

Because the slide is still moving, vegetation grows only sparsely upon it. The movement of the earth breaks the roots of trees that try to gain a purchase on the flow. In some places aspen trees have managed to acquire a toehold. Many of these, however, appear gnarled and twisted. As the earth beneath the trees has moved, it has twisted

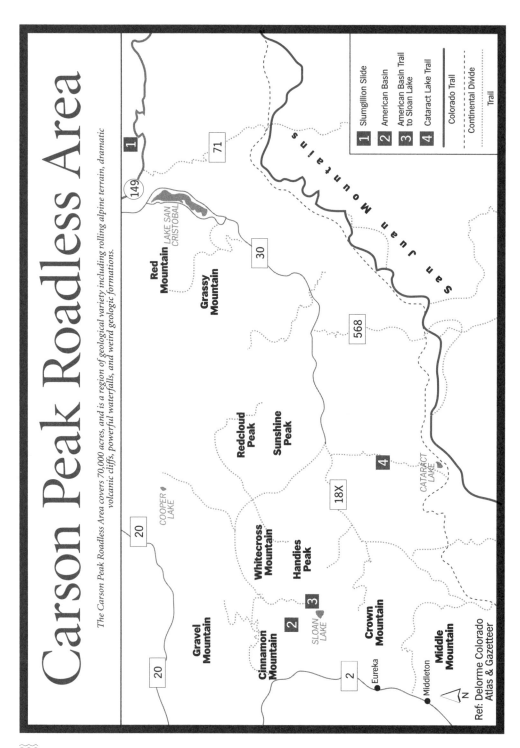

Carson Peak Roadless Area

The Carson Peak Roadless Area covers 70,000 acres, and is a region of geological variety including rolling alpine terrain, dramatic volcanic cliffs, powerful waterfalls, and weird geologic formations.

1 Slumgillion Slide
2 American Basin
3 American Basin Trail to Sloan Lake
4 Cataract Lake Trail

— — — Colorado Trail
········· Continental Divide Trail

San Juan Mountains

LAKE SAN CRISTOBAL

Red Mountain

Grassy Mountain

Redcloud Peak

Sunshine Peak

COOPER LAKE

Whitecross Mountain

Handies Peak

CATARACT LAKE

Gravel Mountain

Cinnamon Mountain

SLOAN LAKE

Crown Mountain

Middle Mountain

Eureka

Middleton

N

Ref: Delorme Colorado Atlas & Gazetteer

them out of vertical position. Each year the crown of the tree adjusts to that twisting by trying to grow vertically. Then the earth moves again, and the tree adjusts again.

Directions: The Slumgullion Slide is best viewed from CO 149, which traverses it immediately east of Lake San Cristobal. If you would like to walk on the slide, drive east 7.1 miles from Lake City to a small dirt road to the southwest (right). Cross the highway to the north to walk on the slide. There is a wide pulloff and interpretive sign 0.5 mile farther east on CO 149. The slide may also be viewed from the Windy Point overlook, 10 miles east of Lake City on CO 149.

Activities: Day hiking, viewing.

Facilities: Restrooms at Windy Point.

Closest town: Lake City, 10 miles west.

For more information: Taylor River-Cebolla Ranger District, Gunnison National Forest, Lake City Office, PO Box 89, Lake City, CO 81235. Phone (970) 944-2500.

CARSON PEAK ROADLESS AREA

[Fig. 48] This roadless area, covering 70,000 acres, is a region of geological variety: vast stretches of rolling alpine terrain, dramatic volcanic cliffs, powerful waterfalls, and weird geologic formations. The headwaters of the Rio Grande lie here on the eastern side of Stony Pass, a rough route through the mountains that once connected the boom towns of Silverton and Creede.

The Carson Peak Roadless Area includes 15 miles of the Continental Divide and is traversed by both the Continental Divide Trail and the Colorado Trail. Although the northwestern corner is being managed as a wilderness study area by the Bureau of Land Management, the Carson Peak Roadless Area is not designated as wilderness. This is unusual in Colorado, where most high country is protected as wilderness if it has not been extensively mined or otherwise developed. Part of the reason this land is not wilderness is that responsibility for the region is divided between three federal agencies: the BLM, Gunnison National Forest, and Rio Grande National Forest.

Wilderness designations are always controversial; the 1993 Colorado Wilderness Bill was the result of a full decade of legislative battles in the U.S. Congress. Wilderness opponents often include individuals or companies that benefit from or enjoy motorized access to an area (such as snowmobilers), or those who hope to profit from exploiting natural resources such as timber, minerals, or water rights. The Carson Peak area has been excluded from past wilderness bills in part because extensive wilderness exists to the north, in the La Garita Wilderness Area, and to the south, in the Weminuche. Protection of the Carson Peak area, however, would create a wilderness land bridge through the San Juans that stretched from Cochetopa Hills to the South San Juan Wilderness. Such a bridge would help ensure the stability of species that need vast, undisturbed terrain, such as mountain lions, black bears and Canada lynx.

Legislation introduced in Congress in early 1999 by Congresswoman Diana

Degette (D-Boulder) proposed giving the Carson Peak area, and 48 other areas around the state totalling 1.4 million acres, wilderness designation. If past is prologue, Degette's bill may need many years to become law.

AMERICAN BASIN

[Fig. 48(2)] American Basin is an alpine valley located east of Cinnamon Pass and west of Handie's Peak, in the northwestern corner of the Carson Peak Roadless Area. It is near the Alpine Loop Scenic Byway (*see* page 320), and is one of the highest valleys accessible by motor vehicle in the San Juan Mountains. The road to American Basin along Henson Creek demarcates the northern edge of the roadless area.

An unnamed, castellated ridge runs around the southern side of the basin, overhanging it with dark volcanic rock. From the upper basin hikers can see 12,600-foot Cinnamon Pass, which connects to the Animas River drainage and the town of Silverton.

Fireweed (*Epilobium angustifolium*) is common along roadsides here and in other sunny, disturbed, and relatively dry sites throughout the montane zone. It's an early colonizer of such sites and is often one of the first plants to bloom in the wake of a forest fire. Topped with showy, fuchsia racemes of flowers, fireweed grows up to 6 feet tall.

Directions: From Lake City, drive south 3 miles on CO 149 to County Road 30 (Lake San Cristobal). Turn right (south) onto this road. Pass Lake San Cristobal and remain on the road approximately 20 miles. At a sharp right-hand hairpin, the road to American Basin bears left (there is a sign). Take this left and drive 1 mile to the American Basin trailhead. South of Lake San Cristobal the road is graded dirt. The entire route is passable in a two-wheel-drive vehicle if you are careful and conditions are good; however, this route is not well maintained and is definitely limited to four-wheel-drive vehicles if you wish to continue above the turn to American Basin toward Cinnamon Pass.

Activities: Hiking.

Facilities: None.

Dates: Open late June to Sept. The road is not plowed.

Fees: None.

Closest town: Lake City, about 25 miles northeast.

For more information: Taylor River-Cebolla Ranger District, Gunnison National Forest, Lake City Office, PO Box 89, Lake City, CO 81235. Phone (970) 944-2500.

AMERICAN BASIN TRAIL TO SLOAN LAKE

[Fig. 48(3)] This trail follows old mining roads through the flower-filled meadows of American Basin to a small lake below the summit of 14,048-foot Handie's Peak.

Trail: Double-track and single-track through alpine tundra.

Elevation: Change of 1,700 feet.

Degree of difficulty: Moderate.

Surface: Dirt and rock.

CATARACT LAKE TRAIL

[Fig. 48(4)] This trail climbs past tumbling waterfalls into the Cataract Lake Basin, which lies under the northern lip of the Continental Divide. Steep volcanic cliffs drop down into meadows of wildflowers. On the way up, look to the west for the 1,000-foot vertical face of Half Peak, which lies northeast of Cataract Lake. The high country here is less vertical than in the San Miguel Mountains or along the Sneffels Range, both to the northwest. It's rounder and flatter than in many of Colorado's other alpine areas, a characteristic seen in other parts of the San Juans (such as in the highlands above the Conejos River [*see* page 309]).

The Cataract Creek Trail connects with the Continental Divide and Colorado trails 1 mile south of the lake.

Directions: From Lake City, drive south 3 miles on CO 149 to County Road 30 (Lake San Cristobal). Turn right (south) onto this road. Pass Lake San Cristobal and remain on the road approximately 10 miles to a fork marking the turn to the town of Sherman, a left. Take this left and drive approximately 1.5 miles to the Cataract Creek trailhead, on the left. Park here and begin climbing the trail.

Activities: Day hiking, backpacking.

Facilities: Restrooms at the trailhead.

Closest town: Lake City, approximately 17 miles northeast.

For more information: Taylor River-Cebolla Ranger District, Gunnison National Forest, Lake City Office, PO Box 89, Lake City, CO 81235. Phone (970) 944-2500.

Trail: 10 miles round-trip.

Elevation: Change of 2,500 feet.

Degree of difficulty: Strenuous.

Surface: Dirt and rock.

Creede Area

[Fig. 49] Creede can arguably be called the booming-est of all of Colorado's mining towns. It was a late bloomer, as silver was not discovered here until 188. But Creede made up lost ground fast. In the summer of 1890, 300 people moved to Creede every day. Five hundred shacks were built in one 90-day period. By 1892 Creede counted a population of 10,000 and was producing $1 million worth of silver ore per month.

A single story illustrates how quickly Creede grew, and why: On February 1, 1892, somebody suggested bringing electric lights to Creede. Five days later, electricity was available throughout town and the lights burned into the night.

The silver ore was found in broad veins, including a very rich one of amethyst quartz, in the steep walls of the Willow Creek valley. Towering cliffs and spires form massive stone gates into the narrow valley. These volcanic intrusions are thrust up

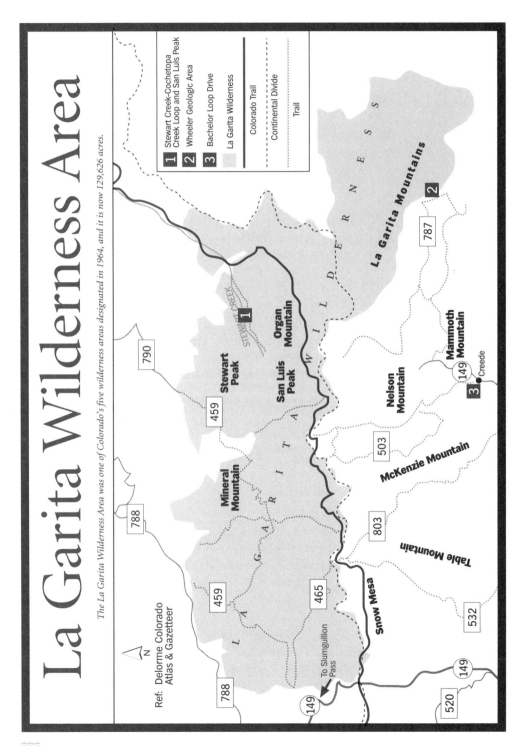

La Garita Wilderness Area

The La Garita Wilderness Area was one of Colorado's five wilderness areas designated in 1964, and it is now 129,626 acres.

N

Ref: Delorme Colorado Atlas & Gazetteer

1 Stewart Creek-Cochetopa Creek Loop and San Luis Peak
2 Wheeler Geologic Area
3 Bachelor Loop Drive
La Garita Wilderness

Colorado Trail
Continental Divide
Trail

La Garita Mountains

WILDERNESS

Stewart Peak
Organ Mountain
San Luis Peak
Mineral Mountain

Nelson Mountain

Mammoth Mountain
Creede

McKenzie Mountain

Table Mountain

Snow Mesa

To Slumgullion Pass

790
459
788
459
465
788
503
803
532
787
149
149
520
149

L A G A R I T A

along the northern edge of a collapsed caldera that lies south of Creede. The Rio Grande River meanders through the floor of the caldera, which was a second-phase volcanic dome that once stood 2,000 feet high.

The caldera, which measures 10 miles across, formed when the dome exploded or collapsed. The flat lands east and west of Creede, where the Rio Grande now runs, are Oligocene lake beds of yellow and white shale. The lake ran in a broad, south-facing U around Snowshoe Mountain, from Wagon Wheel Gap past Creede and extending south of Bristol Head.

Snowshoe Mountain was a more recent, third-phase volcanic intrusion into the old caldera.

Creede's mineralized zones—containing commercial quantities not only of silver but also of gold, zinc, and lead—were produced when heavily mineralized volcanic solutions filled in the fissures of the rim around the caldera.

The quantities of money involved in Creede's mines were astounding. The Amethyst Mine produced $2 million in the first year; some of its ore was worth $5,000 a ton. A miner grubstaked with $25 found the Last Chance while chasing his wandering burros over a hillside. That mine produced $1.6 million in its first year. This was an enormous amount of money at the time; at the turn of the nineteenth century, miners in Telluride would go on strike to try to force mine owners to pay them a fixed wage of $3 a day.

Creede was particularly lawless and wild, in part because it was a long way from anywhere, and in part because county boundaries in the San Juan Mountains were unclear. The result was a no-man's land in which a Mafia-style order was imposed by camp bosses who ensured they made plenty of money in the process.

Law and order came in 1893 when Mineral County was established with Wasson (3 miles south of Creede) as its county seat. That decision didn't sit well with Creede residents, who soon stole the courthouse records, and then the courthouse itself, and moved both up to Creede, which became (and remains) the county seat.

The 1893 silver bust hurt but didn't break Creede. The population dropped to 900 by the turn of the century, but daily train service to Alamosa was still run by the Denver and Rio Grande railway. Commercial mining continued until 1988.

For more information: Creede Chamber of Commerce, POB 580, Creede, CO 81130. Phone (719) 658-2374.

🌼 LA GARITA WILDERNESS AREA

[Fig. 49] This wilderness area is lightly used. Its mountains are long, rolling summits on the northeastern corner of the San Juans. The Wheeler Geologic Area, now contained inside the wilderness, was once designated as a national monument because of its extraordinary geology. That designation was rescinded in 1950 because the area is so remote and difficult to reach. Nevertheless, the geology is still compelling.

La Garita (Spanish for lookout) was one of Colorado's five wilderness areas designated in 1964. Since then its name has been changed (it was originally called Big Blue) and it has been expanded considerably to its current 129,626 acres. La Garita now contains 35 miles of the Continental Divide Trail and one Fourteener, San Luis Peak.

Directions: CO 149 touches on the western edge of the La Garita Wilderness Area at Spring Creek Pass. At Slumgullion Pass, Forest Road 788 runs east between the La Garita and Powderhorn wilderness areas. This road is open only during the summer. Access to the northeastern and eastern portions of the wilderness is relatively difficult and necessitates traversing many miles of forest roads, several of which lead to trailheads from CO 114. These roads are not plowed during the winter months.

For more information: During May to Nov., contact Creede Ranger District, Rio Grande National Forest, 3rd Street and Creede Avenue, Creede, CO 81130. Phone (719) 658-2556. At other times of the year, contact Divide Ranger District, Rio Grande National Forest, 13308 West Highway 160, Del Norte, CO 81132. Phone (719) 657-3321.

WHEELER GEOLOGIC AREA

[Fig. 49(2)] There's no easy way to get to this bizarre volcanic formation, but it's worth the effort. The Wheeler Geologic Area is 60 acres of eroded volcanic tuff that resemble a small city. The tuff, comprised of volcanic ash and breccia from at least 18 nearby volcanoes, has been eroded over the past 26.5 million years into a ghostly city of towers, minarets, and castles in the middle of the forest. This volcanic anomaly seems like the sort of strange rock formation one would find in the deserts of southeastern Utah, rather than high in Colorado's mountains.

The area's existence was documented by Anglo-Americans in 1907. In 1908, President Theodore Roosevelt declared 300 acres around the site a national monument. But access was very difficult. Thirty-five years later, only 43 people visited the monument in a single summer. The lack of both visitation and funding for an improved road led to the monument status being revoked by Congress in 1950. However, the area around the monument was protected administratively by the Rio Grande Forest, which prohibited mining in the immediate vicinity.

In 1993, 25,640 acres of new wilderness, including the Wheeler Geologic Area, were added to the La Garita Wilderness. The rough jeep road to the monument, however, was allowed to remain, and traditional four-wheel-drive access to the Wheeler Geologic Area is still permitted. The wilderness designation surrounds, but excludes, the old jeep road.

Directions: If you wish to drive to the Wheeler Geologic Area, allow at least 7 hours of round-trip driving time. This route can only be driven in a high-clearance, four-wheel-drive vehicle by an experienced driver. In wet conditions it is impassable.

To drive or hike to the area, begin by driving south from Creede approximately 7 miles on CO 149 to Forest Road 600 (Pool Table Road), a left (north) turn. Drive 9.5 miles on Pool Table Road to Hanson's Mill Campground, site of a former timber mill.

Beyond Hanson's Mill the road is a 14-mile four-wheel-drive route. Plan on 3 hours of driving from this point to the Wheeler Geologic Area.

If you are hiking, pick up the East Bellows Creek Trail, which leads out of the north end of the parking lot at the Hanson's Mill Campground. About 1 mile from the Wheeler Geologic Area, the trail joins the jeep road. Follow this road to its end; the tuff formations are located 0.5 mile north of the roadhead along a clear footpath.

Activities: Scenic four-wheel-drive route, day hiking, backpacking.

Facilities: There is camping and a pit toilet at Hanson's Mill Campground.

Dates: Generally June to Sept. The road is not plowed.

Fees: None.

Closest town: Creede, 25 miles west by trail and road from the Wheeler Geologic Area.

For more information: May to Nov., contact Creede Ranger District, Rio Grande National Forest, 3rd Street and Creede Avenue, Creede, CO 81130. Phone (719) 658-2556. At other times of the year, contact Divide Ranger District, Rio Grande National Forest, 13308 West Highway 160, Del Norte, CO 81132. Phone (719) 657-3321.

Trail: Foot **Trail:** 8.5 miles one-way. Jeep road: 14 miles one-way.

Elevation: Gain of 1,600 feet.

Degree of difficulty: Moderate.

Surface: Dirt and rocks. One creek crossing on the East Bellows Trail may not be possible early in the summer, due to high water from snowmelt.

STEWART CREEK-COCHETOPA CREEK LOOP AND SAN LUIS PEAK

[Fig. 49(1)] This route is a pleasant loop hike through the northeastern San Juan Mountains, which overlook the Cochetopa Hills and the West Elk range to the north. It makes for a good overnight trip and provides access to San Luis Peak, 14,014 feet high and one of the easier Fourteeners in the state. Some route-finding is necessary above timberline as you pass from Stewart Creek to Cochetopa Creek because the trail is faint here.

Norway sedge (*Carex norvegica*) is found in the moist meadows along the slopes and creeks. This grass-like plant can be identified by its seedheats, which are a dark, fleur-de-lys shape. The plant rarely grows about 30 centimeters at alpine altitudes.

This unnamed pass is located between Organ Mountain (13,799 feet) on the east, and San Luis Peak on west. Climb to the saddle; if you wish to climb San Luis Peak, follow the ridge north from the saddle to the summit. The main route continues south from the saddle to intersect with the Colorado Trail (also called the Skyline Trail here) in Cochetopa Creek. Turn northeast and follow Cochetopa Creek to complete the loop.

Directions: From Gunnison, drive east on US 50 approximately 8 miles to CO 114, a right (south) turn. Drive approximately 20 miles on CO 114 to County Road NN-14, a right (west) turn (look for the sign for Dome Lakes). Follow County Road NN-14 approximately 4 miles, pass the two small lakes of Dome Lakes on your right, then turn right (west) on Forest Road 794. Follow this road 5 miles to the Stewart Creek trailhead, on your right. If you wish, continue another 0.25 miles to the Eddiesville trailhead and park here; if you hike the full loop, you will emerge at Eddiesville after descending Cochetopa Creek. Begin by hiking up Stewart Creek.

Activities: Backpacking, mountaineering, camping.

Facilities: None.

Dates: Generally May-Oct. The road is not plowed to the trailhead.

Closest town: Gunnison, approximately 37 miles northwest.

For more information: Cebolla-Taylor Ranger District, Gunnison National Forest, 216 North Colorado, Gunnison, CO 81230. Phone (970) 641-0471.

Trail: A 13-mile loop, with a short, steep side trip to San Luis Peak.

Elevation: Change of 2,800 to the saddle between San Luis Peak and Organ Peak; San Luis Peak's summit is 800 feet higher.

Degree of difficulty: Moderate.

Surface: Dirt and tundra, with some sections of very faint trail above timberline.

PHOENIX YURT SYSTEM

Three yurts—Mongolian-style walled tents—are for rent in the high terrain north of Creede. The yurts, which are set on a 100-acre private site surrounded by public land, are insulated and set on wooden platforms. Each sleeps up to six people. Unlike other yurt and hut systems in Colorado in which travelers may spend a day traveling from one to the next, these backcountry accommodations are a single destination from which to strike out on daily adventures.

The yurts are situated 4 miles north of Creede at 10,500 feet elevation. They provide easy access into the surrounding peaks and valleys for hikers, mountain bikers, and backcountry skiers.

The yurts are equipped with furniture, kitchen utensils, wood and propane stoves, solar-powered electric lighting, and firewood.

Activities: Overnight accommodations for self-directed backcountry skiing, biking, hiking.

Facilities: Three furnished and equipped yurts, which may be rented individually or as a group.

Dates: Open mid-May to mid-Oct. and mid-Nov. to mid-Apr.

Fees: There is a fee to use the yurts. Reservations are necessary; directions are provided when reservations are made.

Closest town: Creede, 4 miles south.

For more information: Vertical Reality, PO Box 434, Creede, CO 81130. Phone (800) 984-6275.

BACHELOR LOOP DRIVE

[Fig. 49(3)] The Bachelor Loop is a 17-mile counterclockwise drive through the heart of Creede's gravity-defying mining district. The route follows graded gravel roads; a 2-mile portion north of the East Willow and West Willow creek junctions is very steep and narrow but can be accomplished in good weather in a two-wheel-drive car.

The mining district is punctuated by stunning vertical spires and cliffs, which are the remains of eroded tertiary volcanic intrusions. Although much of the evidence of Creede's mining history is gone, much still remains, including several large buildings that dangle precariously from the sides of the cliffs above West Willow Creek.

Approximately 1 mile north of downtown creek is the junction with East Willow Creek, to the right. This narrow valley was the original site of Creede. First it was called Willow, then Creede, then—as today's Creede rose along the base of the downstream cliffs—it became North Creede.

West (left) of the interpretive sign are the remains of the Humphrey Mill, once an enormous ore-crushing mill that climbed the side of valley. Look for the mill's foundations. Several hundred feet up the talus slope, ore from mines higher up the creek was transported into the mill. The ores were processed with the help of gravity; the concentrated ore came out the bottom of the mill, where it was loaded onto railcars and shipped to smelters.

The tour route proceeds up West Willow Creek. The steep section of road directly ahead of you was known as the Black Pitch by teamsters who had to bring loaded wagons down it. When their brakes failed the wagons leapt out of control, often killing the horses and mules drawing them.

At the top of the Black Pitch, where the road begins to diverge east from West Willow Creek, the Amethyst Mine and Last Chance Mine may be seen. The Last Chance is the one set higher up the steep slope. Both mines sank shafts as far as 1,500 feet into the mountain. A town of 100 people, Stumptown, was located here as well. Wild red raspberry (*Rubus ideaus*) grows among the loose rocks here.

Where the road takes a hard left hairpin turn, look to the right for an old trail. You may park here and walk 1.6 miles to the east along this path, the Campbell Mountain Trail, to the top of the Kentucky Belle Mine, which was perched on a cliff 1,400 feet above East Willow Creek. This, like all mining areas, is a hazardous place: Open vertical shafts and tunnels still exist, so do not venture off the trail.

The driving tour continues up to a crossing over West Willow Creek and then through the remains of Bachelor, a one-time boom town at 10,512 feet elevation that is now all but vanished. The route then winds down into the Rio Grande Valley and back to the southern end of Creede's Main Street.

Directions: Begin the drive at the intersection of CO 149 and the southern end of Creede's Main Street. Drive north through the town to the intersection of East Willow and West Willow creeks, about 1 mile north of downtown Creede. An interpretive sign is located here; interpretive pamphlets are available here for a fee. (Pamphlets are also available at the Creede Chamber of Commerce and Creede

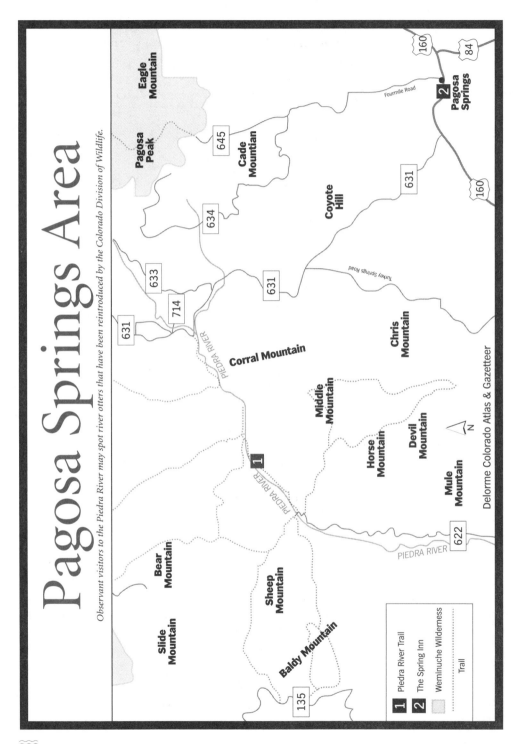

Pagosa Springs Area

Observant visitors to the Piedra River may spot river otters that have been reintroduced by the Colorado Division of Wildlife.

Eagle Mountain

Pagosa Peak

Cade Mountain

Pagosa Springs

Fourmile Road

Coyote Hill

Turkey Springs Road

Chris Mountain

Corral Mountain

PIEDRA RIVER

Middle Mountain

Horse Mountain

Devil Mountain

Mule Mountain

Bear Mountain

Sheep Mountain

Slide Mountain

Baldy Mountain

Piedra River Trail

The Spring Inn

Weminuche Wilderness

Trail

PIEDRA RIVER

Delorme Colorado Atlas & Gazetteer

Ranger District Office at Third and Main in Creede).

Activities: Scenic drive, day hike.

Facilities: None.

Dates: Generally June to Oct.

Fees: There is a fee for the interpretive pamphlet.

Closest town: Creede, at the beginning and end of the tour.

For more information: Creede Chamber of Commerce, PO Box 580, Creede, CO 81130. Phone (719) 658-2374.

Trail: If you take the optional Campbell Mountain Trail, this is a 3.2-mile round-trip hike.

Elevation: Change of 450 feet.

Degree of difficulty: Moderate.

Surface: Old wagon trail and loose rock.

Pagosa Springs Area

[Fig. 50] Fifty-five miles due east of Durango on US 160 is Pagosa Springs, the site of one of the largest hot springs in the United States. The heavily mineralized spring along the bank of the San Juan River in downtown Pagosa Springs produces 700 gallons of hot water a minute at a temperature of 155 degrees Fahrenheit. The water is laden with silica, which precipitates into siliceous sinter, the flowstone formations around the springs. So much of this sinter has been produced that the San Juan River has shifted its bed to the west to pass around the growing rock formation around the springs.

Pagosa Springs lies west of Wolf Creek Pass, where you will find Wolf Creek Ski Area, which receives more snow, on average, than any other ski area in Colorado. To the southwest is the South San Juan Wilderness Area, where Canada lynx (*Felis lynx*) were reintroduced to Colorado in 1999, and where some researchers think a remnant population of grizzly bears still exists.

HOT SPRINGS
THE SPRING INN

[Fig. 50(2)] Several hot springs have been developed in and around Pagosa Springs. The pools at The Spring Inn are sculpted into the banks of the San Juan River in downtown Pagosa Springs and are open to the public all year.

Water temperature in the 10 soaking pools ranges from 95 degrees to 112 degrees Fahrenheit. There is continuous flow-through in the pools, so the water is not chemically treated. The pools are surrounded by the mineral terraces that typify the springs around Pagosa Springs.

Directions: There is only one stoplight in Pagosa Springs; at this light turn south and cross the San Juan River. Bear right; the Spring Inn is on the right, immediately past the visitor's center, about 200 yards from the stoplight.

Activities: Soaking in natural hot springs.

Facilities: Outdoor pools, deck, lockers, showers, dressing room, overnight accommodations.

Dates: Open year-round.

Fees: There is a fee to use the pools and to stay overnight.

For more information: The Spring Inn, PO Box 1799, Pagosa Springs, CO 81147. Phone (970) 264-4168 or (800) 225-0934. Pagosa Springs Chamber of Commerce Visitors Center, 402 San Juan Street, Pagosa Springs, CO 81147. Phone (970) 264-2360.

PIEDRA PROTECTED AREA

Situated between Pagosa Springs and Durango on the southern edge of the San Juans, this critical old-growth forest is one of the lowest elevation areas given protected status in Colorado. Hikers in the region walk through thousands of acres of old-growth ponderosa pine, spruce and fir. Observant visitors may spot river otters (*Lutra canadensis*), which have been reintroduced into the Piedra River by the Colorado Division of Wildlife. River otters were trapped to extinction in Colorado by the early 1900s; reintroduction efforts have been underway in Colorado since 1976, and in the Piedra River drainage since 1978.

Another endangered species, the peregrine falcon (*Falco peregrinus*), hunts and nests in this 62,550-acre protected region.

The U.S. Forest Service had proposed extensive logging for this region, one of the last uncut, lower-elevation

RIVER OTTER
(*Lutra canadensis*)

ponderosa forests in the San Juans. The Piedra Protected Area was spared the ax when it was included in the 1993 Colorado Wilderness Bill. Low-elevation forests such as those encompassed in the Piedra watershed are relatively easily reached by timber companies and are coveted by developers and homeowners. Along the southern flank of the San Juan Mountains, most of this type of habitat has been cut or developed. The Piedra Protected Area, while less dramatic than other parts of the state, is distinctive and valuable for this reason.

The Piedra Protected Area is not an official federal wilderness area because the legislation preserving it did not include reserved water rights. In all other ways, however, the Piedra has been protected against development. Contiguous with the Weminuche Wilderness to the north, the Piedra provides a land and water bridge between the high elevations of the Weminuche and the lower lands around the Piedra. This is critical for species which migrate with the seasons.

PIEDRA RIVER TRAIL

[Fig. 50(1)] This easy hike makes a good point-to-point walk if you are willing to shuttle vehicles, or the trail can be a nice out-and-back hike. The Piedra River runs through two canyons carved through Permian sediments. Here the trail runs at elevations from 7,100 to 7,600 feet through ponderosa pines, gambel oak, and open meadows as it follows the river through Second Box Canyon. In open, moist areas you may find chokecherry (*Prunus virginiana*), a large shrub that produces racemes of wonderful-smelling, white flowers.

Directions: To drop a car at the mouth of Second Box Canyon, drive west on US 160 about 22 miles from Pagosa Springs to the marked turn for Chimney Rock, which lies to the south. Turn north here (right) onto Forest Road 622, which runs on the east side of the Piedra River. Follow this 12 miles to a bridge crossing the Piedra; park here. The trail to Second Box Canyon begins to the right (east) and heads upstream.

To reach the upper end of Second Box Canyon, drive west from Pagosa Springs 2 miles on US 160 to Forest Road 631 (Piedra Road), a right-hand (north) turn. Take this and follow it 14 miles to the Piedra Picnic Ground and the trailhead for Forest Service Trail 596, the trail through Second Box Canyon. This trail begins on the left side of the road.

Closest town: Pagosa Springs, 16 miles from the upstream trailhead, 34 miles from the downstream trailhead.

For more information: Pagosa Ranger District, San Juan National Forest, PO Box 310, Pagosa Springs, CO 81147. Phone (970) 264-2268.

Trail: 10 miles one-way.

Elevation: Change of 500 feet.

Degree of difficulty: Easy.

Surface: Single-track dirt and rock.

South San Juan Wilderness

The moisture of heavy snowpacks combines with rich volcanic soils here to create vast, rich forest lands.

East Fork Road

250

PLATORO RESERVOIR

CONEJOS RIVER

LAKE FORK

S O U T H

Nipple Mountain Road

S A N   J U A N

W I L D E R N E S S

CONEJOS RIVER

Blanco Basin Road

NO NAME LAKE

RUYBALID LAKE

ALVERJONES LAKE

1

NAVAJO RIVER

ROUGH CREEK

250

SPENCE RESERVOIR

CHAMA LAKE

663

RIO DE LOS PINOS

84

1 Ruybalid Lake Hike

South San Juan Wilderness

········ Trail

NAVAJO RIVER

Navajo River Road

121

TRUJULLO MEADOWS RESERVOIR

17

SOUTH SAN JUAN WILDERNESS AREA

[Fig. 51] In his 1995 book, *The Lost Grizzlies: A Search for Survivors in The Wilderness of Colorado*, author Rick Bass comes tantalizingly close to finding proof that a remnant population of grizzly bears (*Ursus arctos horribilis*) exists in the South San Juan Wilderness. The last known grizzly was killed here by a bow hunter in 1979. But evidence, including sightings, large digs, scat, and hairs, suggest that the elusive bear may be holding on in this sprawling wilderness of 158,790 acres.

Lewis and Clark were the first Anglo-Americans to document the grizzly, which was a predator of the western plains before it was extirpated there. Lewis first encountered the grizzly on the high plains of eastern Montana in the spring of 1805 during the Corps of Discovery's expedition to the Pacific Ocean. The bears, which were aggressive and exceedingly difficult to kill, charged even when they had been shot as many as 10 times. The grizzly, Lewis concluded in his journal, was a "much more furious and formidable anamal [sic]" than the black bears of the eastern United States.

Grizzlies or no, the South San Juan Wilderness is a wild place, considered by the Colorado Division of Wildlife to be the best habitat for predators such as grizzlies, wolverines (*Gulo gulo*), and Canada lynx. Several lynx, believed to be extinct within Colorado, were reintroduced to the region by the Division of Wildlife in early 1999.

The moisture of heavy snowpacks combines with rich volcanic soils here to create vast, rich forest lands. The Continental Divide splits the wilderness area north to south. The mountains here are high, but not quite so high as those to the north and west. This wilderness is typified by rolling terrain, much of it forested, cut by deep canyons. It is the beginning of the end of this finger of the Rocky Mountains; south of here the San Juan Mountains level out into high mesas.

Directions: The South San Juan Wilderness Area can be reached via trailheads from Forest Road 250 on the east side; US Highway 184 on the southwest edge; or US Highway 160 on the northern border.

For more information: Pagosa Springs Ranger District, San Juan National Forest, PO Box 310, Pagosa Springs, CO 81147. Phone (970) 264-2268. Conejos Peak Ranger District, Rio Grande National Forest, 21461 US 285, La Jara, CO 81140. Phone (719) 274-5193.

RUYBALID LAKE HIKE

[Fig. 51(1)] This hike begins in the scenic Conejos River valley. The Conejos, a beautiful river meandering through hay meadows and cottonwoods, traces a flat-bottomed canyon about 2,000 feet deep. The canyon cuts through the basalt cap of the surrounding plateau and into the volcanic debris beneath it.

The trail climbs the western side of the valley and provides excellent views to the south down the valley. Once you have surmounted the 27 switchbacks up the side of the Conejos River valley the route turns south to Ruybalid Lake, perched at the lip of the 11,000-foot-high mesa. From the eastern shore of the lake you can look across the Conejos Valley and the diminishing tablelands of the eastern San Juans, then farther across the San Luis Valley to the shimmering western face of the Sangre de Cristo Mountains, 60 miles away.

Once at Ruybalid, an intrepid hiker can strike out cross-country to No Name Lake to the northwest, or backtrack to the main trail and continue west deeper into the wilderness area, which contains a network of 180 miles of trails.

Directions: From Antonito, drive west on CO 17 approximately 15 miles to a right-hand fork onto a gravel road, Forest Road 250. After about 8 miles, at a cluster of houses, turn left (west) across the river at a sign marking "Ruybalid Lake and No Name Lake." Park immediately after you cross the river; the trail for Ruybalid Lake is on your left as you face west.

Closest town: Antonito, 23 miles east.

For more information: Conejos Peak Ranger District, Rio Grande National Forest, 21461 US 285, La Jara, CO 81140. Phone (719) 274-5193.

Trail: 8 miles round-trip.

Elevation: Change of 2,400 feet.

Degree of difficulty: Moderate.

Surface: Dirt and rocks.

WEMINUCHE WILDERNESS AREA
CONTINENTAL DIVIDE TRAIL AT WOLF CREEK PASS

[Fig. 44(2)] This wilderness area is described in detail in the Silverton section of the book (*see* page 267.) The southeasternmost corner of the sprawling Weminuche touches US 160 at Wolf Creek Pass where the Continental Divide Trail crosses the highway. This trail runs for 80 miles through the wilderness area, bearing west to Stony Creek Pass, near Silverton.

By accessing the trail at 10,850-foot Wolf Creek Pass, hikers can access the high country with minimal effort. This route winds along ridges, through patches of Engelmann spruce, and across open meadows and bogs. On the southern horizon, down the San Juan River drainage, distant mesas of northern New Mexico are visible. To the north, the San Juan Mountains seem to roll on forever.

The Continental Divide Trail here is a pleasant day hike, an out-and-back stroll through the high country of the eastern San Juan mountains that can be as long as you want to make it.

Directions: From Pagosa Springs, drive east on US 160 to Wolf Creek Pass, about 15 miles. A few yards east of the summit, look for a dirt road on the north side. Take this road, which heads east, then switchbacks for 3 miles up to the Lobo Overlook. On the northern end of the parking area, pick up the trail beside an interpretive sign.

Closest town: Pagosa Springs, 18 miles west.

For more information: Divide Ranger District, Rio Grande National Forest, 13308 West Highway 160, Del Norte, CO 81132. Phone (719) 657-3321.

The Frémont Disaster Of 1848

John C. Frémont was a military geographer who led exploring expeditions through several states in the West. His Colorado explorations began in 1842 at the behest of Senator Thomas Hart Benton, his father-in-law. Frémont conducted several explorations through the Rockies, seeking suitable passes for settlers headed west. In 1848, employed by Saint Louis businessmen to find a winter railroad route through the mountains, Frémont undertook his last Colorado exploration, a disaster.

Convinced he could cross the Rockies in the winter and so prove the viability of a rail route, he headed west from Pueblo in November of that year. Very heavy snows made crossing the Sangre de Cristo Mountains and San Luis Valley difficult, but Frémont pushed on with 33 men and 120 mules. In December the group bogged down on the high plateaus of the eastern La Garita Mountains.

Frémont sent four men to seek help from Taos, New Mexico, the nearest settlement. A few days later he went himself with four more. Eventually he returned to rescue the remainder, who were straggling across the San Luis Valley. Fully one-third of his men, 11 altogether, died in the mountain snows.

Frémont blamed the disaster on his guide, Bill Williams, who was among the dead. Others have blamed Frémont for being stubborn and bullheaded. Frémont was done exploring Colorado; he eventually became a United States senator for California.

Trail: Out-and-back hikes of varying lengths.
Elevation: Rolling terrain varying in elevation between 11,000 and 12,000 feet.
Degree of difficulty: Easy.

FISHING
THE CONEJOS RIVER
[Fig. 51] The Conejos River (the name is Spanish for rabbits) runs 75 miles from the base of Platoro Peak to the river's confluence with the Rio Grande in the San Luis Valley just north of the New Mexico border. The river contains rainbow, brown, and (in its tributaries) some cutthroat trout. Fish tend to run 10 to 16 inches in size.

Much of the river below Platoro Reservoir (built at an elevation of 10,000 feet, it is the highest man-made lake in the United States) is open to public access, although portions are privately controlled. As always, ask for permission if in doubt. Between Menkhaven Campground and Aspen Glade Campground along CO 17, 3.5 miles of river are managed as catch-and-release, fly-fishing only water. The Lake Fork of the river is a no-kill fishery; threatened cutthroat trout populations are recovering here.

This river is a beautiful stream, 20 to 60 feet wide along the portion north of CO 17, with pools as deep as 10 feet. The section that parallels CO 17 is deeper and wider but still fishable.

Mesa Verde National Park

More than 4,400 archeological sites have been discovered in the 52,080-acre Mesa Verde National Park.

160

← To Cortez

160

● **Morefield Campground**

▲ ‖ 开

开

Indian Ruins Road

Wetherill Mesa Road

‖ ● **Far View Visitor Center**

LONG CANYON

M E S A   V E R D E
N A T I O N A L   P A R K

MOREFIELD CANYON

SPRUCE CANYON

NAVAJO CANYON

Ruins Road

▲ ‖
开

ROCK CANYON

1

| 1 | Petroglyph Point Trail |
| - - - - - - - - - - - - |
| Trail |

N

Ref: NPS Mesa Verde National Park

Directions: The Conejos River can be accessed at many points on CO 17 and on Forest Road 250, which parallel the river for most of its length. There are numerous public access points. Be sure to ask for permission before crossing private land.

For more information: Colorado Division of Wildlife, 0722 South Road 1 East, Monte Vista, CO 81144. Phone (719) 587-8900.

SKIING WOLF CREEK SKI AREA

[Fig. 44(3)] Wolf Creek Ski Area, on the eastern side of the Continental Divide at Wolf Creek Pass, is southwestern Colorado's southernmost ski area. However, it gets more snow, on average, than any other ski resort in the state: 465 inches annually. Wolf Creek is legendary among powder hounds; when snow comes to Wolf Creek, it often comes in vast quantities.

The ski area contains 1,000 acres of terrain. The base lodge is at 10,350 feet; the summit is at 11,775 feet, for a vertical drop of 1,425 feet. Much of the resort's expert terrain lies on ungroomed slopes on the southern side of the resort. This area of the resort is not served by lifts (skiers and snowboarders hike along the ridge), but it is patrolled by ski patrol. In lieu of lifts, snowcats tow skiers and boarders back to the resort base.

Directions: From Pagosa Springs, drive 25 miles east on US 160. The ski area is located just over the summit of Wolf Creek Pass, on the right (south) side of the highway.

Activities: Skiing and snowboarding.

Facilities: Base lodge, picnic area.

Dates: Generally open early Nov. to early Apr.

Fees: There is a fee to use the lifts.

Closest town: South Fork is 18 miles east on US 160. Pagosa Springs is 25 miles west on US 160.

For more information: Wolf Creek Ski Area, PO Box 2800, Pagosa Springs, CO 81147. Phone (970) 264-5639.

MESA VERDE NATIONAL PARK

[Fig. 52] Mesa Verde National Park is a high tableland southwest of the La Plata Mountains. To date, more than 4,400 archeological sites have been discovered in the 52,080-acre park. These sites represent the remains of dwellings built by Native Americans who lived on the Mesa from 550 B.C. to 1300 A.D. The ruins of more than 600 cliff dwellings have been located in the park.

Cliff dwellings and other evidence of the Anasazi Indians (the term means "ancient ones;" some contemporary Indians prefer the term Ancestral Puebloans) are scattered throughout the Four Corners region of Arizona, New Mexico, Utah, and Colorado. Mesa Verde National Park, however, contains the most dramatic and best examples of this archeological treasure trove.

Short-Tailed Weasel

Also known as an ermine, *Mustela ermina* is a resident of the high country above 8,000 feet. The short-tailed weasel measures only 6 inches to 9 inches long but has a reputation as an aggressive predator willing to attack animals several times its size.

This weasel may be spotted in winter bounding across the snow and then diving beneath it. At that time of year the animal is entirely white, except for the black tip of its tail. In summer it is colored a dark brown.

The weasel hunts rabbits, pikas, birds, mice, chipmunks, and ground squirrels, mostly at night.

In 1978, the park was named a World Heritage Site by the United Nations Educational, Scientific, and Cultural Organization. It was the center of an extraordinarily vibrant civilization that flourished in the region, then abandoned it. The Indians who lived on these mesas and cliffs did not vanish. Instead, they moved south, for reasons still unclear. Today's Pueblo Indians of northern New Mexico are believed to be direct descendants of Mesa Verde's residents.

Mesa Verde is an unusual national park for the region. It is not a place to go backpacking or to take in spectacular scenery—although the scenery is impressive. Views from the park include Sleeping Ute Mountain to the west, the Chuska Mountains in northeastern Arizona to the southwest, the La Plata Mountains to the northeast, and a half dozen deep canyons directly south.

Rather, Mesa Verde is a cultural resource, a place to wander among the ruins of an ancient people and marvel at how they made a living from the land, why they chose to do so here, and why they left.

THE GEOLOGICAL KEY

Geology and geography had much to do with the Anasazis' choice of Mesa Verde, a high tableland that angles gently to the south. The northern edge rests at about 8,500 feet elevation, the southern edge around 6,000 feet. Compared to the nearby areas, this mesa is generally 10 degrees Fahrenheit cooler in the summer and 10 degrees Fahrenheit warmer in the winter. It gathers rain and snow from the skies, and—perhaps more critically—it is covered with arable soil.

The soils of the surrounding canyons tend to be sandy and of poor quality. The top of Mesa Verde, however, is covered with a fine, windblown soil called loess (pronounced low-ess), as deep as 17 feet in some places. Loess is what gives the central plains of the United States their remarkable fertility. And loess made Mesa Verde a good place for the Anasazi to grow corn, one of their staple foods.

The mesa itself is a product of intermittent seas and regional uplift. The geologic column here is grounded in thousands of feet of Mancos Shale, the floor of a Cretaceous sea which once covered the area. Above this shale is Point Lookout Sandstone, formed from beach sand as the Cretaceous sea withdrew to the northeast. This sandstone is 80 feet to 125 feet deep. Above this lies the Menefee Formation, 300 feet of sandstone, siltstone, and coal laid down in the littoral of that ebbing and flowing sea.

The last layer is Cliff House Sandstone, forming the top 100 to 300 feet of the mesa. This formation is composed of a layer of sandstone, a layer of shale, and a top layer of sandstone. These layers probably represent two periods when the area was near the edge of the oscillating sea, and one when it lay beneath it. The last of the ancient seas retreated about 75 million years ago. Uplifts in the San Juan Mountains to the north lifted Mesa Verde and tilted it to the south.

The shale of that last, ancient seabed is critical to making Mesa Verde habitable. Moisture from precipitation falls on the permeable Cliff House Sandstone surface of the mesa, percolating through the porous rock until it reaches the impermeable shale layer. Then the water moves laterally until it reaches a cliff, where it appears as a spring or seep. There are no flowing streams on the mesa or in the surrounding canyons; these seeps were the principal water source for Mesa Verde's inhabitants.

Percolating water also created the overhung alcoves where Mesa Verde's most spectacular cliff dwellings were constructed. Water seeping through the sandstone dissolves the calcium carbonate bonding the grains of sand together, so that the alcoves begin to enlarge back and beneath the mesa's top. Anasazi builders constructed retaining walls and backfilled them to create level floors beneath the overhangs, then built multi-roomed villages.

Mesa Verde's Inhabitants

The first human inhabitants to live in the Four Corners region (although not on Mesa Verde itself) in significant numbers were Early Basketmaker peoples, who came to the region around 500 B.C. These people were principally hunters and gatherers who most likely found deer, rabbits, and wild turkey on the mesa, and gathered piñon pine nuts, serviceberries, and acorns from gambel oak.

The Modified Basketmaker period began around A.D. 550, marked by the first settlements on the mesa. These took the form of pit houses dug into the mesa top.

Distinctive pottery began to be made on the mesa in the following centuries, and trade was established. Pacific Ocean sea shells have been found in ruins from this period, suggesting extensive trade networks throughout the Southwest.

By A.D. 750, the beginning of the Developmental Pueblo period, farming methods on the mesa involved water management. Indians of the period constructed check dams to trap runoff water and make the most of the region's limited precipitation.

Population on and around Mesa Verde continued to grow. The Classic Pueblo period began around A.D. 1100. During this time the most spectacular cliff dwellings were built. Villages such as Cliff Palace, Balcony House, and Spruce Tree House were built. The largest, Cliff Palace, contained about 150 rooms that served as living, working, and storage areas for an estimated 100 to 150 residents. Some of these villages were difficult to reach; in some instances the Anasazi chipped shallow hand and foot holds into the surrounding rock to create ladders that appear precarious to today's visitors.

In A.D. 1250, population on Mesa Verde peaked. By 1300, the mesa had been abandoned. No one is sure why. Suggestions include overuse of the area's resources (such as wood and game animals), protracted drought, a worldwide cooling that reduced the growing season and made corn an untenable crop, or some form of war or aggression that forced Mesa Verde's residents to abandon their lands.

A related question is, why did the Anasazi move from the open mesa tops to villages tucked under the cliffs? Some of the location and construction details, such as difficulty of access and limited exterior windows, suggest that the Mesa Verdeans built their cliff dwellings for defensive purposes. Or perhaps they moved into the cliffs for religious reasons, or simply to take advantage of the shelter provided there.

However, if the Mesa Verdeans did use the cliff dwellings defensively, against whom were they defending themselves? One controversial theory suggests that the Indians in Chaco Canyon (located southeast of Mesa Verde in northwestern New Mexico) were immigrants from the violent, hierarchical Aztec society of central Mexico, and that Chacoans tried to control the Pueblo Indians in surrounding lands through violence. Such an imperial projection of power, according to the theory, could not be sustained. Nevertheless, the violence and disruption associated with it may have contributed both to the creation of the cliff dwellings and to their abandonment.

HISTORY OF THE PARK

Mesa Verde was probably first seen by Anglo-American prospectors in the 1860s. The first geologist to visit, John Newberry, arrived in 1859 but only touched on the north edge of the park, and did not see the ruins. A party led by the photographer William Henry Jackson explored the area in 1874. The ruins were rich with buried pots, bones, baskets, stone tools and other artifacts. In 1875 the first collection of Mesa Verde artifacts was sent to the National Museum in Washington, DC.

This bounty attracted pot hunters, who ransacked ruins in search of artifacts to sell. Late nineteenth century tourists did the same thing. For a quarter century, despite active lobbying of Congress by preservation groups, the ruins were given no protection from scavengers. Finally, in 1906, Congress passed legislation to create the park and simultaneously protected its resources through the Antiquities Act.

Many ruins can be seen today in the park, both on the several mesas that together comprise Mesa Verde, and along the cliff faces. Some ruins have been stabilized, and visitors may walk through them. Numerous short walks and overlooks from the park's roads lead to ruins or to views of them. Some of the ruins may be visited only on a ranger-guided tour.

Directions: From Durango, drive west for 36 miles on US 160. Take the exit marked Mesa Verde National Park and turn left (south). The park entrance is 0.5 mile down this road. The park visitors center is 15 miles south of the entrance; park headquarters is 20 miles south of the entrance.

Activities: Scenic drives, day hikes, interpretive talks, guided hikes, and ruins tours. Offerings vary with the season. Interpretive talks are given at the Morefield Campground amphitheater from Memorial Day to Labor Day.

Facilities: Visitor center area facilities include a nearby cafe, restrooms, gift shop, amphitheater, and interpretive museum.

Dates: Open year-round. However, many park facilities, such as Morefield Campground, the road to Wetherill Mesa, Cliff Palace and Balcony House, are closed in winter or during bad weather to protect archeological resources or because climbing in and around the ruins can be dangerous. Surface archeological sites are open year-round from 8 a.m. to sunset.

Fees: There is a fee to enter the park, a fee to camp, and a fee to enter some of the ruins.

Closest town: Mancos, 7 miles east of the park entrance on US 160.

For more information: Mesa Verde National Park, Mesa Verde, CO 81330. Phone (970) 529-4465.

Fire At Mesa Verde

On August 18, 1996, a lightning-caused fire burned across portions of Soda Canyon and Chapin Mesa. This blaze eventually covered 4,781 acres before firefighters controlled it on August 24. Management of the fire was complicated by the presence of both known and unknown archeological sites in the area.

The fire had a silver lining for park archeologists. Ninety-two previously unknown archeological sites were discovered in the wake of the fire, and ongoing research is providing more information.

Please note that visitors may not enter the burned area.

HIKING IN MESA VERDE NATIONAL PARK

In order to protect the fragile archeological resources of the park, hiking is permitted only on designated trails. No cross-country or backcountry hiking is permitted. There are a half dozen day-hiking trails in the park, ranging in length from 1.5 miles to 7.8 miles. Interpretive guide booklets for many of the trails are available at park headquarters.

Although the trails are relatively short, these hikes can be hot and dry, particularly in midsummer. Carry plenty of water, wear a hat, and use sunscreen.

PETROGLYPH POINT TRAIL

[Fig. 52(1)] This trail begins at Spruce Tree House, located immediately behind the park headquarters at Chapin Mesa. Walk down the paved trail to the Spruce Tree

House ruin, approximately 200 yards. Note the small spring on the left; this was the only water source for this village.

Take time to explore Spruce Tree House, a cliff dwelling that was once home to about 100 people. This is the third largest cliff dwelling in the park, after Cliff Palace and Long House. It contains 114 rooms and 8 kivas (kee-vahs), ceremonial underground chambers. It is 216 feet long and 89 feet deep.

The ruin has been cleaned up and stabilized. The Park Service's policy is to stabilize but not rebuild ruins, except in cases where doing so is necessary for stabilization of other parts of a ruin. Spruce Tree House is predominantly original.

Directions: Petroglyph Point Trail leads south from Spruce Tree House to the largest panel of Anasazi rock art in the park. The trail then loops down up onto the mesa top and returns to the park museum.

Trail: 2.8-mile loop.

Elevation: Change of 330 feet.

Degree of difficulty: Moderate.

Surface: Pavement to Spruce Tree House, then dirt.

CAMPING

Camping is permitted in the park only at Morefield Campground, near the park entrance. Backcountry camping is not permitted

Morefield Campground, located 4 miles south of the park entrance, contains 450 campsites. The campground has showers, laundry, a gas station, a grocery store, and a restaurant. These facilities are open from early May to mid-October. Reservations are not accepted

The park also contains a motel, the Far View Motor Lodge, located 15 miles inside the park. The lodge includes a restaurant and bar. It is open from late April until late October.

For more information on the Far View Motor Lodge, phone (970) 529-4421. In the winter months, call (970) 533-7731. For campground and other information, call park headquarters at (970) 529-4465. Camping is available on a first-come, first-served basis.

Scenic Drives

SAN JUAN SKYWAY

The San Juan Mountains form the largest mountain range in Colorado. Not surprisingly, their geography, geology, human history, flora and fauna vary widely. The totality of the San Juans is difficult to grasp, but the San Juan Skyway Scenic Byway is a good introduction.

This loop, more than 230 winding miles in length, splits the middle of the range and circles around its western half. Along the way it travels through five mountain life zones, a half dozen towns and some of the richest, most beautiful, and most environmentally devastated terrain in Colorado. This route takes about eight hours to drive in good weather. The roads in question are open year-round, although the section from Hermosa to Ouray may be treacherous or closed during winter storms or periods of high avalanche danger.

The route begins on the north side of the San Juans in Ridgway, once the headquarters for the Rio Grande Southern Railroad. Much of the byway roughly follows this railroad's route. Built by Otto Mears, the Rio Grande Southern carved a half circle around and through the San Juan Mountains from Durango to Ouray. The railway was completed in 1891 and operated until 1931.

Begin the drive at the intersection of US 550 and CO 62; go west on CO 62 through Ridgway, a town that served as the backdrop for the John Wayne movie *True Grit*. The route climbs up through hay meadows on Mancos Shale, south of a mesa capped with Dakota Sandstone.

The road ascends toward Dallas Divide, elevation 8,899 feet, situated at Mile 10. The northern front of the Mount Sneffels massif is to the left, above a beautiful bowl of aspen and spruce trees. This is one of the most photogenic views in Colorado. Mount Sneffels (14,150 feet) is the prominent, nipple-tipped peak near the western end of the ridge.

West of Dallas Divide the route descends the Leopard Creek valley. gambel oak ecosystems dominate the eastern side of Dallas Divide. Once you cross the divide and begin heading down to the west, aspen and fir lie on the left (north-facing) side of the road. Ponderosa pine is evident on the warmer, south-facing side.

At Mile 24, turn left (south) onto CO 145. The road winds through a narrow canyon along the San Miguel River. Much of the purplish-red sedimentary rock in this canyon is 300-million-year-old Cutler Formation, a Paleozoic stone that is most likely the remains of the ancestral Rocky Mountain range of Uncompahgria.

The road climbs east up Keystone Hill to Telluride's hanging valley, which was created when a lateral moraine from the glacier coming north down the South San Miguel River valley blocked this valley. Telluride is 2 miles straight ahead; the byway bears right (south) toward Rico and Cortez.

As CO 145 climbs south along the flanks of the San Juan Mountains, the San Miguel Mountains and Lizard Head Wilderness Area (*see* page 254) become clearly visible to the west. At Mile 43, a hairpin to the right, you pass the turn to Ophir, a nineteenth century mining town that is being revived as a suburb of modern Telluride.

The settlement of Ames is situated down in the canyon to the west at Mile 43; this was the site of the first industrial alternating current plant. Here in 1891 L.L. Nunn, the manager of the Gold King Mine above Ophir, developed a hydroelectric generating plant and strung wires to his mine. He cut the mine's power costs by 80 percent. The Ames plant still generates electricity today.

At Mile 49 you drive over the easy slopes of Lizard Head Pass (10,222 feet high).

Continue about 2 miles farther on and look back to the northwest for a good view of the Lizard Head, an eroded volcanic intrusion.

The route is now in the Dolores River drainage. Cutler Formation rock appears in the roadsides again. At Mile 57 you pass through the former mining town of Rico. The road continues down the Dolores Canyon, which is characterized by heavy forests on the north-facing slopes and rich bottomlands of wet meadows and willows.

Around Mile 82, the byway leads out of the mountains and into the plateau terrain of the Four Corners region. The sandstone formations above the road—Wingate, Kayenta, and Entrada—are typical of the canyons of southeastern Utah and the western edge of the Uncompahgre Plateau.

This country is marked by piñon pine (*Pinus edulis*), common juniper (*Juniperus communis*), big sagebrush (*Artemisia tridentata*), and rabbitbrush (*Chrysothamnus nauseosus*).

Near Dolores, at Mile 98, the piñon-juniper ecosystem appears. Immediately past Dolores, the byway exits the Dolores Canyon and leads out into a sage desert of upper Sonoran scrub. The views here are broad and expansive. The Abajo Mountains in Utah lie to the northwest; Sleeping Ute Mountain, a lacolith, is to the southeast. Mesa Verde National Park (*see* page 310) is to the south.

Stay on CO 145 until the junction with US 160, immediately east of Cortez. Turn east (left) on US 160. The route runs east past the entrance to Mese Verde National Park, at Mile 127, then climbs through Mancos Shale out of the Sonoran ecosystem and into stands of ponderosa pine, which extend broadly across the southern front of San Juan Mountains.

At Mile 153, on the outskirts of Durango, turn left (north) onto US 550. Follow this around Durango's downtown and north into the Animas Valley. At Hermosa (Mile 164), the road begins to climb sharply. The Hermosa Cliffs, running for several miles along the west side of the road, are of the same Cutler Formation seen in the San Miguel Valley. The Hermosa Roadless Area and La Plata Mountains lie to the west (*see* page 280).

At Mile 179 a very distinctive conical mountain appears ahead: Engineer Mountain, 12,972 feet high. It is a landmark throughout this portion of the San Juans. Purgatory Resort is to the west at Mile 181 (*see* page 284). Beyond this point the road narrows and demands more of the driver's attention.

The route descends slightly, then climbs to 10,640-foot Coal Bank Pass at Mile 188. A precipitous descent to the north leads down to Lime Creek, then up again to Molas Pass, at Mile 195. Look to the southeast to see the Grenadier Range, which is a northwestern extension of the highest peaks in the Weminuche Wilderness, the Needle Mountains. Another steep, winding descent leads to Silverton at Mile 201.

Stay on US 550 North toward Ouray. Between Ouray and Silverton is one of the richest mineral zones in Colorado and some of the most dramatic landscape accessible by automobile. Mining-era relics and avalanche chutes intermingle on the slopes of the mountains. This portion of the road is risky in winter and regularly closed by avalanche hazard.

Red Mountain Pass, once the site of the town of Red Mountain, is at Mile 211. The red tint of the surrounding mountains is the result of high levels of iron ore. Tailings piles and ponds proliferate through the high valley between Red Mountain and Ironton, several miles north. Efforts are ongoing to reclaim the soil and clean up the water here and in the Animas Valley to the east, which has been poisoned by heavy metals released during mining.

A memorial marker has been erected at Mile 219 for travelers and highway workers who have been killed in avalanches on US 550. The road descends steeply along the side of the Uncompahgre River canyon here; just below the marker a snowshed has been built to shelter the highway from the East Riverside Slide, one of the largest and most dangerous avalanche chutes overhanging the road.

At Mile 221 the route enters Ouray, which sits in a natural amphitheater. Continue north on US 550 back to Ridgway, which lies out in the open meadows of the Uncompahgre Valley at Mile 235.

For more information: Telluride Visitors Services, 700 West Colorado Avenue, Telluride, CO 81435. Phone (970) 728-3041. Ouray Chamber of Commerce, 1222 Main Street, Ouray, CO 81427. Phone (970) 325-4746. Ridgway Chamber of Commerce, 150 Racecourse Road, Ridgway, CO 81432. Phone (970) 325-4746. Silverton Chamber of Commerce, 414 Greene Street, Silverton, CO 81433. Phone (970) 387-5654. Durango Chamber of Commerce, 111 South Camino Del Rio, PO Box 2587, Durango, CO 81302. Phone (800) 525-8855 or (970) 247-0312.

🎖 SILVER THREAD SCENIC BYWAY

The Silver Thread Scenic Byway winds through the eastern portion of the San Juan Mountains. It connects Creede, the only incorporated town in Mineral County, with Lake City, the only incorporated town in Hinsdale County, along a 73-mile historic railroad and stage line. Open year-round, this route takes two to three hours to drive.

The mountains on the eastern end of this route are heavily forested and more gentle than in the western San Juans. Although there is some residential development along the banks of the Rio Grande, for the most part the byway winds through unpopulated country. Much of the land to the north and south of the route lies in the La Garita, Powderhorn, and Weminuche wilderness areas.

The western end of the byway drops down into the Lake City caldera, which encompasses some of the more dramatic mountains of the San Juans.

Begin the byway in South Fork, located 48 miles west of Alamosa on US 160. South Fork, situated at the junction of the Rio Grande's main stem and its south fork, was a nineteenth century railhead and lumber town. Drive west on CO 149.

The route follows the Rio Grande upstream. To the right, around Mile 2, are the Palisades, cliffs eroded from the welded tuff deposited by volcanic eruptions. At Mile 14 the highway and river pass through Wagon Wheel Gap, which was cut by the river. Note the columnar jointing (vertical joints in the rock) that was created when the lava flows around the gap cooled and shrank.

At Mile 21 CO 149 crosses Willow Creek and the southern outskirts of Creede. Stay on CO 149. Around Mile 41 the byway turns north up the fault, leaving the Rio Grande, whose headwaters lie to the west near Silverton. At Mile 44 the cliffs of Bristol Head are visible to the north. Bristol Head is the edge of an uplift; the byway and Rio Grande traverse here through a graben, or down-dropped block, in the old Creede volcanic caldera.

Moose (*Alces alces*) were reintroduced to the area around Spring Creek Pass (elevation 10,898 feet), at Mile 55, in 1993 by the Colorado Division of Wildlife. The deep forests and rich riparian zones make this prime habitat for the big, water-loving ungulates.

Spring Creek Pass lies on the Continental Divide. Slumgullion Pass, 11,530 feet high, is at Mile 62. Look for the turnoff to Windy Point, around Mile 63.5, on the north (right) side. This turnoff provides views of the mountains surrounding Lake City, including several Fourteeners in the Uncompaghre Wilderness (*see* page 286) and the Carson Peak Roadless Area (*see* page 292). The Slumgullion Slide is clearly visible to the northeast (*see* page 292).

The road descends across the Slumgullion Slide toward the outlet of Lake San Cristobal, formed in 1270 A.D. by the Slumgullion Slide. Stay on CO 149 and turn west on Third Street to end the byway in downtown Lake City.

For more information: Creede Chamber of Commerce, POB 580, Creede, CO 81130. Phone (719) 658-2374; South fork Chamber of Commerce, 28 Silver Thread Lane, PO Box 116, South Fork, CO 81154. Phone (719) 873-5512.

ALPINE LOOP SCENIC BYWAY

The bulk of this scenic byway can be traversed only in summer and only by four-wheel-drive vehicle, dirt bike, or mountain bike. The Alpine Loop covers approximately 65 miles of historic roads between Silverton, Ouray, and Lake City. It is more of a figure-eight than a true loop.

Although the Alpine Loop is less than 100 miles long, the trip is slowed by the vertical nature of the terrain and the rough roads. Many people drive it over the course of several days, stopping for the night in the small towns along it. The route can be ridden on a mountain bike, although this is a very strenuous undertaking: The climb from Ouray to Engineer Pass, for example, rises 5,000 feet.

Much of the land on either side of the Alpine Loop is privately owned mining claims. The byway does pass a number of hiking trails leading into lands managed by the U.S. Forest Service and the Bureau of Land Management.

The geography of the Alpine Loop is essentially volcanic. Two massive calderas, the San Juan and Uncompahgre, were formed about 25 million years ago by collapsing volcanoes. Smaller calderas (the Silverton and Lake City) subsequently formed and collapsed inside these rims. The Alpine Loop traces between these calderas.

Begin the Alpine Loop 6 miles south of Ouray on US 550 at the left (east) turn toward Engineer Mountain. Follow the dirt road east along the deep canyon of the Uncompahgre

River. At the intersection at Mile 2.5, turn left up the switchbacks toward Engineer Mountain. At Mile 5, turn left again toward Engineer Mountain, not right toward Mineral Point.

The terrain here is mostly alpine tundra, with pockets of spruce and fir. This is beautiful but also fragile country. Tundra is very slow-growing and, as the ruins of the mining era attest, does not easily recover from disturbance. Stay on the roads with your vehicle.

At Mile 7, turn left (north) again toward Engineer Mountain. The right here leads toward Animas Forks and Silverton.

Engineer Pass (12,800 feet) is at Mile 9.5. As you descend to the east, Wetterhorn Peak (14,017 feet), Matterhorn Peak (13,590 feet), and Uncompahgre Peak (14,309 feet) line the horizon ahead. At Mile 18 you come to the junction with the north fork of Henson Creek and the site of Capitol City, a mining camp whose founder once thought it would supercede Denver. Today it is only ruins.

Continue downstream to Lake City, at Mile 27. Turn right (east) onto Second Street, then right again onto Gunnison Avenue (CO 149 South). This portion of the byway, to Mile 30, is the western end of the Silver Thread Scenic Byway (*see* page 319). At Mile 30, turn right (south) onto County Road 30.

Follow County 30 south past Lake San Cristobal, which was formed by the Slumgullion Slide to the east (*see* page 292). Stay on County 30 to Cinnamon Pass (12,840 feet), at Mile 51. Descend to the west; at Mile 54, you may turn right (north) to return to the Engineer Pass Road.

To continue to Silverton and complete the Alpine Loop, turn left at this intersection and travel down the Animas River. This region of the upper Animas Valley has been very heavily mined and was the site of several communities. Some land reclamation work is now being undertaken here. Hard rock mining produces weak acid solutions which leach heavy metals such as lead and cadmium into water supplies, poisoning many high mine sites such as these.

Silverton, the end of the byway, is at Mile 65. You may return to Ouray by taking US 550 north over Red Mountain Pass.

For more information: Ouray Chamber of Commerce, 1222 Main Street, Ouray, CO 81427. Phone (970) 325-4746. Silverton Chamber of Commerce, 414 Greene Street, Silverton, CO 81433. Phone (970) 387-5654.

Major Trails

Two extraordinary long trails traverse Colorado's high country: the Colorado Trail from Durango to Denver, and a portion of the Continental Divide National Scenic Trail, which runs from Canada to Mexico.

Like the better-known Appalachian Trail in the East and the Sierra Crest trail near the

West Coast, these trails offer determined backpackers the opportunity for literally months of uninterrupted hiking. Unlike those trails, however, both the Colorado Trail and the Continental Divide Trail are quite young.

Portions of both trails are discussed throughout the book. These trails can provide a day's worth of enjoyment, or a lifetime's. A few people travel the trails' full length in a single summer of backpacking. Others chip away at them piece by piece over the years.

Although distinctive plastic blazes have been designed for both the Colorado Trail and the Continental Divide Trail, these may not always be in place. Moreover, these trails are neither complete nor well worn in many places. Navigating them requires map and compass skills and self-reliance.

THE CONTINENTAL DIVIDE TRAIL

The Continental Divide National Scenic Trail (CDT) traces, as closely as practical, the great spine of the continent that runs for 8,000 miles from northern Alaska to the Panama Canal. The CDT is a footpath along the 3,100 winding miles between the Canadian and Mexican borders. One-quarter of the route—759 miles—lies within Colorado, where the divide twists and meanders through the state's mountains.

Colorado is the highest region along the continental divide, so it's no surprise that the highest point of the trail lies here: Gray's Peak, 14,270 feet. Much of the trail lies above timberline; in the San Juan Mountains more than 100 miles of it is above 12,000 feet.

Like most good things, the Continental Divide Trail is the result of a few of determined individuals.

The Continental Divide National Scenic Trail was the brainchild of Benton MacKaye, who also conceived of the Appalachian Trail from Maine to Georgia. During the 1960s MacKaye proposed that Congress consider a similar trail through the Rocky Mountains. Congress obliged by authorizing a study in 1968. In 1973 another trails activist, Jim Wolf, hiked a portion of the potential CDT in Montana and began agitating for official designation of the route.

A 1976 study by the Bureau of Outdoor Recreation determined that the CDT was an idea worthy of official support, on the basis that the route in question possessed outstanding scenic qualities. In 1978 the CDT was formally designated by Congress in the legislation of the National Parks and Recreation Act.

The CDT, however, remains a work in progress more than 20 years later. It is largely but not completely finished and, of course, needs regular maintenance as all trials do. Although most of the trail is situated on U.S. Forest Service land, funding for trail construction and maintenance is in short supply. Efforts to complete the trail are being spearheaded by the Continental Divide Trail Alliance, a Colorado organization that raises money and coordinates volunteer work.

The Colorado portion of the CDT runs north from Cumbres Pass through the South San Juan Wilderness to Wolf Creek Pass, then northwest through the Weminuche Wilderness to Stony Pass. It turns northeast here, passing between Creede and Lake City in the

La Garita Wilderness. It drops down into the Cochetopa Hills, crosses Cochetopa Pass, then climbs the spine of the Collegiate Peaks and runs north through the Sawatch Mountains to Copper Mountain Ski Resort.

Here the CDT turns east toward Mount Evans, then north into the Vasquez Peaks Wilderness, across Berthoud Pass, and north through the Indian Peaks Wilderness into Rocky Mountain National Park and across the headwaters of the Colorado River. At the top of the Never Summer Mountains the route runs west across the Rabbit Ears Range and Rabbit Ears Pass before turning north once more through the Park Range and Mount Zirkel Wilderness to Wyoming.

For more information: Continental Divide Trail Alliance, PO Box 628, Pine, CO 80470.

COLORADO TRAIL

An argument can be made that the Colorado Trail exists today largely due to the determination of one woman, Gudy Gaskill. The route runs from Denver to Durango, covering 471 miles. About three-fourths of the trail lies on pre-existing pathways. Additional trails were built to connect the system together, and the whole thing was completed in 1987.

The first acts of the Colorado Trail's story were played out by others. Bill Lucas, director of the Rocky Mountain Region of the U.S. Forest Service in the early 1970s, organized a meeting in November 1973 to discuss the idea of a trail across the state. Out of that meeting came the nonprofit Colorado Mountain Trail Association (CMTA), which hoped to find funding and volunteers to complete a trail between Denver and Durango by 1978.

The association foundered, however, and within a couple of years the completion of the Colorado Trail (CT) seemed to be in doubt. Gudy Gaskill, an early CMTA employee, took over where CMTA left off, slowly organizing volunteers through the Colorado Mountain Club. A 1984 newspaper article on Gaskill's labors drew the attention of Colorado Governor Richard Lamm, who threw his weight behind completion of the trail. Over the next two years, hundreds of volunteers pitched in to finish the CT, which was declared complete in September 1987.

Portions of the Continental Divide Trail and Colorado Trail overlap. The Colorado Trail begins in Durango, where it heads northwest into the La Plata Mountains. It crosses into the Weminuche Wilderness at Molas Divide and roughly follows the Continental Divide northeast past Lake City and Creede and down into the Cochetopa Hills. The trail stays on the divide across Marshall Pass and into the Collegiate Peaks. With the Continental Divide Trail it follows this range north across the flanks of Mount Massive to Copper Mountain Ski Area. Here it turns east across the Ten Mile Range, runs south of Breckenridge into the Kenosha Mountains, and angles northeast through the foothills near Bailey to follow the South Platte River to Denver's outskirts.

For more information: The Colorado Trail Foundation, PO Box 260876, Lakewood, CO 80226.

Appendices

A. Map Sources

Bureau of Land Management, U.S. Department of the Interior, Colorado State Office, 2859 Youngfield Street, Lakewood, CO 80225. Phone (303) 239-3600.

Colorado Atlas & Gazetteer, Delorme Mapping, PO Box 298, Freeport, ME 04032. Phone (207) 865-4171.

Colorado Division of Wildlife, Department of Natural Resources, 6060 Broadway, Denver, CO 80216. Phone (303) 297-1192.

Colorado State Parks, 1313 Sherman Street, Room 618, Denver, CO 80203. Phone (303) 866-3437.

National Geographic Trails Illustrated, PO Box 4357, Evergreen, CO 80437. Phone (800) 962-1643.

National Park Service, Intermountain Region, 12795 Alameda Parkway, Denver, CO 80225. Phone (303) 969-2500.

National Recreation Reservation Service. Phone (877) 444-6777. Reservations at National Forest campgrounds throughout Colorado and the United States may be made in advance through this organization. Reservations are accepted 240 days in advance for individual sites, 360 days in advance for group sites.

U.S. Forest Service, Regional Office, PO Box 25127, Lakewood, CO 80225. Phone (303) 275-5370.

U.S. Forest Service Regional Office, 740 S. Simms Street, Lakewood, CO 80228. Phone (303) 275-5354

U.S. Geological Survey, Denver Federal Center, PO Box 25268, Lakewood, CO 80225. Phone (303) 202-4700.

USGS Topographical Maps, National Cartographic Center, 507 National Center, Reston, VA 22092. Phone (703) 648-6045.

B. Guide & Outfitter Services

GENERAL:

American Mountain Guides Association. Members include qualified guides and guide services. 710 Tenth Street, Suite 101, Golden, CO, 80401. Phone (303) 271-0984. Web site: www.amga.com.

Colorado Outfitters Association. Hunting, fishing, packing, and cattle drive guides. PO Box 1949, Rifle, CO 81650. Phone (970) 876-0543. Web site: www.colorado-outfitters.com.

Colorado River Outfitters Association. Represents more than 50 licensed rafting outfitters and offers a free directory. 730 Burbank Street, Broomfield, CO 80020. Phone (303) 280-2554. Web site: www.croa.org

Colorado Association of Campgrounds, Cabins, and Lodges. Official association for operators of campgrounds, cabins, and lodges. Offers *Colorado Vacations, Adventures and Memories* guide. 43590 Highway 50 West, Canon City, CO 81212. Phone (719) 275-0506. Web site: www.coloradovacation.com.

Colorado Dude and Guest Ranch Association. Offers free directory of Colorado's 38 approved dude and guest ranches and $10 video. Box 300V, Tabernash, CO 80478. Phone (970) 887-9248. Web site: www.coloradoranch.com.

Colorado Travel and Tourism Authority. Phone (800) COLORADO or (800) 265-6723. Web site: www.colorado.com.

NORTHEAST

Outfitters Inc./Eagles Nest Equestrian Center. Hunting, fishing, summer pack trips, trail rides, horse rentals. PO Box 495, Silverthorne, CO 80498. Phone (970) 468-0677.

EAST CENTRAL

Pikes Peak Outfitters. Private property tent camps, lodge, resort. Hunting, fishing, summer pack trips and trail rides. PO Box 9053, Woodland Park CO 80866. Phone (800) 748-2885.

SOUTHEAST

Red Mountain Outfitters. Hunting, fishing, summer pack trips, trail rides, winter sports. PO Box 893, Alamosa, CO 81101. Phone (719) 589-4186.

Wahatoya Base Camp. Peak climbs, llama treks, auto tours, outdoor education in the Spanish Peaks and lower San Luis Valley area. PO Box 589, La Veta, CO 81055. Phone (719) 742-5597.

NORTHWEST

Adams Lodge. Hunting, fishing, summer pack trips, trail rides, winter sports. 2400 RBC Road 12, Meeker, CO 81641. Phone (970) 878-4312.

CDel's Triangle 3 Ranch. Hunting, fishing, summer pack trips, trail rides, winter sports. PO Box 333, Clark, CO 80428. Phone (970) 879-3495.

Sunset Ranch, Inc. Hunting, fishing, summer pack trips, winter sports. Box 770876, Steamboat Springs, CO 80477. Phone (970) 879-0954.

Trappers Lake Lodge. Resort, store, and tent camp. Hunting, fishing, summer pack trips, trail rides, snowmobiling, cross-country skiing. PO Box 1230, 7700 Trapper's Lake Road, Meeker, CO 81641. Phone (970) 878-3336.

WEST CENTRAL

Fantasy Ranch Outfitters, Inc. Fishing, summer pack trips, trail rides, horse rental, winter rides. PO Box 236, Crested Butte, CO 81224. Phone (970) 349-5425.

Four Corners Rafting. Runs trips on Dolores River near Mesa Verde, Colorado. Trips from 2 to 6 days. PO Box 569 - CRN, Buena Vista, CO 81211. Phone (800) 332-7238 or (719) 395-4137.

Gunnison Country Guide Service. Hunting, fishing, summer pack trips, and trail rides. PO Box 1443, Gunnison, CO 81230. Phone (970) 641-2830.

Lazy F Bar Outfitters. Hunting, fishing, pack trips, and winter sports. PO Box 383, Gunnison, CO 81230. Phone (970) 641-0193.

River Runners, LTD. Colorado's largest rafting company. 11150 US Highway 50, Salida, CO 81201. Phone (800) 525-2081.

Rock Gardens Rafting. Half- and full-day trips. Roaring Fork, Arkansas, Blue, and Upper Colorado rivers. 1308 County Road. 129, Glenwood Springs, CO 81602. Phone (970) 945-6737.

Spruce Ridge Llama Adventure Treks. High-mountain llama treks in the San Isabel National Forest. 4141 County Road 210, Salida, CO 81201. Phone (719) 539-4182 or (888) 686-8735.

T-Lazy-7 Ranch. Hunting, fishing, pack trips, trail rides, winter sports. PO Box TT, Aspen, CO 81612. Phone (970) 925-4614.

Wilderness Aware Rafting. Half- to 10-day guided whitewater rafting trips on five Colorado rivers. 702 Yale Avenue. PO Box 1550 Buena Vista, CO 81211. Phone (800) 462-7238 or (719) 395-2112.

Whitewater Rafting, LLC. Full-day and half-day trips. Colorado and Roaring Fork rivers. PO Box 2462, Glenwood Springs, CO 81602. Phone (970) 945-8477.

SOUTHWEST

Astraddle A Saddle, Inc. Hunting, fishing, summer pack trips, trail rides, winter sports. PO Box 1216, 531 County Road 139, Pagosa Springs, CO 81147. Phone (970) 731-5076.

Gateway Durango. Whitewater rafting for families and serious paddlers. 2615 Main Avenue, Suite A, Durango, CO 81301. Phone (800) 828-4228 or (970) 385-4711.

San Juan Outfitting. Hunting, fishing, summer pack trips, trail rides, and winter sports. 186 County Road 228, Durango, CO 81301. Phone (970) 259-6259.

San Pahgre Outdoor Adventures Outfitting. Hunting, fishing, and summer pack trips. 21700 Hwy. 550 S., Montrose, CO 81401. Phone (970) 240-8183

Mild to Wild Rafting. Guided day trips on the lower Animas River and overnight trips on the upper Animas River. 11 Rio Vista Circle, Durango, CO 81301. Phone (800) 567-6745.

Wolf Creek Outfitters, LLC. Hunting, fishing, summer pack trips/trail rides, snowmobile tours, winter sports. PO Box 1918, Pagosa Springs, CO 81147. Phone (970) 264-5333.

C. Books

Libraries have been written about Colorado. The following texts offer readers an opportunity to delve deeper into the state's natural history, geology, human history and sheer physical and spiritual beauty.

1001 Colorado Place Names by Maxine Benson. University Press of Kansas, 1994.

A Climbing Guide to Colorado's Fourteeners by Walter R. Borneman and Lyndon Lampert. Pruett Publishing, Boulder, CO 1984.

A Colorado History Seventh Edition, by Carld Ubbelohde, Maxine Benson, and Duane A. Smith. Pruett Publishing, Boulder, CO 1995.

A Historical Guide to the San Juan Skyway by Ian Thompson. Fort Lewis College, Durango, CO 1994.

Aspen High Country: The Geology, A Pictorial Guide to Roads and Trails by David Laing and Nicholas Lampiris. Thunder River Press, Aspen, CO 1984.

Aspen: The History of A Silver Mining Town 1879-1893 by Malcolm J. Rohrbough. Oxford University Press, New York, NY 1986.

Atlas of The New West: Portrait of a Changing Region edited by William E. Riebsame. WW Norton & Co., New York, NY 1998.

Bicycling The Uncompahgre Plateau by Bill Harris. Wayfinder Press, Ouray, CO 1988.

Bizarre Colorado: A Legacy of Unusual Events and People by Kenneth Jessen. J.V. Publications, Loveland, CO 1994.

Black Canyon of The Gunnison by Rose Houk. Southwest Parks and Monuments Association, Tucson, AZ 1991.

Cadillac Desert: The American West and Its Disappearing Water by Marc Reisner. Penguin Books, New York, NY 1986.

Canine Colorado: Where To Go and What To Do With Your Dog by Cindy Hirschfeld. Fulcrum Publishing, Golden, CO 1998.

Canyon Country Geology by F.A. Barnes. Wasatch Publishers, Salt Lake City, UT 1978.

Colorado 10th Mountain Trails Official Ski Touring Guide by Louis W. Dawson II. WHO Press, Aspen, CO 1989.

Colorado Byways: A Guide Through Scenic and Historic Landscapes by Thomas P. Huber. University Press of Colorado, Niwot, CO 1997.

Colorado High Routes by Louis W. Dawson II. The Mountaineers, Seattle, WA 1986.

Colorado Mining Camps by Dave Southworth. Wild Horse Publishing, 1997.

Colorado Mountain Ranges by Jeff Rennicke. Falcon Press Publishing, Helena, MT 1986.

Colorado Scenic Guide: Northern Region Third Edition, by Lee Gregory. Johnson Books, Boulder, CO 1996.

Colorado Scenic Guide: Southern Region Third Edition by Lee Gregory. Johnson Books, Boulder, CO 1996.

Colorado State Parks: A Complete Recreation Guide by Philip Ferranti. The Mountaineers, Seattle, WA 1996.

Colorado Wildlife by Jeff Rennicke. Falcon Press Publishing, Helena, MT 1996.

Colorado's Continental Divide Trail: The Official Guide by Tom Lorang Jones. Westcliffe Publishers, Englewood, CO 1997.

Creede: Colorado Boom Town by Leland Feit. Little London Press, Colorado Springs, CO 1992.

Curecanti National Recreation Area by Rose Houk. Southwest Parks and Monuments Association, Tucson, AZ 1991.

Cutthroat: Native Trout of The West by Patrick C. Trotter. Colorado Associated University Press, Boulder, CO 1987.

Elk Mountains Odyssey: West Elk Loop Scenic/Historic Byway Guide by Paul Andersen and Ken Johnson. Redstone Press, Carbondale, CO 1998.

Encyclopedia of the American West edited by Robert Utley. Wings Books, New York, NY 1997.

Exploring Our National Parks and Monuments by Devereux Butcher. Eighth Edition. Harvard Common Press, Boston, MA 1985.

Flowers of the Southwest Deserts by Natt N. Dodge and Jeanne R. Janish. Southwest Parks and Monuments Association, Tucson, AZ 1985.

From Grassland to Glacier: The Natural History of Colorado and The Surrounding Region by Cornelia Fleischer Mutel and John C. Emerick. Johnson Books, Boulder, CO 1992.

Guide to the National Wildlife Refuges by William and Laura Riley. Collier Books, New York, NY 1979.

Hiking Colorado by Cary and Peter Boddie. Falcon Press Publishing, Helena, MT 1991.

Hiking the Highest Passes of Colorado Second Edition, by Bob Martin. Pruett Publishing, Boulder, CO 1988.

Hot Springs and Hot Pools of the Southwest by Marjorie Gersh-Young. Aqua-Thermal Press, Santa Cruz, CA 1995.

Land Above the Trees: A Guide to American Alpine Tundra by Ann H. Zwinger and Beatrice E. Willard. Johnson Books, Boulder, CO 1996.

Lions, Ferrets, and Bears: A Guide to the Mammals of Colorado by David M. Armstrong. Colorado Division of Wildlife, Denver, CO 1993.

Mesa Verde: A Complete Guide by Gian Mercurio and Maxymillian L. Peschel. Lonewolf Publishing, Cortez, CO 1991.

Mountain Biking Colorado's Historic Mining Districts by Laura Rosseter. Fulcrum Publishing, Golden, CO 1991.

Peterson Field Guides: Ecology of Western Forests by John C. Kricher and Gordon Morrison. Houghton Mifflin Company, New York, NY 1993.

Peterson Field Guides: Mushrooms by Kent H. McNight and Vera B. McNight. Houghton Mifflin Company, New York, NY 1987.

Peterson Field Guides: Rocky Mountain Wildflowers by John J. Craighead, Frank C. Craighead, and Ray J. Davis. Houghton Mifflin Company, New York, NY 1991.

Peterson Field Guides: Western Birds Third Edition by Roger Tory Peterson. Houghton Mifflin Company, New York, NY 1990.

Plants of The Rocky Mountains by Linda Kershaw, Andy MacKinnon, and Jim Pojar. Lone Pine Publishing, Alberta, Canada 1998.

Roadside Geology of Colorado by Halka Chronic. Mountain Press, Missoula, MT 1980.

Roadside History of Colorado by James McTighe. Johnson Books, Boulder, CO 1984.

Rock Climbing Colorado by Stewart M. Green. Falcon Press Publishing, Helena, MT 1995.

Rocky Mountain National Park: Beyond Trail Ridge by Wendy Shattil and Bob Rozinski. Westcliffe Publishers, Englewood, CO 1986.

Shrubs and Trees of the Southwest Deserts by Janice Emily Bowers and Brian Wignall. Southwest Parks and Monuments Association, Tucson, AZ 1993.

Telluride: A Quick History by Rose Weber. Little London Press, Colorado Springs, CO 1984.

Telluride Hiking Guide Second Edition by Susan Kees. Wayfinder Press, Ridgway, CO 1992.

Tellurides: The Mountain Biking Guide to Telluride, Colorado by Dave Rich. Wayfinder Press, Ridgway, CO 1994.

The Audubon Society Field Guide to North American Birds, Western Region by Miklos D.F. Udvardy. Alfred A. Knopf, New York, NY 1977.

The Audubon Society Field Guide to North American Wildflowers, Western Region by Richard Spellenberg. Alfred A. Knopf, New York, NY 1979.

The Audubon Society Nature Guides: Western Forests by Stephen Whitney. Alfred A. Knopf, New York, NY 1985.

The Best of The West: An Anthology of Classic Writing from the American West edited by Tony Hillerman, HarperCollins, New York, NY 1991.

The Colorado Angling Guide by Chuck Fothergill and Bob Sterling. Stream Stalker Publishing, Aspen, CO 1985.

The Colorado Pass Book: A Guide To Colorado's Backroad Mountain Passes, Second Edition, by Don Koch. Pruett Publishing, Boulder, CO 1987.

The Colorado Trail: The Official Guidebook Fifth Edition by Randy Jacobs. Westcliffe Publishers, Englewood, CO 1994.

The Complete Guide to Colorado's Wilderness Areas by John Fielder and Mark Pearson. Westcliffe Publishers, Englewood, CO 1994.

The Encyclopedia of the Central West by Allen Carpenter. Facts On File, New York, NY 1990.

The Ice-Age History of National Parks in the Rocky Mountains by Scott A. Elias. Smithsonian Institution Press, Washington, DC 1996.

The Kingdom in the Country by James Conaway. Houghton Mifflin Company, Boston, MA 1987.

The Last Ranch: A Colorado Community and The Coming Desert by Sam Bingham. Pantheon Books, New York, NY 1996.

The Lost Grizzlies: A Search for Survivors in The Wilderness of Colorado by Rick Bass. Houghton Mifflin Company, New York, NY 1995.

The Mountain Biker's Guide to Colorado by Linda Gong and Gregg Bromka. Menasha Ridge Press, Birmingham, AL 1994.

The Story of Mesa Verde National Park by Gilbert R. Wenger. Mesa Verde Museum Association, Mesa Verde National Park, CO 1991.

To Aspen and Back: An American Journey by Peggy Clifford. St. Martin's Press, New York, NY 1980.

Tomboy Bride: A Woman's Personal Account of Life in Mining Camps of the West by Harriet Fish Backus, Pruett Publishing, Boulder, CO 1969.

Tree Finder: A Manual for the Identification of Trees by their Leaves by May Theilgaard Watts. Nature Study Guild, Berkeley, CA 1986.

Trees and Shrubs of Colorado by Jack L. Carter. Johnson Books, Boulder, CO 1988.

D. Selected Special Events & Festivals

GENERAL:

Colorado Festival and Events Association. Supports 200 members. PO Box 481674, Denver, CO 80248. Denver, CO. Phone (303) 904-1521.

Colorado Calendar of Events by Ricky Clifton, Thriftsmart Press, $24.95. This guide lists more than 1,500 festivals, fairs, and events. Phone (303) 759-4257.

JANUARY

International Snow Sculpture Championships. Sixteen teams from around the world gather in Breckenridge to create works of art from 20-ton blocks of packed snow. Teams hail from the Netherlands, England, Italy, Mexico, Argentina, Canada, Bulgaria, Switzerland, France, and the USA. Phone (970) 453-6018.

Winterskol. A five-day celebration of winter in Aspen includes downhill ski races, a broomball tournament, uphill races, a canine fashion show, fireworks, bike races, and more. Phone (970) 920-0998.

Annual Gay and Lesbian Ski Week. This party-filled event, more than two decades old, attracts thousands of gay and lesbian visitors to Aspen. Phone (970) 925-9249.

FEBRUARY

Winter Carnival. A ski-season celebration in Steamboat Springs with street events, the Lighted Man, and other local favorites. Phone (970) 879-0880.

Winter Trails Weekend. Test-drive snowshoes, get tips and instruction, and watch demos at this event sponsored by the American Hiking Society in Estes Park. Special snowshoeing nature tours and fitness walks. Phone (800) 44-ESTES.

MARCH

Colorado RV, Sports, Boat, and Travel Show. The Denver region's largest outdoor recreation event. Displays on RVs, boats, water sports, vacation spots, fishing, hunting, four-wheeling, river rafting, hiking, camping, and dozens of other outdoor activities. Phone (303) 892-6800 or (800) 457-2434.

Crystal Carnival Ski Joring. Skiers, pulled behind horses, travel at speeds up to 40 mph and perform obstacle courses in Leadville. Phone (800) 933-3901.

U.S. Comedy Arts Festival. A week-long gathering of nationally celebrated comedians and comedy acts held in Aspen. Phone (800) 778-4633.

APRIL

Peach Blossom Home Tour. Tour elegant Victorian and contemporary homes, enjoy special tastings at award-winning wineries, and see Palisade's famous orchards with pink and white blooming fruit trees. Phone (970) 464-7458.

Shortsfest. An annual festival of short films in Aspen. Phone (970) 925-6882.

MAY

Iron Horse Bicycle Classic. Cyclists race the narrow-gauge steam train from Durango to Silverton. Festivities include mountain bike races, a kids race, and an expo. Phone (970) 259-4621.

Jeep Whitewater Festival. The Vail Valley's annual kickoff to summer is packed with whitewater rafting and kayaking races, on- and off-water activities, and public parties. Phone (800) 525-3875.

MountainFilm Festival. Meet filmmakers and photographers in Telluride amid gallery exhibits, symposiums, picnics, and films about outdoor adventure, exotic cultures, natural wonders, and environmental issues. Phone (888) 783-0264.

JUNE

Annual Fibark Boat Races and Festival. Premier summer weekend festival in historic downtown Salida. Downriver races, whitewater rodeo and slalom, 5K and 10K foot races, parade, arts, fair, food, and live entertainment. Phone (719) 539-2068.

Aspen Music Festival and School. World-class classical music performed daily at several venues. June through August. Phone (970) 925-3254.

Bravo! Vail Valley Music Festival. An annual classical music series featuring visiting symphony orchestras and chamber music programs, including the Rochester Philharmonic and Dallas Symphony Orchestra. Phone (800) 525-3875.

Madame Lou Bunch Day. Celebration of famous madams and sporting-house girls. Includes a parade, live musical entertainment, and bed races down Central City's Main Street. Phone (303) 582-5322.

Strawberry Days. The oldest continuous civic celebration west of the Mississippi.

Includes over 150 artisans and food vendors from all over the country who gather in Glenwood Springs. Phone (970) 945-6589, ext. 103.

Telluride Bluegrass Festival. The nation's best traditional, folk, and country artists jam all day and night. Phone (888) 783-0264.

JULY

Blair Street Arts and Crafts Festival. Juried festival in Silverton showcasing talented artists from around the country. Family entertainment, street performers, live music, and cultural events. Phone (800) 752-4494.

Carbondale Mountain Fair. Free festival with 125 arts and crafts booths, 14 stage performances, children's activities, wood splitting, fly casting, limbo contests, and pie and cake judging. Phone (970) 963-1680.

Crested Butte Wildflower Festival. A full week of botanical activities for all ages. Walks, hikes, art and photography workshops, lectures, and exhibits. Phone (970) 349-2571.

Rainbow Weekend. Fifty brilliantly colored hot-air balloons take to the skies over Steamboat Springs. Downtown, Art in the Park showcases arts and crafts exhibits and vendors. Phone (970) 879-0880.

AUGUST

Gold Rush Days. Pancake breakfast, burro races, melodrama, outhouse races, bed races, gold panning, and food in Buena Vista. Phone (719) 395-6612.

No Man's Land Celebration. An annual celebration of Breckenridge's independence, this festival features a woodcarving competition, gold panning championships, an ice cream social, historical tours, and a lumberjack show. Phone (970) 453-6018.

Doc Holidays. Relive the days of the old West in Glenwood Springs. Highlight is the re-enactment of the shootout at the OK Corral. Phone (970) 945-6589.

SEPTEMBER

Council Tree Pow Wow and Cultural Festival. Western Colorado's premier Native American event, with competition dancing, singing, and craft booths in Delta. Art show by nationally known Western artisans. Phone (800) 874-1741.

Fall Foliage Festival. This Steamboat Springs celebration of cultural diversity and fall colors is complemented by the Mountain Brewfest, with over 30 Colorado breweries represented. Phone (970) 879-0880.

Meeker Classic Sheepdog Trials. One of the most difficult sheepdog trials in North America. Thousands of spectators turn out to watch handlers and dogs compete in sheepherding events. Craft fair, food, calcutta. Phone (970) 878-5510.

Salida Fall Festival. Includes the Banana Belt Loop Mountain Bike Race and Trials, Annual Angel of Shavano Car Show, and Taste of Salida. Held in Riverside Park, alongside the Arkansas in historic downtown Salida. Phone (719) 539-2068.

Telluride Film Festival. World-renowned festival features outstanding films and seminars conducted by industry's top filmmakers. Phone (888) 783-0264.

OCTOBER

Diggity Festival. Experience fall colors in the mountains and celebrate Oktoberfest in Town Park with Bavarian-style beer, wine, food, and music in Telluride. Phone (888) 783-0264.

Durango Cowboy Gathering. A celebration of American cowboy culture including exhibits, art, poetry, storytelling, and a rodeo. Phone (800) 525-8855.

Evergreen Cemetery Tour. A local historian, bedecked in black top hat and cape, leads tours of Leadville's fascinating historic graveyard. Phone (800) 933-3901.

NOVEMBER

Celebrate in Estes Park. A Christmas parade followed by two weeks of carolers and choirs, pony rides and carriage rides, Santa and his elves, band concerts, and special shopping hours. November through December. Phone (800) 44-ESTES.

Mountain Holiday Festival Arts and Crafts Fair. More than 30 artists and craftspersons sell handmade crafts and artworks at the Ute Pass Cultural Center in Woodland Park. Free admission. Soup, sandwiches, fry bread, and baked goods available. Phone (800) 551-7886.

Christmas Mountain. Santa comes to historic downtown Salida to light the 700-foot-tall "Christmas Mountain USA" that towers above Main Street. Phone (719) 539-2068.

DECEMBER

24 Hours of Aspen. Annual endurance ski race and fundraiser that attracts national attention. Phone (970) 925-1220.

Continental Divide Hot Air Balloon Festival and Lighting of Breckenridge. The balloon festival features morning competitions and nighttime luminaries that splash the skies with color. Caroling party and tree-lighting ceremony. Phone (970) 453-6018.

Victorian Home Tour. Locals and visitors, some of whom choose to dress in Victorian costumes, tour Leadville's historic homes and buildings, decorated for Christmas. Brunch and entertainment included. Phone (800) 933-3901.

E. Conservation & Outdoor Organizations

10th Mountain Trail Association, 1280 Ute Avenue, Aspen, CO 81611. Phone (970) 925-5775. Manages the 10th Mountain and Braun backcountry hut systems.

Colorado Environmental Coalition, 777 Grant Street, Suite 606, Denver, CO 80203. Phone (303) 837-8701. Umbrella organization and information clearinghouse for numerous Colorado environmental groups.

Colorado Mountain Club, 710 10th Street, Suite 200, Golden, CO 80401. Phone (303) 279-9690. Club organizes and leads hikes and climbs throughout the state.

Colorado Trail Foundation, PO Box 260876, Lakewood, CO 80226. Volunteer group devoted to maintenance of the Colorado Trail.

Continental Divide Trail Alliance, PO Box 628, Pine, CO 80470. Volunteer group devoted to completion and maintenance of the Continental Divide Trail.

Leave No Trace, PO Box 9977, Boulder, CO 80306. Phone (800) 332-4100. Educational organization that teaches light travel on public lands.

National Off-Road Bicycling Association, 1750 East Boulder Street, Colorado Springs, CO 80909. Phone (719) 578-4717. Governing body for mountain bike competition.

Rails-to-Trails Conservancy, 1400 16th Street NW, Suite 300, Washington, DC 20036. Phone (202) 797-5400. National organization promoting the conversion of abandoned railway lines to public trails.

Sierra Club, Rocky Mountain Chapter, 777 Grant Street, Suite 606, Denver, CO 80203. Phone (303) 861-8819. National conservation organization.

The Nature Conservancy, Colorado Office, 1244 Pine Street, Boulder, CO 80302. Phone (303) 444-2950. National organization devoted to purchase and preservation of critical wildlife habitat.

Trout Unlimited, 655 Broadway Street, Suite 475, Denver, CO 80203. Phone (303) 595-0620. National organization devoted to fly-fishing and preservation of wild trout habitat.

Volunteers for Outdoor Colorado, 1410 Grant Street, Suite B-105, Denver, CO 80203. Phone (303) 830-7477. Clearinghouse for volunteers who perform trail work and similar tasks on public lands.

Wilderness Society, 7475 Dakin Street, Westminster, CO 80210. Phone (303) 650-5818. National organization devoted to protection of wilderness lands.

F. Ski Area Information

Arapahoe Basin Ski Area, Box 8787, Arapahoe Basin, CO 80435. Phone (970) 496-7077.

Aspen Skiing Company (Aspen, Aspen Highlands, Buttermilk, Snowmass), Box 1248, Aspen, CO 81612. Phone (970) 925-1220.

Copper Mountain Resort, PO Box 3001, 209 Ten Mile Circle, Copper Mountain, CO 80443. Phone (970) 968-2318.

Crested Butte Mountain Resort, PO Box A, 500 Gothic Road, Mount Crested Butte, CO 81225. Phone (800) 970-9704.

Cuchara Mountain Resort, 946 Panadero Avenue, Cuchara, CO 81055. Phone (888) CUCHARA.

Eldora Mountain Resort, PO Box 1697, Nederland, CO 80466. Phone (303) 440-8700.

Hesperus Ski Area, PO Box 167, Hesperus, CO 81326. Phone (970) 259-3711.

Howelsen Hill Ski Area, PO Box 775088, Steamboat Springs, CO 80477. Phone (970) 879-8499.

Loveland Ski Area, PO Box 899, Georgetown, CO 80444. Phone (800) 736-3754.

Monarch Ski and Snowboard Area, 23715 US Highway 50, Monarch, CO 81227. Phone (800) 228-7943.

Powderhorn Ski Resort, Highway 65, Mesa, CO 81643. Phone (970) 268-5700.

Purgatory Resort, No. 1 Skier Place, Durango, CO 81301. Phone (970) 247-9000.

Silver Creek Resort, Box 1110, Silver Creek, CO 80446. Phone (800) 448-9458.

Ski Cooper, PO Box 896, 1101 Poplar, Leadville, CO 80461. Phone (719) 486-2277.

Steamboat Ski and Resort Corporation, 2305 Mount Werner Circle, Steamboat Springs, CO 80487. Phone (970) 879-6111.

Sunlight Mountain Resort, 10901 County Road 117, Glenwood Springs, CO 81601. Phone (970) 945-7491.

Telluride Ski & Golf Company, PO Box 11555, 565 Mountain Village Boulevard, Telluride, CO 81435. Phone (970) 728-6900.

Vail Resorts (Vail, Beaver Creek, Breckenridge, Keystone), PO Box 7, Vail, CO 81658. Phone (970) 476-5601.

Winter Park Resort, PO Box 36, Winter Park, CO 80482. Phone (970) 726-1572.

Wolf Creek Ski Area, PO Box 2800, Pagosa Springs, CO 81147. Phone (970) 264-5639.

G. Glossary

Alluvial fan: A conical mass of gravel and sand deposited by a mountain stream where it flows onto a level or nearly level plain.

Anticline: Arching rock fold that is closed at the top and open at the bottom. Oldest rock occurs in the center of an anticline.

Basalt: A dark, volcanic rock often containing small bubbles.

Basement: Precambrian-age igneous and metamorphic rocks originally situated below the sedimentary rock sequence.

Batholith: A mass of igneous rock larger than 40 square miles, intruded as molten magma into overlying layers of rock.

Breccia: Volcanic rock, broken by force, that has been ejected from a volcano and is embedded in volcanic ash.

Butte: An isolated hill or small mountain with steep sides and a flat top.

Caldera: A large basin or depression formed by the violent explosion or collapse of a volcano.

Caprock: Relatively erosion-resistant rock atop softer rock forming the summit of mesas and buttes.

Cirque: A deep, steep-walled bite taken by the head of a glacier from the side of a mountain.

Coniferous: Describing cone-bearing trees, usually evergreen.

Cross-bedding: Laminates slanting obliquely in sandstone relative to the generally horizontal planes of the sedimentary rock.

Deciduous: Plants that shed their leaves seasonally and are leafless for part of the year.

Dike: A thin vertical rock produced when magma intrudes vertically into fractures in overlying rock.

Extirpated: Extinct in a particular area.

Fault: A break in rock along which rocks have moved relative to each other, either vertically or horizontally.

Gneiss: Metamorphic, granitelike rock showing layers.

Granite: Igneous rock composed predominantly of visible grains of feldspar and quartz.

Hanging valley: A valley whose floor is significantly higher than the valley into which it leads. Often the result of a glacier digging more deeply in the larger valley.

Igneous: Rocks formed by cooled and hardened magma within the earth's crust or lava on the surface.

Laccolith: An intrusive body of magma that has squeezed between rock layers, lifting those above it into a dome.

Lava: Magma that reaches the surface of the earth.

Lode: A mineral vein in solid rock.

Magma: Molten rock within the earth's crust.

Monocline: A flex in rock in which all the strata dip or rise from the horizontal in the same direction.

Moraine: Gravel or rock pile pushed or left by a glacier.

Nunatak: A peak or pinnacle that sticks up through an ice cap or glacier.

Orogeny: A geologic process which results in the formation of mountain ranges.

Paternoster lakes: A series of lakes in a glaciated valley, connected by a single stream.

Placer: Sand or gravel deposition in a stream.

Redbeds: Red-hued sedimentary rocks.

Schist: Flaky, metamorphic rock containing parallel layers of mica.

Sedimentary: Rocks formed by the accumulation of sediments (sandstone, shale) or the remains of products of animals or plants (limestone, coal).

Shale: Sedimentary rock composed of clay, mud, and silt grains which splits easily into two layers.

Sill: Igneous rock that intrudes horizontally between rock layers.

Stock: Identical to a batholith, but smaller than 40 square miles.

Syncline: A rock fold shaped like a U that is closed at the bottom and open at the top. The youngest rock is at the center of a syncline.

Talus: Rock debris and boulders that accumulate at the base of a cliff.

Thrust fault: An area where older rock has been pushed horizontally over younger rock.

Tuff: Rock formed by volcanic ash.

Welded tuff: Volcanic ash welded into rock by its own heat and that of the associated volcanic eruption.

Index